THE SACKVILLE ILLUSTRATED DICTIONARY OF
ATHLETICS

TOM KNIGHT AND NICK TROOP

SACKVILLE
BOOKS

First published in 1988
by Sackville Books Limited
Hales Barn
New Street
Stradbroke
Suffolk IP21 5JG

Text © Tom Knight and Nick Troop

Designed and produced by Sackville Design Group Limited
Publisher: Al Rockall
Editorial Director: Heather Thomas
Editor: Jane Berry

British Library Cataloguing in Publication Data
Knight, Tom
 The Sackville illustrated dictionary of athletics.
 1. Athletics
 L. Title II. Troop, Nick
 796.4'2

ISBN 0-948615-12-5

Typesetting and electronic page make-up by Apt Setting, Ipswich
Colour reproduction by Hilo, Colchester
Printed in Spain by Graficas Reunidas, Madrid

The authors would like to thank the following for their assistance
in the compilation of this book: Dave Calderwood; Andy Edwards;
Andy Etchells; Gail Fitzpatrick; Paul Fraser; Roger Gynn;
Peter Matthews; Andy Milroy; Roger Mills; Peter Staunton; Cliff Temple;
Mel Watman; Nicky Williamson; Colin Young

The publishers acknowledge the following picture sources, with thanks:

Allsport UK Ltd: page 91
Associated Press: page 82
BBC Hulton Picture Library: pages 4, 5, 6, 19 (bottom), 27 (bottom), 32, 83, 85, 89, 105 (bottom), 114 (top), 155
Popperfoto: pages 14 (bottom), 24 (top), 26 (top), 49 (top), 58 (bottom), 59, 60 (top), 64 (top), 68 (top), 79, 88 (top), 89 (bottom), 91 (bottom), 117 (bottom), 118 (bottom), 124, 147, 153 (bottom), 154, 159 (bottom)
Mark Shearman: pages 9, 10, 11, 12, 13, 14 (top), 15, 16, 17, 18, 19 (top), 20, 21, 22, 23, 24 (bottom), 25, 26 (bottom), 27 (top), 28, 30, 31, 33, 34, 35, 36, 37, 38, 39, 40, 42, 43, 46, 47, 48, 49 (bottom), 51, 52, 53, 54, 55, 57, 58 (bottom), 60 (bottom), 61, 62, 63, 64 (bottom), 66, 67, 68, 69, 70, 71, 72, 73, 74, 75, 76, 77, 78, 86, 87, 88 (bottom), 90, 91 (top), 93, 94, 95, 96, 97, 99, 100, 101, 102, 103, 104, 105 (top), 106, 107, 108, 109, 110, 112, 114 (bottom), 115, 116, 117 (top), 118 (top), 119, 120, 121, 122, 123, 125, 126, 128, 129, 130, 131, 132, 133, 134, 135, 136, 137, 138, 139, 140, 141, 142, 144, 145, 146, 148, 149, 150, 151, 152, 153 (top), 156, 157, 159 (top), 160
Syndication International: pages 45, 81, 158

Foreword

Athletics is about triumph and failure, health, injury and illness, pleasure and pain, cooperation and combat. It's about life. If you're lucky – and I have been – you get rather more triumph than failure, pleasure than pain. It's about drama; it's live competition. There's a direct historical route from the Coliseum in ancient Rome to stadiums like that in Los Angeles, of the same name, which in 1932 and 1984 housed the greatest contest of all, the Olympic Games.

We don't quite fight for our lives, any more. But it sometimes feels like it. Athletics is a tough business. And therein lies one of the developments of recent years, the commercial side of the sport.

As one who has benefited from athletics' popular success, I can truly say that I'm always more conscious of the traditions than its trappings. I've never made a running decision on financial grounds. The essence of the sport is individual competition – against rivals, against the clock. That remains unchanged. Steve Ovett, Steve Cram, Said Aouita and I have been, and are, as motivated as our illustrious predecessors – men like Herb Elliot, Jack Lovelock, Vladimir Kuts, Harold Abrahams – by running faster, by winning.

This essence of the sport is captured in this book. Here you can read about the respective achievements, records and failures of the major athletes, the ones who have captured the public eye and imagination. The text brings them to racing life again; it reminds you of their great moments; it tracks the important stages of their careers. The pictures capture some of the style, the power – the pleasure, the pain.

I hope you enjoy it. Of course, there's also the future. That's not here: but the imagination is. I feel like running again!

Sebastian Coe
August 1988

The History of Athletics

Man has been running ever since he had to hunt for survival. It is likely that his essentially competitive nature led to contests and races at an early stage in his development.

It is to the Greeks, however, that we must look for the first evidence of athletics organized on a grand scale. Homer's *Iliad* describes the sports of running, jumping, throwing, wrestling, and boxing at the Funeral Games for Patroclus in around 800BC.

Up until 776BC the Olympics been mainly a religious festival in honour of Zeus, followed by the 'dromos', a measured sprint of about 192 yards, the length of the stadium. The Games as a sporting event followed and further sports were introduced. There were longer distance running events, discus and javelin competitions, long jumps, high jumps, and a pentathlon of five events. Also included in the programme were chariot races and non-athletic pursuits such as poetry and music.

The Olympics were permanently based at Olympia, Ellis, a small province in Southern Greece, from 776BC. They were held every four years, a period of time which became known as an Olympiad. The stadium, horse-shoe-shaped and measuring 210m in length and 31m in width, held 40,000 spectators. Such was the importance of the Olympics that all battles were halted for the five days of the competition.

Athletics became almost a full-time pursuit in ancient Greece. Winners at the Olympics were afforded all manner of privileges and material rewards in their native cities. Men and women trained for specific events and, although it was decreed that champions were only able to be rewarded with crowns of garlands, the athletes knew that life after an Olympic win would never be the same again, as athletes became part of the élite in Greek society. The first ever association of professional athletes was formed around 50BC.

The Olympics and the pursuit of

Ancient Greek discus thrower

athletic excellence had moved a long way from their origins. Their eventual decline in many ways reflected the decline of the ancient Greek civilization. In the middle of the second century AD, Greece lost its independence to Rome. The Games were finally abolished by the Roman Emperor Theodosius in AD393. They were not revived until 1896.

Meanwhile, athletics had been developing within other cultures, most notably in Ireland and England. The Tailtean Games originated in Ireland in around 500BC, while in England the earliest references to athletics can be traced to the writings of the Venerable Bede, who said of the seventh century Saint Cuthbert (634-687BC) that he 'excelled in jumping, running and wrestling'. The village green was the setting for running races and throwing contests during the Middle Ages, when prizes usually comprised something to wear or something to eat. It was also possible for men and women to win themselves a wife or a husband in such competitions.

There were attempts – most notably by the Puritans in the seventeenth century – to banish sports, but they met with little success. The first organized meeting took place in 1604: Mr Robert Dover's Olympic Games upon the Cotswold Hills. They included wrestling, cudgel-playing, leaping, pitching the bar, throwing the sledge, and tossing the pike.

Foot races, or pedestrianism, are mentioned by Samuel Pepys in his diary. He describes a race between the Duke of Richmond's footman and a tiler who was a famous runner. Victory apparently went to the footman, even though the tiler had taken most bets as the favourite.

It became a common pastime for servants or footmen to race each other while their masters placed bets on the outcome. By the 1750s, races were taking place at the Artillery Ground in London and promoters charged entry fees for spectators. However, professional runners – those who could actually earn a living from their racing – took on much longer distances, sometimes covering half the length of Britain. Foster Powell ran from London to York and back, 402 miles, in five days 18 hours in 1773.

A young Scottish land-owner called Robert Barclay Allardice, known as Captain Barclay, bet 1000 guineas that he could walk 90 miles in $21\frac{1}{2}$ hours. He lost, but immediately bet a further 2000 guineas and tried again, only to lose a second time. When the wager was increased to 5000 guineas, Captain Barclay dumbfounded the bookmaker by completing the distance with more than an hour to spare!

Captain Barclay later took up running, but before that in 1809 more than 10,000 people went to Newmarket, a regular venue for foot races, to see Barclay walk 1000 miles in 1000 consecutive hours to earn £16,000.

The first track to be laid specifically for running races was at Lords in 1837. The narrow path around the ground was designed for two-man races, and the infield was used for jumping and throwing events. Foot races continued to flourish on the road, but more and more grounds (such as cricket and horse-racing venues) were being utilized for athletics meetings. Tracks were measured, proper time-keepers hired and records kept. Popular distances for races were 100 yards, 440 yards, 880 yards, and one, two, four, six and ten miles. The same year athletics was introduced into the curriculum at Rugby School and Eton College.

Another innovation took place at Exeter College, Oxford in 1850. Disillusioned with riding horses over a steeplechase course, the students adapted it for runners instead. The Exeter College athletics club was formed, and its first event featured 24 runners taking on 24 fences over a two-mile course. The race was treated exactly like a horse race: bets were taken and the more athletic runners made to carry weights. Other colleges followed with their own meetings and the fashion spread to Cambridge University soon after. The professional long jumper John Howard was invited to jump at Cambridge in 1853, and cleared 8.53m (28ft) in front of an audience of dons and students.

By 1864, Oxford and Cambridge were competing against each other. Their first athletics match included running, the 120 yards hurdles, a steeplechase, the high jump and the long jump. Honours were even, with each university winning four events.

Meanwhile, a talented foot racer – or pedestrian – arrived in Britain from America in 1861. English pedestrians had competed against Americans since the 1840s, but when Louis Bennett, an American Indian known as Deerfoot, was brought to England by running impresario George Martin, the sport received a boost from a surprising quarter. After beating the best English runners in London, Deerfoot went to Cambridge as part of a troupe of pedestrians putting on exhibition runs. Among those watching him race at the Fenners Ground in Cambridge was the Prince of Wales, who added £10 to the winner's stakes as a sign of his ap-

preciation. He later invited Deerfoot to lunch at Trinity College.

Athletics continued to grow in popularity, and clubs were formed throughout the country. The first London club opened in 1863, Mincing Lane AC. The name was later changed to London AC. The Amateur Athletic Club was formed three years later.

The first major meeting to attract competitors from around the country took place in Liverpool in 1862. The local club, Liverpool AC, organized

The American runner, Deerfoot

the Olympic Festival, a hugely successful venture which featured several events not yet seen in London. There was pole leaping, throwing the cricket ball and throwing the discus. The event had proved so successful that by 1865 its members considered setting up the first national body, to be called the National Olympian Society.

The first national championships in England came in 1866, organized by the Amateur Athletic Club in Welham Green, London. Events included flat races over 100 yards, 440 yards, 880 yards, one and four miles,

plus a seven-mile walk. There was also a 110 yards hurdles race, high jump, long jump, and pole jump. The cricket ball was replaced by the 16lb hammer and the shot put was also introduced. The championships became an annual event and in 1869 the club acquired the Lillie Bridge ground as its own track.

After much political wrangling between what had become the several strongholds of athletics – London AC, the Amateur Athletics Club, the universities, and the regions – a national governing body, called the Amateur Athletics Association, was eventually formed in 1880. Its first championships – the oldest in the world – took place the same year.

America had already seen its first amateur athletic club formed in 1868. The New York club held its first indoor track and field meeting the same year in the Empire City Skating Rink. American colleges set up the Intercollegiate Association of Amateur Athletes of America in 1875, and held their first championships in New York a year later.

The first national governing body for athletics in America came in 1888. Called the Amateur Athletic Union, it was made up of 17 clubs. In both England and the USA, athletics was a sport for the masses at last.

After the establishment of athletics as a sport in England, America and several European countries, it was only a matter of time before international competition was introduced. There were athletics matches between clubs in the USA and Great Britain, and cross-country internationals between the home counties and France before the end of the nineteenth century. However, it was a Frenchman, Baron Pierre de Coubertin, who brought about the first major international event, whilst pursuing his dream of reviving the Olympic Games. Thirteen nations took part in the Games of 1896, when 311 athletes gathered in Athens.

It took an enormous effort by the

Greeks to stage the five-day event. It was only after collections were made among the Greeks living at home and abroad and a generous donation was made by one of the country's wealthiest businessmen that enough money was raised to stage the Games. The opening ceremony at the rebuilt Panathenean Stadium was watched by more than 80,000 people, and the first modern Olympic Games were an overwhelming success.

Despite initial Greek protests, the Olympic Games were moved to Paris in 1900. The number of countries competing rose to 22, but the Games were beset by political, financial and organizational problems. They eventually lasted for four months and included a confusion of different sports. A full list of winners and medallists was not properly compiled until 1912, and de Coubertin concluded that the Olympic movement had been lucky to survive the 1900 Games.

The setting up of the International Amateur Athletic Federation in 1912 promised to produce a code of laws to govern athletics throughout the world. Its progress was gradual but effective. Both the IAAF and the International

The marble stadium at Athens

Olympic Committee (IOC), however, faced the massive problem of uniting people through sport at a time when the world itself was in turmoil. There were no Olympic Games in 1916 because of the First World War. However, the Games in Antwerp in 1920 were to prove a fitting tribute to those athletes who had died during the war. It appeared that Belgium was hardly in a position to host the Games, but once again the facilities were in place in time, just as they had been in Athens. The same problems later faced wartorn London in 1948, but were overcome to produce a memorable festival of athletics.

While the Olympic movement moved through each Olympiad struggling with the growing problems that hosting such a collosal event inevitably brought, the IAAF had battles of its own. The sport was developing fast. Athletics was a major sport around the world, and the introduction of commercialism and television meant that athletes were becoming stars on a global scale. The definition of amateurism, which had caused so many problems for English administrators at the end of the nineteenth

century, was again an extremely contentious issue.

There were also political problems. The Soviet Union joined the IAAF in 1952 and sent its first team to an Olympic Games the same year; China, however, remained in isolation. It finally became a member federation in 1954, but resigned in 1962 when Taiwan became a member. China was not to rejoin the IAAF until 1967. Germany, although divided into East and West after the Second World War, was represented by just one member federation until 1964, when the German Democratic Republic finally pulled clear and took up separate membership.

The East Germans were to join the Soviet Union in forming a powerful athletics force to rival the Americans' prowess across all the disciplines. The arrival of the African nations into world athletics in the 1960s provided the most potent contrast to the East versus West approach to competition enjoyed by the Americans and Soviets.

Membership of the IAAF now stands at more than 160 countries. The success of the sport as a television spectacle has inevitably meant more commercial sponsorship and more money available for its development around the world. It remains a vibrant and ever-changing sport, and yet is still plagued by problems. Political intrigue still threatens the future of the Olympic Games and the IAAF has yet to find the solution to the growing problems of the misuse of drugs.

Women's athletics

The women of Ancient Greece were banned from watching or competing in the early Olympic Games. The penalty for violating the rule was death. Instead, they enjoyed their own athletics event at the Heraea Games, held every four years at Olympia. While the men's Olympics were dedicated to the god Zeus, the women's festival was dedicated to his wife, Hera. The women's Games consisted of only one event, a 500-foot run, and the races were split into age group categories. The women of Sparta were more fortunate in that they were actively encouraged to train and compete alongside men.

There is little on record of women's participation in athletics until the seventeenth century, when it is known that they took part in foot races during country fairs and wakes. They were rather left out of things with the onset of professional pedestrianism in the eighteenth and nineteenth centuries, when the sport of running and athletics in general was largely a male domain.

The first meetings for women only are thought to be those at the exclusive Vassar College in New York in 1895. The first governing body for women's athletics originated in France, where Alice Milliat set up the Federation Feminine Sportive de France in 1917. Four years later, following an international match between France and Belgium and the first ever multi-national women's meeting in Monte Carlo, Milliat formed the Federation Sportive Feminine Internationale (FSFI). The six original members were France, Britain, the USA, Italy, Spain, and Czechoslovakia. The FSFI promptly requested that women be allowed to compete in the 1924 Olympic Games in Paris, but this was turned down by the International Olympic Committee (IOC). The FSFI duly organized its own games in the same city in 1922. Five countries sent teams.

The Women's Olympics were then held every four years, although the name had to be changed to the Women's World Games after protests from the IOC and the International Amateur Athletic Federation. In 1934, 19 countries sent women to compete.

The IOC did relent, however, in 1928 and added five events for women at the Olympic Games in Amsterdam. Previously, the women had contested races of up to 1000m at their own World Games, but they were not well represented in the Olympic Games' 800m. Several participants collapsed

and it was adjudged that the event was too much for women to handle. As a result, they were not allowed to run any distance further than 200m until the Rome Olympics in 1960.

Women's events were included in the Commonwealth Games in 1934, and in 1936 the FSFI merged with the IAAF. Two years later the first all-women European Championships were held in Vienna, and 18 women's events were given world record status. The first combined men and women's European Championships was in Oslo in 1946. Since then the future of women's athletics has gone hand in hand with that of men's. Nevertheless, the IAAF remained cautious about introducing longer-distance events. The 800m was brought back in 1960 and the 400m in 1964, but it was not until 1972 that the 1500m was added. The first women's 3000m and marathon were part of the 1984 programme, and the 10,000m was contested by women for the first time in Olympic history in 1988.

Sex testing was introduced to international competition in 1966. This was deemed necessary to ensure fair competition at a time when more and more women athletes were following increasingly strenuous training schedules and developing the sort of physiques which raised doubts as to their true sexuality. The test used to be a purely visual one, in which female competitors would be physically examined by a medical officer. Now more sophisticated tests have been introduced, involving the examination of the chromosomes in cells taken from inside the mouth or from the hair.

Inevitably, as women have become as committed as men in their approach to athletics, world records have tumbled with unerring regularity every season. Financial rewards, too, equal those offered to men. Zola Budd, for instance, was paid $90,000 to race against Mary Slaney over 3000m at Crystal Palace in 1985, while Ingrid Kristiansen is reported to have earned more than $200,000 in winnings from road racing since 1980.

Key to abbreviations used

AAA   Amateur Athletic Association
AAU   Amateur Athletic Union (USA)
BAAB British Amateur Athletic Board
FSFI Fédération Sportive Feminine Internationale
IAC   International Athletes Club
IAAF International Amateur Athletic Federation
IC4A Intercollegiate Association of Amateur Athletes of America
IOC   International Olympic Committee
ITA   International Track Association
NCAA National Collegiate Athletic Association (USA)
TAC   The Athletics Congress (USA)
WAAA Women's Amateur Athletic Association

IAAF Country Abbreviations used

Africa
ETH   Ethiopa
KEN   Kenya
MAR   Morocco
SA   South Africa
TUN   Tunisia
UGA   Uganda

South America
BRA   Brazil
GUY   Guyana

Asia
JAP   Japan
PRC   People's Republic of China
TPE   Chinese Taipei (Taiwan)

Europe
BEL   Belgium
BUL   Bulgaria
FIN   Finland
FRA   France
FRG   Federal Republic of Germany
GBR   Great Britain & Northern Ireland
GDR   German Democratic Republic
GER* Germany
GRE   Greece
HUN   Hungary
IRE   Ireland
ITA   Italy
NOR   Norway
POL   Poland
ROM   Romania
SWE   Sweden
TCH   Czechoslovakia
URS   USSR
YUG   Yugoslavia

*GER was used for German athletes before 1964, when East and West Germany began sending separate teams to international events. Now GDR and FRG respectively.

North and Central America
CAN   Canada
JAM   Jamaica
MEX   Mexico
TRI   Trinidad and Tobago
USA   USA

Oceania
AUS   Australia
NZL   New Zealand

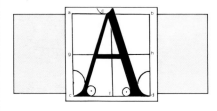

Abrahams, Harold

1899–1978. Born England (GBR)

Immortalized in the Oscar-winning film *Chariots of Fire*, Harold Abrahams is probably better known today than he was in 1924, the year he became the first Briton to win the Olympic 100m title.

Coming from an athletic family (his elder brother Sidney was the AAA long jump champion in 1913), he won the 100 yards and long jump in the 1918 Public Schools Championships, represented Britain (unsuccessfully) at the 1920 Olympics in Antwerp, and scored a record eight wins in the varsity match as a Cambridge student.

The dip finish of Harold Abrahams

Coached by Polytechnic Harriers' Sam Mussabini, he worked hard on his technique before the 1924 Olympics, shortening his stride and perfecting a 'drop' finish. At an inter-club match on 7 June 1924 Abrahams equalled the 100-yard world record of 9.6 seconds (unratified) and went on to set an English long jump record of 7.38m.

Although believing he would be outclassed by the Americans in the 1924 Paris Games, particularly by reigning champion Charley Paddock, and Jackson Scholz, placed fourth in 1920, Abrahams not only equalled the Olympic record of 10.6 in the second round and semi-final, but recorded the same time in the final to win by two feet from Scholz, with Paddock fifth. A silver medal in the 4 x 100m relay made up for any disappointment in coming last in the 200m.

His competitive career came to an abrupt end after a long jump accident in 1925, and he turned his attention to administration and journalism. He was athletics correspondent for *The Sunday Times* from 1925-1967 and a BBC commentator. A member of the AAA general committee from 1926, he was elected chairman in 1976 after seven years as chairman of the British Amateur Athletic Board.

Ackermann, Rosemarie

1952–. Born East Germany (GDR)

Dominant in the high jump during the 1970s, Rosi Ackermann (née Witschas) made history in West Berlin on 26 August 1977, when she became the first woman to clear 2m. It was, however, her last major success, as she struggled to overcome a succession of injuries and fight off the challenge of her main rival, Italy's Sara Simeoni.

The last world record holder to use the straddle technique, Ackermann was Olympic champion in 1976, when her jump of 1.93m proved too much for Simeoni, who took the silver medal with 1.91m. European champion in 1975, when Simeoni took the bronze, and twice the European Cup winner in 1975 and 1977, Ackermann went on to win the gold at the first IAAF World Cup competition in Düsseldorf later in 1977.

Her first major defeat came a year later, in 1978, when she lost her European title to Simeoni in Prague. Despite Ackermann clearing 1.99m, the Italian took the crown with a world record equalling 2.01m. After recovering from an Achilles' tendon injury (one of a succession of similar injuries), Ackermann returned to top form in 1979 to overcome her rival in the European Cup Final in Montreal. However, the injury returned to interrupt her preparation for Moscow in 1980. Ackermann could only finish fourth, as Simeoni took the gold medal with 1.97m. The East German announced her retirement later the same year.

During a glittering career she set seven outdoor world records, was European indoor champion three seasons running (1974-1976), and was GDR national champion six times. Over the years, the shy, unassuming Ackermann enjoyed many head-to-head competitions with the more extrovert Simeoni, eventually ending her career with an eight to five advantage over the Italian.

Adams, Eleanor

1948–. Born England (GBR)

Although she enjoyed running as a youngster, when she represented her county on the track, Eleanor Adams did not take up jogging until after the birth of her third child in 1979. She soon discovered that she had the ability to run long distances, and took to ultra running.

In 1981 and 1982 she watched the six-day race at Nottingham's Harvey Hadden Stadium while she was training on the sidelines. A year later she entered the race, and set a new world best performance of 409 miles. She now holds more than 30 world indoor and outdoor records on the track and on the road, and is acknowledged as the toughest and most accomplished woman ultra runner in the world.

Her records include those for 200 miles (44:44:08) and 500 miles (143:49:00). In one period during 1985, she set world records for 20 and 30 miles, and broke them both just three weeks later. In 1984, she became the first woman to cover 500 miles in a six-day race at Colac, Australia, returning there two years later to add another two miles to what appears to be an unassailable world record.

Her appetite for challenge is unparalleled in ultra running. She has covered the Sydney to Melbourne 1000km race in seven days and 17 hours, with less than eight hours sleep the whole way. She is the first woman to run 140 miles in 24 hours, and in February 1987 she finished second behind James Zarei in a 24-hour race inside the marble-floored shopping mall at Milton Keynes, beating all the other men and finishing 19 miles ahead

John Akii-Bua

of the nearest woman. She holds the women's record for the Spartathlon, a 250km race in Greece, and the Danube Run, a 320km stage race in Austria.

In May 1987, she undertook her biggest challenge, a 1000-mile round-Britain race against the experienced ultra runner Malcolm Campbell. Despite this distance being twice as far as she had ever run before, Eleanor finished an easy winner in 166 hours and 54 minutes, more than 20 hours ahead of the 52-year-old Campbell. She had run the equivalent of two marathons a day to set a new world best for the distance.

A P.E. supply teacher in Nottingham, Eleanor believes women make good ultra runners because they are more determined to keep going when things get tough. 'It's like Everest,' she said. 'The challenge drives you on.'

Akii-Bua, John

1949–. Born Uganda (UGA)

Olympic 400m hurdles champion in 1972, Akii-Bua started his athletics career as an unsuccessful high hurdler, failing to qualify for the 1968 Olympic Games in Mexico. The change to the longer distance produced

almost immediate results, notably fourth place in the 1970 Commonwealth Games in a time of 51.1. A series of good races in 1971 included the year's second fastest time, 49.0, in the Africa v USA international.

Back home, in the winter before the 1972 Olympics in Munich, he ran almost exclusively cross-country, often wearing a weighted vest, as his local grass track was unusable due to persistent rainfall. But even after May, when he was back on the track, he persisted with the vest for intervals over 1000m.

Although his times in the USA and Europe prior to the Games were unremarkable, a time trial of 48.8 one week before left him cautiously optimistic. This feeling was wholly justified by his victory in the final with a new world record time of 47.82. Although drawn in the inside lane – a disadvantage for a right leg leader – he pulled away with 100m to go to win by six metres from the pre-race favourite, Ralph Mann of America, and the defending champion and existing world record holder, Briton David Hemery.

He topped the world rankings in 1973 with 48.5, but did not compete in the 1974 Commonwealth Games. Although lacking motivation throughout the period from 1974 to 1975, he seemed to be back on form prior to the Montreal Olympics in 1976, reducing his 400m flat time to 45.82. But the African nations' boycott deprived him of the chance to defend his title. At the 1980 Olympic Games in Moscow, his progress was halted in the semi-finals.

One of 43 children (his father had eight wives), he also became Ugandan decathlon champion in 1971, scoring 6933 points.

Andersson, Arne

1917–. Born Sweden (SWE)

One of the greatest middle-distance runners of all time, Andersson has to be viewed alongside his great rival, fellow Swede Gunder Hägg. Together they took the world mile record from the 4:06.2 mark, set in 1937, to 4:01.3, set by Hägg in 1945. In Hägg's great year of 1942, when he set ten world records from 1500m to 5000m, Andersson was runner-up on six occasions, having equalled or bettered the previous record three times.

Frustrated, Andersson retired to work on his style through the winter of 1942-1943, emerging with a more economical action and a devastating sprint finish. With Hägg away on a tour of the United States in 1943, Andersson took the opportunity to beat his rival's records for 1500m (from 3:45.8 to 3:45.0) and for the mile (4:04.6 to 4:02.6).

Andersson and Hägg did not meet on the track again until the summer of 1944, first over 1500m in Stockholm on 7 July. With Hägg setting a murderous pace, passing 800 in 1:56.5, Andersson kept on his shoulder, only to see Hägg pull away over the final metres to win in a new world record time of 3:43.0. Far from being discouraged, Andersson prepared for their next clash, over one mile on 18 July in Malmö. This time he unleashed his new finishing sprint to win by three yards in a record 4:01.6, with Hägg second in 4:02.0. 'For me it was the perfect race,' he said afterwards.

Andersson's renaissance lasted throughout 1944, when he beat Hägg on six out of seven occasions. However, in 1945, the roles were reversed, with Hägg regaining all his world records. Their last great battle was over one mile on 17 July in Malmö, where Hägg won by six yards to set a new world record time of 4:01.4.

Towards the end of that season both Andersson and Hägg were banned for life from further amateur competition for receiving excess expenses – a move which abruptly ended the greatest rivalry of the decade.

Said Aouita wins in Los Angeles

Aouita, Said

1960–. Born Morocco (MAR)

Ever since his over-ambitious run for home in the 1500m final of the 1983 World Championships, Said Aouita has made sure that his achievements have matched his own very high expectations. After smashing the world 5000m record in Paris in July 1987, when he was the first man to run under 13 minutes with 12:58.39, he boldly proclaimed himself 'the greatest runner in the world'.

Few would dispute that title, since the Moroccan has won world and Olympic titles with consummate ease, and has broken world records at 1500m, 2000m and 5000m. Between losing to Britain's Steve Cram in an epic 1500m race in Nice in 1985, when Cram himself set a new world record, and a defeat in the final of the 3000m steeplechase at the Mediterranean Games at the end of 1987, Aouita had been unbeaten in 45 races over distances ranging from 800m to 10,000m.

World Student Games 1500m champion in 1981, with a time of 3:38:43, Aouita began making an impact at senior level by lowering his 800m time to 1:44.38 and his metric mile time to 3:32.54. He was, however, an unfancied finalist at the first World Championships in Helsinki, although Steve Cram was advised that Aouita might try and outrun the rest of the field with 500m to go. It was exactly what Aouita did try, livening up a rather dull and uninspired final by sprinting for home at 1000m. He finished a disappointing third, however, after being passed by Cram and America's Steve Scott in the home straight.

The following year, at the Los Angeles Olympic Games, he left the world guessing as to his chosen distance, and was entered for the 800m, 1500m, steeplechase, and 5000m. With very little speedwork behind him, and the prospect of facing the British trio of Cram, Coe and Ovett at 1500m, he chose the 5000m. He sauntered through the early rounds and patiently followed the pacemakers in the final, before choosing his moment to kick away and win with an Olympic record of 13:05.59. He later claimed, in a show of unnecessary arrogance, that Coe's victory in the 1500m had been a hollow one, because he had not been in the race.

In 1985, he turned his attention to breaking records. In July the same year, in Nice, he was defeated by Cram by just four hundredths of a second, which was the spur he needed. He had, in fact, run a faster final 400m than Cram, but had allowed the Englishman too much of a lead going into the last lap. Nine days later, in Oslo, Norway, he lowered the 5000m world record, bettering Dave Moorcroft's mark by one hundredth of a second to record 13:00.4. A month later, in Berlin, denied a race against the absent Cram, he attacked his 1500m world record, despite having run a 3:49.92 mile only two days earlier. Running on his own for the last 300m, he took the record with a time of 3:29.45. He became only the third man, after Paavo Nurmi of Finland and Gundar Hägg of Sweden, to hold world records at 1500m and 5000m simultaneously.

In 1986, Aouita continued to take on the clock at every opportunity. But despite an amazing sequence of wins over the finest runners in Europe, he failed to break records at the mile, with 3:50.35 in Berlin, at 5000m, with 13:00.86 in Cologne, and at 3000m, with 7:32.94 in Zurich. He even took the opportunity to show his potential at 10,000m, trouncing a world-class field in Oslo with 27:26.11, despite being badly spiked in the early laps.

Never content just to shave hundredths of a second off world records, Aouita wanted to put them beyond reach. His obsession continued in 1987, when he finally claimed the 2000m record with a time of 4:50.81 in Paris, and his preparation for the World Championships concluded with his scintillating 5000m world record. In Rome, he calmly announced that he would win the 5000m world title and break his own world record. He said 'It does not matter who else is in the race. I have only the clock to worry about'. In the event, he had virtually talked his way to the gold medal. The rest of the field followed a lack-lustre pace, and could only watch as he sprinted for home with 300m to go to win in 13:26.44.

Ashford, Evelyn

1957–. Born USA (USA)

When Evelyn Ashford won the 100m gold medal at the 1984 Los Angeles Games, in the Olympic record time of 10.97, there were still some detractors who claimed that she might not have won but for the Eastern Bloc boycott. Ashford answered the critics by going to Europe to take on her biggest rival, the East German world record holder Marlies Göhr. On 22 August at Zurich's Weltklasse meeting, Ashford duly beat Göhr by almost a metre to set a new world record of 10.76, proving that she was indeed the world's top woman sprinter.

Coached from the age of 18 by former Olympic pentathlete Pat Connolly, Ashford made her international début for the USA at the Montreal Olympics in 1976, when she was fifth in the 100m in 11.24, behind West Germany's Annegret Richter. In 1977, she was well beaten over 100m and 200m at the inaugural World Cup in Düsseldorf, where Göhr won the shorter sprint in a world record time of 10.88. Ashford's times improved the following year, but it was in 1978 that she became a truly world-class competitor, ending the season ranked world fourth with a best of 11.18.

As American and Pan American champion over 100m and 200m, Ashford went on to win both sprint titles at the second World Cup in Montreal, beating East Germans Göhr and Marita Koch in the process. She repeated the double in the third World Cup competition in Rome in 1981, when she went some way to making up for her sense of loss at missing the Moscow Olympic Games of 1980 because of the American boycott.

She went to Helsinki for the first IAAF World Championships in 1983 as world record holder, after clocking 10.79 at Colorado Springs in July, and was rated joint favourite with Göhr for the 100m title. The final proved dramatic, but for all the wrong reasons. With Göhr just ahead at 50m, Ashford pulled up sharply and collapsed on the track. The East German went on to win in 10.97. The injury was, in fact, a pulled hamstring, although Connolly put it down to 'emotional stress due to personal problems not related to track'. It was later revealed that Ashford's marriage was breaking up.

Her marriage mended, Ashford's 1984 season began with a recurrence of that hamstring injury. She qualified for the Olympics only after having her right leg heavily strapped for the 100m at the American trials. She won that, but had to drop out of the 200m.

Absent from the 1985 season because of the birth of her daughter, Raina Ashley, she returned in 1986 to win 14 of her 15 100m finals, ranking first in the world at this event, and eight out of her nine 200m finals.

Her record includes five US championships at 100m and four at 200m. She has also set five US records at 100m and four at 200m.

Evelyn Ashford

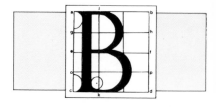

Balas, Iolanda

1936–. Born Romania (ROM)

Never before in the history of athletics has one athlete so dominated his or her particular event as Iolanda Balas did women's high jumping. From December 1956 until June 1967 she won 140 consecutive competitions, winning Olympic titles in 1960 and 1964, European titles in 1958 and 1962, and the first European Indoor Games title in 1966.

She set no fewer than 13 world records, starting with 1.75m on 14 July 1956 in Bucharest to 1.91m on 16 July 1961 in Sofia.

Balas is the only double gold medallist in the history of the Olympic high jump competition. She first participated in 1956, when she finished fifth, her only defeat until her career ended in 1967. In 1960, she won her first Olympic title in Rome by the astonishing margin of 14cm, with a jump of 1.85m. She retained her title in 1964 with a 1.90m jump, 10cm ahead of silver medallist Michelle Brown, of Australia.

Such was Balas' supremacy that by the end of 1963 she had cleared 1.80m in 72 competitions, yet this height was not successfully achieved by another woman until 27 September 1964. By the end of her career, she had jumped clear of 1.80m in no fewer than 93 competitions.

Of her 13 world records, 12 were set consecutively, from 1.78 to 1.91. This last mark stood for ten years and 50 days, the longest time in the history of the event.

Standing 1.85m tall herself, Balas' technique was as unique as her record, being described as a cross between the old-fashioned scissors and the Eastern cut-off. She defended her style

Iolanda Balas

thus: 'Some people think my jumping style is passé. But I wanted to show everyone that it is the best technique for me.' Persistent leg injuries restricted her jumping during 1966, and her winning sequence ended on 11 June 1967, when she was beaten by Dagmar Melzer (GDR). She retired soon afterwards and married her coach, Ion Soter.

Balzer, Karin

1938–. Born East Germany (GDR)

The most capped GDR athlete, with 55 international appearances between 1955 and 1972, Karin Balzer also holds the most world records (six) for the 100m hurdles, taking the record from 13.3 in 1969 to 12.6 in 1971. These records came after she had spent most of her career racing at the shorter distance of 80m, which was changed to 100m after the 1968 Olympics. Balzer was joint world record holder at 80m with 10.5 seconds, set in 1964, and she also went on to win the Olympic

Games title in Tokyo that year.

At 100mh Balzer was the first woman to dip under 13 seconds, and is one of only three women hurdlers to contest three Olympic finals (Australians Shirley Strickland and Pam Ryan are the others). In Mexico, in 1968, she finished fifth, and she also won the bronze medal in 1972 in Munich aged 34.

After finishing second in 1962, she also won three consecutive European titles, in 1966, 1969 and 1971, as well as five European indoor hurdles titles. Besides collecting seven national sprint hurdles titles, she also won two at pentathlon and one each at 200m and the long jump.

Banks, Willie

1956–. Born USA (USA)

Willie Banks and the triple jump event captured the public's attention in 1981. Banks, then touring Europe as part of an American team, asked a leading athletics promoter why so many meetings excluded the triple jump event. When the promoter replied that it was because the event was not exciting, Banks decided to set out to prove him wrong.

During the DN Galan meeting, in

Stockholm, he urged his fellow competitors to jump personal bests to attract the public eye. He then hit upon a much better way to grab people's attention. He warmed up for his jump by listening to music through the headset of his personal stereo. The crowd noticed him moving in time to the music and applauded. Banks proceeded to encourage the crowd and put on a show for the gallery. By the time he stepped on to the runway for his jump, the crowd were clapping in time to Banks' approach. The triple jump event had at last become the focus of attention.

This resulted in the event being increasingly included in the programmes at major meetings, and Willie Banks became a celebrity. Everywhere he competed, the crowd was ready to respond.

He has, however, had mixed fortunes since becoming World Student Games champion in 1979. Runner-up at the 1983 World Championships in Helsinki, where he jumped 17.18m to Poland's Zdzislaw Hoffman's 17.42m, Banks was hot favourite for the Olympic Games in 1984. However, he could only finish sixth in a lack-lustre competition, and immediately turned his attention to breaking the ten-year-old

Karin Balzer (second from right)

Willie Banks

world record of 17.89m, held by Joao de Oliveira of Brazil. He achieved this on 16 June 1985, when he jumped 17.97m at Indianapolis. Later that year, he won gold at the World Cup in Canberra, Australia. Overshadowed by fellow countryman Mike Conley in 1986, Banks failed to qualify for the World Championship final in Rome the following year, where Conley won the silver.

Banks remains a popular figure, however, and the rhythmic clapping that he started in 1981 is a continuing feature of triple jump competitions at major meetings around the world.

Bannister, Roger

1929–. Born England (GBR)

When Roger Bannister broke the four-minute mile barrier on 6 May 1954, at the Iffley Road track in Oxford, clocking 3:59.4, few could have foreseen that his record would last barely six weeks. Yet that one run is enough to ensure that his name passes into athletics immortality, a run that he prepared for over a seven-month period with training partners Chris Brasher and Chris Chataway.

Bannister had shown promise while still a student at Oxford University, and had been offered a chance to compete at the 1948 Olympics in London, an opportunity he turned down on the grounds that he was not yet mature enough. The following year, aged 20, he demonstrated that earlier faith in him was not misplaced, with a mile in 4:11.1, and in the European Championships of 1950 he finished a very close third in the 800m, recording 1:50.7. That same year he also brought his mile time down to 4:09.9, which he improved to 4:07.8 in 1951. But his most impressive run was just before the Olympics – a three-quarter mile time of 2:52.9, over three and a half seconds faster than the unofficial world record.

Yet he could not reproduce this form in the 1500m final at the 1952 Olympics in Helsinki, where he finished fourth, although he did set a UK best of 3:46.0. After mulling over his disappointment and deciding against retirement, he came back to his spar-

kling best in 1954. Although conditions were windy, Bannister and his AAA team mates, Brasher and Chataway, decided to attempt the world mile record in the match against Oxford University. Brasher set the pace for the first two laps, covering 440 yards in 57.4 seconds and 880 yards in 1:58.0, with Chataway taking over the pace to enable Bannister to reach the three-quarter mark in 3:00.5. From 230 yards out Bannister was on his own, with Chataway finishing a distant second in 4:07.2.

Later that year, Bannister won an epic duel against the Australian John Landy, who had broken the Englishman's record with an astonishing run at Turku, in Finland, of 3:57.9 on 21 June. The so-called 'Miracle Mile' took place on 7 August in the Empire Games (later the Commonwealth Games), in Vancouver, with the stage set for a historic confrontation featuring the first two men under four minutes. Allowing Landy to build up an

Bannister breaks the four-minute mile

Daniel Bautista (488)

early lead, Bannister passed the Australian on the final bend to win in 3:58.8, with Landy second in 3:59.6.

Three weeks later, he added the European 1500m title to his collection, but retired at the end of that season to concentrate on his medical studies.

Knighted in 1975, Bannister was Chairman of the Sports Council from 1971-1974.

Bautista, Daniel

1952–. Born Mexico (MEX)

By winning the 20km walk title at the 1976 Olympics in Montreal, Daniel Bautista became Mexico's first-ever Olympic athletics champion, with his time of 1:24.40.6 the fastest yet recorded at a major championship. A photograph of his victory later revealed, however, that he had been 'lifting': both feet had been off the ground at the same time, contrary to the rules. Four years later, in Moscow, Bautista was leading the 20km event with Anatoliy Solomin (USSR), when both were disqualified for this same offence, which allowed the Italian Maurizio Damilano through to win.

However, before this unfortunate incident, Bautista reigned supreme,

setting three world bests on the road: at 15km on 29 September 1979, at Eschborn in Germany, with 58:52.0; at 20km in the same race, when he became the first man under 1:20 with 1:18:49.0; and at 30km on 27 April 1980, at Therkassy, USSR, with 2:03.06. He also set records on the track: at 15km on 26 March 1980, at Monterrey, Mexico, with 59:33.0; at 20km on 17 October 1979, in Montreal, Canada, with 1:20:06.8; and a one-hour total of 15,121m in the Monterrey race on 26 March.

Bautista also won the IAAF Race Walking World Cup (the Lugano Trophy) twice, in 1977 and 1979, setting his world best 20km mark at the latter event in Eschborn, West Germany. He retired soon after the 1980 Olympic Games.

Bayi, Filbert

1953–. Born Tanzania (TAN)

Bayi entered the history books by becoming the first African to break the world mile and 1500m records. However, what was remarkable about his records was the way that he achieved them: he simply ran as fast as he could from the gun, a tactic that

meant he led races from the start and which often proved that he had the stamina and speed to outpace his rivals, even though he was prone to misjudging his early effort and being overtaken on the final lap.

In his most famous victory, however, he timed his run to perfection. He led from start to finish to win the 1500m title at the 1974 Commonwealth Games in Christchurch, New Zealand in 3:32.2, breaking Jim Ryun's seven-year-old world record. Bayi went through 400m in 54.4 seconds, 800m in 1:51.8, and held off the challenge of race favourite John Walker of New Zealand and Ben Jipcho of Kenya with a 55.8 second last lap.

A year later, in Kingston, Jamaica, he broke Ryun's eight-year-old mile record with 3:51, a mark that lasted only three months before Walker took it below 3:50. The two should have met at the 1976 Olympic Games in Montreal, but the African boycott meant that Bayi was absent as Walker took the 1500m gold medal. Bayi's next three seasons were upset by injury and illness, although he was at the 1978 Commonwealth Games in Edmonton, Canada to defend his

Filbert Bayi

1500m title. On this occasion, however, he did not have the necessary strength, and took silver after being passed in the home straight by England's Dave Moorcroft.

In 1980 he won Tanzania's first Olympic medal in Moscow, when he employed his front-running tactic in the steeplechase. In what turned out to be a thrilling race, Bayi built up a 30m lead with two laps to go, but tired noticeably at every hurdle from then on. He was finally caught and passed at the last water-jump by Polish gold medallist, Bronislaw Malinowski.

Beamon, Bob

1946–. Born USA (USA)

With one giant leap for mankind, on 18 October 1968 at the Mexico Olympics, not only did Bob Beamon become the first man to jump over 28 feet (8.53m), but he passed the 29-foot barrier (8.88m) as well. With one jump the record had risen further than it had over the entire 40 years previous to this, the existing record of Ralph Boston being broken by a massive 55cm.

Although Beamon's talent had never been in doubt, his best before

The phenomenal Bob Beamon

his world record being 8.33m, he was also a noted no-jumper. Indeed, during the qualifying rounds on the previous day Beamon only reached the required distance of 7.65m on his third and final attempt after two no-jumps. His third leap, however, although only 8.19, was one at which he gave away at least 30cm on the take-off board, a sign of things to come.

Explanations of Beamon's amazing leap have concentrated on the rarified atmosphere of Mexico City, ideal for explosive activities, and the wind assistance, which was at the maximum permitted level of 2.0m per second. But whatever the explanation, Beamon's jump, his first in the final and the first to count after three other competitors had fouled, totally demoralised the opposition. After a second jump – a more modest 8.04 – Beamon passed on his remaining four attempts.

Unbeaten in 1968, Beamon went to Mexico as slight favourite ahead of compatriot Ralph Boston. He had come to prominence at the previous year's AAU Indoor Championships in America, where he improved his personal best from 7.82m to 8.22. In 1968 he also set a world indoor record

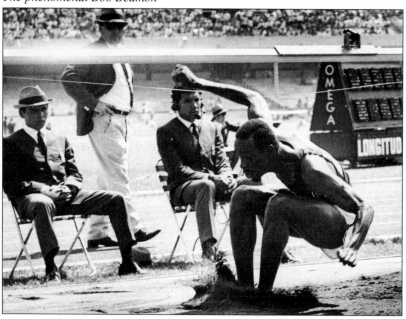

of 8.30, but following his triumph in Mexico he never again jumped over 8.20m. After a serious hamstring injury in 1969, he had to switch his take-off leg and was out of competition until 1973, by which time he had turned professional. That year his best was 8.16m, third in the world for that season.

Beccali, Luigi

1907–. Born Italy (ITA)

When Luigi Beccali romped home to win the 1500m at the 1932 Olympic Games in Los Angeles, recording 3:51.2, an Olympic record and at that time the second fastest 1500m ever, there was little in his previous form to indicate that he would ever reach such heights. Before the 1932 season his best for the distance was a rather mediocre 3:57.2, run in 1930 when losing to that great French runner, Jules Ladoumègue.

Yet in one race, in Milan on 15 May, Beccali's time of 3:52.2 marked him as an Olympic threat; this time had only been bettered by Ladoumègue since 1928. In the 1932 Olympic final, an astonishing last 300 metres, estimated at 41.7 seconds, took him past pre-race favourites Jack Lovelock (NZL) and Glenn Cunningham (USA) to win by ten yards.

Beccali's successes continued throughout 1933. He beat Jack Lovelock again in the final of the 1500m at the Student Games in 3:49.2, which equalled Ladoumegue's existing world record. Later that month, in an international match against Great Britain, he did capture the world record, running 3:49.0 in Milan. He ended the season having run three of the fastest 1500m times ever, and having set a new world record for 1000 yards of 2:10.0.

1934 saw him win the 1500m at the first European Championships, held in Turin, and he started to prepare for the defence of his Olympic title, with several good victories in 1935. Although nearly 29, Beccali was training hard, often running as many as 15

David Bedford

Joan Benoit-Samuelson

World Junior Cross-Country title in Clydebank, and two years later, at the age of 21, he won the senior title, making him only the second person in history to have won both. He won the English National title in 1971 and 1973 and, in an unprecedented display of stamina, won the Southern Counties senior and junior races in the same afternoon in 1970.

His track running was equally impressive, but, although his aggressive front running brought him five consecutive AAA titles at 10,000m from 1970 to 1974, and a memorable world record at the distance in 1973, it proved ineffective in major championships, where he was invariably outsprinted by men with more basic speed.

He finished sixth in the 1971 European Championships 10,000m, and sixth again in the 1972 Olympic final, behind Lasse Viren of Finland, after leading for most of the way. His boyhood hero had been Ron Clarke, the great Australian distance runner, who, ironically, could break records but never won a major title.

Bedford, with his long hair and walrus moustache, became a national hero with his record-breaking exploits. His strict training regime often meant him running 200 miles a week. The high point of his career came in 1973 when, just five weeks after recovering from an injury, and unsure of his fitness, he took almost eight seconds off Viren's 10,000m world record to clock 27:30.80, after going through 5000m in 13:39.74. He maintains even today that, had he been fully fit, he could have brought the record down to around 27 minutes. At one time he held every UK record from 2000m to 10,000m, excluding the two miles but including the steeplechase. In his final full season on the track, he managed fourth place in the 1974 Commonwealth Games 10,000m final, but injury forced him to retire at 25.

Since giving up competing, he has been a businessman and a night-club owner. He is currently actively involved in athletics again, as chairman of the International Athletes Club,

sprints of 300 metres. An excellent win in Budapest on 14 June in 3:50.6 gave him a better than even chance of retaining his Olympic crown.

The final brought together the greatest middle-distance runners of the age, and the race was no disappointment. Five of the first eight home set personal bests, but there was little joy for Beccali, who had no answer to a devastating burst at 1200m by Jack Lovelock, who won in a world record time of 3:47.8. Beccali finished third in 3:49.2.

The Italian's last major honour was a bronze medal in the 1938 European Championships, where he finished in 3:55.2 in a 1500m race won by Britain's Sydney Wooderson.

Bedford, David

1949–. Born England (GBR)

In a top-class career, lasting just six spectacular years, David Bedford won national and international titles, broke world records, and was virtually single-handedly responsible for making athletics popular again as a spectator sport in the UK.

As a brash teenager, he won the

promoter of the IAC's Mobil Grand Prix meeting, member of the Southern Counties AAA and British Amateur Athletic Board General Committee, and deputy race director of the London Marathon.

Benoit-Samuelson, Joan

1957–. Born USA (USA)

Joan Benoit-Samuelson's 2:24:52 win in the inaugural women's marathon at the 1984 Olympic Games in Los Angeles ranks among the best performances of all time. The fact that she made the start line at all was surprising enough, but the manner of her victory was little less than astonishing. Only 17 days before the American Olympic trials in May 1984, she was forced to undergo complex arthroscopic surgery on her right knee, yet she recovered sufficiently to win the race in 2:31:04, and, with it, Olympic selection. In LA, running in the finest all-women field ever assembled, Benoit-Samuelson simply took off after three miles and began a lonely run for the finish line in the coliseum. Rivals like Norway's Grete Waitz, the reigning World Champion, Ingrid

Kristiansen, and Portugal's Rosa Mota realised too late that she was not going to wilt in the heat and were left to battle it out for the minor medals.

Blessed with the strength to sustain a fast, even pace, Benoit-Samuelson has a remarkable marathon record. She won eight of her 13 marathons between 1979 and 1985, and has twice run a world best time: 2:22:43, in Boston in 1983, and 2:21:21, in Chicago in 1985. Her ambition remains to be the first woman to run a marathon inside 2:20.

Like many top-class road runners, she took up running in her teens as a means of keeping fit for another sport. In her case, it was skiing, but that was soon abandoned when her love of running took over. She ran her first marathon in Bermuda in 1979, to satisfy her curiosity about the distance, and finished second in 2:50:54.

She has since won over a variety of distances on the US road racing circuit, three times setting national records for the half-marathon. On the track she is an accomplished 10,000m runner. She won the American national title in 1981 and the Pan American Games 3000m gold medal in 1983.

She married Scott Samuelson in 1984, and missed the Rome World Championships when she had their first child, Abigail, in October 1987.

Beyer, Udo

1955–. Born East Germany (GDR)

Beyer has, without doubt, dominated the shot put event for the last ten years, with a remarkable sequence of championship wins and world record performances. European Junior Champion at the age of 17, he went on to set five European junior records in the ensuing 12 months. At just 20 he won selection for the 1976 Olympic Games in Montreal and, in what was a low standard competition, took the gold medal with a put of 21.05m, a mark that would only have earned him fifth place four years previously.

He followed that by winning the European Championships in 1978 and

Udo Beyer

1982, the European Cup Finals and World Cups in 1977, 1979 and 1981, and the World Student Games title in 1979. He set world records in 1978 (22.15m), 1983 (22.22m), and 1986 (22.64m), and notched up a sequence of ten successive GDR national titles between 1977 and 1986.

A pulled back muscle prevented

Abebe Bikila

him from retaining his Olympic title in 1980, when he won the bronze medal behind Vladimir Kiselyev's championship record put of 21.35m. The Eastern Bloc boycott ruled him out of the 1984 Games.

Beyer went into the 1986 European Championships in Stuttgart as favourite, after setting a new world record just a week before, but finished a disappointing third behind Werner Gunthor, the Swiss European Indoor Champion. He later claimed to have achieved 23m – much better than his world record – in training.

In an exceptionally strong line-up at the 1987 World Championships, Beyer could only finish sixth, with 21.13m, as Gunthor once again took the title.

Bikila, Abebe

1932–1973. Born Ethiopia (ETH)

The first man to retain the Olympic marathon title, he took the distance running world by storm in the Rome Games of 1960 as a complete unknown. Running barefoot – just to attract attention, he later claimed – he fought a classic duel with the Moroccan Rhadi ben Abdesselem from the half-way point, eventually winning by 25 seconds in a world best 2:15:16.2.

A member of Emperor Haile Selassie's Imperial Bodyguard, he started running in 1956, coached by the corps' coach, Swede Onni Niskanen. Training at altitudes above 6000 feet, sometimes barefoot, he had, in fact, run an astonishing 2:21:23 for the 26-mile distance in July 1960.

Between Olympics he raced infrequently, but lost only one of the 13 marathons he contested between 1960-66: the Boston Marathon in 1963, when he suffered leg cramps after 20 miles and finished fifth in 2:24:43. Before the 1964 Olympics in Tokyo, training runs pointed to a successful defence of his title, but an appendix operation six weeks before seemed to rule this out. Incredibly, he destroyed the 68-man field to win by four minutes in a new world best of 2:12:11.2,

Abdi Bile

and waited for the second man to enter the stadium by performing exercises.

In the 1968 Mexico Olympics, a leg injury forced Bikila out after ten miles, and the following year he was seriously injured in a car crash that left him confined to a wheelchair. Stoically accepting his fate, he took up archery and competed in several Paraplegic Games.

He died of a brain haemorrhage on 25 October 1973.

Bile, Abdi

1963–. Born Somalia (SOM)

One of 14 children, Abdi Bile, World Champion at 1500m in 1987, was raised by an uncle, and first went to school in Las Anod in Somalia. He began running at high school in Mogadishu only because it helped him keep fit for playing soccer. He was 18 and playing for the national youth team when he was introduced to 400m running. Wearing football boots, he ran 56 seconds and finished the race exhausted. Encouraged by a teacher, he lowered his time to 55 seconds the following day, and managed 53 seconds later the same week. At first he found running boring, but soon grew to enjoy it as his times improved.

His potential was spotted by Jama Aden, the country's best known athlete, who was studying in the USA. It was Aden who persuaded the coach John Cook to offer Bile an athletics scholarship at George Mason University in Fairfax, Virginia. Bile arrived in America in 1983 with personal bests of 1:50 for 800m and 3:45 for 1500m. Cook immediately set about improving Bile's all-round strength with a course of swimming, cycling and weight training. His first season running in the American college circuit saw him improve his 1500m time to 3:40, and he was picked to represent Somalia at the 1984 Olympic Games in Los Angeles.

He reached the second round of the 800m, but was disqualified from the semi-final of the 1500m race after allegedly impeding Guimares of Brazil in running 3:35.89.

Bile's victory at the second World Championships in 1987 was seen at the time as a shock result, mainly because of reigning champion and race favourite Steve Cram's poor showing, but the Somalian had arrived in Rome with far better credentials than many observers realised. Even Cram, when asked before the race about his rivals, said that Bile was the one who had looked most impressive on the Euro-

pean circuit before the championships. Twice American national collegiate champion in 1985 and 1987, and a respected pace-maker for the likes of Said Aouita and Sydney Maree during the summer of 1986, Bile improved his personal bests in 1987 to 1:44.47 for 800m, 3:31.71 for 1500m, and 3:50.75 for the mile, all run within the space of six days in August.

Only a week after his world championship triumph, he was the star attraction at the IAAF Grand Prix Final in Brussels, when he won the 1500m in 3:31.80, which was an attempt on Aouita's world record of 3:29.46.

Blankers-Koen, Fanny

1918–. Born Netherlands (HOL)

Fanny Blankers-Koen became the most successful female athlete of all time at the 1948 Olympics in London, when she won gold medals in four different events, winning the 100m, 200m, 80m hurdles, and anchoring the 4 x 100m relay team to victory. She did not enter two events at which she was the existing world record holder, the high jump and the long jump. What's more, she was considered, at 30, to be past her best, but continued setting world records until 1951.

Blankers-Koen (far right) wins the 1948 Olympic 100m

Her Olympic career had started 12 years earlier in the Berlin Games of 1936, where she finished sixth in the high jump and helped the Dutch team to finish fifth in the 4 x 100m relay. Married in 1940, by the end of the Second World War she was world record holder in the 80mh, the high jump and the long jump. Her high jump mark, 1.71m, set on 30 May 1943, was a 5cm improvement on the previous record, and was the first jump by a woman over 1.70m.

Between 1938 and 1951 she set official world records at no fewer than seven individual and two relay events, and it is this unique spread of events that assures her place in history: 100 yards, 100m, 220 yards, 80mh, high jump, long jump, and pentathlon.

Blankers-Koen was almost as successful at the 1950 European Championships, winning the 100m, 200m, 80mh, and a silver in the 4 x 100m relay, with a fourth place in the high jump. She also won no fewer than 58 Dutch individual national titles.

At the 1952 Olympics in Helsinki, Blankers-Koen, now aged 34, was a shadow of her former self, partly as a result of medication she was taking for painful boils. She dropped out of the 80mh final, having failed to qualify for the 100m. She retired for good in 1955, aged 37.

Board, Lillian

1948–1970. Born South Africa (GBR)

Although predictions in athletics are as risky as in any other field of life, most athletics experts agree that, had she lived, Lillian Board would have been one of the all-time great middle-distance runners of the 1970s. Although her life was tragically ended by cancer when she was just 22, her talent had already brought her an Olympic silver medal, a European title, and relay world records.

Although she was born in South Africa, her family came to Britain in 1950, and, on moving to London, Lillian was soon running well for her

club, London Olympiades. She first started placing at high level in 1966, coming fourth in the WAAA Championships 440 yards (in a very respectable 54.6), and fifth in the Commonwealth Games final at the same distance. 1967 saw her win the WAAA 440-yard final, and beat a world class field in the USA v Commonwealth match in Los Angeles in July. Her time of 52.8 for 440 yards saw her tipped as an Olympic medallist for the first time.

In Olympic year Lillian also showed her promise at 880 yards, finishing second in the WAAA Championships in 2:02.0 to Vera Nikolic, who broke the world record with 2:00.5, and at shorter distances, being a member of the British quartet who broke the 4 x 110-yard relay world record shortly before the Games in Mexico (45.0). In the 400m final she was beaten in the last few yards by Colette Besson, of France, 52.03 to 52.12.

The following year, a recurring back injury, which got worse the faster she ran, made Lillian choose the 800m for the European Championships in

Lillian Board

Athens. She beat her rival, Colette Besson, by ten yards, avenging her Olympic defeat, in a race where the first four women home broke the 1966 Championship record of 2:02.8 set by Vera Nikolic.

In the 4 x 400m relay, Lillian again overhauled Besson, this time on the line, as both British and French teams set new world records of 3:30.8.

As the winter approached, a nagging stomach pain was diagnosed as cancer. Lillian died in a clinic in Munich on Boxing Day 1970, 13 days after her twenty-second birthday.

Boit, Mike

1949–. Born Kenya (KEN)

Mike Boit has been racing over 800m, 1500m and the mile at the highest international level for 15 years, a record unsurpassed in modern times. Yet, despite a career that includes a Commonwealth title and an Olympic bronze medal, he has been dogged by bad luck. But for Kenya's political boycotts in 1976 and 1980, Boit may well have added to his medal tally.

Born at altitude in Kenya's Rift Valley, he began running at 18 in his second year at a missionary high school run by Patrician Fathers from Ireland. His début at international level came in spectacular fashion in 1972, at the Munich Olympic Games. He won his heat and the semi-final of the 800m, and finished within a couple of strides of gold medallist Dave Wottle in the final. He won the bronze medal with a time of 1:46. He later finished fourth in the 1500m final, won by Finland's Pekka Vasala, in which fellow Kenyan, Kip Keino, the reigning champion, won the silver medal.

In 1973 Boit moved to America on a scholarship at the University of Eastern New Mexico. By the following year, he had improved his times to 1:44.4 for 800m and 3:36.84 for 1500m. At the Commonwealth Games in Christchurch, however, he found himself in exceptionally fast company. He won the silver medal at 800m,

Mike Boit

behind John Kipkurgat's Commonwealth record of 1:43.90, while at 1500m he could only finish sixth, as Filbert Bayi won gold with a world record of 3:32.16.

Ranked number one over two laps in 1975, when he came within nine hundredths of a second of the world record, Boit was gold medal favourite for the Montreal Olympics in 1976. After taking part in the opening ceremony, however, he was reduced to watching Cuba's Alberto Juantorena win in a world record time, when Kenya pulled out over the New Zealand rugby tour of South Africa.

Head-to-head races between Boit and Juantorena came in 1977, confrontations eagerly anticipated by the athletics public. The Olympic champion won the first race in Zurich by a full second – 1:43.64 to 1:44.64 – but their second race, at the World Cup in Düsseldorf, was one of the finest 800m races of all time. Racing neck and neck to the line, the Cuban crossed first in 1:44.04, with Boit just a tenth of a second adrift. A gold medal finally came in 1978, when Boit won the Commonwealth Games 800m title in Edmonton. In 1981 he became the third fastest miler in history, with

3:49.45, behind Sebastian Coe's world record run of 3:47.33 in Brussels.

His last major success was a 1500m bronze medal, behind Steve Cram and John Walker at the 1982 Commonwealth Games in Brisbane. He formally retired in 1985, after struggling to overcome persistent injury problems. Remarkably, he discovered that the injury healed with the enforced rest and he decided to return to international racing in 1987, when he was still able to compete at the highest level on the European road and track circuit.

Bondarchuk, Anatoliy

1940–. Born USSR (URS)

European hammer champion in 1969, Bondarchuk set a world record in this competition of 74.68m, a mark which he increased shortly afterwards in Rovno to 75.48. Although 32 at the time of the 1972 Olympic Games in Munich, he went into the competition having thrown further than any of his rivals during the year. His first throw of the competition won him the gold medal, landing at a distance of 75.50m, although there was a last-minute scare when the penultimate throw of the event, by Jochen Sachse (GDR) landed within a metre of Bondarchuk's mark, which had broken the Olympic record.

Four years later, he succeeded in qualifying for the Olympic team for the Montreal Games, where he took the bronze medal behind one of his pupils, Yiriy Sedykh. He subsequently turned to coaching full-time.

Bondarenko, Olga

1960–. Born USSR (URS)

Despite presenting a tiny figure on the track, Olga Bondarenko is a fiercesome competitor over 3000m, 5000m and 10,000m.

World record holder in 1984 of the 10,000m, with 31:13.78, a distance then rarely run by women, Bondarenko missed the Olympic Games in Los Angeles – where she would proba-

Olga Bondarenko (823)

bly have run 3000m – because of the Eastern Bloc boycott. Nevertheless, she enjoyed an outstanding season in 1985, when she won a 3000m silver medal at the European Indoor Championships and was placed first in the European Cup Final 10,000m. She should have won the World Cup 10,000m in Canberra, but she misjudged the number of laps and set off on a sprint finish, only to find that she had another 400m to run. She eventually finished third in 32:27.70, after being passed by Cunha of Portugal and Knisely of the USA.

There were no such mistakes in 1986, when she sprinted away to the gold medal in the European Championships 3000m in Stuttgart, to win by almost two seconds from Romania's Olympic champion, Maricicia Puica. Two days later, she became the second woman in history to run inside 31 minutes for 10,000m when she won the silver medal behind Ingrid Kristiansen of Norway, who had taken the world record to 30:13.74 earlier that year in Oslo.

At the World Championships in Rome a year later, Bondarenko was not at her best and was, like the rest of the field, left behind when Kristiansen opened up a 25m lead on the second lap of the 10,000m. She finished fourth in a frantic race for the minor medals as silver went to team mate Yelena Zhupiyeva and bronze to Kathrin Ullrich of East Germany.

Borzov, Valeriy

1949–. Born USSR (URS)

Valeriy Borzov achieved the ultimate for a sprinter when he won the 100m/200m double at the 1972 Olympics in Munich, the first European to do so. Four years later, in Montreal, he managed what no other sprinter has done before or since by winning another medal at 100m, albeit a bronze. To this impressive Olympic medal tally a silver can be added for the 1972 4 x 100m relay, and a bronze for the same event in 1976.

In addition to his successes in the Olympics, he also won European titles, three times at 100m (1969, 1971, and 1974) and at 200m in 1971. Indoors, he won seven European titles at 50m/60m, and was the holder of 13 USSR titles, seven at 100m and six at 200m.

Although it is often said that Borzov the sprinter was made and not born, he did show remarkable early promise, winning the European Championships for the first time in 1969 before his twentieth birthday. Since his retirement in 1979, following Achilles tendon operations, the Soviet Union has not managed to produce a worthy successor. It is true to say, however, that his development into the finest sprinter of his generation was largely controlled by a team of scientists at the Kiev Institute of Physical Culture and Sport, and he and his coach, Valentin Petrovsky, meticulously worked on every aspect of his sprinting technique.

His Olympic victories in 1972 proved his superiority, although in the 100m he did not have to face two formidable American sprinters, Eddie Hart and Rey Robinson, both of whom failed to arrive at the stadium in time for their heats. Borzov broke the European record with a time of 10.07 in the heats, and beat the American Robert Taylor by a yard in the final with a time of 10.14. In the 200m final, he set another European record of 20.00, to win by two metres.

Although he intended to compete in the 1980 Games in Moscow, injury forced him to withdraw. His best times were 10.00 for 100m and 20.00 for 200m.

Boston, Ralph

1939–. Born USA (USA)

Holder of six world long jump records and winner of a complete set of medals at the Olympics, Ralph Boston will be remembered equally as the man who finally broke Jesse Owens' world record, which had stood for 25 years.

Owens' 8.13m fell to Boston's leap of 8.21m, set in a pre-Olympic trial on 12 August 1960. Boston's sixth and final world record, set on 29 May 1965, took the mark to 8.35m and lasted until Bob Beamon's amazing leap at the 1968 Mexico Olympics.

Throughout his best years, in the 1960s, Boston's main rival was the Russian Igor Ter-Ovanesyan, with whom he alternated as the world record holder several times. His Olympic record started with gold in 1960, when he became the first man to better Jesse Owens' 1936 winning leap of 8.06m with his 8.12m. Boston, in fact, won by only one centimetre, his compatriot Bo Roberson clearing 8.11m with his last attempt. In 1964, Boston ended four centimetres behind

Valeriy Borzov (828)

Ralph Boston

Britain's Lynn Davies with a last round jump of 8.03m, and he completed his medal set four years later in Mexico with 8.16m, in a competition where his world record was destroyed by the 8.90 mark set by team mate Bob Beamon.

Boston himself jumped further than his own world record unofficially on several occasions. Indeed, the year before at the US Olympic trials he recorded 8.49m, but this was with wind assistance over the legal limit. In 1966 he jumped 8.56, but in falling back reduced his mark to 8.23.

Among his other titles were two Pan American Games victories (1963 and 1967), six outdoor AAU titles from 1961-66, and the indoor title in 1961. He was a talented all-round jumper, with bests of 2.05 for the high jump and 15.89 for the triple jump, as well as 9.6 seconds for 100 yards.

Boyle, Raelene

1951–. Born Australia (AUS)

Winner of seven Commonwealth Games gold medals, and nine medals in all, Raelene Boyle is also the only woman to have run in three Olympic 100m finals, finishing fourth in 1968 (11.19), aged 17, second in 1972 (11.23), and fourth again in 1976 (11.23). Her record at the highest level in the 200m is also impressive: she won two Olympic silver medals at this distance, on both occasions in races where a new world record was set. In 1968, in Mexico, Irene Szewinska lowered the mark to 22.5 seconds (Boyle recorded 22.7), and in 1972 East Germany's Renate Stecher came home in 22.40 to Boyle's 22.45.

It was at the Commonwealth Games that she achieved most success, starting aged 19 at the 1970 Commonwealth Games in Edinburgh, where she won the 100m/200m/ sprint relay treble. She repeated this feat four years later, in Christchurch, New Zealand. In 1978 she won the silver at 100m, and on home ground in Brisbane in 1982 she showed that she could also be devastating at longer distances, winning the 400m. She had a one lap personal best of 51.08, moving up to the distance late in her career at top level, although she had been running it seriously since 1974.

A natural sprinter –, by her own admission she was only training three times a week before the Olympics in Mexico – she was ranked world num-

Raelene Boyle

ber two in the 100m in 1972, and was also number two three times at 200m (1968, 1971, and 1972).

Bragina, Lyudmila

1943–. Born USSR (URS)

A noted front runner, Lyudmila rewrote the women's 1500m record books in 1972, when she broke the

Lyudmila Bragina (leading)

world record no less than four times. At the age of 29, she ran 4:09.6 at the Soviet Championships, six weeks before her amazing performance at the Olympic Games in Munich, where the event was included for the first time. She began by breaking her own record in her heat with 4:06.47, when the first five finishers went inside the previous world record as it had stood at the start of the year.

Bragina improved her record still further in the semi-final three days later, when she clocked 4:05.07. She went even faster in the final, running 2:07.4 for the last 800m to win the gold medal with 4:01.38.

She had made a late start to serious athletics at the age of 21, but made up for it with some stunning performances in her early thirties. In 1974, she set the first of three world records for 3000m, running 8:52.74. After finishing fifth in the Olympic 1500m final in Montreal in 1976, losing her world record to Tatyana Kazankina, Bragina, at the age of 33, produced a sensational run in the USSR v USA 3000m just a few days later. She took 18 seconds off Grete Waitz's (née Andersen) world record with 8:27.12, after covering the final kilometre in 2:87.12.

Brasher, Chris

1928–. Born Guyana (GBR)

Although perhaps best known as the man who, along with Chris Chataway, paced Roger Bannister in the most famous athletics record of all, breaking the four-minute mile, Brasher was Olympic 3000m steeplechase champion in Melbourne in 1956, and continues to this day to be actively involved in running, having been the instigator and race director of the London Marathon since 1981.

Brasher's part in Bannister's record, set on 6 May 1954, was to make the pace for the opening two and a half laps, although he was a fair miler himself, recording 4:09.0 that year. But since 1950, realising his limitations on the flat, he had been concen-

Chris Brasher

trating more and more on the steeplechase, and made the Olympic team for Helsinki in 1952. He finished eleventh out of 12 in the final, but after regular training at Oxford with Bannister and Chris Chataway, improved his steeplechase time of 8:49.2 in August 1956. In the Olympic final of that year he surprised everyone with his victory, although it was a victory that was almost snatched away. Brasher was initially disqualified for obstructing Ernst Larsen of Norway, but was reinstated when the jury of appeal ruled their clash accidental.

Finishing sixth in the Olympic steeplechase final of that year was John Disley, the British number one at the event, who fell ill before the race. It was with Disley that Brasher came up with the idea of a marathon through the streets of London, after seeing the New York Marathon in 1979. At the first London Marathon in 1981, Brasher, then aged 52, set a personal best of 2:56:56.

Briesenick, Ilona

1956–. Born East Germany (GDR)

Without doubt the world's dominant woman shot putter of the late 1970s and early 1980s, Briesenick's career was marred by the positive dope test she had after her 1977 European Cup win in Helsinki, when it was revealed that she had taken anabolic steroids. She was subsequently banned from competition, but, under International Amateur Athletic Federation rules, was allowed to return a year later.

Her first success was as a teenager, when she won the European Junior title in 1973, also coming second in the discus competition. At 1.80m (5ft 11in) and 92.5kg (204lb) she developed into a powerful athlete. In her first Olympic Games, in Montreal in 1976, she finished fifth. Her reinstatement by the IAAF meant that she was able to win her first European Championship title in Prague in 1978. She followed this with a golden year in 1980. In Moscow, she won the gold medal at the Olympic Games by the biggest margin in women's shot putting history. Her winning put of 22.41m (73ft 6in) was a new Olympic record and was 99cm better than the

Ilona Briesenick

best effort of silver medallist Svyetlana Krachevskaya.

European indoor champion in 1979 and 1981, she retained her European outdoor title in 1982. In Helsinki, at the inaugural World Championships in 1983, she finished third. Among her other wins are three World Cup triumphs in 1977, 1979, and 1981, although she was stripped of her title in 1977 after it was revealed that she had failed the drugs test at the European Cup Final the previous month.

Formerly Slupianek, née Schoknecht, she married Hammut Briesenick, the European shot champion of 1971 and 1974.

Brisco, Valerie

1960–. Born USA (USA)

Little known before the 1984 Olympic Games, Valerie Brisco took advantage of the Eastern Bloc boycott to score a unique double by winning gold at 200m and 400m. She won a third gold medal as the third runner in America's winning 4 x 400m relay team.

Inspired in her early years by the 1960 triple Olympic gold medallist, Wilma Rudolph, Brisco began training seriously in 1979, when she was ranked tenth in the world at 200m. In 1980, she married American football player Alvin Hooks.

Living in Los Angeles, she teamed up with coach Bob Kersee, husband of Jackie Joyner-Kersee. Her best 400m time going into the 1984 Olympic year was still only 52.08, although this improved to 49.83 in the American trials. At the Games her 48.83 Olympic record put her fourth on the all-time list. In the 200m, after a hesitant start, she won by two metres from team mate Florence Griffith in 21.81, another Olympic record and the third fastest time in history. She completed a hat trick of titles by running a 49.23 leg in the Americans' Olympic record time of 3:18.29.

Like Evelyn Ashford at 100m, Brisco was eager to show the world that her medals had not been won

Valerie Brisco

cheaply just because of the boycott by Eastern Bloc countries. In 1985, therefore, she joined the European track circuit, and duly beat East Germans Marlies Gohr in the 100m, Marita Koch in the 200m, and Kirsten Emmelmann in the 400m. She ended the season ranked in the world's top ten for each event.

She missed out on selection at the individual 400m for the 1987 World Championships by finishing only fourth in the American TAC meeting at San José, California in 51.28. She did make the relay team, though, running a 49.97 third leg as the Americans finished third behind East Germany and the USSR.

Brown, Doris

1942–. Born USA (USA)

The first notable American woman distance runner, Doris Brown won the World Cross-Country Championships in their first five years, from 1967 to 1971. She also competed in 1973, 1975, and 1976, but her placings were mediocre, fifteenth, seventeenth, and seventeenth respectively. Because of the lack of longer track races open to

women during her career, Brown was restricted to the 800m, a distance at which she set two US records, twice finished second in the Pan American Games (1967 and 1971), and was placed fifth in the 1968 Olympics.

During her career, which stretched from 1960 to 1976, the 1.63m (5ft 4in), 50kg (110lb) housewife from Seattle set 14 American records (two at 800m, five at 1500m, five at one mile, and two at 3000m), won five US national championships, and was three times ranked number one in the USA. She served as an assistant coach to the US team at the 1984 Olympics in Los Angeles and the 1987 World Championships in Rome.

Brumel, Valeriy

1942–. Born USSR (URS)

Holder of six high jump world records between 1961 and 1963, Valeriy Brumel came closer than any other man in history to winning two Olympic titles. As a 19-year-old, in 1960, he cleared the same height as the eventual winner, compatriot Robert Shavlakadze, but had to settle for second place on the count-back. Four years later he beat American John Thomas on the same ruling, both men clearing 2.18m.

Doris Brown

Valeriy Brumel

Brumel's first world record was indoors in Leningrad on 29 January 1961, his 2.25m beating the existing mark by three centimetres. His last world record was 2.28m, set during the USA-USSR match in Moscow in 1963, a height that was not beaten until 1970. Brumel was also holder of ten European records, from 2.17 in 1960 to 2.25 in 1963.

On 7 October 1965 a motorcycle accident necessitated five hours of surgery, and there were fears that Brumel's right leg might have to be amputated due to gangrene. After years of recuperation and further surgery, he made a come-back in 1969, clearing 2.13 in 1970. However, he was never able to recapture his previous form.

An all-round athlete, Brumel had best marks of 10.5 for 100m, 7.65m for long jump, 15.84m for shot, and 4.20m for pole vault.

Bryzgina, Olga

1963–. Born USSR (URS)

Formerly Olga Vladykina, and later married to Russian sprinter Viktor Bryzgin, she emerged from the shadow of the great Marita Koch to win the 400m title at the 1987 World Championships in Rome. In Koch's absence the event was thought to be wide open, and Bryzgina went into the final largely unfancied as a medal winner. But in a race in which only two women broke 50 seconds, Bryzgina had the stronger finish to win in 49.38, after pulling away from East Germany's Petra Muller in the home straight.

Her best time, 48.27, set in 1985, makes her the third fastest 400m runner of all time. She was silver medallist behind Marita Koch, the world record holder, in the 1986 European Championships in Stuttgart.

Bubka, Sergey

1963–. Born USSR (URS)

Since winning his first major pole vault competition at the 1983 World Championships in Helsinki at the age of 19, Sergey Bubka has dominated the event. Not only has he won every major title he has contested, but he has set nine world records since 1984, making him arguably the greatest pole vaulter of all time.

A superb all-round athlete – his speed on the runway is testament to his ability as a sprinter – he was denied the chance of an Olympic gold medal in 1984, when the Soviet Union boycotted the Games in Los Angeles.

In 1985, he began by winning the European Indoor title, and went on to win in the European Cup and World Cup. The following year, he became European Champion, taking the gold medal ahead of his older brother, Vasily, with 5.85m, after entering the competition at 5.65m. He won his second European Cup title in 1987, before going on to win at the second World Championships in Rome, where he made victory look all too easy, taking just two vaults at 5.70m and 5.85m. He later had the bar raised to 6.05m, two centimetres above his world record height, but luck was against him on this occasion in the busy and noisy Stadio Olympico. He took the world record to 6.05m in Bratislava in June 1988 and then to 6.06m in Nice a month later.

Budd, Zola

1966–. Born South Africa (GBR)

As a 17-year-old barefoot runner in her native South Africa, Zola Budd's achievements went largely unrecognized by the rest of the world until she bettered Mary Decker's world record for 5000m by almost seven seconds, with 15:01.83 on 5 January 1984. The record could not be ratified, however, because of South Africa's suspension

Sergey Bubka

from world athletics, but Budd herself became the focus of attention for the world's media. When it was discovered that her dream was to run in an Olympic Games and that she could claim a British heritage through her father's family, the *Daily Mail* newspaper brought her to Britain. She arrived, in secret, in March 1984, and was duly presented with a passport only 13 days after applying, apparently after the intervention of the *Daily Mail*. This immediately incurred the wrath of politicians, anti-apartheid groups, and sections of the general public, who condemned the preferential treatment she had received.

Nevertheless, as a British citizen and living in Hampshire, she made her racing début in a Southern League 3000m, running for her new club, Aldershot, Farnham and District on 14 April. Her time of 9:02.6 was a UK junior record. She easily qualified for the British team for Los Angeles, where she met American favourite and her own idol, Mary Decker, in the 3000m final. Just after 1700m, Decker tripped on Budd's trailing leg and fell into the infield, injured and out of the race. The fact that the Romanian Maricicia Puicia went on to win the gold medal, with Britain's Wendy Sly second, was all but lost on the partisan crowd, which proceeded to boo Budd for the remainder of the race, in which she finished a shattered seventh.

Demoralized, she returned to South Africa and threatened to give up international athletics. But she was back in 1985 for her best ever year, beginning with victory in the World Cross-Country Championships in Lisbon, where she ran barefoot despite the greasy surface. She ran into more controversy that summer. She took a £92,000 appearance fee from American television to run against Decker at London's Crystal Palace in a so-called Olympic re-match, but could only finish fourth to the in-form American, who remained unbeaten all season.

Budd recovered to win the European Cup Final 3000m for Britain in

Zola Budd

Moscow, with a Commonwealth record time of 8:35.32. She later bettered it with 8:28.83 in Rome, to finish third behind Decker and Puicia in the IAAF/Mobil Grand Prix Final. Later, in front of British fans at Crystal Palace, she set a new world record for 5000m, with 14:48.07. Another breakthrough came when she became the first British woman to run 1500m in under four minutes, with 3:59.6 in Brussels.

In the winter of 1986, she retained her World Cross-Country title in Switzerland, but her summer was beset by problems. Ruled ineligible for the Edinburgh Commonwealth Games because she had not lived in Britain long enough to satisfy the residency stipulations, she ended her season after poor performances at the European Championships in Stuttgart, finishing fourth at 3000m and ninth at 1500m.

She spent most of 1987 in South Africa visiting her family, and seeking treatment for a severe leg and hip injury. Back in the UK for the cross-country season, she faced an overwhelming backlash for her protracted stay in South Africa. There were claims by some black African nations that she had violated IAAF rules by

taking part in two meetings in South Africa, and her eligibility to compete internationally was called into question. The IAAF launched an investigation, as did the BAAB. Budd, meanwhile, withdrew from the British team for the World Cross-Country Championships in New Zealand to offset a threatened black African boycott, and protested her innocence of the charges.

In May 1988, the pressure on her became too much. Budd, now almost 22, and suffering from nervous exhaustion, sold her house in Guildford and moved back to Bloemfontein, her international running career seemingly in ruins.

Burghley, Lord

1905–1981. Born England (GBR)

One of England's finest ever hurdlers, Lord Burghley (given the title the Marquess of Exeter in 1956) was also an important athletics administrator, being President of the IAAF from 1946 until 1976, and of the AAA from 1936-1976.

Winner of the 400m hurdles at the 1928 Olympics in Amsterdam, he ended his career in fourth place in the

Lord Burghley

final four years later in Los Angeles. He did, in fact, fun a faster time in the latter race, 52.2 as opposed to his winning time of 53.4. He was also a silver medallist at the 4 x 400m relay in 1932, running his leg in 46.7. At his first Olympic Games, in Paris in 1924, he qualified for the 110m hurdles but was eliminated after falling in his heat.

Lord Burghley also held eight AAA records (three at the 120-yard hurdles and five at the 440-yard hurdles), but his time of 54.2 for the longer distance in 1927 was his first and only world record. At the 1930 British Empire Games he was a triple gold medallist, winning the 120-yard hurdles, the 440-yard hurdles, and the 4 x 440-yard relay.

He had personal bests of 14.5 seconds for the 120-yard hurdles, 24.3 for the 220-yard hurdles, and 52.2 for the 440-yard hurdles.

Busch, Sabine

1962–. Born East Germany (GDR)

Already established as a world class 400m runner, with a personal best of 49.24 set in 1984, Sabine Busch decided to switch to the 400m hurdles event in 1985. The reason, she explained, was that she felt she had little

Sabine Busch

Tamara Bycova

chance of beating team mate Marita Koch, the 400m world record holder and arguably the greatest runner in the history of women's athletics. Busch's personal best had, in fact, come in the GDR National Championships, when she had chased Koch to the line. Her record on the flat had been outstanding: she was European Indoor champion in 1985 and 1986, GDR champion in 1983, and a member of the world record 4 x 400m relay team, which ran 3:15.92 at the GDR Championships in 1984.

However, her début at hurdling was to reveal a remarkable talent for the event. Despite a clumsy technique, she clocked 53.83, the third fastest time ever, to set a new national record. In her second race, in a match against the Soviet Union, she logged the fourth fastest time ever run. In a sensational first season as a hurdler, she went on to run the six fastest times of the year, five of the eight fastest times in history and a new world record of 53.55. Along the way, she won the European Cup Final in Moscow and the World Cup in Canberra.

Her first disappointment came at the 1986 European Championships in Stuttgart, when she was surprisingly beaten by the 36-year-old Russian Marina Stepanova, who, in racing

Busch to the line after being neck and neck at the final hurdle, clocked a new world record of 53.32. Busch herself ran the third fastest time in history, 53.60, to take the silver medal. Stepanova later improved that record to 52.94.

But Busch's moment of supreme triumph came in Rome at the second World Championships in 1987. Inspired by team mate Thomas Schonlebe's victory in the men's 400m immediately before her event, Busch fought off the challenge of Commonwealth Champion, Debbie Flintoff, to take her first major outdoor title in 53.62. She added a second gold medal to her collection by running the anchor leg in East Germany's win in the 4 x 400m relay.

Bycova, Tamara

1958–. Born USSR (URS)

Tamara Bycova emerged as a world-class high jumper just as the rivalry between Italian Sara Simeoni and the West German Ulrike Meyfarth was reaching its height. Not only was she to dramatically interrupt their battle for supremacy, but she was to take over from them both as the world's top high jumper.

With Simeoni, the 1980 Olympic Champion, sidelined through injury, the 23-year-old Bycova took second place behind Meyfarth, the 1972 Olympic champion, at the 1981 World Cup in Rome. The following year, she improved her best to 1.98m in the European Championships in Athens, but it wasn't enough to challenge Meyfarth, who won the gold medal with a new world record jump of 2.02m. Bycova did, however, take the silver ahead of Simeoni.

By 1983, she was ready to take her place among the élite. Her season began with the gold medal and world record at the European Indoor Championships in Budapest. Her leap of 2.03m actually surpassed Meyfarth's outdoor record.

The first World Championships in Helsinki was the setting for the confrontation between the three. Injury caused the early departure of Simeoni, however, leaving Bycova and Meyfarth to dispute the gold medal. Bycova sailed clear at 2.01m, while Meyfarth elected to raise the bar to 2.03m. When she failed all three jumps at that height, the gold medal went to Bycova.

Bycova and Meyfarth moved on to London's Crystal Palace for the European Cup Final in August 1983. It was to prove a memorable competition as the two women forced the bar up to a world record height of 2.03m. Both went clear, although Bycova's first failure at the height was to cost her the title. When 2.05m proved too much for them, the gold medal went to Meyfarth, who had fewer failures.

Bycova, a Russian student of journalism, ended her season by claiming the world record, with a magnificent jump of 2.04m, at an IAAF permit meeting at Pisa, Italy.

After a successful indoor season in the USA, Bycova returned for the Soviet Championships in June 1984 to take the high jump into new territory with a clearance of 2.05m, but the world record did not last long. A month later, after going out of a competition in Berlin at 2m, Bycova had

to watch a new high jump sensation, Lyudmila Andonova, of Bulgaria, clear 2.07m at her first attempt.

Bycova missed the 1984 Olympic Games because of the Soviet boycott, failed to regain her world record, and finished third in Moscow's Friendship Games behind Andonova. It was the start of a lean period for the one-time golden girl of high jumping. She finished second in the 1985 European Cup and second again in the World Cup in Canberra later the same year. She even failed to qualify for the final stages of competition in the 1986 European Championships in Stuttgart. She did return to form in 1987, however, when she went to Rome to defend her World Championship title. But she was no match for the Bulgarian Stefka Kostadinova, who took the world record to 2.09m to win gold. Bycova won the silver medal with 2.04m, her best jump for three years.

Bystrova, Galina

1934–. Born USSR (URS)

A multi-talented athlete in her day, Bystrova's events no longer exist in international competition, the 80m hurdles becoming 100m after 1966, and the pentathlon being succeeded by the heptathlon in 1982. However, Bystrova was supreme at her events in the late 1950s, setting two pentathlon and one 80m hurdles world records. Her first pentathlon record of 4846 points was in 1957. She raised this to 4872 the following year, when she also lowered the hurdles mark to 10.6.

Bystrova is the only double winner of the pentathlon at the European Championships (1958 and 1962), and she added a third gold medal at 80mh in 1958. She was top-ranked pentathlete in the world in 1957 and 1958, and led the hurdles rankings in 1958. Her Olympic record, however, was not so impressive: fourth in the 1956 80mh and fifth in the same event in 1960. She won her only medal, a bronze, in the pentathlon at the 1964 Games in Tokyo.

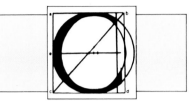

Cacchi, Paula

1945–. Born Italy (ITA)

In an era when the longest Olympic distance for women was 1500m – introduced at the 1972 Games – Paula Cacchi (née Pigni) proved herself stronger and faster the further she ran. She achieved the first women's sub-4:30 mile and went on to set unofficial, i.e. unrecognized by the IAAF, world records at 3000m and 5000m.

She originally concentrated on much shorter distances, however. After struggling with 100m and 200m, she started training specifically for 400m in 1966 and succeeded in lowering her personal best from 58.1 to 55.8 seconds in a season. In her third race at 800m she won the Italian national title, although at that year's European Championships she failed to qualify for the finals at either distance. Soon after, she began working with coaches Enrico Arcelli and Bruno Cacchi.

Cacchi was an advocate of the training methods of Arthur Lydiard – the New Zealand coach – who recommended lots of long, slow distance running to build up stamina and strength. He was eager for his new charge to test the theory. Paula obliged, and the result was an improvement in her times over 800m – from 2:07.2 to 2:05.1 – and in her capacity for hard work. She became as enthusiastic about the training methods as her coach, and often ran far in excess of what was required in her schedule.

In 1968 she ran her first 1500m race, winning in 4:21.2. However, she was restricted to the 400m and 800m in the Olympic Games in Mexico, as the 1500m distance was not introduced until 1972. She bettered her 800m time to 2:04.6 going into the

Paula Cacchi (70)

Olympics, but made too many errors in her semi-final and failed to qualify. She was eliminated in the 400m heats. The following year she returned to the 1500m with mixed fortunes. First came a world record – 4:12.4 in Milan in July – and victory over the former holder Mia Gommers of the Netherlands. At the European Championships, however, Cacchi managed to lose a 15-yard lead with 80m of the 1500m remaining; first the Czech Jaroslava Jehlickova and then Gommers passed her in the home straight. Later that year she ran a world best for 5000m of 15:53.6, to become the first woman to better 16 minutes.

She married Cacchi in 1971. The same year she set her sights on the first-ever women's Olympic 1500m title. However, by the summer of 1972 the world record belonged to Lyudmila Bragina of the Soviet Union, who proceeded to dominate the event in Munich with a series of world record runs in her heat and semi-final. In the final she was too strong for the rest of the field and won the gold medal, improving the record yet again with 4:01.4. Cacchi was third in 4:02.9 – inside the old record – and lost the

silver medal by just 0.1 second to Gunhild Hoffmeister of East Germany.

In 1973 she ran the first women's sub-4:30 mile with 4:29.5 n Milan, taking a massive 5.8 seconds off the existing best. By the end of her career she had also run four world bests for 3000m – although the distance was not recognized by the IAAF until 1974 – and won 13 Italian titles at distances between 400m and 3000m.

Calhoun, Lee

1933–. Born USA (USA)

Calhoun is known mainly as the only man to have won the Olympic title for the 110m hurdles twice, in 1956 and 1960. Both times he won by the smallest of margins: in 1956 in Melbourne he beat compatriot Jack Davis by three hundredths of a second, 13.70 to 13.73. Four years later, in Rome, victory was even slighter as he beat Willie May by one hundredth of a second, 13.98 to 13.99.

Calhoun started his career as a high jumper, but switched to hurdling in 1951, coached by Harrison Dillard, the Olympic champion of the following year. But it was not until Olympic year, 1956, that he finally moved into

Bert Cameron

world class with a time of 13.5 seconds. In the year of his second title he also lowered the world record to 13.2 in Berne on 21 August.

His athletics career took a bizarre turn when, in August 1967, he was married on the TV show Bride and Groom. Gifts that he received on the programme led to his suspension by the AAU, and he missed the whole of the 1958 season before returning to take the AAU 120 yard hurdles title in 1959 and retain his Olympic title the following year.

An assistant coach on the US Olympic team in 1976, Calhoun's best marks include 100 yards in 9.7 seconds, a 1.90m high jump and 220 yard hurdles in 22.8 seconds.

Cameron, Bert

1959–. Born Jamaica (JAM)

As the 1982 Commonwealth and 1983 World Champion, Bert Cameron went into the Los Angeles Olympic Games in 1984 as the firm favourite to win the gold medal. However, although he failed to add the Olympic title to his list of achievements, his extraordinary run in the semi-final remains a lasting memory of the Games.

Drawn in lane two, he was beginning to make up the stagger on Antonio McKay in lane three when, at the start of the back straight, he pulled up sharply as though he had been gripped by cramp or pulled a hamstring. Instead of dropping out of the race, however, he immediately set off in pursuit of the rest of the field, which was already some ten metres ahead. Amazingly, he closed that gap and qualified for the final by finishing fourth in 45.10 seconds. It was an amazing recovery, although the injury – which turned out to be cramp – kept him out of the Olympic final, won by the American Alonso Babers in 44.27.

He had gone into Olympic year as the world's top one-lap runner, and that semi-final run suggested that he might be able to threaten Lee Evans' 16-year-old world record of 43.86, set at altitude in 1968. Since 1984, in what became an increasingly competitive event, Cameron continued to run sub-45-second times, but lost more races than he won. He missed the Commonwealth Games in 1986, because of the boycott by Third World countries, and failed to make the 1987 World Championship final, despite running 45.19 in the semi-final.

Carr, Bill

1909–1966. Born USA (USA)

Winner of the 400m at the 1932 Los Angeles Olympic Games, Bill Carr's career was brought to an end in March 1933 as a result of injuries sustained in a car crash. During his great year of 1932, the highlights were his battles with fellow quarter-miler Ben Eastman, from California's Stanford University. Eastman had taken a full second from his own 440 yard world record of 47.4 on 26 March 1932 on his home track at Stanford, recording 46.4. But at the IC4A (Intercollegiate) championships he was beaten by Carr, 46.99 to 47.19. Carr's previous best for 440 yards had been 48.4, which he reduced to 47.7 in his championship heat.

At the Olympic final Eastman was drawn inside Carr, and he made the pace, with Carr biding his time. Eastman moved into the home straight with a clear lead of three yards, but Carr's final sprint was enough to give him victory by two yards, in a world record time of 46.2, with Eastman also inside the old mark with 46.4. They crossed the line ten yards ahead of the next finisher, Canada's Alex Wilson, who equalled the old record.

At the end of the Games, Carr helped the 4 x 400m relay team to a new world record of 3:08.2, a mark that remained unbeaten for 20 years.

Carr, Henry

1942–. Born USA (USA)

Winner of the gold medal at 200m at the Olympic Games in Tokyo, Henry Carr could probably have been equally successful as a 400m runner. At the

Henry Carr

same Games he helped the 400m relay team to the gold, running the last leg in 44.5. His 200m time of 20.36 is still impressive, although run on a cinder track into a stiff breeze of almost 1m per second.

The National Collegiate Athletic Association 220 yard Champion in 1963, running for Arizona State University, Carr dominated the distance in 1963 and 1964. Although not a good starter, which accounted for his indifference towards the shorter sprints, Carr had a best 100 yard time of 9.3, and clocked 10.2 for 100m. At as young as 17 he had recorded 9.7 for 100 yards and 21.0 for 220 yards. He was unbeaten during his career, strangely enough, at the longest of his specialist distances: he won all eight of his 400m or 440 yard races from 1961 to 1964.

At the Olympics in Tokyo, Carr, who had not been in good form, won by two yards in 20.3 from compatriot Paul Drayton and Trinidad's Edwin Roberts, with defending champion Livio Berruti from Italy fifth. Carr's time was a new Olympic record.

After the Games he turned to American football, playing from 1965-

1967 first with the New York Giants and then with the Detroit Lions.

Castella, Robert de

1957–. Born Australia (AUS)

Noted for his strength and fighting qualities, Robert de Castella became one of the world's most consistent marathon runners after he made his début at the distance in 1979. He has since completed 16 marathons, six under 2:10 and all under 2:15, and has won eight of them. The only one he failed to finish was in Rome in 1987 at the IAAF World Championships, where he was strongly fancied to win.

He put together a spectacular series of wins in the early 1980s, beginning with Fukuoka in December 1981 when his 2:08:18 gave him a world best time. The following year he ran a brilliantly timed race in front of his own Australian fans to win the Commonwealth Games title in Brisbane in 2:09:18. It was a particularly outstanding performance because he refused to be intimidated by the front running of eventual silver medallist Juma Ikangaa, of Tanzania, who had built up a lead of almost a minute by the 20-mile mark. De Castella gradu-

Robert de Castella

ally stepped up the pace over the next four miles and by 24.5 miles the Tanzanian's lead was barely ten yards.

The Australian, nicknamed Deek, went on to run another fast time in Rotterdam in the spring of 1983, when he was able to produce a finishing sprint to beat Carlos Lopes of Portugal by two seconds in 2:08:37. His reputation as being 'unbeatable' gained more credibility when he won the first World Championships marathon in Helsinki later that year by 24 seconds in 2:10:03. He subsequently went to his second Olympic Games in Los Angeles as favourite for the marathon (he was tenth in Moscow in 1980), but suffered in the heat and finished fifth in 2:11:09.

He retained his Commonwealth Games title in 1986, beating a field weakened by the Third World boycott with 2:10:15. Earlier in the year he had run his fastest time ever, 2:07:51, in winning the ninetieth Boston Marathon. The win earned him a total of $60,000 and a Mercedes-Benz. He returned to Boston in 1987 to run against one of the strongest fields ever assembled. This time, however, he was bundled to the ground in a chaotic start and never recovered. He finished fourteenth in 2:14:24. In the second World Championships in Rome he again struggled in the heat and dropped out of the race half-way.

Chataway, Chris

1931–. Born England (GBR)

Although better known as a 5000m runner, it was as a miler that Chris Chataway became recognized at the beginning of 1954, his most successful year. It was he who paced the first two successful attempts to run the mile in under four minutes, the first by Roger Bannister in Oxford on 6 May 1954, and the second by the Australian John Landy in Yurku, Finland, on 21 June.

Chataway was only ranked ninth in the world as a miler that year, and finished those two record-breaking attempts in creditable times, 4:07.2

Chris Chataway wins the 1955 AAA three-mile title

behind Bannister and 4:04.4 behind Landy. He himself broke the four-minute barrier in 1955, clocking 3:59.8.

At the 1952 Olympics, in Helsinki, Chataway was among the leading group in the 5000m final until the last curve, where he fell. He nevertheless got up to finish fifth. He ran 8:49.6 for two miles the following year, and 8:41.0 for the same distance in 1954, ranking him second in the world for both years.

After his successful pacemaking efforts in 1954, he set a world record for three miles with 13:32.2, and then won the Empire Games at the same distance. At the 1954 European Championships, he finished second to Vladimir Kuts (URS), who won in a world record time of 13:56.6. A few weeks later, he beat Kuts at London's White City stadium in what is regarded as one of the finest track races ever: Chataway won in the last stride to set a new world record of 13:51.6 to Kuts' 13:51.7 in front of a crowd of 40,000.

The 1956 Olympics in Melbourne were not a success for Chataway: in the 5000m he finished eleventh after suffering from stomach cramps.

After his retirement he pursued a career in politics, serving as a government minister in the 1970s.

Cheng, Chi

1944–. Born Taiwan (TPE)

Following the standards set by the great Japanese all-rounder, Kinue Hitomi, in the 1920s, Chi Cheng became the greatest Asian athlete of the twentieth century, with a string of national and world records between 1964 and 1973. She also became the first Asian woman to win a track and field medal in a post-war Olympic Games when she won bronze in the 80m hurdles in Mexico City in 1968.

An accomplished all-rounder herself – she held the Asian Pentathlon record in 1968 – her main claim to fame was as a sprinter and hurdler. Her first Asian record was at 100 yards in 1964, when she clocked 11.1 seconds. After moving to live and study in California, she teamed up with the coach Vince Reel, later to become her husband, and her performances improved. After the 1968 Olympic Games, where she was also seventh at 100m, she enjoyed two sensational seasons.

In 1969 she won all but one of her 67 outdoor competitions, broke the 200m hurdles world record and equalled the record over 100 yards. A year later, she won all of her 87 competitions, from 50 yards to 440 yards,

Chi Cheng (centre)

80m to 200m hurdles, long jump and relays. She set 23 Asian records and eight world records, ending the season with personal bests of 10.00 (100 yards), 11.00 (100m), 22.4 (220 yards), 12.8 (100mh) and 26.2 (200mh). Indoors that year she competed 21 times in five meetings, in which she set or equalled her personal bests 17 times.

Her career ended prematurely because of a succession of leg injuries. She missed the 1972 Olympic Games and eventually retired from competition in 1973. She returned to Taiwan in 1980 and in 1981 was elected to the country's national senate. She subsequently became head of Taiwan's national athletics federation and a member of its Olympic Committee.

Chistyakova, Galina

1962–. Born USSR (URS)

An extremely consistent long jumper in recent years, Galina Chistyakova finally emerged from the shadows of her more famous rivals Heike Drechsler (GDR) and Jackie Joyner-Kersee (USA) by setting a new world record of 7.52m on 11 June 1988 in Leningrad.

In fact, she set two records: with her fourth jump she equalled the 7.42m record jointly held by Drechsler and Joyner-Kersee. Her exact series was 7.21m, 7.38m (wind-assisted), 7.21m, 7.45m, foul (measured at around 7.50m), and 7.52m on her final attempt. She thus became the first woman to break the 7.50m barrier, in a competition where four other Soviet jumpers exceeded 7.00m.

Holder of three Soviet long jump records between 1984 and 1986, Chistyakova also set a world indoor best of 7.25m in 1985. The same year she finished first in the European Indoor Championships and the European Cup, second in the World Cup, and was the Grand Prix winner in her event. The following year she was second to Drechsler (7.09m to 7.27m) at the European Championships in Stuttgart, and, in 1987, came fourth in the World Indoor Championships and fifth at the World Championships in Rome, where she could only manage 6.99m (Joyner-Kersee won with 7.36m).

Chistyakova is also the holder of four Soviet triple jump records: 13.58m (1986), and 13.86, 13.96 and 13.98 (1987).

Chizhova, Nadyezhda

1945–. Born USSR (URS)

Holder of a complete set of Olympic medals at the shot (bronze in 1968, gold in 1972, and silver in 1976), Chizhova is the only woman to have won four successive European titles: in 1966, 1969, 1971 and 1974. She also set nine accepted world records, taking the mark from 18.67m in 1968 to 21.20m in 1973. Later that year, on 29 September, she was the first woman to break the 70ft barrier with her throw of 21.45m (70ft 4 $\frac{1}{2}$ in).

As overwhelming favourite to win the gold medal at the 1968 Olympics in Mexico, Chizhova registered her only failure, taking the bronze behind the East German pair, Margitta Gummel and Marita Lange. But four years later, in Munich, she made no mistake, winning with her first throw of the competition, a world record 21.03m. After missing the whole of the 1975 season through injury, she claimed the silver medal in the Montreal Games of 1976, with a throw of 20.96, behind Bulgaria's Ivanka Khristova with 21.16m.

In addition to her Olympic and European successes, Chizhova also won the European Junior shot/discus double in 1964, five European indoor titles, six Soviet titles, and recorded three victories in the European Cup.

Chudina, Aleksandra

1923–. Born USSR (URS)

Holder of five pentathlon world records between 1947 and 1955, Chudina was a superb all-round athlete. At the 1952 Olympics, in Helsinki, she won silvers in the long jump and javelin, and a bronze in the high jump. She would have undoubtedly won gold medals at pentathlon had the event been included (it did not become an Olympic event until 1964).

Her record in the European Championships was equally impressive: in 1946 she first made her mark on the international scene by finishing second; in 1954 she won the pentathlon title and was placed second in the long jump (as well as finishing fifth in the javelin and sixth in the high jump).

Chudina was the holder of 31 USSR

outdoor titles, the most ever won by one athlete, at events ranging from the 400m and 80m hurdles, through her favourite field disciplines, to the pentathlon. She also set a world high jump record of 1.73m in 1954, and was part of a world-record breaking 4 x 200m relay team in 1950.

In all, between 1945 and 1955 she headed the 'best performance' lists for different sports 18 times – eight at pentathlon, four at high jump, three at javelin, two at 400m, and one at long jump.

Cierpinski, Waldemar

1950–. Born East Germany (GDR)

A world class steeplechaser with a personal best of 8:32.4, who turned to marathon running in 1974, Cierpinski astounded the pundits by emulating the great Ethiopian, Abebe Bikila, and winning successive Olympic marathon titles in 1976 and 1980.

In Montreal in 1976 he was hardly recognized as a medal prospect at all when he lined up for the marathon at the Olympic Games. His previous best had been 2:12:22 in winning the East German trial, when his victory had been so emphatic that he was chosen as his country's only marathon

Waldemar Cierpinski

representative. But, as the race unfolded, Cierpinski was the only man to stay with American Frank Shorter, the defending champion, who broke away from the leading pack of runners. Cierpinski finally passed him, opened up a thirty-second lead, and crossed the finish line with a new Olympic record time of 2:09:55.

In the four years before Moscow, the East German looked anything but an Olympic champion. He finished fourth in the 1978 European Championships, and the following year was ranked only third in his own country. His worst performance came at the Fukuoka Marathon in Japan at the end of 1979, when he finished only thirty-second in 2:22:49.

But he was to prove that he could get it right on the big occasion. At the boycott-hit Olympic Games in Moscow, he made his move at 18 miles, leaving the rest of the field to run for the minor medals as he won in 2:11:03. He later admitted that he trained almost exclusively with only the Olympics in mind, and his ambition was to win an historic third title in Los Angeles in 1984. His dream ended when the East Germans joined the Eastern Bloc boycott, and Cierpinski retired from the sport at the end of the 1984 season after a record of 11 wins in 27 marathons.

Clarke, Ron

1937–. Born Australia (AUS)

If world-record breaking were everything, then Ron Clarke would have a fair claim to the title of greatest distance runner of all time. In all he set 18 records, including ten in one year, 1965, which equalled the feat of Swede Gunder Hägg in 1943. But Clarke showed his world-beating talent at a far greater range of distances, from two miles, through three miles, 5000 metres, six miles, 10,000 metres, ten miles, 20,000 metres, and one hour. Far from merely lowering the previous bests, his trademark through the mid-1960s was to pulverize existing world records, and his race opposi-

Ron Clarke

tion had the same treatment.

He took the 5000m world record, for example, from 13:35 to 13:16.6, and the 10,000m from 28:18.2 to 27:39.4, improvements that stunned the athletics world. He first came to the attention of the world as a junior, setting a world record in 1956 as an 18-year-old of 4:06.8 for the mile, and being chosen as the athlete to carry the Olympic flame at the opening ceremony in Melbourne of that year. However, he then disappeared from view to concentrate on his accountancy studies, before making a devastating return at the 1962 Commonwealth Games, where he finished runner-up to Murray Halberg in the three miles.

Yet his record in major championships was consistently disappointing, although he often beat top opposition at less prestigious meets. An overwhelming favourite to win the 10,000m in the 1964 Olympics, he was beaten into third place behind American Billy Mills and the Tunisian Mohamed Gammoudi. Worse was to follow in the 5000m, where he led for most of the race only to be outsprinted by men with fast finishes, eventually finishing ninth.

Three days later, he was in the lead in the marathon, running the first 15km in just 45 minutes until he faded to finish ninth. Nevertheless, he achieved his fastest marathon time of 2:20:26.8.

At the 1966 Commonwealth Games in Kingston, Jamaica he won two silver medals, finishing behind Kenyans Kip Keino and Naftali Temu at three miles and six miles respectively. But perhaps his greatest disappointment was in Mexico for the 1968 Olympics, where his talent was destroyed by the altitude: in the 10,000m he finished sixth and had to be given oxygen after the race, and at 5000m could only manage fifth, behind altitude-trained Kenyans and old rival Gammoudi. In his last major championships, the Commonwealth Games of 1970 in Edinburgh, he finished with yet another silver medal, this time behind Lachie Stewart at 10,000m.

Soon afterwards he retired and was discovered to have a heart problem, which, according to one doctor, made it impossible for him to withstand sudden changes of pace in a race, while allowing him to run for long periods at a steady speed. He underwent open-heart surgery in 1981 and made a complete recovery.

Other best marks include 3:44.1 for 1500m; 4:00.2 for the mile; 7:47.2 for 3000m; 8:19.6 for two miles; 12:50.4 for three miles; 26:47.0 for six miles; 47:12.8 for ten miles; 59:22.8 for 20,000m; and 20,232m for one hour.

Clayton, Derek

1942–. Born England (AUS)

One of only three men to have set two world bests in the marathon (the other two are Jim Peters of Great Britain and Abebe Bikila of Ethiopia), Derek Clayton was nevertheless prevented from fulfilling his potential through recurring injuries. He was operated on for a broken Achilles tendon in 1967, but, astonishingly, set the first of his marathon bests later that year, on 3 December, running the Fukuoka Marathon in Japan to win in 2:09:36.4.

This was the first time that the marathon distance had been completed at an average of less than five minutes per mile.

At the Olympics in 1968 he could only finish seventh, having been plagued by cartilage trouble earlier in the year. He went into the Olympics as only the ninth fastest man that year, with a 1968 best of 2:14:47.8. After another leg operation following the Games, he ran the Antwerp Marathon on 30 May 1969 and set another world best – 2:08:33.6, a time that was not bettered for 12 years until Alberto Salazar's 2:08:13 at the 1981 New York Marathon. There were doubts that the course may have been short, as it was not remeasured after the race, but no concrete evidence had ever been presented.

Clayton, who emigrated to Australia in 1963 and ran under that country's colours, did not finish the Commonwealth Games marathons in either 1970 or 1974 because of injury, and he could finish no higher than thirteenth at the 1972 Olympics for the same reason.

Other best times include 13:45.6 for 5000m, and 28:32.2 for 10,000m.

Derek Clayton

Coe, Sebastian

1956–. Born England (GBR)

Arguably the finest middle-distance runner of all time, Sebastian Coe captured the public's imagination with his three world records in 41 days during the summer of 1979. But his place in the history books was assured when he became the first man to retain the Olympic 1500m title in 1984. He has, through his exploits on the track, become a revered spokesman for the sport and a successful sports administrator, at the forefront of the fight against the misuse of drugs.

His promise as an athlete dates from his schooldays in Sheffield. It was during the early days of his career that his father, Peter, a production manager in a local cutlery works, elected to become his coach. As a schoolboy athlete, Coe won the Yorkshire Schools Intermediate Cross-Country Championships at 14 and, three years later, became English Schools Intermediate 3000m champion. Later, in 1975, he was a bronze medallist over 1500m at the European Junior Championships.

It was in 1977, while an Economics and Social History student at Loughborough College, that he first showed potential at 800m. After twice breaking the UK indoor best for the distance and winning the European Indoor title, he ended his year with a national outdoor record of 1:44.95 and fourth place for Britain in the Europa Cup Final.

In 1978 the public eagerly awaited his clash with the more established Steve Ovett, one year his senior and already an Olympian, over 800m at the European Championships in Prague. It was the start of the so-called rivalry between the two that would claim media and public attention for the next six years.

In a determined effort to win from the front, Coe sped through the first lap in 49.3 seconds with Ovett following. With 200m to go, Ovett proved the stronger and pulled clear of Coe, only to be overtaken himself just yards from the line by the East German Olaf Beyer. Coe ended up with the bronze medal, but both Britons learned not to concentrate their efforts on beating only one man in future.

If Coe had shown promise in 1978, he became a national hero in 1979 with his record-breaking spree on the race tracks of Europe. It started on 5 July in Oslo with 1:42.4, a world record by a second for 800m. On the same track, 12 days later, he won the IAAF Golden Mile in 3:48.95, to take the record from John Walker of New Zealand, in what was only his fourth race over the distance in four years. After winning the Europa Cup 800m on 5 August, Coe moved on to Zurich for his third world record run - 3.32.1 for 1500m.

The rivalry between Coe and Ovett grew more intense as Ovett, who himself was beaten only once that season,

chased Coe's 1500m and mile records. When he equalled Coe's 1500m time in Koblenz, West Germany, the demand was for them to race each other. As the two stars of world athletics, their meeting at 800m and 1500m at the 1980 Moscow Olympics was to become the centre piece of the sporting year.

They arrived in the Soviet Union in superb form. Both had set world records in Oslo at the Bislett Games: Ovett snatching his rival's mile record with 3:48.8 and Coe running 2:13.4 for 1000m. But while Coe was favourite for the 800m, he ran the worst tactical race of his life and was left with far too much ground to make up in the home straight. First blood went to Ovett, gold medallist at 800m with 1:45.4, with Coe second in 1:45.9. The story of Coe's heartbreak was headline news around the world.

However, in the 1500m his response was instant and dramatic. With a telling kick on the final bend, he raced to the gold medal in 3:38.4, with Ovett taking only third behind the East German Jurgen Straub. The confrontation had ended one-all. 'Fear was one of the reasons I came back after losing the 800m,' Coe said. 'I didn't want to go into obscurity. I wanted to win the 1500m because running was my life and I didn't like having something I was good at being taken away from me.'

Ovett and Coe resisted calls for them to meet on the track in 1981, during a season when they were probably both at their peak. Coe lowered his 800m world mark to an astounding 1:41.73 in Florence on 10 June, and spent the rest of the summer swapping the world mile record with Ovett. In all the record was improved three times, ending with Coe's 3:47.33 in Brussels on 28 August.

They finally agreed to race each other in three events in 1982, but the publicity came to nothing as illness or injury to one or both of them meant that they never met. Coe's season ended with a shock defeat in the European Championships 800m final. Subsequent tests showed possible traces of glandular fever, but the real reason for his bad form was not to come to light until the following year.

His 1983 season ended prematurely after a series of defeats in the build-up to the first IAAF World Championships. Medical tests revealed a blood infection called Toxoplasmosis, and Coe spent the rest of the year recovering and resting.

His preparation for the Los Angeles Olympic Games started late and, by the time of the UK 1500m trial, Coe admitted to being only eighty per cent fit. But, despite losing a trial race to aspiring 800m runner Peter Elliott, Coe was picked to defend his title in LA. Six weeks later, he arrived in California at the top of his form. A silver medallist again at 800m (Brazilian Joaquim Cruz took the gold), Coe proved the strongest and fastest

Seb Coe at the Los Angeles Olympics

over 1500m. He hit the front with 200m to go, and his familiar kick, looking even more potent, took him clear of fellow Briton Steve Cram and on to a new Olympic record of 3:32.53. Old rival Steve Ovett dropped out at 1150m, suffering with severe breathing problems.

Coe had a relatively quiet 1985, when he was largely forced out of the limelight by Steve Cram. In the Dream Mile in Oslo, Cram beat Coe and took his world record with 3:46.32. This was now the rivalry that people talked about.

Coe and Cram met again over 800m and 1500m at the 1986 European Championships in Stuttgart, after Coe had earlier withdrawn from the Commonwealth Games because of flu. Coe finally managed a major championship gold medal at his favourite distance with a brilliantly timed run in the 800m final, beating Cram and the Scot Tom McKean in a race for the line. Three days later, he misjudged his final effort and lost the 1500m final to Cram, 3:41.04 to 3:41.67.

Since 1984 Coe has talked about moving up to 5000m, but these plans have been scuppered by years of illness or injury. His 1987 season was ruined by an injury to his Achilles tendon, but he spent the year working in a part-time capacity as vice-chairman of the Sports Council, fuelling speculation that after retiring from competition he will become actively involved in sports administration.

Coghlan, Eamonn

1952–. Born Republic of Ireland (IRE)

After a career of many fast times but near misses in major championships, Eamonn Coghlan was one of the most popular gold medallists at the first World Championships in 1983.

Running in the 5000m – he had moved up from the mile and 1500m a year earlier – Coghlan timed his finish perfectly. In a slow race, with just 20m covering the entire field at 4000m, Dmitriy Dmitriyev of the Soviet Union ran the penultimate lap in 58.2

Eamonn Coghlan

seconds, opening up a 12m lead at the bell. Coghlan gave chase on the final lap and eventually caught the tiring Soviet as they rounded the last bend. The look on the Irishman's face said it all. He smiled at Dmitriyev and then at the crowd before sprinting for the line. He could not believe how easy it had been as he crossed the line in 13:28.53. It was Ireland's first major track title since Ron Delaney's surprise 1500m win at the 1956 Olympics.

Coghlan finished fourth in the 1500m at the 1976 Olympic Games, when New Zealander John Walker took the title, and he was fourth again in Moscow four years later in the 5000m, as Miruts Yifter of Ethiopia won the gold medal. Between these events he achieved second place behind Great Britain's Steve Ovett in the European Championships 1500m of 1978.

Coghlan's major success, however, has been indoors in America, where he spent much of his time while studying at Villanova University. Nicknamed the Chairman of the Boards by the American public, Coghlan won 52 of his 70 races at 1500m and the mile

between 1974 and 1987, and his 3:49.78 mile time in 1983 still counts as a world indoor best.

Outdoors he has won 11 Irish titles (five at 800m, five at 1500m, and one at 5000m), but has missed several seasons since 1983 because of injury.

Connolly, Harold

1931–. Born USA (USA)

Olympic hammer champion in 1956, Harold Connolly also set six world records, and his rivalry with Russian Mikhail Krivonosov dominated the sport before the Olympics in Melbourne. Connolly had thrown 66.71m in Boston, a mark that remained unratified, although it broke the world record. Krivonosov replied a few days later with 67.32 in Tashkent, but Connolly had the last word before Melbourne, with 68.54m in Los Angeles. The hammer final was no disappointment, with Krivonosov's 63.03m leading until Connolly's fifth round 63.19m.

Connolly went from strength to strength after his win, increasing the world record to 68.68m in 1958 before becoming the first man to break the 70m barrier on 12 August 1960 with 70.33. But he never again managed to break the Russian domination at the Olympics, finishing in eighth place in the Rome Games of 1960, and sixth in Tokyo in 1964. Despite such setbacks, he still managed to set another world record in 1965 of 71.26m.

Winner of nine national titles (1955-1961 and 1964-1965), Connolly almost made the team again for the 1972 Games in Munich, finishing fifth in the trial.

Consolini, Adolfo

1917–1969. Born Italy (ITA)

When Adolfo Consolini took the Olympic oath on behalf of his fellow competitors in Rome in 1960, he was about to take part in his fourth Games. Although he only finished seventeenth, he had been one of the top discus throwers in the world for over 20 years. He had won the Olympic title as far back as 1948 in London, although the two Olympic Games that were cancelled because of the Second World War would have found him just as dominant.

Consolini took up athletics at the relatively late age of 20 in 1937, and won his first national Junior title the same year with 41.77m. He first exceed the 50m mark in 1940 in Turin, and between 1941 and 1948 he set three world records, each time in Milan, improving the distance from 53.34m in 1941, to 54.23m in the spring of 1946, and finally to 55.33m in the autumn of 1948. In Europe he was almost unbeatable, only losing once, to compatriot Giuseppe Tosi, between September 1941 and June 1955. He won three European titles in five attempts, in Oslo in 1946 (52.23m), Brussels in 1950 (53.75m), and Berne in 1954 (53.44m).

Consolini held the European record six times, setting the last of these – 56.98m, his best mark ever – in December 1955 when nearly 39.

In the Olympics, Consolini followed the gold he won in London in 1948 (52.78m) with a silver in Helsinki in 1952 (53.78), then finished sixth in Melbourne in 1956 with 52.21m, before his final appearance on home ground in 1960 to finish seventeenth (52.44m).

He was Italian champion no fewer than 15 times: in 1939, 1941, 1942, 1945, 1949, 1950, and then from 1952 to 1960.

Cova, Alberto

1958–. Born Italy (ITA)

Renowned for his scintillating turn of speed over the final 200m, Alberto Cova set the world of 5000m and 10,000m running alight in the 1980s. He led a spectacular revival in Italian distance running by winning all the major championship titles between 1982 and1985, becoming European, World, and Olympic Champion.

Alberto Cova wins in Helsinki, 1983

A member of the famous Italian club Pro Patria, Cova's first important win was in the 1982 European Championships in Athens, when he took the 10,000m title. The following year, he burst through a crowd of runners in the final 400m and passed still more in the home straight to claim the World Championship 10,000m title in Helsinki, just inches ahead of the East German Werner Schildhauer.

At the Los Angeles Olympic Games in 1984, Cova was the only man to stay with Martti Vainio when the Finn made the all-important break in the 10,000m final. After tracking Vainio, the former European Champion, for the next 14 laps, Cova simply shifted into another gear with 150m to go to win the gold medal in 27:47:54. He had covered the second 5000m in 13:26:98. Vainio, who had done so much to dictate the outcome of the race, was later stripped of the silver medal when he failed a drugs test.

Not known for running particularly fast times – he was ranked only twenty-second on the all-time list for 10,000m in 1984 – Cova repeatedly showed that he was a true champion, capable of running well when it mattered and where championships were at stake. In 1985 he scored a notable double

when he won the 5000m and 10,000m titles in the space of two days at the Europa Cup Final in Moscow. Earlier that summer, he had run his fastest ever time for 5000m – 13:10:06 – behind Said Aouita's world record in Oslo.

By 1986, however, his fellow Italian distance runners were catching him up. In what was an emphatic exhibition of Italian supremacy at 10,000m at the European Championships in Stuttgart, when Italians won all the medals, Cova was finally outsprinted to the line by his rival, the 23-year-old Stefano Mei. Such was his standing, however, that Cova's defeat brought more press attention than Mei's victory.

An ankle injury kept him away from the World Championships in 1987, after a poor season in which he suffered the indignity of being lapped by countryman Francesco Panetta in a 10,000m race in Stockholm.

Cram, Steve

1960–. Born England (GBR)

While Britain was enjoying the gold medals and world records of its two middle distance stars, Steve Ovett and Sebastian Coe, in the late 1970s and early 1980s, Steve Cram was rapidly developing into the runner who would eclipse them both.

European Junior 3000m Champion in 1979, and holder of several UK age best times over 1500m, Cram quickly graduated to the international circuit, lining up alongside Coe and Ovett in the top races in Europe. He never beat them, but a mile time of 3:53.8 behind Ovett's world record of 3:48.8 in the 1980 Dream Mile in Oslo was enough to win him, at the age of 18, a place in Britain's 1500m team for the Olympic Games in Moscow. He finished eighth and last in the final, won by Coe with Ovett third, but the experience proved invaluable.

The following year, as Coe and Ovett swapped the mile world record, Cram's times improved behind them. When Coe claimed the record with 3:48.53 in Zurich, for example, Cram clocked 3:49.95 - the first time he had run below 3:50.

With Coe ill and Ovett injured, Cram at last graduated to the big time in 1982, when he revealed a fine tactical awareness as well as a finishing kick to win both the Commonwealth Games and European Championship 1500m titles. But it was not until 1983 that he could claim to have finally stepped out of the shadow cast by Coe and Ovett. He silenced his critics, who pointed out that his success had come only when his main rivals were missing, by beating Ovett to win the 1500m title at the inaugural World Championships in Helsinki. Ovett, running a poor tactical race, could only finish fourth, while Coe was ruled absent through illness.

Cram and Ovett met again that season, over a mile at Crystal Palace, in a race both needed to win to assert their superiority. Cram was World Champion, but Ovett had just reclaimed his 1500m world record with 3:30.77 in Rieti, Italy. Cram took the initiative with a lap to go, taking the lead and kicking for home. Ovett chased all the way, but could not catch him, and victory went to Cram by a stride in 3:52.56.

By now he had become one of the most sought-after athletes in the world, but, despite hopes of the Olympic 1500m title in Los Angeles, Cram went to the Games in 1984 after a season trying to overcome a recurring calf injury. While Ovett was forced to drop out of the final after succumbing to severe bronchial problems, Cram had to be content with second place behind Coe, the defending champion, who had timed his preparation to perfection.

The defeat spurred Cram to a momentous season in 1985, when he set three world records in 19 days. He broke the 1500m world record with 3:29.67 in Nice on 16 July, when he beat Said Aouita, the Olympic 5000m champion, in a frantic dash for the line. Nine days later, in Oslo, he beat Seb Coe, and took his world mile

Steve Cram

record with 3:46.32, and, in Budapest on 4 August, he defied a strong head wind to take the 2000m record with 4:51.39. He ended his season by lowering his best 800m time to 1:42.88 in beating Joaquim Cruz, the Olympic champion.

He went into 1986 with his sights set on the 800m/1500m double at both the Commonwealth Games and the European Championships, and ended up with three of his targetted gold medals. The only one to elude him was the 800m in Stuttgart at the European Championships, where Coe, who had withdrawn from the Commonwealth Games through illness, proved superior. Cram took the bronze medal behind Scotsman Tom McKean, as Britain scored a clean sweep of the medals.

World Championship year proved a massive disappointment after so much success. While his training appeared to be going well, Cram could not get things right in races. His season began with defeat over 1500m in the European Cup Final in Prague, when he was genuinely shocked at being passed by the Spaniard José Luis Gonzáles in the home straight. He never really recovered from that loss and went to Rome for the second World Championships after a series of defeats and less than impressive performances. In the 1500m final, a disconsolate Cram did not show his customary finishing speed, and was passed by seven athletes in the last 100m.

His title went to the Somalian, Abdi Bile. Cram's disappointing showing was put down by some as being due to lack of motivation after five world-beating seasons. If there were any other reasons Cram kept them to himself.

Crawford, Hasely

1950–. Born Trinidad (TRI)

Trinidad's first Olympic gold medallist, Hasely Crawford was the winner of the 100m title in Montreal in 1976. Facing an impressive field, including defending champion Valeriy Borzov

Hasely Crawford (far right)

of the Soviet Union, Don Quarrie of Jamaica, and Harvey Glance of the USA, Crawford's winning time of 10.06 seconds placed him sixth on the all-time list.

This was Borzov's first-ever defeat in a major competition. Four years earlier he had won the title as the 21-year-old Crawford was forced to pull up after only 10m because of injury. Crawford had qualified convincingly for the 1972 final and considered that he had a good chance of winning, even though Borzov was at top form.

Crawford, a bronze medallist behind Quarrie at the 1970 Commonwealth Games and a runner-up to Silvio Leonard of Cuba in the 1975 PanAmerican Games, went into the Montreal Olympics with a season's best time of 10.1 seconds. He had actually been credited with a wind-assisted 9.8 seconds a year before. Also, although unfancied by the media as a potential champion, he had been tipped by both Borzov and Quarrie as a threat.

Four years on in the boycott-hit Moscow Olympics, Crawford was once again picked out by fellow sprinters as a potential winner. However, the defending champion was eliminated in his heat – running 10.42 – as his title went to Britain's Allan Wells.

Cruz, Joaquim

1963–. Born Brazil (BRA)

At the age of 14, running against athletes four years older than himself, Joaquim Cruz clocked 4:02.3 for third place in the 1500m at the Brazilian Junior Championships. However, the exertion made him physically sick immediately after the race, and the young Cruz vowed never to run again and to return to his first love, basketball. After being persuaded to continue by his coach, Luiz de Oliveira, Cruz went on to become World Junior record holder at 800m in 1981 and, three years later, the first Brazilian runner to win an Olympic gold medal, when he beat the finest 800m field ever assembled at the 1984 Games in Los Angeles.

At the age of 20, after moving to live and study in the USA, he won a bronze medal at 800m in the first World Championships in Helsinki. A year later he won the Olympic title after putting together a remarkable series of runs in the strongest of 800m competitions. He won his heat in 1:45.66, his quarter final in 1:44.84, and his semi-final in 1:43.82 in consecutive days, before finishing well clear in the final with an Olympic

record of 1:43.00, the third fastest time ever recorded. Running with a long, loping stride - he wears special shoes because his right leg is shorter than his left - he hit the front with 80m to go, and won by five metres from Sebastian Coe, the world record holder and pre-race favourite.

Cruz's hopes of winning the 1500m title as well ended when the onset of a cold prevented him from lining up for the semi-final of the longer distance. After the Olympics, however, he took his talent to Europe, intent on breaking Coe's world record of 1:41.73. He came close, recording 1:41.77 in Cologne at the end of a week in which he had run 1:42.34 in Zurich and 1:42.41 in Brussels. It had been an exceptional season, in which he had also won American National Collegiate titles at 800m and 1500m.

His strong front-running took him to further successes on the European Grand Prix circuit in 1985, when he again set his sights on the world record over two laps, although the closest he got was 1:42.49.

Joaquim Cruz (093)

Injury kept him out of most of the 1986 season and, despite winning the Pan American Games 1500m title in 1987, he was a non-starter at the second World Championships in Rome, when injury again ruled him out.

Cunningham, Glen

1909–1988. Born USA (USA)

One of the greatest milers of the 1930s, Glenn Cunningham first took up running to gain strength after a childhood accident – a fire at his school – in which he received burns so horrific that at first amputation was proposed.

Cunningham ran more than 20 sub-4:10 second mile races in seven years, finished fourth in the 1932 Olympic Games 1500m in Los Angeles, and came second in this event four years later in Berlin behind New Zealand's Jack Lovelock, both men beating the existing world record of American Bill Bonthron.

Cunningham first came to prominence in the 1932 National Collegiate (NCAA) Championships, where his mile victory in 4:11.1 was not only a new American record but the fourth fastest time ever at that point. Although he finished out of the medals in the 1932 Olympics, the following year saw him 20 times unbeaten in Europe, only losing once at the mile, and running the second fastest mile ever at that year's NCAA Championships on 17 June, to win in 4:09.8. His European tour ended with him fourth fastest on the 1500m all-time list.

His rivalry with Bill Bonthron was one of the highlights of 1934: at the Amateur Athletic Union (AAU) 1500m final, which was indoors, Cunningham won in 3:52.2, a new world indoor record, with Bonthron given the same time. On 17 March Cunningham set a new world indoor mile record of 4:08.4, the second fastest ever, and at the Princeton Invitational on 16 June, racing against Bonthron, he smashed the outdoor world record, clocking 4:06.8. In a season where both men had beaten the other twice, the deciding rubber was a match in

Milwaukee, where Bonthron came back from a seemingly impossible position to win the 1500m with Cunningham second, both inside Luigi Beccali's world record. Bonthron clocked 3:48.8, Cunningham 3:48.9.

At the 1936 Games in Berlin, a superbly timed surge by Jack Lovelock after 1200 of the 1500m gave him the gold over Cunningham, who nevertheless finished second in an American record time of 3:48.4.

Cunningham continued to run and win important races in the late 1930s, although a new generation of sprinters that included American Archie San Romani and Briton Sydney Wooderson was hard on his heels. But in his late twenties he was as fast as ever: in a special handicap race on 3 March 1938 he ran 4:04.4 for the mile, a time that was never ratified, and he continued racing until 1940. His last race, the AAU 1500m, was one in which he ran his fastest time – 3:48.0 – but he could only finish second to Germany's Walter Mehl.

Cuthbert, Betty

1938–. Born Australia (AUS)

The golden girl of the 1956 Olympics in Melbourne, Betty Cuthbert, aged only 18, won three gold medals, taking the 100m/200m sprint double then anchoring her team to victory in the 4 x 100m relay. Later, after a succession of disappointing major championships, she returned to win the 400m title at the 1964 Games in Tokyo.

Cuthbert was a natural sprinter, discovered by her high school physical education teacher, June Fergurson, herself an international competitor at the 1948 Olympics in London. By the time she was 15, Cuthbert's best 100 yard time was 10.8 seconds. She reduced this to 10.6 at the beginning of 1956 at the New South Wales Championships, where she also clocked 24.2 for 220 yards. Picked for the Olympic team, she set her first world record, at 200m, in a warm-up meet for members of the Australian

Olympic squad on 16 September.

In the Olympic 100m final, Cuthbert hit the tape at full speed, running open-mouthed, as though in agony, as was her style, to win in 11.5. The 200m she won by four yards in 23.4, equalling the Olympic record. In the relay, Australia set a world record of 44.5, having set the previous one of 44.9 earlier in the season.

After Melbourne, the inexperienced Cuthbert found it difficult to come to terms with her new-found fame. At the 1958 Commonwealth Games, in Cardiff, she lost out to team mate Marlene Mathews in the 220 yards, and could only finish fourth in the 100 yards. But it was on this European trip that Cuthbert first experimented with the longer one-lap distance, winning a race in Sweden in August in 54.4: the fastest time of the year at her first attempt! Early in 1959 she equalled the world record of 55.6, and reduced this two months later to 54.3.

Named for both sprints and the relay at the 1960 Olympics, and as women's team captain, Cuthbert was in good form before the Games, but during the preceding summer a troublesome leg injury grew steadily worse and she had no option but to withdraw.

After this setback, Cuthbert withdrew from the athletics stage, only returning for the 1962 Commonwealth Games in Perth, where she did not make either sprint final, although she did run the last leg in the 4 x 110 yard relay team to help win the gold.

During the 1962 season she returned more and more to the longer distance, setting world records at both 400m and 440 yards in 1963. In the Olympic final in Tokyo in 1964 she was not a favourite, but a tremendous burst of speed from about 180 metres out brought her home in an Olympic record 52.0, ahead of Britain's Ann Packer in 52.2.

As she had intended, Cuthbert retired after the 1964 Olympics, saying she wanted to be remembered for her 400m victory: 'the only perfect race I ever ran'.

Da Silva, Adhemar Ferreira

1927–. Brazil (BRA)

In a country noted for its triple jumpers, Da Silva was the most successful of them all. The first Brazilian to hold a world record in any event, he dominated the triple jump between 1951 and 1956, winning two Olympic titles and remaining unbeaten in 60 consecutive competitions.

His first record came in 1950, when he equalled Naoto Tajima's 14-year-old mark of 16.00m in Sao Paulo to win the Brazilian national title. A year later, at the same championships in Rio de Janeiro, he improved the record to 16.01m. At the 1952 Olympic Games, in Helsinki, he twice improved the world record, first to 16.12m and then to 16.22m. He won the title from Leonid Shcherbakov of the Soviet Union, who set a European record of 15.98m. After Shcherbakov had taken the record to 16.23m in 1953, Da Silva responded with a mighty leap of 16.56m at the Pan American Games at altitude in mexico City in 1955.

It was his third Pan American Games title – he also won in 1951. His second Olympic win was in 1956 in Melbourne. He was undefeated between 1951 and 1956.

Damilano, Maurizio

1957–. Born Italy (ITA)

The roar of appreciation which greeted Maurizio Damilano's arrival at the Stadio Olympico in Rome on 30 August 1987 revealed just how popular his World Championship 20km walk victory was. It brought Italy's first gold medal of the championships, and it marked Damilano's first major win since his surprise victory in the 1980

Maurizio Damilano

Olympic Games in Moscow.

In that race he had been lying third, as defending champion Daniel Bautista of Mexico led in the approach to Moscow's Lenin Stadium. When Bautista was disqualified for lifting, it looked as if Damilano would get the silver medal behind Anatoliy Solomin of the USSR. However, Solomin was also disqualified, and the Italian was left to win the race and the gold medal by more than a minute in 1:23:35.5. His twin brother, Giorgio, was eleventh. Both are coached by their older brother, Sandro.

Four years later, Damilano, established as Italy's greatest ever walker, went to the Los Angeles Olympics to defend his title. Despite opening up an eight-second lead on his pursuers at 15km, he was finally caught and passed, first by Ernesto Canto, the Mexican World Champion and favourite, and then by his countryman Raul Gonzales. Damilano won the bronze medal behind the two Mexicans in 1:23:26.

Damilano's World Championship victory, in an Italian and Championship best time, came with a final 5km of 19:41. He celebrated by throwing

his shoes to the crowd – only to publicly ask for them back later. He has won 15 Italian championships (six at 10kmw, seven at 20kmw, and two at 50kmw) and holds track world records for 25km (1:44:54), 30km (2:06:07.3), and the two hours walk (28.565km).

Danek, Ludvik

1937–. Born Czechoslovakia (TCH)

Winner of a complete set of medals for the discus in the Olympics – silver in 1964, bronze in 1968, and gold in 1972 – Danek is one of only two men to have competed at six European Championships (the other is the Italian walker Abdon Pamich).

From 28 July 1963 until 15 October 1964 he won 45 competitions in a row, before losing to American Al Oerter at the 1964 Games in Tokyo. He looked certain to take the gold, leading until the fifth round with 60.52m, but Oerter, under doctors' orders not to compete because of torn cartilages in his rib cage, produced a throw of 61.0 to win his third gold medal. After this defeat, though, Danek was beaten only once in 47

Ludvik Danek

competitions, before losing to Oerter again on 28 May 1966. He followed this with a string of 26 more victories. He set three world records between 1964 and 1966 but produced his best ever throw as late as 1974, when he recorded 67.18.

A veteran of 47 internationals, Danek won 13 national titles and the 1965 AAU title. His complete record at the European Championships is: 1962, ninth (52.12m); 1966, fifth (56.24m); 1969, fourth (59.30m); 1971, first (63.90m); 1974, second (62.76); 1978, fifteenth (58.60m).

Davenport, Willie

1943–. Born USA (USA)

Willie Davenport is the only man to have run in three 110mh finals at the Olympics. He won the title in 1968, came fourth in 1972, and third in 1976. Davenport competed in the 1964 Games in Tokyo, but failed to reach the final because of a leg injury, finishing seventh in his semi-final.

In 1969 in Zurich he ran a world record 13.2, one tenth of a second faster than his winning time in Mex-

Willie Davenport

ico, an Olympic record 13.3, in a race where he successfully challenged team mate Ervin Hall and Italian Eddy Ottoz for the gold. He had, in fact, been injured before the Games and, in his first come-back race, clocked an unimpressive 14.9. However, he regained his form to tie for the world record 120-yard hurdles (13.2) at the end of August, and also to win the US Olympic trials.

In 1972 in Munich he was fourth in a race won by team mate Rod Milburn, with France's Guy Drut second. Four years later, in Montreal, Drut finished ahead, winning in 13.3 seconds, ahead of Cuba's Alejandro Casanas (13.33) and Davenport (13.38). Contesting his fourth final at the age of 33, Davenport pronounced himself happy after the race: 'I gave it the best I had. I'm happy. I got a medal.'

Davies, Lynn

1942–. Born Wales (GBR)

The only man ever to hold simultaneously the Olympic (1964), European (1966), and Commonwealth (1966 and 1970) long jump titles, Davies became the first British athlete to win a field

Lynn Davies

event when, in Tokyo in 1964, he unexpectedly beat the overwhelming favourites Ralph Boston (USA) and Igor Ter-Ovanesyan (USSR) to take the Olympic title. Davis' mark of 8.07m, a personal best, was just four centimetres ahead of the final jump by multi-world record holder Boston.

In 1966 he won his first Commonwealth title, with 7.99m, and went on to beat Ter-Ovanesyan at the European Championships the same year, with a last-round leap of 7.98m. The Russian gained his revenge three years later in Athens, when he beat Davies 8.17m to 8.07m.

At the Olympics in Mexico, in 1968, any hopes that Davies had of retaining his title were dashed by the extraordinary leap of America's Bob Beamon: Davies had for the first time that year passed the 27 feet barrier with 8.23m, but when Beamon launched himself past the 29 feet mark a dejected Davies could only finish ninth.

Davies also won the European Indoor Championships in 1967 and was second in 1969, and he went on to retain his Commonwealth title in 1970 in Edinburgh with a wind-assisted 8.06m. He failed to qualify for the 1972 Olympic final in Munich.

Davies won 41 international caps, was AAA champion five times outdoors and three indoors, and set eight UK records in a career where he raised the UK record by almost two feet and jumped over eight metres more than 20 times in competition.

His best marks include 9.4 seconds for 100 yards; 10.4 seconds for 100m; 21.2 seconds for 220 yards, and 15.43m for the triple jump. He served as Britain's assistant team manager at the 1980 Moscow Olympics.

Davis, Glenn

1934–. Born USA (USA)

The only man ever to retain the Olympic 400m hurdles title, winning in both 1956 and 1960, Davis was also an exceptional sprinter on the flat, and won a further Olympic gold as part of the American 4 x 400m relay team. He ran his leg in 45.4 seconds to contribute to a new world record of 3.02.2.

Although talented at a variety of sports in high school, Davis did not turn to hurdling until April of Olympic year 1956, when he recorded an unexceptional 54.4. Less than two months later, however, at a meeting in Los Angeles on 29 June, he became the first man to dip under 50 seconds when he set a new world record of 49.5 in only his ninth race at the event.

Davis' Olympic victories were clear-cut: the first, in Melbourne, won in 50.1, broke the existing Olympic record, and in Rome, four years later, his mark of 49.3 was just 0.1 seconds outside his own world record, which he had improved to 49.2 in 1958. That year he also set new world records for 440 yards flat (45.7) and 440 yard hurdles (49.9), and just before the 1960 Olympics he equalled the world record for 200m hurdles (22.5).

Davis won four NCAA hurdling titles and one at 440 yards (1958). Other best marks include 100 yards in 9.7; 100m in 10.3; 120 yard hurdles in 14.3, and a high jump of 1.92m (indoors).

After the 1960 Games he retired from athletics to play American football, first for the Detroit Lions and then for the Los Angeles Rams.

Davis, Jack

1930–. Born USA (USA)

In an event which lasts barely 13 seconds, Jack Davis can count himself one of athletics' unlucky losers, twice being runner-up in the 110m hurdles, firstly at the 1952 Olympic Games in Helsinki, then again four years later in Melbourne.

In 1952, Harrison Dillard, the great hurdler who had won the 100m flat race four years before in London after sensationally failing to make the US hurdles team, was looking for the gold medal that most thought was rightfully his. Jack Davis had other ideas, however, and the two men were neck and neck until the eighth barrier, which Davis hit slightly. He finished a yard down, but was given the same hand time of 13.7, 0.2 second under the old Olympic record.

Four years later, in Melbourne, Davis faced Lee Calhoun, with whom he had tied for first place at the US Olympic trials. Again they were level at the eighth hurdle, but the photo-finish evidence made Calhoun the winner. Both were given the same time of 13.5, one tenth of a second outside Davis' own world record.

Delany, Ron

1935–. Born Republic of Ireland (IRE)

Olympic 1500m champion in 1956, Delany was an unexpected winner in a fiercely contested race in Melbourne. The favourites were undoubtedly Australians John Landy and Mervyn Lincoln, with New Zealander Murray Halberg. But in the back straight Delany stormed into the lead to win by six yards, coming with 0.6 second of the world record, and covering the last 100m in 12.9 and the final 300m in 38.8, with a last lap of 53.8. At the finish he fell to his knees and offered up a prayer, before accepting the congratulations of bronze winner and mile record holder John Landy.

Delany had shown little form before the Games, although he had an impressive pedigree, making the final of the 1954 European Championships when aged only 18. He was unbeaten indoors over the mile during the winter of 1956, and started his outdoor season with an impressive 4:04.9. But he reserved his best pre-Melbourne performance for the Compton Invitational race in the USA, which he won in 3:59.0. Before the Games, however, he returned to Eire and suffered an injury, only racing twice and losing both times.

After the Olympics he came second in one of the greatest mile races of all time: at London's White City stadium on the night Derek Ibbotson broke Landy's world mile record with 3:57.2. Delany was second in 3:58.8. His habit of competing in world-record-breaking races continued on 6 August 1958, in Dublin, when Australian sensation Herb Elliot broke Ibbotson's mile record with 3:54.5, with Delany third in 3:57.5.

At the 1958 European Championships, in Stockholm, Delany finished third in the 1500m, running the last lap in a quick 54.6 but with too much ground to make up.

In 1959 he was undefeated indoors at the mile, and lowered his own indoor world record to 4:01.4, before an Achilles tendon injury effectively ended his career.

Didrikson, Mildrid

1914–1956. Born USA (USA)

Voted the greatest woman athlete of the first half of the twentieth century in an Associated Press poll in 1950, Mildred 'Babe' Didrikson's athletics career was relatively brief, before she moved on to even greater success as a golfer. She won gold medals at the 1932 Olympics in Los Angeles at the 80m hurdles and the javelin, and a silver at the high jump.

She set her first world record aged just 16 when, in 1930, she was the first woman to exceed 40 metres throwing the javelin, achieving 40.62m

(133ft 3¼in) on 4 July. At the 1932 Games both she and second-placed Evelyne Hall took 0.1 second off the 11.8 world record at 80mh, which Didrikson had equalled in the heats. In the high jump she broke another world record, as did team mate Jean Shiley. Both cleared 1.65m (5ft 5in) and went into a jump-off, where both cleared 1.67m (5ft 5¾in). Rules at that time, though, said that no world records could be set in a jump-off. Furthermore, Didrikson's jump was rendered invalid by the judges, who took exception to her head-first style.

In 1932 she won the AAU women's team title single-handedly for her club, Employers' Casualty of Dallas, taking part in eight events and winning six: 80mh, shot, javelin, baseball throw, long jump, and first equal in the high jump. She was also fourth in the discus and third in a semi-final of the 100 yards. Her prowess with the baseball earned her the nickname 'Babe' after baseball star Babe Ruth, and she set a world record on 25 July 1931, throwing the ball 90.22m (296ft).

Harrison Dillard

She also excelled at basketball and, after the AAU declared that she was no longer an amateur after apparently allowing a photograph of herself to be used in a car advertisement, she turned to professional golf and, as Mrs George Zaharias, won 17 international titles between 1934 and 1950, including the US Women's Open in 1948, 1950, and 1954.

She died of cancer aged 42 on 27 September 1956.

Dillard, Harrison

1923–. Born USA (USA)

When Harrison Dillard hit three hurdles in the trials for the 1948 Olympic Games, it was one of the greatest surprises in athletics history, going totally against form. In 82 competitions, between 31 May 1947 and 26 June 1948, Dillard was unbeaten at either flat sprints or hurdles, a winning streak that included a world record at 120 yard hurdles of 13.6 seconds.

Fortunately, he had qualified for the Olympic team by virtue of finish-ing third in the 100m race, and in London he sensationally won the short sprint in 10.3 seconds, to equal the Olympic record of his boyhood hero and early coach, the great Jesse Owens. He was a member of the gold-medal-winning 4 x 100m relay team in both the 1948 and 1952 Olympics, and his domination of the high hurdles continued until Helsinki, where he won the gold medal that should have been his four years earlier, beating compatriot and long-time rival Jack Davis in an Olympic record 13.7 seconds. Indeed, it was Davis who ended Dillard's indoor record of 37 consecutive wins from 1949 to 1954.

Dillard attempted a come-back for the 1956 Games in Melbourne, but could finish no higher than sixth in the Olympic trials. During his college career he won no fewer than 201 out of 207 sprint and hurdles finals, and was AAU sprint hurdles champion three times outdoors and eight times indoors, winning the NCAA Championships twice.

He had bests of 9.4 seconds for the 100 yards; 10.3 seconds for the 100m; 20.8 seconds for the 200m; 13.6 seconds for the 120 yard hurdles; 22.3 seconds for the 220 yard hurdles (straight); 23.0 seconds for the 220 yard hurdles (turn); and 53.7 seconds for the 400m hurdles.

Donkova, Yordanka

1961–. Born Bulgaria (BUL)

In a glorious season of sprint hurdling in 1986, Yordanka Donkova put together the finest series of races by a woman ever seen. She ran 11 sub-12.50-second times, improved the world record for 100mh three times, and ran the fastest ever time, a hand-timed wind-assisted 12 seconds dead.

She hit top form in August. On 11 August she set a new Bulgarian record, with 12.38 for 100mh, and, at her national championships two days later, equalled Grazyna Rabsztyn's world record of 12.36. On a balmy night at the Weltklasse meeting in Cologne, on 17 August, she twice improved the

Yordanka Donkova

world record, with 12.35 in a heat and 12.29 in the final.

At the European Championships in Stuttgart, at the end of the month, there was no stopping her. She took the gold medal with 12.38 from Cornelia Oschkenat of East Germany and Bulgarian rival Ginka Zagorcheva, whose best season was to come in 1987. Donkova also won a silver medal, running the anchor leg in the Bulgarian 4 x 100m relay team. She ended the season with a fourth world record of 12.26 at the Balkan Games, and the overall women's title at the IAAF/Mobil Grand Prix Final in Rome.

She started 1987 by winning the European indoor 60mh title at Lievin, France with 7.91. Next came a silver medal in the inaugural World Indoor Championships in Indianapolis, clocking 7.85 behind Oschkenat. In February, she crowned a fine winter by setting a new world indoor record – recognized for the first time that year by the IAAF – of 7.74, in Sofia.

Despite starting her summer season by beating Zagorcheva in their first seven races over 100mh, and running 17 times under 12.70, Donkova missed her main target when she finished fourth, out of the medals,

at the World Championships in Rome. Zagorcheva won the gold medal in 12.34.

Drechsler, Heike

1964–. Born East Germany (GDR)

Heike Drechsler (née Daute) literally leapt into the record books with her surprise win in the 1983 World Championships long jump competition. At just 18, she became the youngest champion that year, with a remarkable series of jumps including a wind-assisted 7.27m, which bettered her personal best by 13cm. The world record holder, Anisoara Stanciu (née Cusmir) of Romania, was well beaten in second place in one of the biggest upsets of the championships.

A few days later, she was able to win the Europa Cup long jump final in London with a jump of 6.99m. She had already won the European Junior long jump and heptathlon titles in 1981.

While the 1984 Olympic long jump was won with a leap of 6.96m by Romania's Anisoara Stanciu, Drech-

Heike Drechsler

sler – absent from Los Angeles because of the Eastern Bloc boycott – showed just how much she was missed by clearing 7.40m, the second longest jump of all time, in Dresden while the Games were still on.

She leapt even further in 1985, claiming Cusmir's record with 7.44m. The same year she won the World Cup competition in Canberra with 7.27m, beating the Russian, Galina Chistyakova, who had beaten Drechsler in the Europa Cup Final in Moscow earlier in the season.

She began by capturing the European indoor long jump title. She went on to complete a sensational summer, achieving four world records and two gold medals in the European Championships in Stuttgart, in the long jump and 200m. In the latter competition, she brushed aside a world class field in only her fourth race at the distance to equal Marita Koch's world record of 21.71 seconds for the second time that summer. She had only turned to sprinting to improve her long jump approach, but could now include it among her specialist events. In only her third race over 100m, for instance, in 1986, she ran the world's fastest time that year. She ended her season having improved her long jump world record to 7.45m.

Her gold medal successes continued in the 1987 indoor season, when she won the European long jump title and became the first world indoor champion at the long jump and 200m in Indianapolis.

The winning streak came to an end that summer at the second World Championships in Rome. She took the silver medal behind fellow East German Silke Möller (née Gladisch) in the 100m – the timetable did not allow her to compete at 200m – and the bronze medal behind an irrepressible Jackie Joyner-Kersee of America in the long jump. Nevertheless, at the age of 23, after only four years at the top, she was named the world's top long jumper of all time in a poll of more than 1000 journalists and sports specialists in an IAAF survey.

Drut, Guy

1950–. Born France (FRA)

Born in the same street in Oignies, near Calais, as national miling hero Michel Jazy, Guy Drut became the first Frenchman in 56 years to win an Olympic gold medal on the track when he won the 110mh in Montreal in 1976.

Acknowledged as a superb technician, who was especially quick between the barriers, Drut reached his first Olympic final at the age of 21 in Munich in 1972. On that occasion he was beaten into second place by the American Rod Milburn, who continued his country's stranglehold on the event by clocking a world record 13.24 to Drut's 13.34. Drut spent most of 1973 working to improve his technique, and emerged in 1974 to win the European Championship title in Rome and equal Martin Lauer's long-standing European record of 13.2 seconds.

By 1975 he was established as a world-beater. Running for France, he won his third consecutive European Cup title and went on to improve his times with manually clocked 13.1 and 13.0 seconds at Saint-Maur, near Paris, and Berlin.

He readily accepted that he was the favourite to win the gold medal in Montreal. 'I will win, of course, without problem,' he said. True to his word, he became the first European to

Guy Drut

win the Olympic 110mh, with 13.30 seconds, from Casanas of Cuba and the American Willie Davenport, the 1968 champion.

An accomplished all-round athlete, he had designs on becoming a decathlete after Montreal, but his revelations in a magazine interview led to his suspension by the IAAF for infringing amateur rules. Calling for track and field athletics to be made open – something that did not happen until 1981 – he admitted being paid to compete in races. He was not reinstated as an amateur until 1980.

Dumas, Charles

1937–. Born USA (USA)

The first man to clear seven feet in the high jump, Dumas went on to take the 1956 Olympic title in Melbourne. His barrier-breaking leap was made at the Olympic trials on 29 June 1956. Dumas, a freshman at Compton Junior College, broke the existing world record, set by Walt Davis in 1953, by nearly an inch on his second attempt at the height. He then decided not to try beyond that mark.

Dumas had come to prominence as a schoolboy, jumping 1.88m when aged only 16. He improved that to 1.97m a year later, and then to 2.09m aged 19. He remained unbeaten until 1958 and in the process won Olympic gold in 1956, America's first track

and field victory of those Games. In a long drawn-out competition that lasted for more than ten hours, Dillard leapt six feet 11 $^1/_4$ inches on his final try, exceeding Walt Davis' mark set at the 1952 Helsinki Games by three inches.

Dumas continued jumping after finishing sixth at the 1960 Olympic Games in Rome, even though he did not compete in 1961, 1962 or 1963. In April 1964 he made a startling come-back, with a leap of 2.14m.

Winner of the American Championships for five successive years (1955-1959), and Pan American champion in 1959, Dumas was also a talented high hurdler with a best of 14.1 seconds for 120 yards.

Dumbadze, Nina

1919–1983. Born USSR (URS)

Dumbadze was one of the all-time great women discus throwers, setting seven world records over 13 years. Since her early records were set at a time when the USSR was not part of the IAAF, they were not put forward for ratification. However, between 1939 and 1952 Dumbadze increased her throwing capability from 49.11m to 57.04m. Her unratified marks included 49.10m and 49.54m in 1939, 49.88m in 1944, and 50.50m in 1946. Those accepted by the IAAF, after the Soviet Union joined in 1947, were 53.24m in 1948, 53.36m in 1951, and 57.04m in 1952.

This last improvement, well over the mark of 53.61m set by fellow Russian Nina Ponomaryeva in 1952, was the largest ever seen in the event and remained unbeaten for eight years.

In international competition, Dumbadze suffered from the lack of Olympics during the Second World War. However, she was the first double gold medallist in women's discus at the European Championships, winning in 1946 and 1950. Each time her victories were decisive: by 4.06m in 1946 and 5.78m in 1950. In her first Olympics in 1952, aged 33, she took the bronze medal.

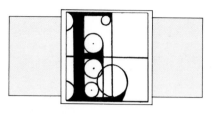

Edwards, Phil

1907–1971. Born Guyana (GUY)

If one remembers the Olympic motto that to take part is the most important thing, there can be no better example of this philosophy in action than Phil Edwards. In the Olympics of 1932 and 1936 he won no fewer than five bronze medals, two at 800m, one at 1500m, and two in the 4 x 400m relay.

Having emigrated to Canada, he showed promise in the AAU Championships, winning the 600m indoors in 1928. That same year he won the Intercollegiate Association of Amateur Athletes of America (IC4A) and the AAU 880 yards outdoors, and was placed fourth in the Olympic 800m in Amsterdam. He won the AAU 600m title again the following year, and repeated his successes at the IC4A and AAU 880-yard championships.

In 1932 he improved his position in the Olympic 800m to third, behind Britain's Thomas Hampson and Canada's Alexander Wilson. Then, apparently while waiting for heats of the 4 x 400m relay, he entered the 1500m heats, never having run the distance seriously before. Not only did he make it to the final, but he led the great Luigi Beccali of Italy and the American Glenn Cunningham, in a world class field, at the 1200 mark, and went on to take the bronze medal in 3:52.8, the sixth fastest time of that year.

He entered the 1500m again in Berlin, once more without any serious preparation, after having won his fifth bronze medal with third place in the 800m behind John Woodruff (USA) and Mario Lanzi (Italy). In a very fast 1500 race, won by New Zealand's Jack Lovelock, Edwards could only finish fifth, but he recorded a personal best time of 3:50.4.

In 1934, representing British Guyana, Edwards was the first black man to win a Commonwealth title, taking the 880 yards.

Ehrhardt, Annelie

1950–. Born East Germany (GDR)

The 100m hurdles event replaced the 80mh for women in 1969. Annelie Ehrhardt (née Jahns), European Junior champion over the shorter sprint in 1968, joined the ranks of the world class performers over 100mh in 1970, when she recorded her best time of 12.9 seconds and shared the 200mh world record of 25.8 seconds. This event was subsequently replaced by the 400mh in 1974.

Ehrhardt finished runner-up in the 1971 European Championships 100mh, when victory went to three-times champion Karin Balzer. Then 33 years old, Balzer, the 1964 Olympic champion, was nearing the end of her hugely successful career as a major force in sprint hurdling. Her position as world number one went to Ehrhardt in 1972.

After clocking a new hand-timed world record of 12.5 in Potsdam in June, Ehrhardt went on to win the gold medal at the Olympic Games in Munich in September. Her time of 12.59 in the final gave her a quarter-second victory margin over Romania's

Annelie Ehrhardt

Valeria Bufanu and Balzer.

The hand-timed world best went again in 1973, when Ehrhardt reduced it to 12.3 in Dresden. The following year she won the European Championships 100mh in 12.66. A back injury prevented her from showing any convincing form in the 1976 Olympic Games at Montreal and, running against medical advice, she was eliminated after managing only 13.71 for fourth place in her semi-final.

Elliott, Herb

1938–. Born Australia (AUS)

In a brief but spectacular career, Herb Elliot laid claim to the title of the greatest middle-distance runner the world has ever seen: between 1954 and 1960 he was undefeated in 44 races at 1500m or the mile, his only loss in a race coming when he was only 14 years old. He broke the world record for 1500m with 3:35.6, and 3:54.5 for the mile. He also won the 1958 Commonwealth Games mile title and the 1960 Olympic 1500m title.

Herb Elliott became the eighteenth man to break the four-minute mile barrier on 25 January 1958, but he was the first teenager to do so. By the end of that year he was the world record holder and had run five of the ten fastest ever times at the distance, reducing his personal best to 3:54.5 in Dublin on 6 August. In that race, against Olympic 1500m champion Ron Delany, top New Zealander Murray Halberg, and fellow Australians Mervyn Lincoln and Albert Thomas, Elliott strode away to win by 12 yards and take 2.7 seconds off Derek Ibbotson's world record.

Following his racing successes in 1958, his low profile in 1959 was misinterpreted by some rivals as a case of the youngster having burned himself out. But Elliott proved them all wrong in the final of the 1960 Olympic 1500m, producing a race that many experts still regard as the finest ever. With 600m to go Elliott surged ahead to win in 3:35.6, bettering Michel Jazy's world record by 2.8 seconds.

The unbeaten Herb Elliot

In the month following his Olympic success, Elliott ran four further sub-four-minute miles before ending his career in London on 13 May 1961 with an easy mile victory, despite many tempting financial offers from promoters to continue running. He was aged just 22.

In addition to his solo successes, Elliott also ran a leg of 4:4.6 seconds for the Australian 4 x 1 mile relay team that broke the world record on 22 March 1959.

European Championships

The first European Championships took place over three days at the Stadio Communale in Turin in 1934. They were staged at the insistence of the Hungarian Szilard Stankovits, a member of the IAAF's European Committee which had been formed in 1932. Absentees from the first championships, which were for men only, included Great Britain and the Soviet Union.

Great Britain joined the championships in 1938, but the Soviet Union did not enter a team until 1946, when women's events were included. Previously, in 1938, women competitors had taken part in separate championships in Vienna.

Since 1970, the championships have been organized by the European Athletic Association, which replaced the IAAF's European Committee, and have been held generally every four years, although there were championships in 1969 and 1971.

Since 1934, the championships have taken place in the following cities: Paris and Vienna in 1938; 1946 Oslo, after a break because of the Second World War; 1950 Brussels; 1954 Berne; 1958 Stockholm; 1962 Belgrade; 1966 Budapest; 1969 Athens; 1971 Helsinki; 1974 Rome; 1978 Prague; 1982 Athens; 1986 Stuttgart.

The Soviet Union continues to be the most powerful athletics nation in Europe. East Germany puts on the pressure in second place, although the strengths of the two nations lie in different areas. The Soviets are particularly strong in the men's field events and the women's track events, while the East Germans have the most powerful women's track and field teams. Great Britain remains the third force in Europe, although this ranking is entirely due to the British athletes'

tremendous success on the track.

At the 1986 European Championships in Stuttgart the Soviet Union men won only seven medals on the track, yet they dominated the field events with five gold medals, six silver, and four bronze. While Britain had only one finalist in the men's field events, the team won nine medals on the track, with five gold medals, two silver and two bronze. In the decathlon, Britain's Daley Thompson won his third European title. These championships also showed that women's athletics in Europe continue to be dominated by the East Germans. They won 12 track medals (five gold) and eight in the field (four gold).

Evans, Lee

1947–. Born USA (USA)

Arguably the greatest 400m runner of all time, his world record of 43.86 seconds, set at altitude on 18 October in the 1968 Olympic Games in Mexico, still stands today. He had actually improved the world record to 44.06 at the US Olympic trials at Echo Summit, South Lake Tahoe in California, again at altitude, but his time was dis-

Coe (326), Cram (328) and Tom McKean (351), Stuttgart 1986

allowed because he was wearing illegal 'brush' spikes.

Evans had won the 1967 Pan American title in 44.95 seconds, and in 1968 won all his major races, including NCAA and AAU finals. At the 1968 Olympics, however, he very nearly did not run following the expulsion from the American team of Tommie Smith and John Carlos after their 'black power' demonstration on the rostrum after the 200m (Smith won the gold, Carlos the bronze). However, both Smith and Carlos persuaded him to run, and he produced the race of a lifetime with splits of 10.7, 10.4, 11.1, and 11.6, although it has been calculated that the rarified atmosphere was worth perhaps as much as 0.4 second.

At the same Games Evans was a member of the 4 x 400m relay team which set another world record, running the last leg in 44.1. This record time of 2.56.16 still stands. On the victory rostrum the quartet of Vince Matthews, Ron Freeman, Larry James, and Evans gave a muted demonstration of black power solidarity, taking off their berets but not giving the famous clenched fist salute during their national anthem.

1968 saw Evans running a world best 1.14.3 for 600m, and he retained his AAU title at 400m the following year. However, injury led to him being placed only fourth in the Olympic trial before the 1972 Games, although a relay medal was a distinct possibility until 400m team mates Vince Matthews and Wayne Collett, first and second in the individual event, were disqualified by the International Olympic Committee following their behaviour during the playing of the American national anthem. They had stood on the winners' rostrum and chatted, causing the crowd to boo their apparently casual attitude.

Evans turned professional in 1972, but was reinstated in 1980 and managed to run 46.5 seconds aged 33.

Ewry, Ray
1873–1937. Born USA (USA)

If one includes the unofficial Olympic Games of 1906, then Ray Ewry is the holder of more gold medals than any other athlete in history, yet none of his events remain in the modern athletics calendar. Ewry specialized in standing jumps, i.e. jumping without a run-up. He won gold medals at the standing high jump in 1900, 1904, and 1908, at the standing long jump in 1900, 1904, 1906, and 1908, and at the standing triple jump in 1990 and 1904.

Ewry was paralysed while a boy and confined to a wheelchair, but through exercise developed exceptional leg power. His standing long jump record of 3.47m (11ft 4$^7/_8$in), set in 1904, remained on the official world record list until the event was dropped in 1938. Other world records included a standing high jump of 1.655m (5ft 5$^1/_4$in) in 1900, and a standing triple jump of 10.58m (34ft 8$^1/_2$in) in 1900.

Lee Evans

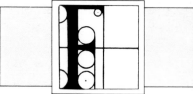

Felke, Petra
1959–. Born East Germany (GDR)

But for the presence of Britain's Fatima Whitbread, Petra Felke would be the dominant force in women's javelin throwing. As it is, these two women have to share that role, since they are the only two capable of throwing beyond 70m. But while Felke holds the world record, with 78.90, she has had to settle for second place in all their recent meetings at major athletics championships.

World Student Games Champion in 1981, Felke was runner-up that year to the world record holder Antoaneta Todorova in the World Cup in Rome. At the World Championships in Helsinki in 1983, Felke finished barely noticed in ninth place, as the crowd were enthralled by the battle for the gold medal between Whitbread and the Finnish favourite, Tiina Lillak.

As world record holder, Felke was among the favourites for the gold medal in Los Angeles in 1984 until the boycott by the Eastern Bloc countries denied her the chance to compete. Victory there went to Tessa Sanderson, who beat Whitbread. The following year, 1985, the two top competitions were the European Cup Final in Moscow, where Felke beat Whitbread, and the World Cup in Canberra, where both were beaten by Olga Gavrilova of the Soviet Union.

At the 1986 European Championships in Stuttgart, Felke led the final for three rounds until Whitbread let go a throw of 72.68m to edge past her. While the East German rallied to find a final throw of 72.52, Whitbread, in terrific form after smashing the world record in the qualifying round, increased her margin of victory with a closing throw of 76.32m, the second best throw of all time.

Petra Felke of East Germany

The scenario was similar in Rome a year later at the World Championships. Again, the Briton proved too strong and was probably mroe competitive than Felke, whose 71.76m was almost five metres short of Whitbread's best. Bronze medallist Beate Peters, of West Germany, was three metres further back with 68.82m. The one consolation for Felke was that she had regained the world record five weeks earlier with 78.90m in Leipzig.

Fibingerova, Helena

1949–. Born Czechoslovakia (TCH)

Helena Fibingerova has competed at the very highest level in women's shot putting for some 15 years. She has broken world records, won a record number of European indoor titles, and competed at two Olympic Games, but it was not until the inaugural World Championships in 1983 that she finally won a major outdoor competition.

A giant of a woman at 1.78m (5ft 10in) and 96kg (218lb), Fibingerova, who is married to her coach, Jaroslav Smid, first burst onto the international scene in 1972, when she improved her best to 19.18m and finished seventh at the Munich Olympics. She claimed

her first world record in 1974 with 21.57m and, having lost it in 1975, recaptured it in 1976 with 21.99m.

At the Montreal Olympics, she left it until the fifth round before unleashing a put of 20.67m, snatching the bronze medal from East Germany's Marianne Adam. She won other medals indoors, most notably in the European Championships. In a rec-

Helena Fibingerova

ord six appearances dating back to 1969, she won silver medals in 1978 and 1982, and a bronze in 1974. There was also success in the World Cup (second place in 1977, 1979 and 1981, and third in 1985) and in the European Cup (first in 1983, second in 1985, and third in 1987).

Indoors she seemed almost unbeatable, winning the European title a record eight times since 1973. She still holds the world indoor record with her put of 22.50m, achieved at Jablonec in 1977. But a major honour eluded her until Helsinki in 1983. At the age of 34 she competed with her right knee heavily strapped and won the World Championship title with a final round effort of 21.05m, grabbing victory from Helma Knorscheidt of East Germany. It was the first time that Fibingerova had beaten her arch rival Ilona Briesnick (née Slupianek), and her joy at the end of the competition was understandable.

Flanagan, John

1873–1938. Born Republic of Ireland (IRE)

Known as the father of modern hammer throwing, John Flanagan won the first three Olympic hammer gold medals and set no fewer than 14 world records. He emigrated from Ireland to the USA in 1896, having already set a world best of 44.47m at Clonmel on 9 September 1895, a mark which he improved to 56.19m at New Haven, Connecticut on 24 July 1909. He set his last world record aged 41 years 196 days, which is itself a record that still stands.

Flanagan's Olympic titles were in 1900, 1904, and 1908, and his winning throws were 49.73 (from a 2.74m circle), 51.23m, and 51.92m respectively, the last two victories from the now standard 2.13m circle. His world bests were set over a record time span of 13 years 318 days, and he topped the world rankings no fewer than 13 times (1895-1901, 1904-1906 and 1908-1910).

In addition, Flanagan also came fourth in the discus at the 1904 Games, and second in throwing the 56lb weight. He won the AAA title in 1896 and 1900, seven AAU hammer titles, and six with the 56lb weight.

Until the advent of Al Oerter in the discus in the 1950s, Flanagan was the only athlete to win three successive gold medals in a standard event. He returned to his native Ireland in 1911, and won the hammer for Ireland against Scotland in his final international appearance.

Fosbury, Dick

1947–. Born USA (USA)

Few athletes are assured of immortality on the strength of their performances, and fewer still are remembered for shaping the destiny of their own event. Dick Fosbury was one such man, however, for although he achieved greatness by winning the high jump gold medal at the 1968 Olympics in Mexico, his technique, dubbed the 'Fosbury Flop' ensures that his name lives on.

Before this, most top high jumpers either straddled the bar with one foot following the other, or used the 'Western roll', where both feet crossed the bar together. Dick Fosbury had been experimenting with his own style since the age of 16, when he discovered that he could only clear 1.78m with the Western roll style. On 26 January 1968, he jumped 2.13m (seven feet) for the first time, in Oakland, California, and placed third just before the Olympics in the trial with a best of 2.21m (7ft 3in).

His style involved running into the bar on a curved approach, then turning to go over the bar backwards, arching the back and bringing the legs over, a method that at first sight looked almost suicidal. In the Olympic final, team mate Ed Caruthers, jumping straddle-style, matched Fosbury until the bar was at 2.24m (7ft 4½in). Fosbury cleared at the third attempt, Caruthers failed. Afterwards, Fosbury tried three times for a world record at 2.29m (7ft 6¼in) but without success, although his winning jump was an Olympic record.

Fosbury faded into obscurity after the Games, trying his hand for a while, unsuccessfully, as a professional, but his style is now the most common in top level high jumping. On 11 July 1973, American high jumper Dwight Stones set the first world record using the 'flop' style in Munich, clearing 2.30m (7ft 6½in).

Foster, Brendan

1948–. Born England (GBR)

Now recognized as Britain's last great 10,000m runner after his performances in the 1970s, with a reputation akin to that of a folk hero in his native northeast, the name of Brendan Foster is one of the best known in athletics.

His running career brought him national and world records, Commonwealth and European titles, but in his Olympic Games appearances he came up against even greater talents than his own: John Walker at 1500m and Lasse Viren at 10,000m.

He was a dogged runner, rarely seen without a grimace, but an athlete who was successful over a variety of distances. His first international appearance was at the 1970 Commonwealth Games in Edinburgh, where he won a bronze medal at 1500m in 3:40.6. Still at the metric mile, he won another bronze medal in the 1971 European Championships, while at the 1972 Olympic Games in Munich he finished fifth in 3:39.0, behind Finland's Pekka Vasala.

The following year he stepped up in distance. His season began well with a two-mile world record of 8:13.68 at Crystal Palace, and he scored a sensational win in the European Cup Final 5000m in Edinburgh, when he injected a 60.2 second eighth lap to open up a lead he never lost. The tactic became his trade mark, and he used it to devastating effect in Nice in 1975, when he retained his European Cup title with mid-race laps of

Dick Fosbury, 1968 Olympic high jump champion

Brendan Foster

59.4 and 61.30. He finally won by 20 seconds in 13:36.18.

He attempted a 1500m/5000m double at the 1974 Commonwealth Games, with mixed fortunes. He finished a close second to Kenya's Ben Jipcho at 5000m in a UK record 13:14.6, and was seventh in the 1500m in another UK record of 3:37.6, while victory went to Filbert Bayi of Tanzania in a new world record of 3:32.16. Later that year, he marked the opening of the new Gateshead Stadium – built through his encouragement and inspiration – in fine style by breaking Emiel Putteman's 3000m world record with 7:35.2.

He climaxed a glorious season by winning the European Championship 5000m title in Rome in 13:17.21. Such was the impact of his running that year that he was voted BBC TV's Sports Personality of the Year.

He moved up in distance yet again in 1975, making his début at 10,000m with 27:45.4. He went for a 5000m/10,000m double at the following summer's Olympic Games in Montreal, and was rewarded with a bronze

medal at the longer distance behind Finland's Lasse Viren and Portugal's Carlos Lopes. But he was run out of the 5000m final, as Viren completed his historic 'double-double' of winning four gold medals.

The winter of 1977 saw him extend his range further by winning the nine-mile English National Cross-Country Championship. In 1978, with two major championships to aim for, he elected to run the 5000m and 10,000m at the first, the Commonwealth Games in Edmonton. He won the 10,000m title and finished third at 5000m, but by the time he lined up for the 5000m at the European Championships in Prague, his season's racing had taken its toll. He was never able to compete over the final lap and, despite running 27:32.65, finished out of the medals in fourth place.

He won his third European Cup title in 1979, this time at 10,000m. However, his third attempt at an Olympic gold medal ended in disappointment in 1980, when he struggled to overcome illness and the heat to finish eleventh in the 10,000m, won by Ethiopia's Miruts Yifter.

Foster retired from competitive racing in 1980, but stayed within the sport to launch the Great North Run, a half-marathon from Newcastle to South Shields designed to cater for the growing numbers of fun-runners.

It is now Britain's biggest mass-participation event, with annual entries of 25,000.

He later joined the shoe company Nike and became UK managing director, before leaving in 1987 after a one year sojourn at its American headquarters. He is known to millions of athletics fans as a commentator for BBC Television.

Foster, Greg

1958–. Born USA (USA)

Greg Foster's record at 110m hurdling – in an era when the overall standard is so high – makes him one of the all-time great athletes. He has had his rivals – most notably Nehamiah and Campbell of the USA, McKoy of Canada, Bryggare of Finland, Caristan of France and, latterly, the British duo of Ridgeon and Jackson – but Foster's consistency has kept him ranked in the world's top ten for 11 successive years. He has been ranked in the top two for nine years.

Foster made his breakthrough at world level only after the retirement of Renaldo Nehamiah, the world record holder who gave up athletics for American football in 1981. His best time, in fact, dates back to 1981, when he beat Nehamiah in 13.03 seconds, Foster took his place in America's World Cup team that year in Rome,

World champion Greg Foster

and claimed victory by the narrowest of margins – just 0.04 seconds – from Alejandro Casanas of Cuba. He won the World Championship title in 1983, despite hitting the last three barriers and only just managing to hold off the challenge of Bryggare at the line.

Favourite for the Olympic title in 1984, Foster had to take silver, while team mate Roger Kingdom continued America's domination of the event with the gold medal in a Games record of 13.20. Foster claimed he had hesitated after what he thought was a false start. Kingdom, relatively unknown before the Olympics, acknowledged that Foster was still the world's number one.

The following year was marred by tragedy, as Foster struggled to get over the death of his mother and three other members of his family in a car crash. For a time in 1987 he became known for his spectacular falls during races. He crashed out of the World Indoor Championship in Indianapolis and the Pan American Games 110mh final. However, his technique was impeccable in Rome, where he retained his World Champion's crown with a 13.21 victory over Ridgeon and Jackson.

Fuchs, Ruth

1946–. Born East Germany (GDR)

From 1970 to 1980 the women's javelin event was dominated by the consistent throwing of Ruth Fuchs. She won 11 East German titles, was ranked world number one for eight successive years, and at the end of her career had notched up 113 wins in 129 competitions.

She won her first GDR title in 1967, and in 1970 won the first of four European Cup titles with a throw of 60.60m. In what turned out to be a remarkable day in 1972, Fuchs claimed her first world record with a mighty 65.06m throw in Potsdam, bettering the 62.70m record throw of Poland's Eva Gryziecka 30 minutes earlier at a meeting in Bucharest. Both women had at last wiped out the world record of 62.40m by Yelena Gorchakova of

the Soviet Union, which had stood for eight years. Fuchs' season ended with the Olympic gold medal at Munich, where she threw 63.88m. Her domination of the event grew more emphatic each season. She set further world records in winning her second European Cup title in 1973 (66.10m) and her first European Championships gold medal in 1974 (67.22m). A third European Cup win came in 1975.

Fuchs became the first woman to retain her Olympic javelin title in 1976, when she took the gold medal with her opening throw of 65.94m. Earlier that year, she had improved her world record to 69.12m in Berlin.

In 1977 she won the inaugural World Cup competition in Düsseldorf. A second European Championship victory was secured with a European record throw of 69.16m. When she won the second World Cup in Montreal in 1979 and improved the world record – snatched briefly by Kate Schmid of the USA with 69.32m in 1977 – to 69.96m in April 1980, she looked certain to win her third Olympic title in Moscow. But it was not to be. The gold medal went to Maria Colon of Cuba, who upset the competition with an Olympic record throw of 68.40m in the first round of the final. Fuchs was unable to respond and finished eighth.

Ruth Fuchs

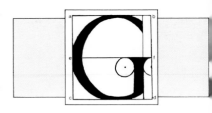

Gammoudi, Mohamed

1938–. Born Tunisia (TUN)

Gammoudi was Tunisia's most successful athlete after the country gained independence from France and first competed in the Olympic Games in 1960. He won the 5000m in 1968 and took a bronze the same year in the 10,000m. Four years earlier he had come second at this distance.

He first made his mark internationally at the 1963 Mediterranean Games, where he won the 5000m in 14:07.4 and the 10,000m in 29:34.2, both Tunisian records. He achieved the same double four years later.

At the 1964 Olympics in Tokyo in the 10,000m, Gammoudi was out ahead with American Billy Mills and Australian multi-world record holder Ron Clarke at the start of the last lap, and the three were neck and neck until Mills' final surge took him to the line first with Gammoudi second. There were no heats before this race, which caused traffic problems as the leaders tried to thread their way through lapped runners.

Four years later, at altitude in Mexico City, he turned the tables most notably on the altitude-trained Africans, beating overwhelming pre-race favourite Kip Keino into second place in the 5000m with the fastest time ever seen at altitude, 14.05. Kenyan Naftali Temu, winner of the 10,000m a few days earlier, was third. In the longer race Gammoudi had been in contention until the last two laps with Temu and Ethiopia's Mamo Wolde, but when Wolde struck for home only Temu had the finishing power.

In 1972, the 10,000m Olympic final saw a new world record from Finland's Lasse Viren after he had got up from a fall. However, Viren's fall had

Tunisia's Mohamed Gammoudi (904)

brought down the gallant Tunisian, and Gammoudi was forced to drop out of the race.

Garderud, Anders

1946–. Born Sweden (SWE)

When Anders Garderud won the European Junior 1500m steeplechase title in 1964, it was assumed, in Sweden at least, that he would go on to one day win an Olympic gold medal. He finally made it with his last attempt at the age of 30, after one of the most thrilling Olympic steeplechase finals of all time. In the meantime he repeatedly had to overcome being branded a failure after poor performances at major championships.

He followed up his first European title with a junior world record of 4:00.6 for the 1500m steeplechase, but was, surprisingly, eliminated in the heats of the senior European Championships in 1966. He got no further in Mexico at the 1968 Olympics, and failed to win selection for the Swedish team at the 1969 European Championships in Athens. He fared better in the 1971 Championships, however, when he reached the final of the 3000m steeplechase. He finished tenth,

though, seemingly unable to cope with the pressure of being expected to do well.

He began training with the Finnish distance runners Juha Vaatainen and Pekka Vasala in preparation for the 1972 Olympics in Munich. Once again he failed to live up to expectations and did not survive the semi-final. Just a few weeks later, however, he showed his true form by beating the Olympic bronze medallist Tapio Kantanen (FIN) in Helsinki, with a new world record of 8:20.8.

The record went to Kenyan Ben Jipcho in 1973, who improved it firstly to 8:19.00 and then to 8:13.91 eight days later. Garderud and Jipcho raced each other in Stockholm a week later and, although the Swede had to be content with second place behind the Kenyan, he did achieve a new European record of 8:18.39.

A year later, at the 1974 European Championships, Garderud finished runner-up to his great rival Bronislaw Malinowski of Poland. He then became the first man to break 8:10 for the steeplechase in 1975, when he ran 8:09.70 in front of his home fans, who immediately installed him as favourite for the Olympic title in 1976.

The Montreal Games in 1976 represented Garderud's last chance of a major title, and he made no mistakes. In the final, he hit the front with 300m to go, leaving Malinowski and the East German Frank Baumgartl to chase him to the line. Baumgartl, in fact, almost caught him, but misjudged the final barrier and crashed to the track, leaving Garderud to win the gold medal in a new world record time of 8:08.8. Malinowski took the silver medal and the luckless Baumgartl the bronze.

George, Walter

1858–1943. Born UK (GBR)

The greatest British athlete at the end of the nineteenth century, Walter George as an amateur set world records over several distances: the mile in 4:18.4 in 1884, two miles in 9:17.4 the same year, three miles in 14:39.0, six miles in 30:21.0, and 18,555m in one hour. After this, heavily in debt and with nothing left to prove, he turned professional in order to face his great rival, William Cummings, a Scot who had turned professional in 1876.

Their first clash was on 31 August

Anders Garderud

1885 in front of more than 30,000 spectators at the Lillie Bridge stadium in London's Chelsea. George set a fast pace and ran the first three-quarters in a world record time before Cummings gave up on the last lap. George won in 4:20, although he walked himself when he was far enough ahead. His boast that he could have run 4:12 proved not to be an idle one when the pair met again almost a year later on 23 August.

Neck and neck until the final 350 yards, Cummings then surged ahead. But George methodically caught him up and passed him on the back straight, and Cummings again collapsed, allowing George to coast home. His time was near his prediction: 4:12.75.

Yet he had run even faster before his first meeting with Cummings, during a time trial in Surbiton in 1885. He ran 4:10.2 against three local runners with handicaps, a time that was not bettered until 1931.

He was also reputed to have run a time trial of 49:29 for ten miles as a professional in 1886. The first amateur to break the 50-minute barrier was Finland's Viljo Heino in 1945.

In all, George won British titles at four different events: one mile and four miles in 1880, then 880 yards, one mile, four miles, and ten miles between 1882 and 1884.

Göhr, Marlies

1958–. Born East Germany (GDR)

Along with her great rival, Evelyn Ashford, Marlies Göhr ranks as one of the greatest women sprinters of all time. Ever since she made her Olympic debut as an 18-year-old, Göhr has been remarkably consistent in her 12 years in international athletics. Her distinctive short striding sprinting style has taken her to 26 major outdoor titles, five indoors, three individual and eleven relay world records. She has, however, failed to win an Olympic gold medal in her favourite 100m event, and there have been significant defeats.

Marlies Göhr

Göhr began winning gold medals in 1975, when she was part of the victorious East German relay team at the World Junior Championships in Athens. She also picked up a silver medal in the individual sprint. After finishing eighth in the 1976 Olympic final, Göhr astonished the world by becoming the first woman to run an electronically-timed sub-11-second 100m, when she clocked 10.88 at the East German Championships in 1977. It was a phenomenal run which catapulted her into world class.

She won the first of six European Cup titles later that year and – something which has become a formality over the years – went on to anchor the GDR to a relay gold medal. The following year brought European Championship success in Prague, although her plan to add the 200m gold to her 100m title was dashed by Lyudmila Kondratyeva of the Soviet Union, who would inflict another, more important defeat on her at the 1980 Olympics.

In fact, the Soviet athlete beat Göhr again over 200m at the European Cup in Turin in 1979. Göhr had already won the 100m, and ended the competition by helping the GDR to a new

world record of 42.10 in the 4 x 100m relay race.

There was little she could do against an inspired Evelyn Ashford at the 1979 World Cup in Montreal, where the American completed a momentous 100m/200m double. Hopes that the two rivals would meet in Moscow at the 1980 Olympics ended when America boycotted the Games over Russia's invasion of Afghanistan. Göhr was still denied the gold medal at 100m, however, when she lost out by 0.01 seconds to Kondratyeva. A relay gold medal was little consolation.

The 1981 season began with yet more European Cup success in Zagreb, and Göhr was eager to redress the balance with Ashford at the forthcoming World Cup in Rome. Once again, though, Ashford was in sparkling form, and sprinted to another double as Göhr finished only third behind Britain's Kathy Cook (née Smallwood) in the 100m.

There were no such disappointments in 1983, when Göhr completed a clean sweep of gold medals at the European Indoor Championships (her fifth title), the World Championships, and the European Cup. There was also a world record of 10.81 in Berlin in June. However, Ashford later took that world record, with 10.79 in Colorado Springs, and should have provided the strongest opposition in Helsinki at the World Championships. But the American crashed out of the final after 50m, crumbling to the track with a pulled hamstring.

The world was still waiting for the Ashford-Göhr show-down in 1984, when the Eastern Bloc countries boycotted the Los Angeles Olympics after fears for their athletes' safety. Gold went to Ashford who, keen to test herself against the absent East Germans, went to Europe in search of a confrontation. It came at the Weltklasse meeting in Zurich in August, where victory went to Ashford in 10.76, a new world record.

It had been a frustrating year for Göhr, but she went into the relatively quiet 1985 season with her usual meticulous preparation. With no Ashford to contend with – she was having a baby – Göhr won the World Cup in Canberra and anchored the GDR team of Möller (née Gladisch), Gunther-Reiger, and Auerswald to another 4 x 100m relay world record of 41.37.

Her third set of European Championship medals came in 1986, when she won the 100m in 10.91, a time bettered only by herself and Ashford. It was thought that Göhr would retire at the end of that season, but the prospect of meeting her old rival in the following year's World Championships may have convinced her that, at 28, she was too young to stop. She began 1987 in good form, winning her sixth European Cup 100m and sprint relay titles. But injury upset her build-up for the Rome World Championships. With Ashford absent with her own injury problems, Göhr had to give way to a new set of young East German sprinters. Silke Möller became the new sprint queen with a 100m/200m double, while Göhr, recovering from injury, was eliminated in the 100m semi-finals.

Golubnichiy, Vladimir

1936–. Born USSR (URS)

One of the most consistent race walkers of all time, with easily the best championship record, Vladimir Golubnichiy competed in no less than five Olympic Games between 1960 and 1976.

Physically very strong, Golubnichiy set his first world record over 20km – 1:30:35.2 – at the age of 19. Five years later, he made his international championship début at the 1960 Rome Olympics and won the 20km walk gold with 1:34:07.2, in hot and humid conditions, from Freeman of Australia and Vickers of Great Britain.

Britain's great hope in 1960, Ken Matthews, had his revenge in 1964 in Tokyo, winning the gold medal while Golubnichiy finished third in 1:31:59.4. In Mexico City in 1968, Golubnichiy's strength powered him to his second gold medal, less than

two seconds ahead of the home favourite, José Pedraza.

With gold and bronze medals in his collection, Golubnichiy added a silver with his time of 1:26:55.2 in Munich in 1972. His last Olympic appearance was in Montreal in 1976, when he finished seventh, despite clocking 1:23:55, his fastest ever.

He was no less successful in European Championships, winning bronze in 1962, silver in 1966 and, finally, gold in 1974 at the age of 38. He was runner-up in the Lugano Cup, the trophy contested every two years by the world's top walkers, in 1967 and again in 1970.

Gonzales, Raul

1952–. Born Mexico (MEX)

Three-time winner of the Lugano Trophy over 50km and the Olympic walking champion of 1984, Raul Gonzales qualifies as probably the greatest race walker of all time. Regarded by walkers as the perfect stylist, his record includes the world track record for 50km of 3:41:38.4, set at Fana in Norway in 1979. In a remarkable career spanning four Olympic Games, he has clocked under 3:50 no less than 15 times for the 50km distance, a feat equalled by no other walker.

At his first Olympics, in Munich in 1972, he finished twentieth. Four years later, at the Montreal Games, where the 50 km walk was not included, he finished fifth over 20km in a race won by his compatriot Daniel Bautista. He was the favourite in Moscow in 1980, when the 50km distance was restored, but after leading for most of the way he blew up in the final stages and was forced to pull out. It was a major disappointment for him and his Mexican fans but, determined to win an Olympic gold medal, he returned to the Games in Los Angeles in 1984. There, in front of legions of Mexicans, he finally won the title he had been seeking for so long. He finished more than five and a half minutes

ahead of his nearest challenger in an Olympic record time of 3:47:26. He also finished second to team mate Ernesto Canto in the 20km walk.

He completed a memorable hat trick of Lugano Trophy victories in 1977, 1981 and 1983. He should have won the title in 1979, but fell victim to his own fast early pace and had to drop out after building up a five-minute lead.

A similar fate befell him at the first World Championships in 1983, when he again set off too quickly and struggled in the closing stages to finish fifth. The title went to Ronald Weigel of East Germany.

He retired after the 1984 Olympics for a career in politics, only to reappear in 1987 when he was runner-up in the Pan American Games 50km walk and eleventh in the World Championships in Rome after leading to the half-way mark.

Raul Gonzales

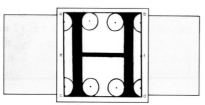

Hägg, Gunder

1918–. Sweden (SWE)

With 16 world records in all, ten of them set in a single season (1942), Gunder Hägg thrilled the athletics world during the Olympics-starved war years, three times reducing the world 1500m record and three times lowering the mile mark, until, in 1945, it stood at a tantalizing 4:01.3.

Hägg's greatest rival for the very highest honours was compatriot Arne Andersson, who himself set three world mile records and one at 1500m. Between the two of them they not only revised the record books, but produced some of the best 1500m races the world has ever seen. In Stockholm, on 10 August 1941 Hägg clocked 3:47.6, a new 1500m world record by a fifth of a second, with Andersson second in 3:48.6. Hägg improved this time on 17 July the following year to 3:45.8, with Andersson again second, in 3:49.2. Andersson then reassessed his training, and come storming back to set a world record of 3:45.0 at Göteborg on 17 August 1943. However, Hägg had the last word the following year, again at Göteborg, running 3:43.0, with Andersson second in 3:44.

At the mile, Hägg's time of 4:06.2, set on 1 July 1942, was equalled nine days later by Andersson. Hägg's time of 4:04.6, set in Stockholm on 4 September 1942, had no less than two full seconds removed from it by Andersson on 1 July 1943 in Göteborg, a time he himself bettered the following year on 18 July 1944 in Malmö, when he ran 4:01.6 with Hägg second in 4:02.0. Hägg's time of 4:01.4, set almost a year later at the same venue, was their final great confrontation, as both were suspended from amateur competition in 1946, allegedly for claiming

Gunder Hägg

excessive travel expenses.

From 1945-1948 Hägg held all seven world records from 1500m to 5000m, even though he was no longer competing. The records were: 1500m, 3:43.0; the mile, 4:01.4; 2000m, 5:11.8; 3000m, 8:01.2; two miles, 8:42.8; three miles, 13:32.4; 5000m, 13:58.2.

At all distances he beat Andersson 15-8, and the score stood at 11-5 at 1500m or mile races.

Halberg, Murray

1933–. Born New Zealand (NZL)

Halberg overcame the handicap of a withered left arm, the legacy of a boyhood rugby accident, to become one of the best middle-distance athletes of his day, and Olympic 5000m champion in 1960. From 1951 he was coached by the New Zealander Arthur Lydiard, having been an excellent miler at school. Under Lydiard, he ran a 4:04.4 mile in 1954, and bettered this in 1956, winning races in 4:02.4 and 4:01.8. His international career started

in 1954, when he was fifth at the Commonwealth Games in the mile, but his greatest successes came when he moved up to longer distances.

He won the three mile title at the Commonwealth Games in 1958 and 1962, and set world records at two miles (8:30.0) and three miles (13:10.0) in 1961. He had a mile best of 3:57.5, set in Dublin on the night that Herb Elliott stormed to a new world record of 3:54.4 on 6 August 1958. At a time when his rivals included Elliott, Mervyn Lincoln, Ron Delany and Derek Ibbotson, among others, Halberg decided to move up in distance. By the end of 1958, he had run three of the 12 fastest mile races ever.

At the end of the 1960 Olympics in Rome, Halberg was entered for both 5000m and 10,000m. In the 5000m he was content to run with the pack until, with three laps to go, he put on a burst of speed that left his rivals standing. With 800m to go, he was almost 20 metres clear after a lap of 61 seconds, followed by one of 64. Struggling to maintain his lead over the final 400m, and being slowly reeled in by Germany's Hans Grodotski, Halberg managed to hang on to win by eight

Murray Halberg (left)

yards. Not surprisingly, after this effort he made little impression in the 10,000m, and finished in fifth place, well behind the medal winners.

Halberg had a best time of 13:35.2 for 5000m, set in 1961. He won his Olympic title in the relatively slow time of 13:43.4, but commented afterwards: 'I am not concerned about records – only winning'.

Hampson, Thomas

1907–1965. Born England (GBR)

Hampson was the first to win both Commonwealth and Olympic Games titles. He won the inaugural 880 yard race at the British Empire (later Commonwealth) Games in Hamilton, Canada in 1930, then continued Britain's winning ways in the 800m at the Olympics. He followed Albert Hill (1920) and Douglas Lowe (1924 and 1928) as Olympic champion, winning in a world record 1:49.7.

Hampson began to show promise as a half-miler when he was an undergraduate at Oxford University, winning matches against Harvard and Yale on a North American tour in 1929. He continued winning in 1930, beating world 800m record holder Sera Martin (France) in the AAA Championships over 880 yards, then again three days later. At the British Empire Games, in Hamilton, he uncorked an 880 yard time of 1:52.4, the fastest time in the world that year over the distance, to win ahead of team mate Reggie Wilson and Canadian Alex Wilson.

It was Wilson who Hampson beat on the line to win in Los Angeles and become the first man ever to go below 1:50 for 800m. The final was an extraordinary example of Hampson's even-paced running, which he was convinced was the secret to 800m running. At the end of the first lap, which leader Phil Edwards (Canada) completed in a very fast 52.8, Hampson was in fifth place, nearly 20 metres adrift. Yet he covered the second lap in almost exactly the same time as the first, (54.9 to 54.8), even catching

Thomas Hampson

Wilson with 50 metres to go, then surging ahead to win by a metre. Hampson's time was a full nine-tenths of a second lower than Sera Martin's world record, and was a personal best by around two seconds.

Harbig, Rudolf

1913–1944. Born Germany (GER)

Before being tragically killed on the Eastern front on 5 March 1944, Rudolf Harbig did enough during his short career to ensure being remembered as one of the all-time great middle-distance runners. He set world records at 400m, 800m, and 1000m, winning 55 competitions in a row at all events from August 1938 until September 1940. During a career lasting from 1934 to 1942, he took part in 233 races, winning 201.

At the 1936 Olympics in Berlin, he was part of the bronze medal-winning 4 x 400m team, and he went on to win the 800m at the 1938 European Championships in a German record of 1:50.6.

His most famous world record came at 800m, in Milan on 15 July 1939, against his great rival, Mario Lanzi of Italy, winner of the silver medal at 800m in the 1936 Games. Harbig's

best had improved to 1:49.4, and Lanzi had recently set an Italian record of 1:49.5. However, although evenly matched on paper, on the day Lanzi had no answer to the German's finishing speed as he powered his way to 1:46.6, almost two second's off the world record set by Sydney Wooderson of Britain the previous year, a time that remained unbeaten until 1955.

Harbig beat Lanzi twice more in 1940, but his defeat by the Italian on 28 September of that year ended Harbig's winning streak of 48 successive 800m races.

A few weeks after his 800m record, Harbig raced to another world record, this time at 400m, which he covered on 12 August in Frankfurt in 46.0. Despite reducing his training as a result of being called up, he still managed to set a further world record over 1000m in Dresden on 24 May 1941, clocking 2:21.5.

Hardin, Glenn

1910–1975. Born USA (USA)

Hardin was a superb runner on the flat or over hurdles. He has the unusual distinction of having set a world record when coming second. It happened at the 1932 Olympic Games, when the 51.7 second time of winner Bob Tisdall (IRE) was not accepted for ratification as he had knocked over the final barrier. Hardin's time of 51.9 was rounded up to 52.0 for his first world record, a mark he improved to 51.8 in 1934 to win the AAU title. Then, on 26 July 1934 in Stockholm, he ran 50.6, a record that stood for 19 years and was the biggest ever improvement in the event's history.

In the same year, 1934, he was also rated number one on the flat running 440 yards in 46.8 seconds, equivalent to a 46.5 at 400m. At the 1936 Olympics, in Berlin, he won the gold at the 400m hurdles in 52.4 seconds.

From his second place at the 1932 Olympics, Hardin was unbeaten at 400m or 440 yard-hurdles until his retirement. He won three AAU titles,

Armin Hary

and was also an excellent runner over the 220 yard-hurdles, with a best of 22.7 seconds. In 1935, Jesse Owens beat him over this distance at the NCAA Championships.

Hary, Armin

1937–. Born Germany (FRG)

Winner of the 100m title at the 1960 Olympics in Rome, Armin Hary was also the first man to run exactly 10.0 seconds for the distance. He achieved this feat twice at the same meeting in Zurich on 21 June 1960. The first race was rendered null and void after Hary was judged to have false started, but the second was allowed as a world record, even though the electronic device being used as a back-up gave the time as 10.25.

Hary was well-known for his fast starting; indeed, he caused a false start in the final of the Olympic 100m in 1960, but got away at the second time of asking to win in 10.2 (auto 10.32), the first European since Harold Abra-

hams (1924) to win the 100m title.

In addition to his individual gold, Hary also helped his team to the 4 x 100m relay title, opening up a big lead while running the second leg. Faulty baton-passing between two of the American team led to their disqualification, even though Dave Sime had charged passed Germany's Martin Lauer in the home straight. The German team's 39.5 seconds equalled the world record.

Hary also won the European title in 1958, in Stockholm, with yet another good start, finishing in 10.3. He rarely raced other distances, but had a best at 200m of 20.5 on a partially-curved track. He retired in 1961.

Hayes, Bob

1942–. Born USA (USA)

The first man to run under ten seconds for the 100m – although on both occasions the wind was over the permitted limit – Hayes also won the 100m at the Tokyo Olympics of 1964, clocking 10.06 seconds, a full 0.19 seconds ahead of his nearest rival.

Before his Olympic gold, Hayes had contested and won 49 finals at 100m or 100 yards in a row, and his disjointed style and heavily muscled

physique seemed an unbeatable combination. Although a relatively poor starter, after 10-30m he would get into his stride. It has been estimated that at full speed he must have been travelling close to 25.6mph. In the 1964 Olympic 4 x 100m relay final, Hayes, running the last leg, picked up the baton in fourth position three metres behind the leader. By the time he had completed a third of his leg he was in the lead, and went on to win by an incredible three metres, in a race where seven of the eight teams involved equalled or bettered the 1960 Olympic record.

Hayes' first dip under ten seconds was on 27 April 1963 at Walnut, California, where he ran 9.9 seconds, albeit with wind assistance of 5m/s. The second time was in the Olympic final in Tokyo, where he was automatically timed at 9.91, with the wind well over the legal limit at 5.3m/s.

Hayes won the American title three years running for the 100m and 100 yards (1962-1964), and in 1964 was the first man to go under six seconds for the 60 yard indoors. He held the world record both for the 100m (10.00) and 100 yards (9.1), and equalled that for the 220 yards (20.5, on a curve), although this was not ratified. He retired from athletics after Tokyo and went back to his first sport, American

Bob Hayes (far right) wins the 1964 Olympic 100m

football, turning professional in 1965 and enjoying great success with the Dallas Cowboys. In 1979, however, he was convicted of drug trading and sentenced to five years imprisonment.

Heino, Viljo

1914–. Born Finland (FIN)

Double world record holder at six miles and holder of eight world records at distances from six-miles to 20,000m, Viljo Heino was the leading Finnish distance runner of the 1940s, following in the footsteps of the great Paavo Nurmi. Although wounded in the leg at the start of World War Two, which curtailed his training until 1943, Heino was able to produce the leading time of that year for 10,000m: 30:15.2.

In August 1944, in Helsinki, he became the second man to achieve under 30 minutes for 10,000m, recording 29:56.2 and almost breaking the world record of Taisto Maki. Three weeks later, again at the Olympic stadium, he did break it, running 29:35.4. The Olympic Games in London, however, proved to be a disaster. Facing the Czech Emil Zatopek in the 10,000m, Heino, who had missed most of the year through injury, was forced to drop out with stomach trouble. In the marathon, his first and last, he finished eleventh.

Heino is credited as being the first amateur to break 50 minutes for ten miles, recording 49:41.6 in Turku, Finland on 30 September 1945. He set a one-hour record on 19,339m/12 miles 29 yards in the same race.

Heino retired from racing in 1951 aged 37.

Hemery, David

1944–. Born England (GBR)

Although his greatest successes came at the 400m hurdles, Hemery was also an excellent high hurdler, having tried both while studying in the United States at Boston University. He won the 400mh at the 1968 Mexico Olympics,

David Hemery

setting a world record in the process, and four years later, in Munich, took the bronze. At the shorter distance he took the gold at the 1966 Commonwealth Games in Kingston, Jamaica, and retained his title four years later in Edinburgh.

Hemery concentrated on the one lap race for Olympic year 1968, reducing his time to 49.6, and also winning the American collegiate title in Berkeley, California on 15 June. Going into the final in Mexico, Hemery was the fourth fastest of the year on paper, but he led from the second hurdle and came in three yards clear, setting a new world record of 48.1. The rarified atmosphere led to a spate of fast times, and the first seven were inside the old Olympic record of 49.3, set by the American Glenn Davis in 1960.

After injury had ruled him out of competition completely in 1971, Olympic year 1972 began inauspiciously with a mediocre 54.6 in Philadelphia on 28 April. But he had reduced this to 49.3 by the time of the Olympics, and in the final ran 48.5, faster than any other European ever, and the same time as American Ralph Mann, who stormed through to take the silver medal. Neither David Hemery nor Ralph Mann was close to winner John Akii-Bua of Uganda, however, who

set a new world record of 47.8.

At the same Games Hemery produced a 45.1 relay leg that helped Britain take the silver medal in the 4 x 400m relay, the team finishing in a European record time of 3:00.5. Just after Munich, at Crystal Palace, he set a world best 300mh in 34.6.

In 1973 Hemery started on a different athletics career, winning the television Superstars competition, placing second in 1974 and winning again in 1976. He also competed for a time as a professional hurdler on the ITA circuit.

Hill, Albert

1889–1969. Born England (GBR)

Ten years after winning his first British title, the AAA four-mile championship, 31-year-old Albert Hill won both the 800m and 1500m Olympic titles at the 1920 Games in Antwerp. The next man to achieve this feat was the New Zealander Peter Snell, over 40 years later in the 1964 Olympic Games in Tokyo.

Hill, a railway guard who had served in the Royal Flying Corps throughout the First World War, faced a tough schedule of racing in Antwerp, with five races in as many days: three rounds of the 800m, and the heat and final of the 1500m. He displayed a superbly even temperament before races, eating an early lunch and then sleeping soundly for three hours.

In the 800m, the favourite was the South African Bevil Rudd, who had already taken gold in the 400m. But after leading for the first 600m, he apparently went over on an ankle 20 metres from the tape, and was passed by the sprinting Hill, who finished in 1:53.4 seconds. In the 1500m, American Joie Ray from Illinois was a firm favourite, and he set the pace, but from 100 yards out both Hill and another Englishman, Philip Noel-Baker, sprinted for the line to finish inches apart, Hill winning in 4:01.8, six seconds outside the world record.

Hill also won a silver medal at the 3000m team event at the same Games.

Hill, Ron

1938–. Born England (GBR)

Ron Hill has been running virtually all his life, and is probably as enthusiastic now as he was in the days when he was European and Commonwealth marathon champion.

Now a successful businessman selling his own range of sports goods, he still runs every day and has not missed a day's training since 1964. His best time – 2:09:28, set when he won the Commonwealth Games title in 1970 – still ranks among Britain's all-time top ten, and he still commands celebrity status wherever he races.

His early successes were on the track and at cross-country. A British international from 1962, he has set numerous UK and even world records at six miles, ten miles, 20,000m, 15 miles, 25,000m, and the marathon. He represented Britain at three Olympic Games, four European Championships, and three Commonwealth Games. His seventh place at 10,000m in the rarified atmosphere of Mexico City in 1968 was especially noteworthy, since

Ron Hill (right)

he had spent the minimum amount of time acclimatizing.

He twice won the English National Cross-Country Championship and, in 1964 and 1968, came close to winning the international title. His greatest success, though, came in the marathon. His first was in 1961 and he has since run more than 110 around the world – all under 2:50. Victory at the European Championships in 1969 and the Commonwealth Games in Edinburgh a year later made him one of the favourites for the Olympic marathon in 1972. But after obsessively concentrating all his training on that one race in Munich, he had, in his own words 'a lousy day', and finished only sixth. It was his greatest disappointment.

A textile chemist by profession – his formal title is Dr Ron Hill – he has always tested his own designs in races. He introduced the string vest and freedom shorts, and even ran the Olympic marathon in 1972 wearing specially made heat-reflective kit. He was also largely responsible for pioneering the carbo-loading diet many marathon runners now use.

Hines, James

1946–. Born USA (USA)

Hines was the first man to be electronically timed at under ten seconds, recording 9.9 in the 100m final at the 1968 Olympics in Mexico. He was also the first man to run hand-timed under ten seconds if one disregards the efforts of compatriot Bob Hayes four years earlier, who had twice dipped under the magical barrier in wind-assisted races.

Hines' run was in a semi-final of the AAU championships at Sacramento, California on 20 June 1968. Second-placed Ronnie Ray Smith was also given 9.9, as was Charlie Greene, the winner of the other semi-final, but the automatic timings were respectively 10.03, 10.14, and 10.10. Hines had previously won his heat in a wind assisted 9.8.

In the Olympic final, Hines won by 9/100 second over Jamaica's Lennox

Jürgen Hingsen

Miller, with arch-rival Charlie Greene third. He also helped his country to the 4 x 100m relay gold medal, running the last leg, to set a team world record of 38.23.

Hines equalled the world record for 60 yards three times in 1967, and the world-best mark for the 100 yards (9.1) the same year, as well as having a good 220 yard personal best of 20.3. He was capable of running a 440 yard relay leg in 45.5 to show his ability over longer distances.

Like his great predecessor Bob Hayes, Hines' ambitions were always to play American football, which he did for the Miami Dolphins from 1969-1970, without, however, achieving the same success.

Hingsen, Jürgen

1958–. Born West Germany (FRG)

A great all-round athlete, Jürgen Hingsen's fate was to contest the decathlon in the era of Britain's world record breaking Daley Thompson. As a result, Hingsen has had to be content with silver medals in all his competitions against Thompson before 1987.

Despite being world record holder in 1982, 1983 and 1984, and being the first man to exceed 7000 points in a decathlon, he has been consistently unable to beat Thompson, who has taken all of those records and has been able to show a greater degree of competitiveness when necessary.

At 1.97m (6ft 6in) tall and 101kg (224lb), Hingsen has been an awesome opponent for Thompson, who is 1.80m (5ft 11in) and 88kg (14st). His stronger events are the 1500m (4:12.3), the pole vault (5.10m), the shot put (16.57m), the discus (50.82m), and javelin (67.42m). Such is the rivalry between the two that the decathlon - ten events spread over two days - has been a major feature of championships in recent years.

Unfortunately for Hingsen, the one occasion when he might have beaten Thompson was in Rome at the 1987 World Championships, when the reigning champion was not at his best because of injury. But the West German had his own injury problems, and withdrew from the event at the high jump. The title, in fact, went to East German Torsten Voss, while Daley Thompson finished ninth.

Hitomi, Kinue

1908–1931. Born Japan (JAP)

In the days before the IAAF governed women's athletics, Kinue Hitomi was perhaps the greatest female all-rounder. In the Women's World Games, organized by the Federation Sportive Feminine Internationale (FSFI) at four-yearly intervals from 1922 to 1934, she won eight medals, more than any other woman. In 1926 she was first in the long jump and the standing long jump, second in the discus, and third in the 100 yards. In 1930 she won the long jump, came second in the pentathlon, and came third in the 60m and the javelin.

She was the first Asian athlete to set a world record and the first to win an Olympic medal. On 20 May 1928, in Osaka, she set a long jump world record of 5.98m, and the following year she became the first woman to jump over 6m when, on 17 October in Seoul, she achieved 6.16m (20ft 2 in), a mark that remained unratified, however. She followed this with a pentathlon world record of 3841 points in 1930.

At the Olympics in 1928, she was second in the 800m in 2:17.6, and the following year, on 5 May in Myashino, she was the first woman to break 60 seconds for 400m.

She set Asian records at ten standard events: 100m, 200m, 400m, 800m, 80mh, high jump, long jump, discus, javelin, pentathlon, as well as at 60m, 100 yards, and 220 yards. She died in 1931 of tuberculosis, just 23 years old.

Hohn, Uwe

1962–. Born East Germany (GDR)

The first man to throw the javelin further than 100m, Uwe Hohn signalled the end of the old-style javelin with his 104.80m at the Olympic Day meeting in East Berlin in 1984. With men of his talent – and strength – around, it was becoming very difficult for officials to keep the javelin competition inside the confines of athletics stadiums. As from 1986, therefore, the IAAF introduced a new style javelin, with its centre of gravity shifted to make it drop sooner. However, Hohn was unhappy with the rule change, claiming that it would prevent the javelin from 'flying' and the whole event would subsequently become less attractive and exciting.

In fact, Hohn never competed with the new javelin because a serious back injury brought his career to a premature end in 1984. He had just enjoyed an unbeaten season, which included his world record - an improvement of 5.08m on American Tom Petranoff's 1983 mark - and a succession of throws over 90m.

His record breaking began in 1981, when he set a European junior record to win the European junior title. He secured the senior European Championship title with a personal best of 91.34m in 1982. But he had his problems. There was a motorbike accident in 1981 and an operation to remove a cartilage which forced him to miss the 1983 World Championships. There seemed little doubt that he would have mastered the new javelin but for his back problems.

He is now a coach to East German javelin throwers.

Hohne, Christopher

1941–. Born East Germany (GDR)

Hohne started his Olympic career with a disappointing sixth place at the 50km event in Tokyo in 1964, although he is

Uwe Hohn, the first man to throw the javelin beyond 100m

now regarded as one of the most successful race walkers of all time. Four years later in Mexico, however, he was unstoppable, winning by the greatest margin ever seen, 10:03.4 ahead of second-placed Antal Kiss (Hungary) in a time of 4:20:13.6. The race, which started in the early afternoon during the hottest part of the day, saw many competitors dropping out, including defending champion Abdon Pamich of Italy.

Coincidentally, Hohne and Pamich are the only two double winners at walking in the European Championships. Hohne won in 1969 and 1974, and finished second in 1971. He set two world records for 50km, 4:10:51.8 in 1965 and 4:08:05.0 in 1969, and had a road best for the distance of 3:52:53, set in 1974.

In his early years, Hohne concentrated on the 20km event, with a best of 1:34:56.2 in 1960, before moving up to 50km in 1962. He won three Lugano Trophy (also known as the IAAF Race Walking World Cup) 50km finals, in 1965 with 4:03:14, 1967 (4:09:09), and 1970 (4:04:35.2), and was third in 1973. Before his win at the Olympics,

Christopher Hohne (white cap)

his best result had been in the Lugano Trophy, when he won the 100km race with the best recorded road performance, in a time of 9:15:58 on 29 October 1967.

In 1972, at the Munich Olympics, he could finish no better than fourteenth in 4:20:43.8.

Holden, Jack

1907–. Born England (GBR)

Four-time winner of the International Cross-Country Championships (admittedly before the event became dominated by the altitude-trained Africans), Jack Holden turned to marathon running in his forties and met with equal success there, winning Commonwealth and European titles in 1950.

Winner of the English National Cross-Country title in 1938, 1939 and 1946, with supposedly his best running years denied him by the Second World War, Holden won the International race a record four times, in 1933, 1934, 1935 and 1946, finishing six times in the top three, and ten times in the top ten in 12 appearances.

In 1947, aged 40, he turned to marathon running, and won his first two races before taking the AAA title that year in 2:33:20.2. He retained his title the following year, in what was the AAA Championship/Olympic trial, winning the Polytechnic Marathon in London in 2:36:44.6. However, he was forced out of the 1948 Olympic marathon race with blistered feet at the half-way point.

After the Games, though, came his best period: he did not lose a race in 1949, and in 1950 ran five marathons, again winning them all. He became the oldest Commonwealth Games medallist when, aged 42 years and 335 days, he won in Auckland, New Zealand in 2:32:57, an amazing personal best considering that he ran the last eight miles barefoot after his shoes split, and he was attacked by a Great Dane when he had two miles to go.

Improving his personal best to 2:31:03.4 while winning the National

Clarence Houser

Championship in July of that year, he then became the oldest medallist in European Championships history when, aged 43 years and 163 days, he beat the Finn Veikko Karvonen by 32 seconds to win in 2:32:13.2.

Houser, Clarence

1901–. Born USA (USA)

Clarence Houser was the last man to win both the shot and the discus in the Olympics, a feat he achieved in 1924. Four years later, he retained his discus title. Although today the two events are not considered close, Houser was the leading American participant at a time when such a mixture was not uncommon.

In Paris, in 1924, he threw 46.14m (151ft 4in) to take the discus title, and 14.99m (49ft 2½in) to win the shot. In Amsterdam he took the discus with 47.32m (155ft 3in). His best year was 1926, when he set a world discus record of 48.20m (158ft 1¾ in), and his shot put best came later in the same year, with 15.42m (50ft 7in).

A student at the University of California, Houser was the first athlete to show how important speed in the circle was to the discus thrower - he used to do one and a half turns, moving in a rapid sequence of steps.

Hunty, Shirley de la

1925–. Born Australia (AUS)

Winner of no fewer than seven Olympic medals (the most by any woman other than Poland's Irena Szewinska, who also won seven), Shirley de la Hunty (née Strickland) also has the honour of being Australia's first woman medallist in any Olympic Games. Her first medal was in the 1948 London Games, dominated by Holland's Fanny Blankers-Koen. The 23-year-old Australian won bronze in the 100m behind Blankers-Koen and Britain's Dorothy Manley. In the 80m hurdles she recovered from a poor start to almost overtake second-placed Maureen Gardner (GB) who was herself given the same time (11.2 seconds) as winner Blankers-Koen.

De la Hunty also finished fourth in the 200m, although an examination of the photo-finish showed clearly that she won the bronze medal ahead of Audrey Patterson (USA). However, because the photo-finish equipment was only used experimentally at these Games, the verdict of the officials stood.

In the 4 x 100m relay, de la Hunty was part of the silver-medal-winning team, finishing one tenth of a second behind the all-conquering Dutch.

In Helsinki in 1952 she won the 80mh by two metres, to win in a new world record time of 10.9 seconds in a race where defending champion Blankers-Koen failed to finish. She became the first woman to retain her title at any event, and is still the only female hurdler to have done so, in Melbourne in 1956. Winning in a time of 10.7 seconds, ahead of world record holder Zenta Gastl (FDR) and Norma Thrower (AUS), de la Hunty set Olympic

records in each of the four rounds.

In the 4 x 100m relay, with de la Hunty and double sprint champion Betty Cuthbert on the team, Australia were the overwhelming favourites, and it came as no surprise when they set a new world record of 44.5 seconds.

At the Commonwealth Games, too, de la Hunty had an excellent record: at the 1950 Games in Auckland she won five medals: gold at 80mh and two relays, and silver at both the short sprints.

She did not compete in the 1954 Games, however, not being selected by her national federation after the birth of a son and a serious case of influenza, a decision she opposed forcefully but to no avail.

As well as her superb record of wins in major championships, she also set more Olympic records than any other athlete, five at 80mh and three at the 4 x 100m relay. Two of her 80mh records at the 1952 Games were also world records, and she added the 100m (11.3 seconds) in 1955, a mark not bettered until 1961. At 31 years and 136 days, she became the oldest woman sprinter to win gold when the Australian 4 x 100m relay team swept to victory at the Melbourne Games of 1956. In 1960, aged 35, she was still in good enough shape to clock a 10.9 100 yards although she had retired after the 1956 Olympics.

Hyman, Dorothy

1941–. Born England (GBR)

One of Britain's most successful sprinters, Hyman's medal collection started at the 1958 Commonwealth Games in Cardiff, where she was part of the gold medal winning 4 x 110 yard relay team. After winning British titles at both sprint distances in 1960, she went on to the Olympics in Rome. In the 100m she finished second, behind Wilma Rudolph of the USA, beaten 11.0 to 11.3. In the 200m she ran a fast time, 23.7, to win her heat, but Rudolph powered her way to 23.2, a new Olympic record, and in the final Rudolph

was out on her own, winning in 24.0. Germany's Jutta Heine overtook Hyman in the last 30 metres to take silver in 24.4.

In 1962, at the Commonwealth Games in Perth, Hyman was the leading medallist, winning the 100 yard and 220 yard titles, and a silver in the 4 x 100 yard relay. At the European Championships, that same year in Belgrade, she collected a full set of medals, winning the 100m, taking silver in the 200m, and bronze in the sprint relay.

She was twice ranked first in the world at 100m (1962 and 1963, the latter being the year she set her personal best of 11.3 seconds) and once at 200m (1963), but she failed to qualify for either sprint final in the Tokyo Olympics of 1964.

Dorothy Hyman (right)

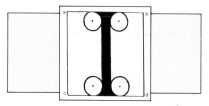

Ibbotson, Derek

1932–. Born England (GBR)

When Derek Ibbotson powered his way to a new mile record of 3:57.2 on 19 July 1957 at London's White City stadium, taking more than half a second off that set by Australian John Landy three years earlier, he could not have known that his own record would last barely a year, broken by the masterful Herb Elliott by almost three seconds.

Ibbotson had been a good junior miler even with his haphazard training. He first came to national attention in a 2000m race, when he lost to Gordon Pirie on the last lap, nevertheless passing the mile mark in 4:08.8. That same year he lost the AAA 3 Mile Championship to Chris Chataway, and went into the winter determined to improve his finishing speed. The next year he beat Chataway into second place in the same three-mile race, clocking 13:32.6.

On 6 August he was persuaded to run in the Emsley Carr Mile in London, even though he protested that he was not really a miler with a best of only 4:07. Nevertheless he won, in a time that equalled Bannister's British record of 3:59.4.

At the 1956 Olympics in Melbourne he won a bronze medal in the 5000m, in a race dominated by the Russian Vladimir Kuts, with Gordon Pirie second. Ibbotson started 1957 in great style, running 4:00.6 for the mile in his first race at the distance on 14 May. This he improved the following month to 3:58.4, the second fastest mile ever run. He claimed that following Kuts' method of training – very fast intervals with only a little rest between each – was improving his speed, and this was clear on 19 July at

Derek Ibbotson (3)

London's White City stadium where, against Olympic 1500 champion Ron Delany and new 1500m world record holder Stanislav Jungwirth (TCH), he stormed away in the back straight to win the mile race in 3:57.2, a new world record.

He ended his great year of 1957 having run the fastest and the third fastest mile ever, but he never really came back to this form, opting to run longer distances, with a best of eight minutes flat for 3000m.

Iharos, Sandor

1930–. Born Hungary (HUN)

The best year for this versatile Hungarian runner, who set world records from 1500m to 10,000m, was 1955. The following year his country was in a state of revolt that led to occupation by Soviet forces – and Iharos was never the same runner again, only finishing tenth and eleventh in the 5000m and the 10,000m respectively at the 1960 Olympic Games in Rome.

A captain and a physical training instructor in the army, Iharos came to prominence in 1954 in the international match against Norway, where he won the 1500m in 3:42.4, covering the last 300m in 41 seconds to set a new European record. In May of the following year, he broke the 3000m world record on his club track in Budapest, clocking 7:55.6, and two weeks later on 30 May set a world record at two miles at the British Games, running 8:33.4. But he reserved his most impressive performance for 28 July in the match against Finland in Helsinki: he broke the Australian John Landy's year-old

1500m record, finishing in 3:40.8.

Overall, he set seven world records in 1955, including one at 10,000m at only his second race at the distance. Along with Vladimir Kuts (URS), he took over ten seconds off Kuts' 1954 record of 13:51.2, running 13:50.8 and an astonishing 13:40.6 (set on 23 October, once again in Budapest), while Kuts held the record again briefly with 13:46.8 that year.

Ilg, Patriz

1957–. Born West Germany (FRG)

Runner-up to double champion Bonislaw Malinowski at the 1978 European Championships, West Germany's Patriz Ilg peaked at exactly the right time to claim the title for himself four years later in Athens. In a championships noted for the quality of a number of West German performances, Ilg timed his run to perfection in the 3000m steeplechase, winning comfortably in 8:18.52 from Boguslaw Maminski of Poland.

The physical education teacher had already won the third of his five West German national titles earlier that summer, and the European indoor title over 3000m during the winter. The following year, he became the first steeplechase world champion, after beginning his sprint for the line with 300m to go in the final in Helsinki. The race proved a disaster for American Henry Marsh, who chased Ilg along the finishing straight but fell at the final barrier and let in Maminski and Reitz of Great Britain for the minor medals.

Sadly, Ilg missed most of the 1984 season because of injury, but returned in 1985 to capture his first European Cup Final title in Moscow, when once again he proved too strong for Maminski, who finished second. In 1986, he became the only steeplechaser to win a medal at three European Championships when he took the bronze in a thrilling finish behind Hagen Melzer of East Germany and Francesco Panetta of Italy. The three finished well clear of the rest of the field after Mel-zer and Ilg had spent much of the race closing the lead that the Italian had built up with his front running.

Beset by injury problems, Ilg finished twelfth in the 1987 World Championships in Rome as his title passed to Panetta in 8:08.57.

Iso-Hollo, Volmari

1907–1969. Born Finland (FIN)

Following the ban on the great Paavo Nurmi for alleged professionalism before the 1932 Olympics in Los Angeles, Finnish hopes rested on Volmari Iso-Hollo, a long-distance runner with an equal liking for the flat and the steeplechase. While not continuing Nurmi's winning ways in the 10,000m, where he lost by just 1.2 seconds to the Pole Janusz Kusocinski, he made up for this in the 3000m

Patriz Ilg (258)

steeplechase, which, because of an error by the official counting the laps, became the 3450m steeplechase. Iso-Hollo was way out in front even at the start of the extra lap, and he went on to beat Britain's Thomas Evenson and American Joseph McCluskey in a time of 10:33.4. In the heats he had set an Olympic record of 9:14.6.

Between Los Angeles and the 1936 Berlin Games he ran the second fastest 3000m race ever, finishing in 9:09.4, and in Berlin he set a new world record of 9:03.8, an Olympic record that was not beaten until 1952. In the 10,000m he finished third in 30:20.2 in a race where the Finns took a clean sweep of the medals.

Other times included 51.6 for 400m, 3:54.3 for 1500m, 8:19.6 for 3000m flat, and 14:18.3 for 5000m.

Itkina, Maria

1932–. Born USSR (URS)

One of the most versatile sprinters Europe has ever produced, Maria Itkina suffered from the fact that her best event, the 400m, did not become an Olympic event until the Tokyo Games of 1964, in which she finished fifth. Nevertheless, she won the first two European Championships at the distance, in 1958 and 1962, to go with her 200m victory in 1954.

In addition, she won a sprint relay gold at the 1954 European Championships in Berne, and completed her European medal tally with a bronze in the 200m in 1958. The 400m was only added to the IAAF official list in 1957, two years after Itkina had already run 53.9. She claimed an official record with 54.0 in 1957, and lowered it three more times until it was 53.4 in 1962, a time that she equalled in winning the European title in Belgrade that same year.

Winner of 14 Soviet titles, four each at 100m and 400m, and six at 200m, Itkina ran her best ever 400m in 1965, clocking 52.9. She withdrew from competition following the introduction of more sophisticated sex tests at the 1966 European Championships.

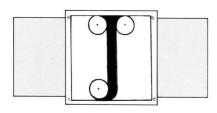

Jackson, Marjorie

1931–. Born Australia (AUS)

Marjorie Jackson, known as the 'Lithgow Flash', became Australia's first Olympic gold medallist in Helsinki in 1952. She succeeded the great Fanny Blankers-Koen as the world's fastest woman by winning the 100m/200m sprint double.

Just 20 years old, she set a new world record of 11.5 seconds in her 100m heat and then equalled it in the final, easily beating Daphne Hasenjager of South Africa and fellow Australian Shirley Strickland. Three days later she equalled the 17-year-old 200m world record of 23.6 seconds in winning her heat, before reducing it to 23.4 in the semi-final. Her second gold medal of the Games came with a 23.7 second run in the final. Jackson anchored the Australian relay team to a 46.1 world record in the 4 x 100m heats, but a fumbled last baton exchange in the final ruled the team out of the medals. The Australians finished fifth.

Jackson went to the Olympics as double Commonwealth sprint champion after winning the 100 yards and 220 yards in Auckland in 1950, equalling the world record at both distances. She also won gold medals in the 4 x 440 yards and 660 yards relays. It made her the first woman to hold Olympic and Commonwealth titles at the same time. She retained her Commonwealth sprint titles in 1954 in Vancouver, where she also won a 4 x 110 yards gold medal. Her seven gold medals are the most won in Commonwealth Games history.

In her career, Jackson set the greatest number of officially-ratified world records. At 100 yards she ran 10.8 (twice) and 10.7 in 1950, 10.4 in 1952,

Marjorie Jackson (30) wins the 1952 Olympic 200m

and clocked a wind-assisted 10.3 in 1953.

Jahl, Evelin

1956–. Born East Germany (GDR)

As Evelin Schlaak in 1976, Jahl scored a major surprise at the Montreal Olympic Games when her first throw in the discus competition sailed out to a lifetime best of 69m, an Olympic record. No one else came near it and the gold medal was won. It was as much a surprise to her as it was to everyone else. Reigning champion Faina Melnik of the Soviet Union threw 68.60m in the fifth round of the final, but it was adjudged to have been a foul throw after officials examined a video of the competition. She eventually placed fourth, a major upset since she was regarded as unbeatable after 52 successive wins.

European Junior Champion in 1973, Jahl threw a European junior record of 63.26m in 1974. She followed her Olympic success by winning the European Championship title in 1978, and both the European and

World Cups in 1979. She actually took Melnik's world record with a throw of 70.72m in 1978, and improved it to 71.50m in 1980 before losing it to Maria Vergova of Bulgaria, the silver medallist in Montreal.

The two met in competition in Moscow later that year at the Olympic Games, and the result was exactly the same as it had been four years previ-

Evelin Jahl

ously. It was the first time a woman had won two successive Olympic gold medals in the discus.

Her second World Cup win in 1981 came after a topsy-turvy competition in which the lead changed hands three times. Jahl emerged the winner with a fifth round throw of 66.70m, gaining revenge over Maria Petkova of Bulgaria and Galina Salvinkova of the Soviet Union, who had beaten her in that season's European Cup Final.

Järvinen, Matti

1909–1985. Born Finland (FIN)

From a nation of great javelin throwers, Järvinen was possibly the greatest of them all. He held ten world records – a record in itself – and dominated the event during the mid-1930s.

His first world record came on 8 August 1930 in Viipuri, then part of Finland, where he threw 71.57m. Three more records came in 1930, one in 1932, three in 1933, one in 1934 and, in 1936 in Helsinki, he took the record to 77.23m.

He took the Olympic title in Los Angeles in 1932 with 72.71m, in a Finnish clean sweep of the medals. Matti Sippala took the silver, Eino Penttila the bronze. A back injury prevented him from repeating his success at the 1936 Games in Berlin, where he finished fifth.

His greatest rival, Yrjo Nikkanen, another Finn, beat him twice in 1938, both times with world record throws. The second of these, 78.70m, was to stand for 15 years, the longest span in javelin history. But Järvinen had the better of Nikkanen when he took the European Championship title ahead of him in 1938. Järvinen was also the winner at the first European Championships four years earlier, when he threw a world record 76.66m in Turin.

Between 1933 and 1940 he threw the javelin over 75m in 20 competitions, and between 1929 and 1942 amassed eight Finnish titles. Järvinen was part of an exceptionally talented family. His brother Akilles was a double Olympic silver medallist in the decathlon and holder of three world bests, while another brother, Kalle, held the Finnish shot put record with a throw of 15.92m in 1932.

Jazy, Michel

1936–. Born France (FRA)

Michel Jazy secures his place in athletics history as one of the 12 men to have held the world record for the mile since Roger Bannister first crashed through the four-minute barrier. His part in the story came on 9 June 1965, when he shaved half a second off Peter Snell's record to advance it to 3:56.6. It was a performance timed to perfection, and came less than a year after he had threatened to quit athletics following his defeat over 5000m at the Olympic Games in Tokyo.

There he had opted for the 5000m instead of the 1500m, the distance at which he was European Champion. It was a mistake. He simply did not have the strength to maintain his long run for home, and was left behind as the medals went to Bob Schul of America, Harald Norpoth of West Germany, and another American, Bill Dellinger.

Jazy later proved himself at 5000m by winning the European title in 1966, when he also won a silver medal at 1500m after being outsprinted by West German Bodo Tummler.

But Jazy's talent really lay at shorter distances. His second place behind the great Herb Elliott at the Rome Olympics in 1960 had inspired him to

Michel Jazy in the 1964 Olympic 5000m final

train harder, and in subsequent years he set world records at 2000m (5:01.6) and 3000m (7:49.2) in 1962, and at two miles (8:29.6) in 1963.

His world mile record came in a season when he set ten European records. There were also two more world records, at 3000m (7:49.0) and two miles (8:22.6), achieved in the same race at Melun on 23 June 1965. The only one of his seven world records not set in the month of June was in 1966, at the end of his career, when he arranged a special two-mile race at St Maur des Fosses in October. His time, 4:56.2, was to survive for ten years.

Jenner, Bruce

1949–. Born USA (USA)

With two world record scores behind him, Bruce Jenner went to Montreal for the 1976 Olympic Games decathlon with a sure sense of his own destiny. It was to be his final competition

Bruce Jenner

Ben Jipcho (second right)

before retirement, and he was confident of victory.

But even Jenner was surprised by the manner of his win. Not only did he start with five personal bests in the first day's events, but he ended the competition with a world record tally of 8618 points, 207 clear of Guido Kratschmer of West Germany in second place. Defending champion and previous world record holder, Nikolay Avilov, of the Soviet Union, was third.

In eighteenth place in his first Olympics was the 18-year-old Daley Thompson of Great Britain, who would take over from Jenner as the world's greatest decathlete. In fact, he developed into a much stronger competitor than Jenner in most of the ten events, although he cannot match the American's best of 4:12.16 for 1500m.

Since retiring, Jenner, the golden boy of American track and field, has become a millionaire through a sports promotion company, television and film appearances, and public relations work. He also has a meeting named after him, the Bruce Jenner Classic in San José, California, which is part of the IAAF/Mobil Grand Prix series.

Jipcho, Ben

1943–. Born Kenya (KEN)

Ben Jipcho first made a name for himself in the 1500m final at the Mexico Olympics in 1968. It was Jipcho who paced fellow countryman Kip Keino through the tortuous opening laps of his victory over the American Jim Ryun in 3:34.9. Jipcho helped him to a first 800m of 1:55.3, which was thought much too quick for the heat and altitude.

Keino was to lead African athletes to the very top in world athletics, where their flair and natural talent would change the face of distance running. But the Kenyans were late to mature in terms of their performances. Jipcho was 30 and had been running for 11 years when he finally began breaking world records in 1973. An officer in the Kenyan Prisons Department, he was allowed the privilege of time off to train, and his first success came at the 1972 Olympic Games. He finished second in the steeplechase final in 8:24.6, as Keino, who had moved up to longer distances, took the title in 8:23.6.

He achieved his greatest successes

over the next two years. In 1973 he lowered the world record for steeplechase three times to 8:13.91 (improving his own record by a massive 5.8 seconds) and went through the entire season undefeated. He also demonstrated his enormous reserves of stamina by running two races in quick succession, sometimes at the same meeting. He ran a 3:36.6 1500m the day after his 8:13.92 steeplechase world record, for instance, and in Oslo ran 3:37 for 1500m and 13:34.6 for 5000m within an hour.

At the following year's Commonwealth Games in Edmonton he was at his most impressive. There were glorious gold medals at 5000m, when he beat Britain's Brendan Foster in a thrilling finish, and at the steeplechase, and a bronze medal in the 1500m, as Tanzanian Filbert Bayi broke the world record with 3:32.2. Jipcho's own time, 3:33.2, moved him to fourth on the all-time list.

Later that year Jipcho joined the professional circuit, run by the International Track Association. He earned a great deal of money during the ITA's two years in existence, often running two races a night. He once ran 8:27 for two miles followed 45 minutes later by a 3:56.2 mile.

Johnson, Ben

1961–. Born Jamaica (CAN)

Ben Johnson is, quite simply, the fastest man the world has ever seen. In Rome, at the 1987 World Championships, he beat arch rival Carl Lewis of the USA by more than a metre, covering 100m in 9.83 seconds. He had improved Calvin Smith's 100m world record, set at altitude, by a full tenth of a second, an incredible margin. On a sensational second day of the championships, his remarkable performance briefly shared the limelight with Stefka Kostadinova's high jump world record which followed within minutes, but Johnson's run will remain one of the great track records of all time.

The race also proved that Johnson – a Canadian after leaving Jamaica in

Ben Johnson (145) becomes world champion in world record time

1976 – had finally achieved the number one world ranking over Lewis, the World and Olympic champion. Lewis had opted out of the 200m to face Johnson and, despite equalling the old record himself, could never get to grips with his rival, who had secured a clear lead within ten metres of the gun. Johnson, a renowned fast starter, was found to have had a 0.129 second reaction time at the gun and was out of his blocks and into his stride faster than anyone. Even in the middle of the race, where Lewis has always been at his most powerful, Johnson was able to find more speed, and actually accelerated at 70m.

He had an exceptional year in 1987, winning all 21 of the finals that he contested, running four sub-four-second times, setting four indoor records over 55m and 60m, one outdoor record, and winning two world titles.

His rivalry with Lewis dates back to 1983, when he was eliminated in his semi-final at the inaugural World Championships in Helsinki, while Lewis went on to win three gold medals. In 1984, Lewis repeated Jesse Owens' feat of winning four gold medals at the Los Angeles Olympics,

while Johnson won only a bronze at 100m and the 4 x 100m relay. A breakthrough came at the 1985 World Cup in Canberra, where Johnson won the 100m in 10.00.

In 1986 he lost just once, ran ten sub-10.10 times, and beat Lewis three times. The two men represent a fascinating contrast of styles: Lewis tall and elegant with a long stride, Johnson short and stocky with a powerful build. Their races had always been close until that decider in Rome.

Johnson is now sampling the fame and fortune that he watched Lewis enjoy after his Olympic triumphs. Sponsorship, endorsements and appearance fees mean that the world champion is capable of 'earning' around $1 million a year.

Johnson, Rafer

1934–. Born USA (USA)

Olympic decathlon champion in 1960, Johnson had been heavily favoured to win the title four years earlier, but had taken the silver medal behind team mate Milton Campbell. The world record holder at the time, having set a mark of 7985 points in 1955, Johnson had a knee injury that forced him out of the long jump competition, for which he had also qualified.

Johnson won nine decathlons, including the 1955 Pan-American title and three AAU titles, and set three world records. This sprang from unlikely beginnings, however. As a child he suffered near crippling injuries after an accident in which he caught his left foot in a conveyor belt, but he recovered after several weeks on crutches. His decathlon début in 1954 was disappointing – 5874 points only a year before he set his first world record. The 1956 Games saw the second of his two defeats.

At the 1960 Olympics, in Rome, Johnson had a terrific struggle for the gold medal with Chuan-Kwang Yang of Taiwan. Yang actually beat Johnson in seven of the ten events, but he still needed to beat him by 60 metres in the final discipline, the 1500m, to make sure of the gold. He failed, and Johnson scraped home by a mere 58 points after more than 26 hours of competition.

Johnson's best marks for the ten events were: 100m, 10.3; long jump, 7.76m; shot put, 16.75m; high jump, 1.90m; 400m, 47.9; 110mh, 13.8; discus, 52.50m; pole vault, 4:10m; javelin, 76.74m; 1500m, 4:49.7.

He retired after the 1960 season to make a career in films.

Jones, Steve

1955–. Born Wales (GBR)

If one race can change an athlete's life, then that is exactly what the 1984 Chicago Marathon did for Steve Jones. In only his second marathon – he had dropped out of the same race 12 months previously – he slashed eight seconds off the world best to win in 2:08.05, and beat the likes of World Champion Rob de Castella and Olympic Champion Carlos Lopes. The race rocketed him to a level of fame and fortune he could never have dreamed of. As an aircraft technician with the RAF he earned a modest salary, but success in Chicago meant that he could

Steve Jones

command massive appearance fees in races where prize money ran into thousands of dollars. Estimates put his earnings from road racing around the world at $194,000 in prize money alone between 1984 and 1988.

Up until 1984, he had been a much-travelled world class 5000m and 10,000m runner, with personal bests of 13:18.6 (1982) and 27:39.14 (1983). His record at 10,000m included seventh place in the 1982 European Championships, eleventh in the 1982 Commonwealth Games, twelfth in the 1983 World Championships, and eighth in the 1984 Olympic Games. He was one of a growing number of track athletes who took up the marathon after a degree of success at 10,000m, including the 1984 Olympic medallists Carlos Lopes, John Treacey, and Charlie Spedding. The distance held no fear for him, and he was unaware of just how close he was to a world best time in 1984 until he was within yards of the finish.

He won the following year's London Marathon in April with a UK all-comers best time of 2:08:16, a day after Lopes had improved the world best to 2:07:11 in Rotterdam. Not to be outdone, Jones went back to Chi-

cago in October to produce another astounding run, only to finish an agonising one second outside Lopes' time.

His new-found confidence transferred well to the track in 1986, when he won his first major championship medal: a 10,000m bronze at the Commonwealth Games. At the European Championships in Stuttgart, later that year, he started the marathon as clear favourite. However, it all went wrong.

His aggressive front running put him on world-best pace and gave him a two-minute lead at half-way. But he was unable to drink the fizzy mineral water provided at the feed stations and, as a result, suffered badly from dehydraton from 20 miles. He was eventually caught by the pursuing pack and struggled home in twentieth place in 2:22:12.

There is no doubt about the long term effect of that experience, and he has since failed to run anywhere near his best. He was selected for Britain's World Championship team after a 2:12:37 clocking for second place in the Boston Marathon in 1987, but was unable to go to Rome because of injury. He failed to make the Olympic team in 1988, after only managing 2:14:07 when finishing ninth in his second attempt at winning Boston, one of the classic marathons. He left the RAF soon afterwards to concentrate on his running career.

Joyner, Florence

1959- Born USA (USA)

On a remarkable day at the American Olympic trials in Indianapolis in 1988, Florence Joyner (née Griffith) took women's sprinting into a new era with a sensational time of 10.49 seconds for 100m. The wind speed was nil and Joyner simply flew from gun to tape to take 0.27 seconds off Evelyn Ashford's (USA) four-year-old record, a massive margin in sprinting. Her personal best before the trials had been 10.99 seconds.

Joyner's world record came in the quarter final of the women's 100m competition, but she later won her place in the US team for Seoul by winning the final in 10.61, again inside the old record. Ashford herself also made the team in second place.

Joyner's previous major achievements on the track have been at 200m. She was Olympic silver medallist in 1984 and was second behind East Germany's Silke Möller (née Gladisch) at the World Championships in Rome in 1987, where she also won a gold medal in the 4 x 100m relay.

Joyner-Kersee, Jackie

1962–. Born USA (USA)

Married to her coach, Bob Kersee, Jackie Joyner-Kersee demonstrated her clear superiority at the 1987 World Championships by winning the heptathlon by 564 points from her nearest challenger. She also came within 30 points of her own world record score. She completed the double by winning the long jump with a leap of 7.36m. This was well clear of Yelena Belyovskaya of the Soviet Union and Heike Drechsler of East Germany, who is her greatest rival and who shared her world record of 7.45m until it was broken in 1988 by Galina Chistyakova (7.52m).

Joyner-Kersee had failed to finish the heptathlon event at the 1983 World Championships in Helsinki, pulling out at the fifth event, the long jump, because of injury. The event was dominated subsequently by the East Germans, who took all the medals. A year later, when the heptathlon was included in the Olympic programme for the first time at Los Angeles, Joyner-Kersee was second. The East Germans were not there – absent because of the Eastern Bloc boycott – and this time the gold medal went to a surprise winner, the Australian Commonwealth Champion Glynis Nunn, who beat Joyner-Kersee by just five points.

The following year, the American began an unbeaten run of heptathlon competitions, winning seven with her win in Rome. She is the sister of triple jumper Al Joyner.

Jackie Joyner-Kersee

Juantorena, Alberto

1950–. Born Cuba (CUB)

Victory at 400m and 800m made the long-striding Alberto Juantorena the sensation of the 1976 Olympic Games in Montreal. It was a unique double. The Cuban, almost 1.98m (6ft 6in) tall with a shock of fuzzy hair, was an awesome runner, with the strength and sprinting speed to suddenly open up winning leads over the rest of the field with what often seemed like only a few strides.

He did not seriously take up 800m running until 1976. Before that he was a 400m runner, placed fifth in the 1972 Olympic semi-final in Munich. A former basketball player, he won the World University Games 400m in 1972. He had improved so much by 1974 that his 44.7 led the world.

He went to Montreal with a best 800m time of 1:44.9, but there were doubts from some – America's favourite Rick Wohlhuter included – that Juantorena would have the stamina for three races in three days. The Cuban proved them wrong by easily qualifying for the final, where he led into the second lap before surging away with 300m to go. The rest of the field gave chase, but Juantorena strode to victory in a new world record of 1:43.5.

His 400m victory three days later

in 44.26 was a low altitude best time, and he went on to run his eighth race of the Games in the 4 x 400m relay, in which Cuba finished seventh.

One man who might have challenged Juantorena over 800m was missing from the Games because of the African boycott: Mike Boit of Kenya. The two met twice in 1977 after Juantorena had improved the world record to 1:43.44. At their first encounter in Zurich, the Cuban won by a second in 1:43.64 after a 49.65 opening lap. Their second race, in the World Cup in Düsseldorf, was much closer, with the Cuban just pipping Boit to the line, 1:44.04 to 1:44.14. He remained unbeaten throughout 1976 and 1977.

The arrival of Steve Ovett (fifth in Montreal) and Sebastian Coe at world level, plus a series of injuries, meant that Juantorena's career effectively tailed off from 1978.

In 1980 he chose to defend only his 400m title and finished fourth. In 1983 he withdrew from the World Championships 800m after the semi-final, stretchered off the track after tripping over the inner kerb. He finally retired after some lack-lustre performances in 1984.

Alberto Juantorena

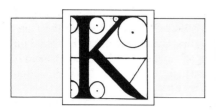

Kazankina, Tatyana

1952–. Born USSR (URS)

A triple Olympic champion, and the first athlete to successfully defend a 1500m title, Tatyana Kazankina was a major force in world middle-distance running for eight years until 1984, when she was banned by the IAAF for refusing to take a drugs test after a 5000m race in Paris.

She did not really emerge as a potential Olympic champion until a few weeks before the Montreal Olympics in 1976. Her previous best at 1500m had been 4:05.9, dating back to 1974, but six weeks before the Games she claimed the world record with 3:56.0 in Podolsk. Due to run only the 1500m in Montreal, she was picked at the last minute to double up in the 800m as well, after clocking 1:56.6 at a pre-Games meeting in France. She justified the faith of the Soviet team management by winning the 800m title in 1:54.9, a world record. Also, with a devastating kick off the final bend, she added the 1500m title in 4:05.5 after a last lap of 56.9 seconds.

The following year she won the inaugural World Cup 1500m title in Düsseldorf, but raced sparingly throughout the summers of 1977 and 1978. She gave birth to a daughter early in 1979, and started later that year began preparing for the 1980 Olympic Games in Moscow. She clipped a second off her own world record with 3:55.0 in Moscow before the Games, and in the Olympic final made her run for home with a lap and a half to go to win in 3:57.8.

Shortly after the Games she lowered her 1500m world record yet again, beating American star Mary Decker in the process, with a solo run of 3:52.47. The time was faster than any

Tatyana Kazankina

men's Olympic champion before 1932, and faster than the great Paavo Nurmi ever ran in his life.

After 1980 she moved up in distance to 3000m, an official world record distance since 1974, although it would not be included at the Olympic Games until 1984. She lowered her best at the distance to 8:36.54 in 1982, but at the age of 31 had to give way to Decker at the first World Championships in Helsinki in 1983. Kazankina finished third, as Decker won in 8:34.62. The Soviet was pipped for the silver medal in a thrilling finish by Brigitte Kraus of West Germany. She did win one title at 3000m, however, in 1983 – the European Cup Final at Crystal Palace.

There was also a world record – 8:22.62 in Leningrad in August – after Kazankina had missed the Los Angeles Olympics because of the Eastern Bloc boycott. Her career effectively came to a halt in Paris later that season when, after running 5000m in

15:23.12, she refused to take a drugs test. Since IAAF rules state that refusal to take a test implies that the athlete is guilty of using a prohibited substance, she was subsequently banned from international competition for 18 months. She was reinstated in 1986 and finished fifth in the Women's World 15km Road Race Championship in Portugal.

Keino, Kip

1940–. Born Kenya (KEN)

Kip Keino has a special place in athletics history as the most popular Kenyan to emerge during the 1960s. His loping stride, toothy grimace and unpredictable race tactics meant that he was much loved by his fans.

He came to prominence in the golden summer of 1965, when he joined Australia's Ron Clarke and France's Michel Jazy in breaking world records on the race tracks of Europe. Keino took on all distances. He set a world record of 7:39.6 in his first ever 3000m, beat Clarke twice at 5000m, and clocked 3:54.2 for the mile. He won the 1500m and 5000m at the first African Games, and claimed Clarke's 5000m world record with 13:24.2.

His first major championship wins came at the 1966 Commonwealth Games in Jamaica, where he won the three miles and the one mile. Perhaps his most famous victory came in the heat and altitude of Mexico City in 1968, when he upset the 1500m form books at the Olympic Games. He won in a staggering 3:34.91, with a first 800m of 1:55.91, to leave the favourite, Jim Ryun of the USA, floundering 2.9 seconds behind at the finish. Amazingly, he had already won a silver medal in the 5000m and run in the 10,000m.

There were more medals at the 1970 Commonwealth Games in Edinburgh: gold at 1500m and silver at 5000m. In Munich, in 1972, Keino surpassed himself by winning the Olympic steeplechase title in 8:23.6 from team mate Ben Jipcho, but was well-beaten by

Kip Keino (1)

the fast-finishing Finn Pekka Vasala in the 1500m.

Kipkoech, Paul

1963–. Born Kenya (KEN)

With his team mate John Ngugi, Paul Kipkoech is becoming known more through his road and cross-country running than for his massive talent over 10,000m on the track.

However, it was at the 1987 World Championships in Rome that he gave the perfect demonstration of 10,000m running the Kenyan way. After following the slow early pace, he suddenly opened up with a 62.58 sixteenth lap which produced telling gaps through the field of 30 as everyone responded to the move. Only the Italian favourite, Francesco Pannetta, stayed in touch as Kipkoech injected intermittent fast laps of around 63 seconds. The pressure proved too much even for Pannetta, and the Kenyan soldier cruised to victory - despite the confusion over the lap

counter, which left some runners sprinting for the finish one lap too soon. His first major title came in 27:38.63.

His talent encompasses many distances. He was fifth in the 1984 Olympic 5000m final behind Said Aouita, and has a best 1500m time of 3:41.41. Three times he has finished runner-up in the World Cross-Country Championships, once to Lopes of Portugal in 1985 and twice, in 1987 and 1988, to Ngugi.

Klim, Romuald

1933–. Born USSR (URS)

One of the most consistent hammer throwers of the 1960s, Klim won 42 straight hammer competitions from 1965-1968, and in total picked up six major championship medals: Olympic gold in 1964, silver in 1968, European gold in 1966, silver in 1969, and two European Cup victories, in 1965 and 1967.

At the 1964 Olympics, in Tokyo,

Klim set a new Olympic record of 69.73m (228ft 9in) beating the Hungarian Gyula Zsivotzky. He beat him again in the 1966 European Championships, and in the 1967 European Cup final.

The final of the 1968 Olympics, in Mexico, brought the prospect of a classic battle between the two. Although Zsivotzky had never beaten Klim in competition, he had set a new world record of 73.76m (242ft) in 1968, and was throwing near to 76.2m (250ft) in practice. Klim in his turn had overshot the training area in the Olympic village!

Klim threw an Olympic record 72.82m (238ft 11in) in the third round, and victory seemed assured when in the next round he improved this to 73.28m (240ft 5in). However, Zsivotzky, silver medallist in the two previous Olympics in 1960 and 1964, unleashed an Olympic record 73.36m (240ft 8in) with his fifth round throw, to inflict defeat on Klim for the first time in two years. Klim set a world record in 1969 of 74.52m.

Paul Kipkoech

Koch, Marita

1957–. Born East Germany (GDR)

When the 20-year-old Marita Koch finished second to the Olympic champion and world record holder Irena Szewinska over 400m at the 1977 World Cup in Düsseldorf, a new era in women's sprinting was just beginning. Koch showed that she was ready to take over from Szewinska as the world's greatest 200m and 400m runner. It turned out to be the East German's last defeat over one lap for four years, as she went on to dominate women's sprinting for a decade, amassing 26 major titles, 16 world records, and 14 world indoor bests.

Prior to 1977 she had already shown her potential, setting two world indoor bests for 400m in one day, winning the European Indoor title, and taking her first GDR 400m title outdoors in 51.47 seconds. In 1978 she continued to improve at all the sprints, breaking Szewinska's 200m world record with 22.06 in May, her 400m world record with 49.19 in July, and lowering the latter to 49.03 in August. The climax of a marvellous season came at the European Championships in Prague, when she not only beat Szewinska, who finished third, and the rest of the field by some 12m, but she also stopped the clock at 48.94 to become the first woman in history to break 49 seconds. She added to her medal tally with another gold after a stunning 48.1 anchor leg in the 4 x 400m relay.

The following year brought more world records. She brought her 200m record down to 21.71 in early June and her 400m mark down to 48.89 in July. She reduced the latter to 48.60 at the European Cup Final in Turin in August. A rare defeat came at the World Cup in Montreal, when Evelyn Ashford, who had already beaten Koch's team mate Marlies Gohr over 100m, scored a notable double by taking the 200m title as well, running 21.83 to the East German champion's 22.02. In the 400m Koch faced Szew-

Marita Koch wins the 1982 European 400m title

inska for the last time, beating her once again in 48.97, the fourth fastest time ever.

Olympic year brought a world best 100m indoors of 11.15, followed by a 6.11 world best for 50m. The Olympic final in Moscow's Lenin Stadium provided her with the perfect stage to demonstrate her superiority over the rest of the world at 400m. Her 48.88 – the second fastest of all time – put her well clear of the Czech Jarmila Kratochvilova in second place, although the two were to experience closer confrontations after the Games. On this occasion, the GDR did not win the 1600m relay gold medal, but took silver behind the Soviet Union. Soon after the Games, however, Koch played her part in a 4 x 200m world record for the East Germans of 1:28.15.

At the World Cup in Rome in 1981, Koch suffered her first 400m defeat in four years when Kratochvilova proved too strong for her in the home straight to win in 48.61, just 0.01 seconds outside the world record. A year later the two met again, this time at the European Championships in Athens. Victory went to Koch with a new world

record of 48.16, as she proved yet again that she was the undisputed world number one. She capped a fabulous championships by running a 47.9 final leg in a world 400m relay record for the GDR of 3:19.04.

Koch prepared for the 1983 World Championships in Helsinki with a lifetime best 100m of 10.83 in the GDR championships, followed by a 21.82 200m and a part in a new 4 x 100m relay world record of 41.53. In Helsinki, she won a silver medal behind Gohr at 100m and three gold medals: at 200m and in the two relays. Kratochvilova took advantage of her absence in the 400m by clocking a world record 47.99 and beating Koch to the first sub-48 second time. A week later the Czech beat Koch over 200m at the European Cup Final in London.

Missing from the 1984 Olympics because of the Eastern Bloc boycott, Koch nevertheless equalled her 200m world record that year and ran the third fastest 400m of all time. Her Olympic title went to America's Valerie Brisco-Hooks in 48.83.

Her 1985 season focused on the

World Cup in Canberra, and she began by taking the 200m title in 21.90, seven metres clear of the rest of the field. She surpassed herself in the 400m, winning with another world record of 47.60. The following year, she rounded off her extraordinary career by winning her third European Championship 400m title in Stuttgart, followed, of course, by another gold medal in the 4 x 400m relay.

Kolehmainen, Hannes

1889–1966. Born Finland (FIN)

If young Hannes Kolehmainen needed any sporting heroes, he had only to look at his own family. His older brothers Tatu and William had both set world bests, William running a marathon on the track in 2:29:32.2 in 1912 for a world professional best, and Tatu achieving the same for the 20,000m in 1913.

With a solid background of running and skiing, Hannes Kolehmainen became the first foreigner to win the AAA 4 Mile Championships in 1910, and he dedicated himself to preparing for the 1912 Olympics in Stockholm. There his performances made him instantly the most successful of the three brothers: between 7 and 15 July he won three gold medals (at 5000m, 10,000m and cross-country) and took a silver in the team cross-country competition.

In the 10,000m he took off on his own and reached half-way in 15:11.4 (the 5000m world record was 15:01.2!), then slowed down to jog to victory in 31:20.8. It is his 5000m victory against Frenchman Jean Bouin, however, that many regard as one of the best races of all time – both became the first men to go under 15 minutes, and Kolehmainen's time of 14:36.6 beat the world record by 25 seconds. With one lap to go, Bouin was slightly in front, but they both sprinted neck and neck down the finishing straight before Kolehmainen crossed the line first to win by 0.1 second. His world record lasted for ten years until broken by the next great

Finnish runner, Paavo Nurmi.

Although he held world records from 3000m to 30,000m, many people thought that Kolehmainen had given up serious training by the time of the 1920 Olympics in Antwerp. However, aged 30, he won the marathon course (which was about 600m over the now standard distance) in 2:32:35.8, a world amateur best and equivalent to about $2^1/2$ hours for the now accepted 26 miles 385 yards.

Kolehmainen continued running in his thirties, competing in the Olympic marathon trials of 1924 and 1928.

Kostadinova, Stefka

1965–. Born Bulgaria (BUL)

Stefka Kostadinova added to the crescendo of noise in the Olympic Stadium in Rome at the 1987 World Championships by taking the women's high jump record to 2.09m.

It was a brilliant performance, coming as it did after her battle with defending champion, Tamara Bycova, for the gold medal. Bycova a former world record holder herself, went out of the competition at 2.04m, while Kostadinova cleared it at her third attempt and went on to jump 2.06m before her world record. For a while it had looked as if the Bulgarian was

beaten, as Bycova put together a series of first-time clearances.

Kostadinova has shown herself to be both a supreme high jumper and a tough competitor, winning 34 successive competitions between 1984 and 1986. That sequence was interrupted briefly by the West German Heike Redetzky at Munich in 1986, but Kostadinova went on to win a further 19 competitions until 1987, when she was beaten three times. She has jumped 2m in 46 competitions, winning the European and World Indoor championships in 1985 and 1987, the World Cup and European Cup in 1985, and the European Championships in 1986, when she was the only one to master the rain-soaked run-up and took the gold medal with 2.00m. She has set three world records outdoors, taking the mark from 2.07 in 1986, and holds the world indoor record with 2.06m.

Kouros, Yiannis

1956–. Born Greece (GRE)

Yiannis Kouros' ultra running début was so spectacular that many observers thought he had cheated. He won the Spartathlon – a race over 245km from Athens to Sparta – by two and a half hours! His great ability was later

Stefka Kostadinova

confirmed when he won a 200-mile stage race in Austria. The following year he established himself as one of the finest ultra runners of all time by breaking George Littlewood's 96-year-old record for a six-day event with 635 miles. He broke his own record later the same year at Colac, Austria, when he ran 1023.2km (639.5 miles).

In between these two runs he also added the world 24-hour road best to his growing collection of achievements. In 1985 he set world track bests for 24 hours and 48 hours in the same race in Montauban, France – 176 and 281 miles respectively – before winning the arduous Sydney to Melbourne 1060km race for the first time. Later that year, he broke his own 24-hour road best with 178 miles in New York.

Since then he has focused on the Sydney to Melbourne race, winning it in 1987 in five days, 14 hours and 47 minutes. He ran 272km in 24 hours, followed by 452km in 48 hours, apparently taking a break of just six hours to sleep! Injuries and illness have restricted his performances in shorter ultra races. In 1988 he won the International Association of Ultra runners (IAU) 100-mile World Championships in ten days, ten hours, 30 minutes and 35 seconds, an amazing average of 96 miles a day. Currently he holds every world best from 200km (124 miles) to 1000 miles, apart from the track 1000 miles.

Kraenzlein, Alvin

1876–1928. Born USA (USA)

The winner of the most individual gold medals at any Olympic Games, Kraenzlein won the 60m, 110mh, 200mh and the long jump at the 1900 Games in Paris. At three of these events he also held world records: 15.2 seconds for the high hurdles, 23.6 seconds for the low hurdles (a mark unbeaten for 25 years), and a long jump score of 7.43m.

The 1900 Olympic Games were as far removed as it is possible to imag-ine from the well-organized global spectaculars of today. The track was grass, there were no provisions to speak of for the field events, and the crowds were able to wander about freely. The Games were totally dominated by the Americans, who were almost exclusively college students from the East Coast.

Kraenzlein, from the University of Pennsylvania, won his heat of the 60m in seven seconds, and repeated this time in the final to beat team mate Walter Tewksbury. A bizarre incident made his long jump victory easier than he might have wanted: many of the college authorities refused to allow their athletes to take part in the field events scheduled for Sunday, asking instead that they might be allowed to do their events alone on the Monday, with their scores counting towards the final result. The French authorities refused, and many of the American athletes were thus deprived of medals. However, five members of the university of Pennsylvania carried on, including Kraenzlein. Thus he had six further jumps on the Sunday in which to beat the mark set by Myer Prinstein from the University of Syracuse in the heats the previous day. This he duly did, winning by one centimetre, 7.18m to 7.17m. He refused to meet an angry Prinstein in a head-to-head the next day.

Jarmila Kratochvilova (411)

After his 200mh victory Kraenzlein declared: ' I am through with athletics and intend to devote myself to something more serious'.

Kratochvilova, Jarmila

1951–. Born Czechoslovakia (TCH)

At the age of 32, Jarmila Kratochvilova staged a sensational double gold medal performance at the first ever World Championships in Helsinki in 1983. It was the highlight of a career that started late but put her among the great names in track history.

Kratochvilova had already entered the 400m and was not, in fact, considering competing in the 800m. However, this changed when she ran a world record 1:53.28 at a warm-up meeting in Munich just before the championships. The timetable in Helsinki allowed for her to run in both events – although only just – and she needed all her strength to manage her demanding schedule of races. First came the heats for the two events, followed a day later by the quarter final of the 400m and the semi-final of the 800m. On the third day she won her 400m semi-final in 51.08 seconds, and 35 minutes later secured her first World Championship title with victory in the 800m in 1:54.68. If there were any questions about her stamina, she answered them all by winning the 400m the following day with a world record 47.99, making her the first woman to break 48 seconds.

Kratochvilova's record at 400m is outstanding. She came second to the great Marita Koch of East Germany at the 1980 Olympic Games, but reversed these placings at their meeting in the 1981 World Cup in Rome. It was Koch's first defeat over 400m since 1977, but the East German reasserted her supremacy over one lap a year later when she beat Kratochvilova into second place at the European Championships in Athens. Kratochvilova later ran the fastest ever 400m relay leg in 47.6, but the GDR took the gold medal.

The Czechoslovakian went on to

Ingrid Kristiansen wins the world cross-country title in 1988

run world best times and to win a succession of European indoor titles, including the 400m in 1982 and 1983, and the 200m in 1984. She missed the 1984 Olympic Games because of the Eastern Bloc boycott, and claimed to have retired from international competition after the 1985 World Cup in Canberra where, running for the European team, she finished a distant fifth in the 400m behind Koch. However, to the delight of her supporters, she reappeared in 1987 to win an 800m silver medal at the European Cup Final in Prague. The pace was much too hot for her in Rome, though, where she went to defend her World Championship 800m title. She qualified for the final as the fastest loser in her semi-final and finished fifth in 1:57.81.

Kristiansen, Ingrid

1956–. Born Norway (NOR)

The only woman to hold world records at 5000m, 10,000m and the marathon, Ingrid Kristiansen has taken over from her former rival Grete Waitz, who is also from Norway, as the world's leading distance runner. Such is her record over recent years that she can probably lay claim to the title of the greatest woman distance runner of all time.

She started running as a youngster, with a world age best of 4:22.6 for 1500m as a 15-year-old. However, for several years after that her main priority was cross-country skiing, in which she achieved some success. By 1977 she had made her marathon début, with 2:45:14 in Trondheim.

Three years later she won the Stockholm Marathon in 2:38:45, then finished third in New York, behind Grete Waitz. By 1981 she had reduced her time to 2:30:09 in New York, but that year the race was won in a world best 2:25:29 by Alison Roe (NZL).

Up until 1984, it was her fellow Norwegian Grete Waitz who had taken all the honours at distance running: on the track, at cross-country, and in the marathon. She was so revered in Norway that her statue was placed outside the famous Bislett Stadium in Oslo. But Kristiansen improved fast, winning the Houston Marathon in January 1984 in 2:27:51 – and only five months after the birth of her son, Gaute. She finally overtook Waitz on the world rankings with her first London Marathon win that spring. Her 2:24:26 was a European record, coming just a couple of weeks after she had beaten Waitz in the Norwegian National Cross-Country Championships – her first domestic defeat for 14 years.

The two Norwegians were favourites to take medals at the 1984 Olympic Games in Los Angeles, where the women's marathon was included for the first time. However, America's Joan Benoit outsmarted both of them by setting a pace neither was prepared to follow. Waitz did eventually give chase, and won the silver medal, but Kristiansen suffered in the hot weather and finished a disappointed fourth.

She made amends in 1985. First came a world best in the London Marathon, when she ran at sub-2:20 pace for much of the race to finish in 2:21:06, easily inside Benoit's old mark. It was a time that would have won every men's Olympic marathon until 1960. She followed it up with a sensational 10,000m run on the Bislett track, where her 30:59.42 was 14 seconds inside the previous record of the Soviet Union's Olga Bondarenko. Her year ended, however, with a second defeat by Olympic Marathon champion Joan Benoit-Samuelson in Chicago, when once again the American proved too strong over 26.2 miles.

Since 1986 Kristiansen has enjoyed an unparalleled run of success. There was a world best 10km on the road in the Ekiden Relay in Japan, where her 30:39 was 21 seconds inside Waitz's best, victory in the Boston Marathon in 2:24:55, and a 10km win over Benoit-Samuelson in New York. With her home fans screaming their encouragement and clapping out a deafening rhythm, Kristiansen shattered her own 10,000m record with 30:13:74 at the Bislett Stadium in June. Next came wins over Bondarenko and Olympic champion Maricicia Puica in two 3000m races, and a further world record, this time at 5000m, with 14:37:33 in Stockholm. She duly took the European Championships 10,000m title in Stuttgart in August, when she ran on her own from the second lap to clock 30:23:25. She won the Chicago Marathon in October.

Her sights were now set on being the first woman to run a sub-2:20 marathon, an ambition shared by Benoit-Samuelson. In London in 1987 she made a heroic attempt, but started too quickly and finished in 2:22:48, hampered by a painful foot injury. The injury persisted for most of the summer, but Kristiansen, under-prepared and not her usual confident self, gambled in the 10,000m at the World Championships in Rome. She raced into a 25m lead at the end of the second lap, silently daring the rest of the field to stay with her. None of them did, and she won on her own in 31:05:85.

That winter was her best ever. She won the Women's World 15km Road Race Championship in November and again the following March, the World Cross-Country title, also in March, and her fourth London Marathon in April. Each time, her only opposition was the clock.

Krzesinska, Elzbieta

1934–. Born Poland (POL)

Krzesinska is the only woman to have won two medals in Olympic long jump competition, winning the gold in 1956

with world record 6.35m and coming second eight years later in 1964.

Four years prior to her Olympic triumph, she took part in the Games in Helsinki, finishing twelfth. Two years later she had improved enough to win a bronze at the European Championships in Berne.

She was ranked number one in the world in 1956, and set one other world record of 6.35m several months before the Olympics prior to equalling that mark in the final. In the 1960 Olympics in Rome she lost by ten centimetres to Vera Krepkina (URS), 6.27m to 6.37m.

Second at the European Championships of 1962 in Belgrade, she was rated the world's number two three times: in 1957, 1960, and 1962.

She now works as a coach in the United States.

Kuts, Vladimir

1927–1975. Born USSR (URS)

Many experts rate Kuts' 1954 duel with Briton Chris Chataway over 5000m at London's White City as one of the classic races of all time. Chataway reduced Kuts' existing world mark to 13:51.6, just a step ahead of the Russian, who finished in 13:51.7. Yet this was one of Kuts' few defeats over 5000m or 10,000m, in a career where he showed himself to be the toughest competitor of the 1950s.

In addition to the 1954 European and the 1956 Olympic 5000m titles, Kuts also completed the distance double at the 1956 Games in Melbourne by taking the 10,000m as well. In his career he set four world records at three miles and four at 5000m.

Kuts experienced several arduous years during the Second World War, during which time he was forced to work for the German occupying forces before escaping to fight against them. He then joined the Russian navy. Here he discovered his talent for sports, particularly distance running.

His first major international meeting was the 1954 European Championships in Berne, where at 5000m he

Kuts and Chataway, White City, 1954

reduced Emil Zatopek's record to 13:56.6, ahead of Chris Chataway in second place by nearly the length of the home straight. After his defeat by Chataway at White City, Kuts regained the 5000m world record ten days later, running 13:51.2. He also ran 13:46.8 in 1955 to take the record back from the Hungarian Sandor Iharos.

1956 saw Kuts beaten by Briton Gordon Pirie in Norway in June, in a race where Pirie set a new 5000m world record, with Kuts second, 13:36.8 to 13:39.6. Their races at both 5000m and 10,000m at the Olympics later that year, however, showed Kuts' supremacy. In the 10,000m they were out in front after a very fast first lap, and Kuts repeatedly tried to break the Briton with a series of punishing bursts. This continued until lap 21,

when the Russian finally broke free and went on to set a new Olympic record of 28:45.6, with Pirie finishing an exhausted eighth.

In the 5000m Kuts dominated the race to win ahead of Pirie in 13:39.6, a new Olympic record by almost 30 seconds, with Derek Ibbotson of Britain third. In 1957, two years to the day that he had been beaten by Chataway in London, Kuts regained the 5000m world record in Rome for the third time, clocking 13:35.0, a time that stood for over seven years until beaten by Australian Ron Clarke.

Kuts three-mile world records date from 1953, when he had set an unratified mark of 13:31.4. This was followed by three official marks in 1954, including 13:26.4 in Prague on 23 October, en route to regaining his

world record for 5000m for the first time with 13:51.2.

Kuts, who trained himself almost to complete exhaustion, fashioned a regime where he could maintain sustained speed against more natural finishers like Pirie. Before the 10,000m in Melbourne, for example, in training he did 25 fast quarter-miles with only 30 seconds of jogging between each.

Kuznyetsov, Vasiliy

1932–. Born USSR (URS)

Twice Olympic bronze medallist in the decathlon, and three times European champion, Kuznyetsov is one of the event's most consistent performers. He set two world records, 8014 points in 1958 and 8357 in 1959, and was winner of the Soviet decathlon title ten times.

At the 1956 Games in Melbourne he finished third with 7461 points, behind favourite Rafer Johnson (7568 for the silver), and winner Milt Campbell. Four years later he could only finish third again, as Rafer Johnson and Chuan-Kwang Yang (Taiwan) battled for the gold right up until the last event, the 1500m.

Kuznyetsov won the European title in 1954, 1958 and 1962, winning his final title against Werner von Moltke (West Germany) by 8026 points to 8022. This very close victory was based on the current 1952 tables, but when the calculation is done using the 1962 tables, von Moltke actually comes out in front, 7786 to 7770.

Kuznyetsov's first world record of 8014 points was set in Krasnodar over 17 and 18 May 1958. It comprised: 100m, 11.0; long jump, 7.30m; shot, 14.49m; high jump, 1.75m; 400m, 49.1; 110mh, 14.5; discus, 47.50; pole vault, 4.00; javelin, 66.16; 1500m, 4:50.0.

His second world record of 8357 points, set in Moscow over 16 and 17 May 1959 included: 100m, 10.7; long jump, 7.35; shot, 14.68; high jump, 1.89; 400m, 49.2; 110mh, 14.7; discus, 49.94; pole vault, 4.20; javelin, 65.06; 1500m, 5:04.6.

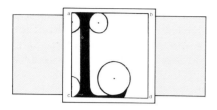

Ladoumègue, Jules

1906–1973. Born France (FRA)

In the years when the great Paavo Nurmi (FIN) was beginning to fade at the 1500m and mile, Jules Ladoumègue was one of the finest runners to fill the void. By the end of 1931 he was world record holder for the 1000m, ³/₄ mile, 1500m, 2000m and the mile, but was ruled ineligible for the 1932 Olympics and banned for life by the French athletics federation after receiving illicit payments.

Ladoumegue had been a 5000m runner primarily (third in the French Championships of 1926) until advised that his style would be better suited to shorter distances. He made no real breakthrough until joining the Stade Francais where the coach was Charles Poulenard. Poulenard had coached, among others, 800m world record holder Sera Martin. In June 1927 he ran the two fastest 1500m of his career – 3:58.0 and 3:55.2 – and the following month won the French Championships in 3:52.2, the third fastest time ever.

At the 1928 Olympic Games in Amsterdam Ladoumègue finished second in the 1500m behind the Swede Harri Larva, losing in the final 20 metres by 3:53.8 to 3:53.2. This defeat affected him badly, and in 1929 he lost both confidence and races, but he returned to form in 1930 with a mile in 4:15.2 and 1500m in 3:53.7. In October 1930, at his home track at Stade Jean Bouin, he decided to try for the 1500m world record and succeeded, becoming the first man under 3:50 for the distance, clocking 3:49.2. On 19 October, he went on to set a 1000m world record of 2:23.6.

World records were attacked and broken by Ladoumègue in 1931 – first on 2 July the 2000m in 5:21.8, then on

Landy looks inside as Bannister (329) passes him on the outside

13 September the ³/₄ mile in 3:00.6. Almost a year to the day after becoming 1500m world record holder he decided to go for Nurmi's mile world record. On 4 October 1931 he crossed the line in 4:09.2, a world record by 1.2 second. He ran the last 120m in 16.8 second and passed the 1500m mark in 3:52.4, the fastest time that year, in a race which proved to be his last.

Landy, John

1930–. Born Australia (AUS)

John Landy will forever be known as the second man to break the four-minute barrier for the mile, but at the beginning of 1954 it was a two-horse race between him and Roger Bannister (GBR), the man who did eventually run under the magic time, running in 3:59.4. Not that the two men raced each other for the privilege – Landy's attempts were made virtually unpaced in Australia and later Finland – but when the two did meet at the British Empire Games in August 1954 they produced one of the greatest races of all time. Bannister won 3:58.8 to 3:59.6 in the first race to have two men under the four-minute-mile mark.

Landy was eliminated from the 1952 Olympic Games 1500m heats, but trained harder than any middle-distance runner before him to shock the world by clocking the third fastest mile of all time on 13 December 1952 in Melbourne, finishing in 4:02.1. A month later he tried again in windy conditions and clocked 4:02.8. A year later, still in Melbourne, he ran 4:02.0, a time that put him equal with Bannister, and three more times at the start of 1954 he went for the record, clocking 4:02.4, 4:02.6 and 4:02.6.

In desperation he travelled to Turkey, Finland to try again on the fast track and in more favourable conditions. Arriving on 3 May, he was in Europe to hear of Bannister's achievement on 6 May. Nonetheless he put in a month's hard training before running 4:01.6, 4:01.6, then on 21 June, helped by Bannister's pacemaker Chris Chataway, 3:57.9, a new world record.

The so-called 'Miracle-Mile' was set for 7 August 1954 at the Empire Games in Vancouver. Landy led until half-way, and did not slow even when caught by Bannister. But coming into the home straight he allowed himself a look inside just as Bannister stormed through on the outside, winning by five yards.

At the 1956 Olympics in Melbourne, Landy could finish no better than third in the 1500m behind Ron Delany and Germany's Klaus Richtzenhain, his confidence badly shaken by Delany's late burst through to win.

Lauer, Martin

1937–. Born Germany (FRG)

Martin Lauer was an excellent sprinter either on the flat or over hurdles. He finished fourth at 110mh at the 1956 and 1960 Olympics, and set a world record at this distance and at 200mh in 1959 after winning the European Championships 110mh title in Stockholm. But Lauer's greatest success came as part of the West German sprint relay team: between 1958 and 1960 he ran in teams that equalled the world record of 39.5 seconds three times.

At the 1960 Olympic Games in Rome the German team won the sprint gold medal after the USA team had been disqualified. Lauer was running the final leg and started two metres up against Dave Sime, but the American, in a devastating burst of speed, reached

the line one metre in front. However, with faulty baton-passing between Ray Norton and Frank Budd after Norton had overrun the exchange zone, the judges awarded the gold to the Germans, their time of 39.5 seconds equalling the world record.

Lauer's world individual records were set in Zurich on 7 July 1959. Firstly, in the 100mh his hand-timed 13.2 seconds was only 13.52 seconds on automatic timing, then in the 200mh he set a time of 22.5 seconds that remained the final world record at this distance, as the race was superseded by the 400mh.

Leather, Diane

1933–. Born England (GBR)

A little more than three weeks after Roger Bannister broke the four-minute barrier for the mile on 6 May 1954, Diane Leather became the first woman to dip under five minutes for the distance. In all she set five world

Diane Leather

records, reducing the mark from 5:07.6 to 4:45.0. She was also world record holder at 1500m (twice) and 880 yards, and won the National Cross-Country title four years in succession, from 1953-1956.

Her first mile world record came during an Invitation Race in the international match between Great Britain and Holland at White City Stadium on 30 September 1953. She finished in 5:02.6, after passing 880 yards in 2:37.8. The following year, on 26 May, she came tantalizingly close to five minutes, clocking 5:00.2 in a Birchfield Harriers meeting race which she led from start to finish. Three days later, at the Midland Championships, she did go under five, with 4:59.6, passing 440 yards in 1:08.8 and 880 yards in 2:27.0.

She continued her dominance in 1955, reducing the mark to 4:50.8 at White City on 24 May, and then slicing a huge five-second chunk off her own record on 21 September, clocking 4:45.0.

In addition, she set two 1500m world records in 1957, firstly at the National Championships on 16 May with 4:30.0, then with 4:29.7 on 19 July, an intermediate time during a mile race. Her time of 2:09.0 for 880 yards, set at the WAAA championships at White City on 19 June 1954 was briefly a world record until beaten by Nina Otkalenko (USSR) in Moscow on 18 July the same year.

Lehtinen, Lauri

1908–1973. Born Finland (FIN)

Lehtinen was one of the runners to follow in the wake of the great Paavo Nurmi. While never approaching the heights of his predecessor, he still managed to win the 5000m at the 1932 Olympics in Los Angeles, and to finish runner-up four years later at the Olympics in Berlin.

Lehtinen also set a world record for 5000m, on 19 June 1932 in Helsinki, taking over 11 seconds off the previous best mark, finishing in 14:16.9. In the same race he also passed the three-mile mark in 13:50.6 to become the first man to break 14 minutes for the distance outdoors.

He was the overwhelming favourite for the 5000m gold in Los Angeles, but was involved in one of the best, and most disputed, finishes of all time against the American Ralph Hill. Coming off the final bend, the unfancied Hill was still very much in contention and tried to pass the Finn. Lehtinen appeared first to move out into lane 2 to block him, then to move back when Hill tried to go inside. Lehtinen crossed the line first but both runners were awarded a new Olympic record time of 14:30.0. An inquiry by the judges was held and after an hour they concluded that Lehtinen did not 'wilfully interfere' with Hill, and there was no official protest from the American team. The American public was not so understanding, and it was only after the admonition by the stadium announcer Bill Henry, who reminded the outraged home spectators that 'these people are our guests', that the jeers subsided.

In 1936 in Berlin Lehtinen lost his Olympic crown to fellow Finn Gunnar Hoeckert who came home in 14:22.2 after a tremendous burst of speed in the last lap. Lehtinen was second, well inside his old Olympic record, in 14:25.8.

Lemming, Erik

1880–1930. Born Sweden (SWE)

A fine all-round athlete at the beginning of this century, Erik Lemming had his greatest successes at the jardin, winning four Olympic titles, setting nine world records and being the first man to break the 50m barrier.

At the 1900 Olympics in Paris, Lemming finished fourth in the pole vault and fifth in the high jump. Sweden did not compete in the 1904 Games in St Louis so Lemming had to wait until the 1906 Games in Athens to start his medal winning. He won the javelin in 1906, retaining his title in 1908 and in 1912. On all three occasions he set world records – 53.90m in

Carl Lewis

1906, 54.82m in 1908 and 60.64m in 1912. He also won the 'freestyle' javelin competition in the only year it was held, 1908. Choosing to hold the javelin in the middle, he won with 54.44m. In 1912 he was fourth at throwing the javelin with either hand, reaching 58.33m with his right but only 40.26m with his left.

In all Lemming won 25 Swedish national titles at various events: ten javelin, six shot put, five hammer, three discus, and one at pole vault. He won bronze medals at pentathlon and shot events at the 1906 Olympics.

His world records at javelin were set over a period of 13 years, starting

with his 49.32m at Gothenburg on 18 June 1899 and ending with 62.32m on 29 June 1912 in Stockholm. In 1902 he was the first man over 50m, reaching 50.44m in Jönköping.

Lewis, Carl

1961–. Born USA (USA)

A supremely gifted sprinter and long jumper, Carl Lewis entered the annuls of the all-time greats with his four gold medals at the 1984 Olympic Games. He repeated the achievement of the legendary Jesse Owens, and yet it seems unlikely that Lewis will be remembered with the same reverence as his boyhood hero. Such have been the enormous improvements in standards of track and field athletics that Lewis' feat in Los Angeles was almost expected by a public which viewed it with a certain degree of cynicism once he began capitalizing on his athletics success by recording pop songs and grooming himself for a future career in the media.

But Lewis' display in the Los Angeles Coliseum was majestic. There is no finer sight in athletics than that of Carl Lewis accelerating to full power in a 100m or 200m race. In the 100m final, for instance, he started poorly, opened up at 50m and won by 2.5m – the biggest winning margin ever – in 9.99 seconds. He upset the crowd by taking only two jumps in the long jump final, even though his first round 8.54m was enough to win by 30cm from Australia's Gary Honey. His 200m victory is rated as one of the finest runs of all time and his anchor leg in 8.94 helped the USA to a world record 37.83 in the 4 x 100m final.

A year before Lewis had given notice of his awesome talent by taking three gold medals at the first World Championships in Helsinki, when he omitted the 200m from his schedule. It was the culmination of years of spectacular improvement in the USA.

The last time he was beaten in a long jump competition was in 1981 at the US Indoor Championships, where he finished second to Larry Myricks, 8.13m to 8.06m. He has since won 52 competitions in succession and his four low altitude world bests of 8.79 suggest that he might be the one to eclipse the 20-year-old world record of 8.90m, set by Bob Beamon at altitude in Mexico City in 1968.

But while Lewis is still the world's leading 200m runner – although he opted out of running the distance at the 1987 World Championships – he has had to accept second place at 100m behind Canada's Ben Johnson, the new world champion and world record holder. Johnson beat Lewis in three races in 1986 and two in 1987, the last

of which was their World Championship clash in Rome. Johnson, who was third in the 1984 Olympic final, proved too quick off his blocks for Lewis who, although into his flowing stride by 50m, was unable to catch the Canadian. Ironically, Lewis equalled Calvin Smith's old world record set at altitude, but the time of 9.93 seconds still left him a metre down on Johnson at the finish. Lewis went on to win the long jump with two jumps of 8.67m, 14cm better than Robert Emmiyan's effort in second place. At the US Olympic trials in July 1988, Lewis ran the fastest 100m ever seen when he clocked a wind-assisted 9.78 seconds.

Liddell, Eric

1902–1945. Born China (GBR)

Although better known as a sprinter, his 100-yard time of 9.7 seconds set in 1923 a British record for 35 years, Eric Liddell achieved his greatest success at 400m, winning the Olympic title in Paris in 1924. This achievement was immortalized in the film *Chariots of Fire*, which depicted – with some artistic licence – the preparations of Liddell and Harold Abrahams, who went on to win the 100m in Paris.

Liddell, a deeply religious man, was a Scottish rugby international in 1922 and 1923. Although in the film he changes from the short sprint to the 400m during the journey to Paris on learning that the heats were due to take place on a Sunday, in reality he knew this well in advance and had been preparing for a year. Even so he went to Paris with a personal best of only 49.6 seconds for 440 yards, his winning time at the AAA Championships of 1924. He improved this to 48.2 in winning his heat, and then set a flying 47.6 in the final to win in a new world record time, the third time the record had been broken in the competition.

Having already taken the bronze medal in the 200m (in which a very tired Abrahams finished last), Liddell ran the one-lap race exactly the same way, building up a large lead in the outside lane then hanging on to win by two yards from American Horatio Fitch.

Three years running Liddell won

Eric Liddell is fêted after his 1924 Olympic 400m victory

the 100-yard, 220-yard and one-mile relay (for Edinburgh University) at the Scottish Championships, in 1921, 1922 and 1923. In 1924 and 1925 he won the two short sprints and added the 440 yards, gaining a fourth relay victory as well in 1925. Overall in the years 1922-1925 he was unbeaten in 14 races at 440 yards or 400m.

Eric Liddell did not race seriously after 1925. He went to China as a missionary, where he died in 1945 in a Japanese prisoner of war camp.

Lightbody, James

1882–1953. Born USA (USA)

James Lightbody won the 800m and 1500m titles at the 1904 Olympics in St Louis, a fet not achieved again until the performance of Albert Hill (GBR) in the Games of 1920. Lightbody, however, had the enormous advantage of appearing on home ground, and very few of the top 1500m runners were present to compete. Indeed, only nine men contested the final, but Lightbody, who had won the 800m two days earlier in 1:56.0, finished in a world record 4:05.4. He had also won the 2500m steeplechase an come second in the four-mile team race for his club, Chicago AA.

At the unofficial Games of 1906 in Athens – which were paradoxically much more successful than the three previous Games – Lightbody retained his 1500m title, striding out on the home straight to win in 4:12, a good time on a poor track. The next day he lost the 800m by two feet.

In London for the 1908 Games, Lightbody, seemingly unaware that only one man would qualify from each 1500m heat, carelessly allowed himself to be beaten by team mate J. P. Sullivan.

Lillak, Tiina

1961–. Born Finland (FIN)

Finland, a country famous for its javelin throwers, enjoyed one of its greatest moments in athletics history on 13 August 1983, when Tiina Lillak won

Tiina Lillak

the World Championship title with her very last throw of the competition.

Her throw of 70.82m was enough to overhaul the 69.14m posted by Britain's Fatima Whitbread in the first round. Her best before that was 67.46m, and it was a moment of pure drama when the crowd in the Helsinki stadium roared Lillak to her last throw. While Whitbread was consoled by her mother, who is also her coach, Lillak celebrated with the 50,000 fans who were all too ready to applaud Finland's only gold medal of the championships.

Lillak made her first impression on the event in 1982, when she threw a world record 72.40m at the same Helsinki stadium in the World Games. It was the stadium's first ever world record in a field event. Lillak reclaimed the record a year later with 74.76m after Sofia Sakorafa of Greece had taken it to 74.20m in September 1982.

In Los Angeles at the 1984 Olympic Games she had to face the British once more, and in particular an in-form Tessa Sanderson. Despite hav-

ing to withdraw from the competition after the second round with an injury, Lillak's 69m was enough to win her the silver medal behind Sanderson and ahead of Whitbread. Injury disrupted her 1985 season and a throw of 66.66m left her in fourth place at the 1986 European Championships, won by Whitbread. She threw 16cm further in Rome at the World Championships in 1987, but it was only good enough for sixth place, again behind Whitbread.

Litvinov, Sergey

1958–. Born USSR (URS)

Sergey Litvinov was a silver medallist at the 1980 Olympic Games. He has spent his hammer competitions since then trading blows with countryman Yuriy Sedykh. It was not until 1983 that the younger Litvinov beat the double Olympic champion.

Soviet champion in 1979 and 1983, Litvinov was the first man to beat Sedykh in a major competition when he threw 82.68m at the first World Championships in Helsinki. Sedykh's reply was more than a metre down for the silver medal and for the first time in a decade his supremacy at the event was under threat.

Sergey Litvinov

Litvinov had in fact taken Sedykh's world record in 1982 with 83.98m, and further improved it a year later to 84.14m. Sedykh had responded by firstly winning the 1982 European title – when Litvinov was third – and then by improving the record three times to 86.74m. The last throw was his winning effort at the 1986 European Championships, when Litvinov threw over 85m for the second time in his career only to end up with the silver medal. He had previously thrown over 85m in Cork in 1984 when, once again, Sedykh went one better with a world record 86.34m.

In 1987, with Sedykh enjoying a less competitive year in his build-up to the 1988 Olympics, Litvinov had it all his own way. He won the European Cup Final in Prague in June and his second World Championship title in Rome in September, when 83.06m put him two metres clear of the rest of the field.

Ljunggren, John

1919–. Born Sweden (SWE)

In an international career than spanned five Olympic Games from 1948-1964 and five European Championships from 1946 to 1962, Ljunggren collected a complete set of Olympic medals and European gold and silver medals.

He won more Olympic medals at the 50km walk than anyone else in the event's history. He came first in London in 1948 (4:41:52), third in 1956 (4:35:02) and second in 1960 (4:25:47) aged 41, 17 seconds behind Britain's Don Thompson. He also competed at the 1952 Games in Helsinki, finishing ninth in 4:43:45.2, and in 1964 in Tokyo where, in his fifth Olympics, he finished sixteenth.

At the shorter 20km distance he competed three times. His best placing was fourth in 1956 which, combined with his bronze medal in the longer event, is the best ever double in the discipline.

In the European Championships his record was only marginally less

Dallas Long

impressive. He won in 1946 in 4:38:20, came second in 1950 in 4:43:25, fourth in 1954 with 4:38:09.6, ninth in 1958 in 4:42:40.8, and fifth in 1962 in 4:30:19.8.

Long, Dallas

1940–. Born USA (USA)

When Dallas Long threw 19.25m in the shot put in the Santa Barbara Easter Relays on 28 March 1959 he ended Parry O'Brien's domination of the event since May 1953. Long went on to better the existing world record six more times in a career that lasted until 1964 and included the Olympic title in Tokyo.

At the Olympic Games in Tokyo Long was up against the young Texan Randy Matson. Matson threw an Olympic record 20.20m in the first

round, but this lasted only three minutes as Dallas Long's first throw sailed out three centimetres further.

Long's final world record, 20.68m, was set in the USA-URS international match on 25 July 1964, in a meet where he broke the 20m barrier with four of his six puts, totally dominating the event. Second-placed Viktor Lipsnis (URS) finished with 19.34m. Randy Matson was third on 19.17m, but he took the world record the following year.

Lopes, Carlos

1947–. Born Portugal (POR)

Just when the rest of the field thought that Carlos Lopes' best running was behind him, the little man from Portugal gave his finest ever performance in the 1984 Olympic marathon: he won the gold medal at the age of 37.

It was only his second full race at the distance, but he put all his experience of track, road and cross-country running into practice as he stayed with the leaders until 37km. Then Lopes pushed hard for home and no one was able to stay with him. His 2:09:21 was an Olympic record and he became a national hero.

Lopes was no stranger to Olympic Games competition. He made his first appearance at that level in 1972 when he failed to qualify for the finals of the 5000m and 10,000m in Munich. In 1974 he failed to finish the 10,000m at the European Championships. His running improved dramatically over the next couple of years as he began to benefit from the Portuguese government's interest in the country's top athletes. Lopes was found a job in a bank and his training was intensified. His first major victory came at the World Cross-Country Championships at Chepstow, Wales in 1976. Later that year at the Montreal Olympics, he led the 10,000m for most of the 25 laps, only to be outsprinted by Lasse Viren of Finland in 27:40.4. Lopes' time for the silver medal was 27:45.2.

In 1977 he finished second to Belgian Leon Schots in the World Cross-

Country Championships, but then succumbed to a series of injuries which ruled him out of the track season. As Lopes got older, so his times improved. He missed the 1980 Olympics when Portugal joined the Western boycott, but was back with a vengeance in 1982, clocking 27:24.39 for 10,000m and 13:17.28 for 5000m. Another second place in the World Cross-Country Championships in 1983 was followed by his first completed marathon in Rotterdam. His first attempt had ended at 21 miles a year before when he dropped out of the New York race with a leg cramp. But in Rotterdam he fought a race-long duel with Rob de Castella of Australia, losing by just two seconds in 2:08.39.

At the Helsinki World Championships 10,000 in 1983 he again allowed himself to be outkicked on the last lap and finished sixth.

But 1984 was his year. In New York he reclaimed his World Cross-

Jack Lovelock

Country title after eight years, and the second fastest 10,000m of all time behind countryman Fernando Mamede's world record 27:13.81. He then went on to that momentous marathon win in Los Angeles. There was more to come in 1985. He took his third World Cross-Country title in Lisbon and a month later ran a world best 2:07:12 to win the Rotterdam Marathon. The time stood for three years until Belayneh Dinsamo achieved 2:06:50 in 1988.

Louis, Spyridon

1872–1940. Born Greece (GRE)

Spyridon Louis won the marathon at the first Olympic Games in Athens in 1896, and became a symbol of sporting triumph to an otherwise disappointed Greek nation. His winning margin of seven minutes 13 seconds was the biggest in international marathon history until that of Rosa Mota in the women's marathon in Rome in the 1987 World Championships.

Louis was a peasant who used to sell water in his village in nearby Athens. He came fifth in an Olympic trial race from which the marathon team was picked on 24 March 1896. Of the 17 starters for the marathon proper on 29 March, 12 were Greeks. The foreigners entered had more experience of much shorter distances – Flack of Australia and Lemursiaux (FRA), two expert runners, were more at home with 800m and 1500m. None of the field had run a marathon before. Lemursiaux led until almost the three-quarter mark before he had to retire with cramps, being overtaken by Flack who himself dropped out after 37km. Of the non-Greeks, only Hungary's Gyula Kellner finished. He was in fourth place but was awarded a special bronze medal. Louis was not particularly fast, but he trotted through to complete a weary victory, to the delight of his countrymen.

Louis was offered free shaves and even free meals for life, and when asked by Prince George, who had accompanied him on the last few

Carlos Lopes

hundred metres of his journey, to name a gift, he asked for a horse and cart to carry water. He never took part in another competition after his victory, which he completed in 2:58:50 for the 25-mile course.

Lovelock, Jack

1910–1949. Born New Zealand (NZL)

Winner of the Olympic 1500m title in 1936, Jack Lovelock was called the greatest runner of his era by, among others, American middle-distance world record holders Glen Cunningham and Bill Bonthron. Bonthron lost to him when the New Zealander set a new world mile record in 1933. Cunningham was defeated when Lovelock won the 1500m title in Berlin in a new world record time.

Jack Lovelock boxed and ran at school, and by the time he went to Oxford University as a Rhodes Scholar in 1931 he was capable of a 4:22 mile, a time he ran in the Varsity match of that year against Cambridge. The following year in a match against the AAA he set a British mile record of 4:12.0, but lost the AAA Championships to fellow Oxford student Jerry Cornes, who won in 4:14.2.

Chosen for the 1932 Olympics, Lovelock finished seventh, unable to respond to the fast pace set by Canadian Phil Edwards and maintained by Italian Luigi Beccali who won in a new world record time.

Lovelock raced well after Los Angeles and made the conscious decision to do just as much work for his medical studies as was needed to pass and to concentrate on winning gold in Berlin.

His world mile record of 4:07.6 was set against American miler Bill Bonthron on 15 July 1933, while visiting the USA with the Oxford and Cambridge team. In September he faced Beccali at the World Student Games in Turin and once again felt the power of the Italian's final kick, losing in 3:49.8 to Beccali's 3:49.2.

In 1934 he won the AAA mile championships against an ever-improving Sydney Wooderson, but lost to Bonthron in a meeting at White City on 21 July. The following year in the Princeton Invitational in front of a 40,000 crowd he beat both Bonthron and Glenn Cunningham, but finished the year exhausted from too much racing. He took four months off with boxing as his only sport and returned refreshed for Olympic year 1936, losing a very close AAA mile championship race to Sydney Wooderson, 4:15.2 to 4:15.0.

Although Wooderson was injured and withdrew from the Olympic 1500m final in Berlin, the competition was first class – Americans Glenn Cunningham and Archie San Romani, Italian Luigi Beccali, and Canadian Phil Edwards among others. In a race that caused BBC commentator Harold Abrahams (1924 Olympic 100m champion) to forget completely his traditional neutrality, Lovelock decimated

the field with a superbly timed break with 300m to go, winning in a new world record of 3:47.8 by six metres from Glenn Cunningham and Beccali. 'It was the most perfectly executed race of my career,' said Lovelock afterwards.

He retired from athletics later in 1936 and became a doctor, but he died tragically after falling under a train in New York on 29 December 1949.

Lowe, Douglas

1902–1981. Born England (GBR)

The first man to retain the Olympic 800m title, Douglas Lowe followed the British win of Albert Hill in Antwerp (1920) with victories in Paris (1924) and Amsterdam (1928). A schoolboy champion over 880 yards, he won his first Olympic title while still a student at Cambridge University before he had even won a British title.

In 1924 in Paris Lowe beat Paul

Douglas Lowe

Martin (SUI) after a battle in the final straight, coming home in 1:52.4. Two years later at the AAA 880-yard Championships he lost in a thrilling race to the German Otto Pelzer, who won by three yards in a new world record of 1:51.6, with Lowe also estimated at just inside the old record although he received no official time. At the 1928 Olympics in Amsterdam in the 800m he beat not only the current world record holder Sera Martin (FRA) but also the favourite from the USA, Lloyd Hahn, coming from behind from 100 metres out to beat leader Erik Bylehn (SWE) by 10 metres in a personal best and Oympic record time of 1:51.8.

Lowe won the 440-yard/880-yard double at the 1927 and 1928 AAA Championships, and in 1926 set a world record at 600m (a distance then recognized by the IAAF) of 1:10.4. His best time at 800m came shortly after his 1928 Olympic victory in Berlin against Otto Pelzer, where he won in 1:51.2 by four metres. His best at 440 yards was a respectable 48.8, and he came fourth in the 1924 Olympic 1500m in 3:57.0.

From 1931-1938 he was Secretary of the British Amateur Athletic Board.

Lusis, Janis

1939–. Born USSR (URS)

One of the most consistent javelin throwers of all time, Janis Lusis stands alone among male athletes in having won four consecutive European titles, in 1962, 1966, 1969 and 1971. He also won a full set of medals at the Olympics, bronze in 1964, gold in 1968 and silver in 1972.

He went undefeated in five seasons, 1962, 1963, 1966, 1968 and 1969, and from 1967 to 1970 won 41 competitions in a row. He was ranked number one in nine seasons, 1962-1963, 1965-1969, 1971-1972, and is one of only two men to have competed in four Olympic javelin finals (the other is Janusz Sidlo of Poland).

In Mexico in 1968 Lusis was the first favourite to win in the javelin since Matti Järvinen in Los Angeles in 1932, taking the title in an Olympic record of 90.10m ahead of Finland's Jorma Kinnunen. He came as close as was humanly possible to retaining his title four years later in Munich: his opening throw of 88.88m was only bettered by his own third round throw of 89.54m until, in the fifth round, home favourite Klaus Wolferman hurled the javelin beyond the 90m line to set a new Olympic record of 90.48m. Lusis concentrated his efforts for his final throw, and appeared to have equalled Wolferman's mark until the scoreboard announced 90.46m – he had lost his title by barely an inch.

Lusis was the second man to throw over 300 feet, which he managed when he broke Norwegian Terje Pedersen's world record in 1968 with 91.98m. Although 1968 Olympic silver medallist Jorma Kinnunen (FIN) had the longest ever throw in 1969 (92.70m), Lusis regained the record in 1972 with 93.80m. In the 1974 European Championships he failed to make five wins in a row by finishing sixth with 83.06m, and at the Montreal Olympics he was eighth.

Lusis was an excellent decathlete in his youth with a best of 7483 points. He won 12 USSR titles between 1962 and 1976. He married the 1960 Olympic javelin champion Elvira Ozolina.

Janis Lusis

Maki, Taisto

1910–1979. Born Finland (FIN)

Taisto Maki was one of the generation of Finnish distance runners to follow the great Paavo Nurmi. He was unfortunate to be just reaching his peak at the outbreak of the Second World War.

In 1938 he set his first world record at 10,000m, coming tantalizingly close to breaking the 30-minute barrier. He had travelled to Tampere from Helsinki during the afternoon, then slept for an hour before going onto the track to beat compatriots such as Lauri Lehtinen, Volmari Iso-Hollo and Ilmari Salminen in 30:02:0.

A year later, on 17 September in Helsinki, he set his second world record at the distance and did achieve the first sub-30-minute time, 29:52.6, in the Olympic stadium. Three months previously, on 16 June, he had broken Lauri Lehtinen's world 5000m record at the same venue: Maki ran 14:08.8, taking over eight seconds from Lehtinen's 14:16.9 set in Helsinki on 19 June 1932. During his record-breaking run Maki passed the three-mile mark in 13:42.4, another world record.

Maki also held the two-mile world record, set in Helsinki on 7 July 1939, completing the distance in 8:53.2, run in two halves both of 4:26.6. During his record-breaking 10,000m run of 29:52.6 he actually ran the second half faster than the first, 14:54.4 to 14:58.2.

Malinowski, Bronislaw

1951–1981. Born Poland (POL)

Although tragically killed in a car crash in September 1981, Bronislaw Malinowski will be remembered for his win at the 1980 Olympic Games in the 3000m steeplechase, when he chased the Tanzanian Filbert Bayi for almost

Bronislaw Malinowski

the entire race before passing him with only 150m to go.

Winner of the European 2000m junior steeplechase in 1970, Malinowski finished fourth in the senior event at the 1972 Olympics in Munich, behind Kip Keino of Kenya. He won his first European Championship title in 1974, after a race-long battle with his great rival Anders Garderud which was only decided in the last few strides. Also, at the same championships, he finished fourth at 10,000m.

His second chance of Olympic glory came at the 1976 Games in Montreal. But after following Garderud through a world record pace, it looked as if he would only get a bronze medal when the East German Frank Baumgartl went past him after the final water jump. With Garderud stretching out for the gold medal Baumgartl fell at the last barrier, leaving Malinowski a clear run for second place. His time of 8:09.2 was well inside the old world record but it still left him almost a second behind Garderud, the new Olympic champion.

His second European title came in 1978, making him the only steeplechaser to win two. His battle with Bayi at the Olympic Games in 1980 was a classic duel. Bayi, formerly a front-running mile and 1500m world record holder, had a 35m lead in the 3000m steeplechase after 2000m, but Malinowski pursued him relentlessly. As Bayi visibly tired at every barrier, the Pole made his final effort and eventually caught him just before the last water jump. He finished in 8:09.7, almost three seconds ahead of an exhausted Bayi.

Manoliu, Lia

1932–. Born Bulgaria (BUL)

At the age of 36 and in her fifth Olympics, Lia Manoliu finally won the gold medal for throwing the discus that she had been striving for since finishing 30 feet behind the winners at her very first Games in 1952. Then she was sixth behind Nina Ponomaryeva. In 1956 she came ninth, before winning two bronze medals in 1960 and 1964.

In 1968 in Mexico City Manoliu's prospects of another medal were strong, although with Liesel Westermann, the world record holder, Christine Spielberg, the European Champion, and Karin Illgen, who had beaten both of them, in the field, she was still unfancied as a winner. Her first throw was 58.28m and, with the favourites throwing beneath their best, Manoliu proved unbeatable. It was her only decent throw of the competition. The only other one she succeeded with landed at 46.82m.

Manoliu was back for her sixth Olympics in 1972, when she finished ninth.

Mathias, Bob

1930–. Born USA (USA)

Bob Mathias won all 11 decathlons in which he competed, including the 1948 and 1952 Olympic titles. He retired aged just 22 and in 1954 starred in a Hollywood film of his life. He is still the youngest Olympic champion in any athletics event, winning the 1948 title in London when just 17.

In fact, in the London Games, he was the winner in only one out of the ten disciplines, the discus, which remained his strongest event. He tied for first place in the pole vault and high jump. Yet, after setting a world record of 7287 points in 1950 and another of 7543 in 1952, he retained his Olympic title in devastating fashion, setting a third world record of 7731 points, winning by 912 points ahead of fellow American Milton Campbell. (Campbell won four years later.) Mathias had injured himself during the long jump on the first day and looked unlikely to beat his own world record set at the Olympic trials until, in the penultimate discipline, he hurled the javelin well over 194 feet to leave himself the relatively simple task of beating 4:55.3 in the 1500m. In almost complete darkness on the track he ran 4:50.8.

His best marks in his career were: 10.8 - 100m; 50.2 - 400m; 4:50.8 - 1500m; 13.8 - 110mh; 1.90m - high jump; 4.00m - pole vault; 6.98m - long jump; 16.05m - shot put; 52.84m

Bob Mathias

Randy Matson

- discus; 62.20m - javelin.

After retiring from athletics, Mathias became a US Congressman in 1966 and, as a Republican, represented California's 18th District.

Matson, Randy

1945–. Born USA (USA)

A giant of a man, 2m (6ft 6in) tall and around 118kg (260lb), Randy Matson was still at school with little formal athletics traninng when he broke through the 60-foot barrier in the shot put, a mark that had only been reached by the top athletes in the event a decade before. He went on to win a silver medal at the 1964 Olympics and win the title in 1968, and to be the first man to put beyond the magical 70-foot barrier, a mark he achieved on 8 May 1965 reaching 21.52m (70ft 7$\frac{1}{4}$ in) at College Station, Texas.

His silver medal behind Dallas Long in the 1964 Tokyo Olympics came in a season when he had already defeated Long for the American title. During 1965 at the same meet where he smashed the world record, his sequence of puts broke the previous record of 20.68m by Dallas Long no fewer than four times. At the same meet he also set a US National Collegiate record in the discus.

The following year on 22 April he improved his own shot record to 21.78m (71ft 5 $\frac{1}{2}$in), set on his final appearance for Texas A & M at College Station. After this performance coach Clyde Hart predicted he would win the Olympic Games the following year in Mexico: 'We'll see Matson standing on the middle platform at the Olympics...he'll peel off his A & M warm-up suit and underneath he'll have on a cape and a big 'S' on his chest. Then he'll fly away and we'll all wonder whether we really saw him.'

In the event Matson kept his feet firmly on the ground to win the gold with 20.54m, ahead of team mate George Woods. Four years later he was sensationally beaten for an Olympic team place by Brian Oldfield (USA). Oldfield was placed sixth in the Munich Games, but he went on to throw a series of world bests as a professional in 1973.

Matson retired from amateur competition in 1972.

Mauermayer, Gisela

1913–. Born Germany (GER)

World record holder at three Olympic events – pentathlon, discus and shot put – Gisela Mauermayer won the 1936 Olympic Games discus title, setting a new Olympic record of 47.63m. She was an extremely versatile athlete who first appeared on the scene aged 19 in 1933, when she set her first pentathlon world record of 3991 points.

Having increased her pentathlon total to 4155 in 1934, she also set a world shot put record on her international début against Poland in Warsaw on 15 July, a record (14.38m) that lasted for over 14 years.

From 44.34m Mauermayer increased the world best mark for discus to 47.12m in 1935, giving her a total of six world records. She concentrated on the discus for the 1936 Games

in Berlin, as neither the shot nor the pentathlon were included in the women's programme. She added three more discus records in Olympic year 1936, finishing with 48.30m, the only record that was ever ratified by the IAAF, who started to record women's world records only that season.

Mauermayer won the discus at the 1938 European Championships in Vienna, and came second in the shot. The same year she increased her pentathlon total to 4391, which was not bettered for nine years.

Overall Mauermayer had a run of 65 unbeaten competitions at discus during 1935-1942. She won 20 outdoor German titles – a record – with nine discus, seven shot put, three pentathlon and one sling ball throwing during the period 1934-1942, and also won five gold medals in the World Student Games Championships, taking high jump and discus in 1935 and 1937, and adding the shot put in 1937.

McGrath, Matt

1878–1941. Born Republic of Ireland (USA)

McGrath was another of the great Irish-born immigrants who dominated hammer-throwing for the United States at the beginning of the twentieth century. He took the silver medal at the 1908 Games in London behind the great John Flanagan, but four years later in Stockholm threw 54.74m to win and set a new Olympic record, beating the previous best set by Flanagan by about 3m.

McGrath was also the world record holder at this time, having in 1911 thrown 57.10m at Celtic Park. After coming fifth at the Antwerp Games of 1920, McGrath became the oldest medallist in the throwing events in Olympic history. Aged 45 years and 205 days he won the silver medal at the 1924 Olympics in Paris behind team mate Fred Tooteil.

McGrath won seven AAU titles between 1908 and 1926, the last when nearly 50, and he was still competing seven years later throwing 57lb.

McKenley, Herb

1922–. Born Jamaica (JAM)

The greatest 400m runner never to have won an Olympic title, Herb McKenley took the silver in 1948 and 1952, and was regarded by many as the best 400m runner of all time. He was the first man to run under 46 seconds for the distance, and set 440-yard world records of 46.2 in 1946 and 1947, improving to 46.0 the following year. In Milwaukee on 2 July 1948 he ran 45.9 for 400m (auto time 46.0). In addition to his successes at 400m, he also took the silver medal in the 100m at the 1952 Olympics.

McKenley's 400m style was to go all out and then hang on: in the 400m final in the London Games of 1948 he covered the first 200m in 21.4 but was gradually reeled in by compatriot Arthur Wint who went on to win 46.2 to 46.4. They were both part of the silver-medal-winning relay team for Jamaica at 4 x 400m.

In 1952 McKenley lost the 100m to the American Lindy Remigino, although the first four men were given the same time of 10.4, and McKenley himself always believed he had crossed the line first, although he did not protest. In the 400m he started more slowly than usual, but lost to fellow Jamaican George Rhoden by a metre, 46.09 to 46.20.

Rhoden and McKenley joined forces with Arthur Wint and Leslie Laing to take the relay gold in a world record time of 3:03.9, McKenley running the third leg in an astonishing 44.6 seconds.

While at university in the USA, at Boston and Illinois, McKenley won the AAU 440-yard title in 1945, 1947 and 1948, and NCAA title for Illinois in 1946 and 1947.

Melinte, Doina

1956–. Born Romania (ROM)

Since Romania was the only Eastern Bloc country to defy the boycott of the Los Angeles Olympic Games in

Doina Melinte

1984, Doina Melinte was able to take advantage of the absenteeism to win gold and silver medals at 800m and 1500m. Along with the 1984 3000m champion, Maricica Puica, Melinte has worn the yellow vest of Romania on race tracks around the world, scoring major victories and running fast times both indoors and out.

In the absence of the Soviet and East German athletes, Melinte was easily the fastest going into the 800m final in Los Angeles. She followed Italian Gabriella Dorio until the 600m mark, when she opened up a powerful drive for the line, winning by more than a second in 1:57.60. Dorio had her revenge at 1500m, when she allowed Melinte to pass her with 150m to go only to kick past the fading Romanian on the home straight.

At the 1986 European Championships Melinte was edged out of the silver medal position in the 1500m by the Soviet Union's Tatyana Samolenko, but she won bronze in 4:02.44. It was Samolenko who took the gold medal at 1500m in the World Championship final in Rome, where Melinte was eventually awarded third

place after Switzerland's Sandra Gasser was a subsequently disqualified for failing a drugs test. Melinte also moved up a place in the IAAF/Mobil Grand Prix rankings at the end of the 1987 season after Gasser's disqualification from that competition as well. She finished top miler and became the joint top points scorer overall with sprinter Merlene Ottey of Jamaica.

A powerful runner indoors, Melinte won the European indoor title at 800m in 1982 and 1984, and at 1500m in 1985. In 1987 she won the World Indoor 1500m title and began the 1988 season with a world indoor record for the mile of 4:18.86.

Melnik, Faina

1945–. Born USSR (URS)

With a world record-breaking final throw of 64.22m, Faina Melnik won her very first international discus competition at the 1971 European Championships. After improving her record four times to 66.76m by the summer of 1972, she was automatically the favourite for the Olympic Games in Munich. She won with a

Faina Melnik

fourth round throw of 66.62m over Argentina Menis of Romania. Menis snatched the world record from Melnik with 67.32m at the end of the season. Melnik broke the world record 11 times between 1971 and 1976, improving it to 70.50m and becoming the first woman to throw beyond 70.00m in 1975. Her second European Championship title was won with a 69.00m throw in 1974.

Melnik's run of 52 successive wins came to a bizarre end at the 1976 Olympic Games in Montreal. Chasing Evelin Jahl's (née Schlaak) 69.00m mark and preparing for her fifth round throw, Melnik twice moved across the throwing circle without letting go of the discus. She was initially given a red flag, indicating a foul throw, but after protesting that she hadn't exceeded the legal time limit she was eventually allowed to continue. Her throw reached 68.60m to put her in second place ahead of Vergova of Bulgaria and Hinzmann of the Soviet Union. But officials overturned the result after studying a video of the event, claiming that her fifth round throw was interrupted and must count as a foul. Her next best throw of 66.40m was counted instead and she ended up in the official result as fourth.

She never repeated her earlier successes, and was placed fifth at the European Championships and failed to qualify for the 1980 Olympic final.

Mennea, Pietro

1952–. Born Italy (ITA)

Nicknamed 'The Blue Arrow', after the Milan to Bari express train, Pietro Mennea became world record holder, European and Olympic champion at 200m in a career spanning 13 years. In that time he raced against the likes of Valeriy Borzov of the Soviet Union, Allan Wells of Great Britain and, latterly, Carl Lewis of the USA, who was to succeed him as the world's top 200m runner. His competitive record was enough to give him top spot in a poll of the world's athletics writers conducted by the IAAF in 1987, ahead

Pietro Mennea

of Lewis and Tommie Smith, the man who clocked the astounding world record of 19.83 seconds at altitude in 1968.

It was that world record and the prowess of Borzov at the 1972 Olympic Games that gave Mennea his drive to become the best. He won the first of his 11 Italian 200m titles in 1971, the same year that he won his first champ-ionship medal, a 4 x 100m relay bronze at the European Championships. In the following year's Olympics he finished third behind Borzov with an Italian record of 20.30. But his first major title came two years later at the European Championships in Rome, where he took the 200m gold medal, beating Borzov to clock 20.60. He had already claimed a silver medal behind the Soviet at 100m. Another silver came in the relay.

An uninspired Mennea finished only fourth at 200m at the Montreal Olympic Games in 1976, but by 1978 he was on top of his form. A 400m European indoor title in the winter was followed by the sprint double at

the outdoor championships in Prague. In 1979 he finally achieved his ambition by taking Tommie Smith's 200m record with 19.72, although he had to go to Mexico City to do it at the World Student Games.

His crowning glory came in 1980 at his third Olympic Games in Moscow. In a thrilling finish he edged out Allan Wells, the 100m champion, for the 200m title, 20.19 to 20.21. He later added a 4 x 400m relay bronze medal to his collection. The two were the closest of rivals and Mennea once more squeezed past Wells to snatch the 200m bronze medal at the World Championships in 1983.

Both men were at the Los Angeles Olympics a year later, but both were in the twilight of their careers. Mennea, the only sprinter to contest four Olympic finals, finished seventh in 20.55 as his title went to Carl Lewis in an Olympic record of 19.80 seconds.

Metcalfe, Ralph

1910–1978. Born USA (USA)

Metcalfe was an outstanding sprinter. He and compatriot Eddie Tolan were the first black Americans to win an Olympic sprint medal. Tolan finished an inch ahead of Metcalfe in the 1932 100m final in Los Angeles. Both men shared a world record 10.3 seconds but the new photo-finish equipment showed that Tolan had breasted the tape first. Four years later in Berlin, Metcalfe had the misfortune to come up against Jesse Owens and, after an atrocious start, he could not make up enough ground to improve on his silver of 1932.

Metcalfe was the first man to run 200m in under 20 seconds, achieving 19.8 in Toronto on 3 September 1932 in a wind-assisted race. He had a best-ever straight 220-yard time of 20.3, set in 1933. He was an outstanding college sprinter, winning the NCAA championships three times at both short sprints (in 1932, 1933 and 1934) and winning the AAU sprint double championships in the same years.

In 1932 he finished third in the

200m, again losing to Eddie Tolan, and just failing to catch George Simpson on the line. Metcalfe's action just after the start often left him with a lot of ground to catch up – his reactions were quick, but his first strides were too short.

He set an unofficial world record of 10.2 on 11 June 1932, and at the 1936 Games was part of the gold medal relay team that went under 40 seconds for the first time to set a new world record of 39.8.

In 1970 Metcalfe was elected to the US House of Representatives as a Democrat for Illinois.

Meyfarth, Ulrike

1956–. Born West Germany (FRG)

Ulrike Meyfarth leapt into the record books in 1972 when she became the youngest ever Olympic champion at the age of 16. She won the high jump title with a new world record of 1.92m. She made history again 12 years later by regaining her Olympic title in Los Angeles. She equalled the record of Iolanda Balas by winning two Olympic gold medals and the time-span between her wins had only ever been equalled by Al Oerter, the American four-time discus champion.

Her win in 1972 caused a minor sensation when she was the first woman to use the Fosbury Flop style of jumping to set a world record. Her early success did bring its problems, however, and Meyfarth found it difficult to combine athletics and her education. The result was a poor series of performances following the Olympics. She could only finish third in the European Junior Championships a year later and failed to qualify for the Olympic final in 1976. She was seventh at the European Championships in 1974, when the event was won by Rosemary Witschas (later to be Ackermann), and fifth in 1978 when the competition was won by the Italian Sara Simeoni.

It was Simeoni who took the Olympic title in 1980, when Meyfarth missed the Games because of the

Ulrike Meyfarth

Western boycott. But the year after the Olympics saw her re-emergence as a real force in women's high jumping. She won the European Cup Final in Zagreb and the World Cup title in Rome, beating, among others, Tamara Bycova of the Soviet Union who was to become her greatest rival.

She proved that she was back to her very best form at the 1982 European Championships in Athens, when she beat Simeoni and Bycova at 2.0m and went on to claim a new world record with 2.02m. But Bycova was to better Meyfarth's world record by jumping 2.03m indoors and beat her again at the World Championships in Helsinki in 1983. The two then met in one of the finest high jump competitions of all time at the European Cup Final in London. They pushed each other to a new world record height of 2.03m, but victory went to Meyfarth as she had cleared it with her first attempt. The Soviet responded by improving the record to 2.04m in Pisa at the end of the season.

In Los Angeles at the 1984 Olympics, Meyfarth repeated her 1972 success with an Olympic record of 2.02m to beat Simeoni, the defending champion.

Mickler, Ingrid

1942–. Born West Germany (FRG)

Although a multi-talented athlete who had competed in four Olympic Games, Ingrid Mickler did not win a gold medal in an individual event until the European Championships in 1971. The gold medal finally came in the long jump when she faced the strongest of fields, including the Commonwealth champion Sheila Sherwood, the 1966 European champion Irena Szewinska, the Olympic champion Viorica Viscopoleanu, and the world record holder Heide Rosendahl. At 28, she won with the longest jump of her career, 6.76m.

Mickler went into the competition as Olympic pentathlon champion after winning the title – as Ingrid Becker – with 5098 points in Mexico City in 1968. At the 1972 Olympics in Munich she won another gold medal as part of the West German 4 x 100m team which clocked a world record 42.18 seconds in the final. She took part in her first Olympics in 1960 in Rome, when she was ninth in the high jump. She took up the pentathlon in 1961 after making her name as the West German record holder at the high

jump. A fine sprinter, Mickler finished second to Renate Stecher (GDR) at the 1971 European Championships, and was one of the few women to beat the East German in the early seventies. Her best-ever time was 11.35.

Milburn, Rod

1950–. Born USA (USA)

In a relatively short but explosive career as an amateur Rod Milburn set five world records at the 120 yards and 110m hurdles and enjoyed his most successful season in 1971 when he had a series of 28 consecutive wins.

During that season he was first timed at 13.0 seconds for 120-yard hurdles with an illegal wind and then given the same time with a legal wind just three weeks later. His third world record, the first with automatic timing, came as he won the 1972 Olympic 100mh title in Munich in 13.24, from Guy Drut and Tom Hill.

He ran another 13.0 for 120-yard hurdles in 1973 and further improved his 110mh record with 13.1. He turned professional in 1975, joining the International Track Association (ITA) circuit, and established another win-

Rod Milburn

ning streak, this time of 31 races. When the ITA folded in 1976, Milburn, along with several other athletes, applied for reinstatement as an amateur. He ran his first race after reinstatement in 1980 but, despite ranking sixth in the world with 13.40, he missed the US Olympic trials – held before America's decision to boycott the Games.

Mimoun, Alain

1921–. Born Algeria (FRA)

In another other age Alain Mimoun would have been the number one distance runner in the world, but he had the misfortune to be competing at the same time as the great Czech runner Emil Zatopek. Mimoun finished behind Zatopek at the 1948 Olympic 10,000m, again in 1952, and also in the 5000m in Helsinki when Zatopek was a double winner.

Mimoun got his revenge in 1956, when both he and Zatopek competed in the marathon. Zatopek, winner of the marathon in 1952 and arguably past his best, was never in contention as Mimoun crossed the line in 2:25:0, a minute and a half ahead of his nearest rival. When he had finished Mimoun calmly waited for Zatopek, who finished sixth, to cross the line and the two old rivals embraced.

Algerian-born Alain Mimoun-o-Kacha, to give him his full name, ran for France and excelled on track, road and cross-country. He won the World Cross-Country Championships four times, in 1949, 1952, 1954 and 1956, and was six times placed in the first three in 11 championships.

In the 5000m final of 1952 the world saw one of the best finishing laps ever as Zatopek, trailing Mimoun and Herbert Schade (GER), stormed through to win in 14:06.6. Mimoun was second in 14:07.4. In the earlier 10,000m Mimoun had trailed in behind the Czech 29:32.0 to 29:17.0, although he himself was as far ahead of third-placed Aleksandr Anufriyev (USSR) as Zatopek was ahead of him.

Mimoun's victory in the 1956

Dietmar Mögenburg

marathon was all the more unexpected because he had damaged his foot while running off road prior to the Games, and could finish no higher than twelfth in the 10,000m race won by Vladimir Kuts (USSR).

Mimoun went on running into middle age, and not just at cross-country. In 1972, aged 51, he ran 10,000m in 32:14.0, and a 2:34:36.2 marathon for world age bests. He was placed sixty-fourth in the 1980 Paris Marathon, aged 59.

Mögenburg, Dietmar

1961–. Born West Germany (FRG)

At 2m (6ft 7in), Dietmar Mögenburg is the tallest of the outstanding high jumpers currently contesting major titles, and his array of titles and world records over recent seasons reveals him to be one of the most competitive athletes in the event.

Winner of the European Cup Final competition in Turin aged only 17, Mögenburg went on to win the first of six West German titles in 1980. The same year he won his first European Indoor Championship title and, later,

equalled the world record of 2.35m set by Jacek Wszola of Poland only the day before. He won his first major outdoor title at the 1982 European Championships in Athens, when 2.30m was enough to secure the gold medal.

He finished fourth equal with Igor Paklin of the Soviet Union at the World Championships in 1983, when the title went to another Soviet, Gennadi Avdeyenko.

With the Eastern Bloc countries absent from the Olympic Games in Los Angeles the following year, Mögenburg enjoyed his best ever competition. He took the gold medal with 2.35m after clearing every height at the first attempt. He ended the competition with a failed attempt at a new world record height of 2.40m.

In 1986 Mögenburg's European title went to Paklin, while he finished only fourth. His 1987 season was disrupted because of injury and he was not in the best of form for the World Championships in Rome. In the circumstances he jumped remarkably well to finish fourth with 2.35m. Patrik Sjoberg – silver medallist in Los An geles – took the gold medal with 2.38m after scoring more first time clearances than Avdeyenko and Paklin, who shared second place.

Möller, Silke

1964–. Born East Germany (GDR)

Following in the wake of Marlies Gohr and Marita Koch, Silke Möller (née Gladisch) established herself as their possible successor with a sensational sprint double victory at the World Championships in 1987.

Up until 1987 Möller had been a member of the GDR's world-record-breaking 4 x 100m relay squad, and won gold medals at the 1983 World Championships, the 1985 World Cup and the 1986 European Championships. She ran in the GDR's world record run of 41.53 in 1983 and in their 41.37 clocking in 1985. In 1985, however, she pushed Marita Koch to 21.78, the fifth fastest time in history, in the 200m at the GDR national championships, and the following year finished fourth behind Gohr in the European Championships 100m and third

Silke Möller

Dave Moorcroft (leading)

behind team mate Heike Drechsler's world-record-equalling run in the 200m.

She began the 1987 season with a 200m win at the European Cup Final in Prague and went to the World Championships as one of several sprinters tipped for the gold medals. Her 10.86 and 21.79 topped the rankings before the competition and she rose to the occasion by beating Drechsler and Merlene Ottey, the Commonwealth champion in the 100m in 10.90. In the 200m she held a three-metre lead at the start of the straight to win from Florence Griffith of the USA and Ottey in 21.74. She led off the GDR 4 x 100m relay team but its 41.95 was only good enough for the silver medal behind the Americans' time of 41.58.

Moorcroft, David

1953–. Born England (GBR)

In a career disrupted by a catalogue of injuries, Dave Moorcroft discovered his full running potential one night in Oslo in 1982. On the tiny, six-lane track in Bislett he ran the race of his life over 5000m, when he improved his own best time by 20 seconds to slice an amazing six seconds off the world record. His time of 13:00.41 made him an instant superstar and sparked off his finest ever season.

He had started his track career as a 1500m runner and miler, and was seventh in the 1976 Olympic final, which was won by John Walker in Montreal. A serious back injury kept him out of competition for the whole of 1977 and hampered him further in 1984. After a winter in New Zealand, he was back for the 1978 season in which he won the Commonwealth Games 1500m in Edmonton in 3:35.48 after edging past defending champion Filbert Bayi just before the line. But missing from that final was the British record holder Steve Ovett, who had chosen to prepare exclusively for the European Championships in Prague in September. Ovett duly won in Prague, where Moorcroft finished third in 3:36.70.

The arrival on the world-class running scene of Ovett and Sebastian Coe at 1500m and the prospect of a tough selection battle to get in to the British team prompted Moorcroft in 1979 to move up a distance to 5000m in preparation for the 1980 Olympic Games in Moscow. The transition went well, with Moorcroft winning the UK title and qualifying for the Olympic team. But the combination of a stomach bug before the Games and further illness when he reached Moscow left Moorcroft in poor shape for the races ahead. He was eventually eliminated after finishing ninth in his semi-final.

The following year he won the European Cup Final 5000m in Zagreb before spending another winter in New Zealand preparing for two major championships in 1982.

In his autobiography *Running Commentary* Moorcroft describes starting 1982 feeling more aggressive than usual and, after a good winter's training with no injuries, of having to face up to his 'moment of truth'. The first indication of his form came in Oslo on 26 June, when he ran his first sub-3:50 mile to finish third behind American Steve Scott.

His so-called moment of truth came two weeks later at the same Bislett Stadium. Running on his own from the third lap, he passed 2000m in 5:12.6, 3000m in 7:50, before finishing with a 58.04 last lap to enter the record books as the fastest 5000m runner of all time. He went on from Oslo to win a 3000m race in London the following weekend in a European

record 7:32.79 and to lower his bests for 1500m and 800m. He finished third in the European Championships 5000m in Athens and travelled to Brisbane to take the Commonwealth Games title in 13:33.00.

Hepatitis ruled out his 1983 season and, although pre-selected for the 1984 Olympic Games in Los Angeles, he was reduced by a back injury to simply jogging through the 5000m final. He finished a distant last, almost lapped by the Moroccan Said Aouita, who won the gold medal in 13:05.59. Moorcroft returned to low-key competition in 1986 but his 5000m world record had already been lowered by Aouita to 13:00.41 in 1985 and improved still further to 12:58.39 in 1987.

Morrow, Bobby-Joe

1935–. Born USA (USA)

Bobby-Joe Morrow was the supreme sprinter at the 1956 Olympics in Melbourne, and the last white athlete to dominate the event. Between 1955 and 1958, while a student at Abiline Christian College, he lost only one championship race in a record that included the 100m/200m double in Melbourne and a gold in the 4 x 100m relay.

On 29 June 1956 Morrow won the US Olympic trials at both 100 and 200m, equalling the world record of 10.3 for the shorter distance in the heats. His time of 20.6 to win the 200m trial race was the same time he produced in the 1956 Melbourne Olympics in a devastating finishing burst that beat not only 1952 champion Andy Stanfield (USA) but also Jesse Owens' 1936 Olympic record.

In the 100m at Melbourne he won through four heats, again equalling the world record of 10.3. In the final, against a strong wind of over 5 metres per second, he won in 10.5 against Thane Baker (USA) and, although both were officially given the same time, the photo-finish picture clearly showed Morrow ahead by a metre.

In the 4 x 100m relay he ran the anchor leg and emulated the feats of

hero Jesse Owens, running a quick anchor leg after some poor baton passing by his team mates.

In the year following the Melbourne Games Morrow equalled the then world record of 9.3 for 100 yards three times, and had a best for the 200m (curve) of 20.6, another world record.

But he could not repeat his successes at the 1960 Tokyo Games. After a season of leg injuries, he finished just short of the medal positions in the 200m in a race where Ray Norton broke the world record with 20.5 to win the gold.

Moses, Edwin

1955–. Born USA (USA)

The record of Ed Moses in the 400m hurdles is quite simply the best of any athlete in any event in any era. For almost ten years, from the end of 1977 to the beginning of 1987, he not only won every major competition, he won every race as well. His unbeaten run ended after 122 races on 4 June 1987 when he was second to fellow American Danny Harris, 47.56 to 47.69. His reputation of invincibility was gone, but Moses proved later in the season that he was far from finished.

His hurdling career began with a flourish at the start of 1976. A mediocre performer on the flat, he started the year over 400mh with a 50.1 clocking, and by the time he went to Montreal for the Olympic Games he had reduced his best to 48.30. After a semi-final 48.29, he won the final by more than a second in a world record 47.64. It had been a remarkable rise for an athlete who had been a novice only six months before.

He lost three times that year, but by the time he went to Berlin for an international meeting at the end of the 1977 season he had already put together a winning streak of 18 races. The man who beat him that night, Harald Schmid, was to dominate the event in Europe but he has never beaten Moses since.

Moses himself went on to win three World Cup titles in 1977, 1979 and

Ed Moses

1981, two World Championships in 1983 and 1987 and another Olympic title in 1984. He missed the 1980 Olympics becausee of the Western boycott and was sidelined with injuries in 1982 and 1985. He also won five US national titles.

At the World Championships in 1983 he beat the luckless Schmid by nine metres in 47.50 to discover that he had run the last 200m with one of his shoelaces undone. Schmid was third in the 1984 Olympic final behind Danny Harris and it was these two who almost denied Moses his second World Championship title in 1987. In the fastest 400mh race ever

seen – seven men ran inside 49 seconds – with easily the most exciting finish, all three bore down on the line together, Moses was finally adjudged to have sneaked home first by just two hundredths of a second – or the thickness of his vest.

Moses – running with a unique 13 strides between each hurdle – has improved the world record three times since 1976 to 47.02 in 1983, and has run the 12 fastest times in history. A well-respected statesman within the athletics community, he was chosen in 1984 as one of three American representatives to the IAAF and was selected to take the Olympic oath on

behalf of those taking part at the start of the Games in Los Angeles.

Mota, Rosa

1958–. Born Portugal (POR)

When Rosa Mota and her coach José Pedrosa pursuaded the Portuguese athletic federation to let her run the marathon at the 1982 European Championships, it changed the course of her running career. It was her first marathon and she won it in 2:36:04. Up until then she had been a modest track runner at distances up to 10,000m.

Since then she has won eight of her 11 marathons, won the European Championship title a second time in 1986 and won the World Championship marathon in 1987. Norway's Ingrid Kristiansen has run fast times and won 11 of her 20 marathons, Grete Waitz, also of Norway, has won 11 of her 15 marathons, Joan Benoit-Samuelson has won the Olympic title, but Mota's record since that marathon début stands comparison with the best and has made her the most competitive road runner of them all.

Her time improved in each of her first seven marathons, which included her only three defeats over 26.2 miles. The first defeat was at the 1983 World Championships in Helsinki, where the women's marathon was included in a major championship for the first time. Mota finished fourth in 2:31:50 behind Grete Waitz of Norway. At the 1984 Olympic marathon in Los Angeles, Mota overtook a tiring Kristiansen in the closing stages to claim the bronze medal with another personal best of 2:26:57, behind Benoit-Samuelson and Waitz. Mota's third defeat – at the hands of Benoit-Samuelson in Chicago, 1985 – gave her a two-and-a-half minute improvement with 2:23:29.

Mota's wins include Rotterdam, 1983, Chicago, 1983 and 1984, Tokyo, 1986, and Boston 1988. But her most famous victory to date was in Rome at the World Championships in 1987, where her winning time of 2:25:17 gave her a 7:21 margin of

Rosa Mota

victory – the best in championship history – over Zoja Ivanova of the Soviet Union in second place. Even the absence of Waitz (injured), Benoit-Samuelson (pregnant) and Kristiansen (running in the 10,000m instead) could not detract from her victory as her tiny 1.58m (5ft 2in), 44kg (97lb) frame apparently proved the perfect build for the heat and cobblestones of the Italian capital.

Munkelt, Thomas

1952–. Born East Germany (GDR)

Thomas Munkelt became the first East German male to win a track gold medal when he won the Olympic 110m hurdles title in Moscow in 1980. He benefitted from the absence of the top Americans who fell victim to their country's boycott of the Games.

Among the names missing from the Olympic final was the world record holder Renaldo Nehemiah, the American who had consistently beaten Munkelt, although the East German had pushed him hard in the previous year's World Cup in Montreal. Mun-

kelt's main opposition in the 1980 Olympic final came from the Cuban former world record holder, Alejandro Casanas, who had won the silver medal behind Guy Drut in 1976. But Munkelt, a strong and consistent hurdler, took the gold medal by just one hundredth of a second from Casanas, 13.39 to 13.40.

European champion in 1978 and 1982, Munkelt had started his athletics career unusually late for an East German. His talent was spotted only after he had run at an athletics meeting as a break from his soccer training at the age of 17. Advised that his chances of progressing very far were slim because of his late start, Munkelt made up for lost time by immersing himself in rigorous training.

He was third in the European Cup Final in 1973, fourth in the 1974 European Championships and fifth in the 1976 Olympic final. In 1975 he won the first of nine East German national titles and went on to win three European Cup Finals (1977, 1979 and 1983), four European indoor titles at 60mh and to clock a personal best of 13.37 in 1977.

Myricks, Larry

1956–. Born USA (USA)

Larry Myricks missed his best chance

Thomas Munkelt

of winning an Olympic long jump title when the USA boycotted the 1980 Moscow Games over the Soviet Union's invasion of Afghanistan. As the world's leading long jumper, he would have been a gold medal favourite.

At the 1976 Games he had to scratch from the long jump final after breaking a bone in his ankle during the warm-up. The injury kept him out of competition for 19 months. He returned to Montreal for the 1979 World Cup event to jump a low-altitude world best of 8.52m, second only to Bob Beamon's leap of 8.90m at the Olympics in Mexico, 1968.

Myricks was the last man to beat Carl Lewis in the long jump, indoors in 1981. Since then his form has faltered, while Lewis has maintained a winning sequence of 52 long jump competitions. His only major victory in recent years was at the 1987 World Indoor Championships where he jumped 8.23m to take the title from Paul Emordi of Nigeria and Giovanni Evangelisti of Italy.

Evangelisti won the bronze medal ahead of Myricks in the 1984 Olympic long jump competition, which was won by Lewis. Ironically, he was also awarded the bronze medal ahead of Myricks at the 1987 World Championships in Rome. Investigations after the event revealed that Evangelisti

Larry Myricks

never reached the 8.38m that went onto the scoreboard after his sixth and final jump. Italian officials had placed the marker in the sand before the jump was taken, which explained why the athlete and the crowd around the pit were surprised at the distance when it was announced. The bronze medal was belatedly offered to Myricks.

Myyra, Jonni

1892–1955. Born Finland (FIN/USA)

The pioneer of javelin throwing in Finland, Myyra won Olympic titles in 1920 and 1924. He set five world records from 63.29m in 1914 to 68.56 in 1925 but only one was ratified by the IAAF, 66.10m set in August 1919.

He entered the Stockholm Olympics of 1912, finishing eighth, but eight years later in Antwerp he won easily with 65.78m, Finns taking the first four places. In that event the first five men all exceeded the Olympic record of 60.64m set by Erik Lemming (SWE) at the 1912 Stockholm Games.

Myyra retained his title easily in 1924 in Paris, winning with 62.96m, although he was aged 32 at the time. He later emigrated to the USA where he continued to excel, achieving an unofficial distance of 68.55m at Richmond, California in 1926. He threw the discus 48.80m in New York the same year.

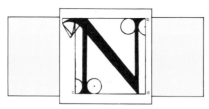

Nehemiah, Renaldo

1959–. Born USA (USA)

Renaldo Nehemiah had been an outstanding high hurdler even as a youngster, and had become the world record holder by the time he was 22. In 1980 he would have been hot favourite to win the Olympic 110m hurdles but for the US boycott, and his only consolation was to spend his season running a succession of very fast times. By the end of that year, he had run 11 of the 15 fastest times in history. The following year, on 19 August, in Zurich, he became the first man to dip below 13 seconds for the event when he clocked 12.93.

Nehemiah was nicknamed 'Skeets' because of his speedy crawl as a toddler. He broke the world junior 110mh record five times in 1978, improving it to 13.23, and the following year

Renaldo Nehemiah

added the world record with 13.16. He ran even faster a month later, clocking 13 seconds dead at Westwood on 6 May. Nehemiah won all of his major races between 1979 and 1981. He took the World Cup title in Montreal with victory over Thomas Munkelt, the European champion, and Alejandro Casanas, the former world record holder. In Nehemiah's absence at the Moscow Olympics a year later Munkelt took the gold medal.

In 1979, Nehemiah also won the Pan-American Games title and the National Collegiate title in America.

However, Nehemiah caused a major upset in 1980 when he resigned from his university track team, relinquished his athletic grant, and signed a lucrative deal with Puma, the sports shoe company, to act as a consultant and spokesman. It was the first sign that, as one of America's top athletes, he was prepared to cash in on his fame and talent. Two years later he gave up his amateur status to play American football with the San Francisco 49ers, a route followed by many top sprinters in the USA.

In 1986, though, he returned to the

Miklos Nemeth

high hurdles, was reinstated as an amateur, and won his first return race at Viareggio in Italy. However, his place at the top of the world rankings had been taken by fellow American Greg Foster and, in an event where the standard is consistently high, Nehemiah has been unable to make the impact he might have hoped for. He has also suffered from injury problems since his return.

Nemeth, Imre

1917–. Born Hungary (HUN)

Olympic hammer champion in 1948, Imre Nemeth won the bronze four years later in 1952 and also set three world records. His son, Miklos, won the 1976 Olympic javelin title.

In London in 1948 Imre Nemeth won by 1.8m over fellow Hungarian Ivan Gubijan 56.07m to 54.27m – just half a metre short of the Olympic record. He became the first Hungarian to take an Olympic title since Rudolf Bauer won the discus in 1900. In 1948 he also set the first of his world records, 59.02m in the National Championships in Tata on 14 July. In an

international match against Poland the following year he improved this mark to 59.57m, and in 1950 achieved 59.88m in the National Championships in Budapest, his third world record.

At the 1952 Olympics in Helsinki he finished behind Jozsef Csermak, also from Hungary, and Germany's Karl Storch. Two years later at the European Championships in Berne he finished behind Csermak again, only this time both were less successful than at the Olympics, Csermak finishing third with 59.72m and Nemeth sixth with 56.86m.

After his retirement from competition Nemeth became an MP, and later the manager of the Nepstadion in Budapest.

Nemeth, Miklos

1946–. Born Hungary (HUN)

Throwing the javelin in his third Olympic Games in 1976, Miklos Nemeth silenced those who thought he might not have a winner's temperament. He hurled the javelin to a new world record, effectively wrapping up the competition before it had begun.

The son of the 1948 Olympic hammer champion, Imre Nemeth, Miklos Nemeth had his father's reputation to live up to. However, he continually failed to throw at his best in major competitions. He did not succeed in qualifying for the 1968 Olympic final at all, and came a disappointing seventh in 1972. In the European Championships in 1971 he was ninth, followed by seventh place in 1974. By the summer of 1975, though, it looked as if he was throwing well enough to make him a medal contender in Montreal. He broke the national record with 91.38m, and was throwing 90m in training.

Everything came right at last in Montreal, when Nemeth opened his account with his record 94.58m throw. The winning margin – more than 6.5m – was the widest in Olympic field event history. The Nemeths went into the record books as the first father and son to win Olympic gold medals.

Nemeth never recovered his Olympic form. He did throw 94.10m in 1977, but at the World Cup in Düsseldorf he finished only third, suffering with a shoulder injury. The title went to West Germany's Michael Wessing who threw 87.46m. Nemeth was later sixth in the 1978 European Championships and eighth in the 1980 Olympics in Moscow.

Neubert, Ramona

1958–. Born East Germany (GDR)

A talented all-round athlete, Ramona Neubert finished fourth in the five-event pentathlon at the 1980 Olympic Games. She then went on to dominate the women's heptathlon after it was introduced in 1981. The event comprises the 100mh, the high jump, the shot put, the 200m, the long jump, the javelin, and the 800m.

Neubert was undefeated throughout 1981, 1982 and 1983, and captured the European Cup titles in 1981 and 1983, the European Championship crown in 1982, and the World Championship gold medal in 1983. She also improved the world record

Ramona Neubert

four times – on the last occasion in 1983 to 6836.

She won the European Combined Events Cup in 1981 and 1983. At the long jump – her strongest event – she was East German champion in 1982. The best long jump performance of her career was 6.90m in 1981, when she also jumped a wind-assisted 7.00m.

Neubert's first and only defeat in a heptathlon came in her tenth competition in 1984, when she was beaten by Sabine Paetz in Potsdam. She was forced to miss the 1984 Olympic Games because of the Eastern Bloc boycott and, after a season disrupted by injury, she retired in 1985.

Newton, Arthur

1883–1959. Born England (SA)

One of the greatest-ever ultra distance runners, Arthur Newton did not start his sporting career until he was 38. Settled in South Africa from 1901, he was the owner of a cotton and tobacco farm. However, this means of livelihood was taken away from him in 1922, when his land was put into a

'native territory' belt. To draw attention to his plight, Newton turned to running, his first training effort being no more than two miles.

Five months later, he won the second Comrades Marathon – 54 miles from Durban to Pietermaritzburg – a feat which he repeated four times in all (1923,1924, 1925,1927), bringing the course record down by over two hours to 6:40.

In 1924 he returned to Britain and became the first man to break six hours for the 52 miles between London and Brighton (5:53:43), long before there was an official race over the distance. A fanatical runner, who covered many miles in training each day, Newton forfeited his amateur status by taking part in the Trans-America race in 1928. During this race, however, he pulled out after 550 miles, 9½ hours ahead of his nearest rival. The following year stomach cramps forced him to retire. To add to his distress, he was knocked over by a car shortly after.

Newton took part in many races in his career over a variety of distances, but was officially world record holder over 50 and 100 miles. In 1934 he set a record for the 100 miles (between Bath and London) of 14:22:10.

Ngugi, John

1962–. Born Kenya (KEN)

In 1988, John Ngugi became the first man to win the World Cross-Country title three times since the Briton Jack Holden had achieved the same feat in the 1930s. In Holden's days the race was an international event, but mainly confined to European athletes. Ngugi, however, has proved himself unbeatable against the very best runners in the world. His margin of victory in 1988 showed just how dominant he had become: he was 22 seconds clear of team mate Paul Kipkoech. The Kenyans took eight of the first nine places in the senior race and six of the first seven in the junior race.

Ngugi, African Games 5000m champion in 1987, was thought to be

John Ngugi (149)

one of the few men who might beat Said Aouita at the World Championships later that year. However, the Kenyan's challenge proved unsuccessful and he finished twelfth as Aouita won in 13:26.44.

Nikolic, Vera

1948–. Born Yugoslavia (YUG)

Although she has one of the best championship records at 800m, Nikolic failed to win a medal at the Olympics in both 1968, when she was overwhelming favourite, and in Munich in 1972. She was twice European champion, in 1966 and 1971, and won a bronze medal in 1969. She set a world record in winning the WAAA title in 1968, clocking 2:00.0, ahead of Lillian Board (GBR).

She won her first European title in Budapest in 1966 aged 17, with a championship best of 2:02.8. Four years later in Athens, the first four girls home, headed by Lillian Board in 2:01.4, broke this 1966 mark, including Nikolic herself. Two years later in Helsinki, she won with another championship record, 2:00.0,

Vera Nikolic (974)

Wolfgang Nordwig

covering the last half lap in a burst of 30.3 seconds to break the field.

Nikolic's 1971 European victory was in sharp contrast to her disastrous performance at the 1968 Olympic Games. The firm favourite and world record holder, she dropped out of the semi-final after 300m, apparently suffering from the pressure and the heavy training load she had been undertaking. Four years later in Munich, she scraped into the final by a centimetre, but could only finish fifth.

She set her best-ever time in 1972, clocking 1:59.62.

Nordwig, Wolfgang

1943–. Born East Germany (GDR)

One of the all-time great pole vaulters, Wolfgang Nordwig went to the Olympic Games in 1972 as the European Champion three times over and holder of two world records in 1970. He had previously won the bronze medal in 1968, when he had been beaten by the American Bob Seagren.

His 1972 victory was with a clearance of 5.50m, after one of the quick-

est and most controversial Olympic pole vault competitions, making him the first non-American to win the title. The controversy came with the banning by the IAAF of a new lightweight pole, developed earlier in 1972 and used by Seagren among others. With a final decision on the issue only being announced the day before the competition, 14 of the 21 vaulters in the qualifying competition had to vault with unfamiliar poles. Seagren, the defending champion, used a pole he did not even have time to practise with.

Nordwig remained unaffected by the controversy, since he did not use the new type of pole. He cleared 5.50m at the third attempt, having already won the gold medal with 5.45m. Between them, Nordwig and the top four vaulters had taken the Olympic record from 5.20m to 5.50!

Nordwig's three European titles constituted a record in themselves, as he was the first person to achieve this. There were also four European indoor titles – another record – and three European Cup Finals. He won the World Student Games title in 1970, the same year that his 5.45m and 5.46m clearances in Berlin and Toronto constituted world records. He won eight GDR titles.

Norpoth, Harald

1942–. Born West Germany (FRG)

A very consistent runner at 1500m and 5000m, Norpoth's greatest successes came in the European Cup. He won the 5000m in 1965, 1967, and 1970, came third in 1973, and was placed fifth at 1500m in 1970.

By their very nature, in that teams are competing for points, European Cup races have tended to be tactical battles. Norpoth showed himself equal to this challenge on many occasions, often bringing in a devastating burst of speed over the last few laps. In 1967, for example, the pace was a very gentle 84/85 seconds per lap, until Norpoth took off and completed the last 800m in 1:53.4.

Harald Norpoth

Norpoth's finishing speed made him a very versatile performer. In 1964 he won the Olympic 5000m silver medal, one second behind Bob Schul (USA). In 1966 he lost only one 1500m race all season, until the 1500m European Championship final where he finished third behind rising star Bodo Tummler (West Germany) and Michel Jazy of France. He finished second to Jazy in the 5000m at the same championships.

In good form, Norpoth lowered the European 5000m record to 13:24.8 in 1967. On 10 September he broke the world 2000m record in Hagen, becoming the first man to go under five minutes for the distance, clocking 4:57.8.

In Mexico for the 1968 Olympics, he failed to finish in the 5000m, dropping out with a stitch (no doubt altitude-induced), but in the 1500m he finished fourth behind Kenyan Kip Keino, Jim Ryun of the USA, and West Germany's Bodo Tummler.

In the 1971 European Championships in Helsinki, he took the bronze, pipped in the finishing straight by France's Jean Wadoux in a race won by Finland's Juha Vaatainen in 13:32.6. He competed at the same distance in the 1972 Olympics and finished sixth in 13:32.6, six seconds behind the winner, Lasse Viren.

Nurmi, Paavo

1897–1973. Born Finland (FIN)

Nurmi is acknowledged as the greatest athlete of his age, and perhaps any age. He won a record 12 Olympic medals (nine gold and three silver), and set 29 world records from 1921 to 1931.

He took up running seriously after his idol Hannes Kolehmainen won the marathon at the 1912 Stockholm Olympics. He started training three or four times a week, running distances from two to six kilometres. His training intensified during his 18-month stint of military service, which began in April 1919. He timed himself on the track with a stopwatch, and became an expert judge of pace.

Nurmi opened his Olympic account in the 1920 Games, at 5000m, where he won the silver behind Frenchman Joseph Guillemot. He beat Guillemot in the 10,000m to take his first gold, and followed this with a cross-country victory. After 1920 he was virtually unbeatable at all distances from 1500m to 20,000m. At the 1924 Olympics he won five gold medals, a figure that remains the most ever won in athletics at one Games, taking the 1500m, the 5000m (with only an hour between the two!), the cross-country (team and individual), and a share of the 3000m team victory.

By the end of 1928 he held all 12 world records from one mile to one hour. Following his Olympic triumphs of 1924, he was invited to compete in the USA. There he won 55 races (45 indoors) and lost only twice, improving the indoor mile record to 4:13.6, the two-mile record to 8:58.2 and the 5000m to 14:44.6.

In 1928 he won the Olympic 10,000m, ahead of compatriot Ville Ritola, the 1924 champion. This was something of a grudge match, as Nurmi

Nurmi (centre) tracks Ville Ritola in the 1928 Olympic 10,000m

had not run this distance in Paris, reportedly excluded by the Finnish Olympic Committee. In fact, legend has it that Nurmi ran the distance by himself on the Olympic training track the same day in 29:45.0 (Ritola's world record and gold medal-winning time had been 30:23.2). When they finally faced each other, Nurmi won in 30:18.8 against Ritola's 30:19.4. However, the position was reversed in the 5000m. Ritola won in 14:38.0 to Nurmi's 14:40.0, after both had suffered injury in the steeplechase.

Although he raced with less frequency after the 1928 Olympics, he still hoped to end his career with a victory in the 1932 marathon in Los Angeles. However, he was banned by the IAAF for alleged professionalism during the 1929 season and was unable to compete. In Finland, however, he was still regarded as a 'national amateur' and won his last important race in 1933, aged 36 – the Finnish 1500m title which he took in 3:55.8.

Almost 20 years later, he was given the honour of carrying the Olympic torch at the opening ceremony of the 1952 Games in Helsinki, and a statue of him stands outside the Olympic stadium.

Among his world records, his best times were: 1500m, 3:52.6 (1926); one mile, 4:10.4 (1923); 2000m, 5:24.6 (1927); 3000m, 8:20.4 (1926); two miles, 8:59.5 (1931); three miles, 14:02.0 (1924); 5000m, 14:28.2 (1924); four miles, 19:15.4 (1924); five miles, 24:06.2 (1924); six miles, 29:07.1 (1924); 10,000m, 30:06.1 (1924); 15,000m, 46:49.5 (1928); ten miles, 50:15.0 (1928); one hour, 19210m (1928); 20,000m, 1:04:38.4 (1930); 4 x 1500m relay, 16:11.4 (1926).

The full list of his Olympic medals is: 1920, three gold medals (10,000m, cross-country team, and cross-country individual), and one silver (5000m); 1924, five gold (1500m, 5000m, cross-country team, cross-country individual, 3000m team); 1928, one gold (10,000m), two silver (5000m, 3000m steeplechase).

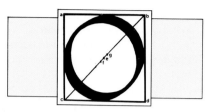

O'Brien, Parry

1932–. Born USA (USA)

The greatest shot-putter of all time, Parry O'Brien won the Olympic title in 1952 and 1956, came second in 1960, set 16 world records (ten ratified by the IAAF) and, between 1952 and 1956, won 116 consecutive competitions. He also pioneered a new style of throwing, starting with his back towards the throwing direction and his right foot behind, then executing a turn of 180° before releasing the shot.

O'Brien became USA champion for the first time in 1951, ending the supremacy of Jim Fuchs. Two years later he broke Fuch's world record of 17.95m with 18.00m on 9 May 1953, and by 1 November 1956 had taken

Parry O'Brien

the mark to 19.25m. He was thus the first man beyond 18m, 60 feet and 19m. He won his first Olympic title in Helsinki in 1952 with 17.41m, and retained it in 1956 with 18.57m.

Dallas Long took the title in 1959 briefly before O'Brien came back with marks of 19.26m and his final world record 19.30m, set on 1 August in Albuquerque. He finished second in the Rome Olympic Games in 1960 behind Bill Nieder, but continued to improve his marks even though younger men had since taken his world record.

He made it onto the US team for the 1964 Games and finished fourth, throwing 19.20m, further than he had ever done before in Olympic competition. He set his best mark two years later in 1966, reaching 19.69m, although by this time the world record had been raised to 21.52m.

Winner of a record 17 AAU titles, both indoors and out, at the shot, he also won the AAU discus title in 1955.

O'Callaghan, Pat

1905–. Born Republic of Ireland (IRE)

The first Olympic gold medallist to represent Ireland, and one of the few giants of the throwing events not to emigrate to the United States, Pat O'Callaghan won Olympic hammer titles in 1928 and 1932.

After a period of non-specialization, O'Callaghan started to concentrate on the hammer in 1927 and was not seen as a threat at the 1928 Olympics in Amsterdam. However, he threw 51.39m on his fifth attempt to take the gold. Four years later in Los Angeles he won with his final throw of 53.92m, beating Ville Porhola (FIN). O'Callaghan's victory was all the more impressive because his ability to turn in the circle was hindered by his long-spiked shoes. Assiduous filing throughout the competition left him with more responsive footwear.

He was not allowed to defend his title at the Berlin Games of 1936 as he was a member of the National Athletic and Cycling Federation of Ireland, a body not recognized by the ruling IAAF. For the same reason his best throw of 59.55m set in 1937 was not recognized as an official world record, although this was about two metres further than the official distance set by Pat Ryan (USA) in 1913. Moreover, when reweighed, O'Callaghan's hammer was found to be 170g overweight.

Winner of the AAU hammer title in 1933 and the AAA title the following year, O'Callaghan had a high jump best of 1.88m, and could put the shot 14.75m.

O'Connor, Peter

1872–1957. Born Republic of Ireland (IRE)

Peter O'Connor was the first IAAF-ratified long jump world record holder. He leapt a remarkable 7.61m in Dublin on 5 August 1901, a mark that was not beaten until Edward Gourdin (USA) jumped 7.69m in 1921. Just how far ahead of its time O'Connor's leap was can be seen by the fact that the first Briton to better it was Lynn Davies with 7.72m on 26 November 1962, more than 61 years later!

O'Connor had improved the record four times already in the previous year, bettering Myer Prinstein's (USA) 7.50m by one centimetre on 29 August 1900, then improving it to 7.51m, 7.54m and 7.60m (twice). Although his first ratified record had been set from a broad wooden runway, it was accepted by the IAAF in 1913.

O'Connor's Olympic ambitions were somewhat thwarted when he finally met Prinstein at the 1906 Games in Athens. Prinstein took the gold with 7.20m to O'Connor's 7.02m. O'Connor, however, showed the typical versatiality of the early 20th century jumpers by winning the triple jump with 14.07m, ahead of Con Leahy (GBR) on 13.98m.

Six times AAA long jump champion (1901-6), O'Connor's 7.61m long jump is still an Irish national record.

Oerter, Al

1936–. Born USA (USA)

The greatest-ever discus thrower with-out a doubt, Al Oerter won four successive Olympic titles between 1956 and 1968, and was four-times world record holder.

In 1956 in Melbourn, as a 20-year-old, Oerter won with his first throw of 56.36m in the final, a personal best and an Olympic record. This came barely two years after he had set an American schoolboy discus record of 56.14m. In Rome in 1960 he beat rival Rink Babka (USA) with 59.18m to 58.02m, over-taking Babka in the fifth round.

Oerter's most remarkable victory was his third, in Tokyo in 1964. He was competing against doctor's orders after tearing cartilages in his lower ribcage. Heavily strapped and using ice-packs repeatedly, he nevertheless managed to set a new Olympic record in the qualifying rounds. In the final he was lying third behind world record holder Ludvik Danek of Czechoslovakia and American Dave Weill until the fifth round, when he overtook Danek's 60.52m with a spectacular 61.00m.

In Mexico in 1968 Oerter's victory was even more surprising: his best for the year was only 62.74, while the favourite Jay Silvester (USA) had improved the world record to 68.40m. Silvester threw an Olympic record 63.64m in the qualifying round, but Oerter, lying fourth after two rounds, unleashed a personal best of 64.78m in the third, and followed it with two more throws over 64m. Silvester could only finish fifth with 61.78, and the silver medallist Lothar Milde (GDR) was over a metre and a half behind Oerter on 63.08m. Oerter's supremacy on the day when it really counted had once again led him to beat men who, on paper at least, should have out-thrown him.

Oerter was not a world record chaser, being the supreme competitor, but he did gain his first world record in 1962, throwing 61.10m. After losing it quickly to Vladimir Trusenyov (URS) he regained it four weeks later with 62.44m, improving to 62.62m in 1963 and 62.94m the following year.

The incredible Al Oerter

Oerter decided not to compete in the Olympics of 1972 or 1976, but in 1976 he began throwing again, hoping to be included in the US team for the Olympics in 1980. He even improved his personal best to 69.46m in 1980 – second in the world for that year – and was placed fourth in the US Olympic trials, before the USA decided to boycott the Games held in Moscow. In 1985, aged 49, Oerter had a season's best of 64.38m.

However, Oerter never won the US Olympic trials, coming second in 1956, 1960 and 1964 and third in 1968. He won the AAU discus title six times between 1959 and 1966, and the Pan American title in 1959.

Oldfield, Brian

1945–. Born USA (USA)

Brian Oldfield caused a sensation in 1975 when, as a professional athlete in an International Track Association meeting, he took three throws in the shot competition and they all landed far in excess of the amateur world record mark. The accepted world record was Al Feuerbach's 21.82, but Oldfield reached 21.94m, 22.25m and finally 22.86m.

His previous best as an amateur was 20.97m and his amazing series of throws at the meeting in El Paso in May 1975, was greeted with some scepticism; the professional circuit was known not to have the stringent checking procedures of amateur competitions. But Oldfield's good form continued and he produced further throws of 22.28m in Edinburgh and 22.45m in El Paso again in 1976. Prior to Oldfield's efforts, the best distance ever achieved in the shot put was George Woods' indoor mark of 22.02m, but indoor competitions did not have world record status.

Oldfield used a revolutionary rotational technique he had seen used by Aleksandr Baryshnikov of the Soviet Union at the 1972 Olympic Games, where Oldfield had placed sixth. Baryshnikov set a world record of 22.00m in 1976.

Joao Carlos de Oliveira

When the ITA folded in 1976, Oldfield, along with many other professionals, applied for reinstatement as an amateur and was finally granted his wish in 1980. At the age of 34 he carried on competing and won the American national title with 21.82m. He improved the American record to 22.02m in 1981 and again to 22.19m in 1984.

Oliveira, Joao Carlos de

1954–. Born Brazil (BRA)

Following in the hops, steps and jumps of Brazil's great triple jumpers, Da Silva and Prudencio, Joao Carlos de Oliveira joined them in the record books with a distance of 17.89m, achieved at altitude in Mexico City in the Pan American Games of 1975. It was 45cm further than the record set by the triple Olympic gold medallist Victor Saneyev of the Soviet Union. Prior to this world record, de Oliveira's best was 16.74m and, although little was known of him outside Brazil, he was South American champion and holder of the Brazilian long jump record.

This was the first of four gold medals de Oliveira won at the Pan American Games. He also won the long jump competition and repeated the feat four years later when the American Willie Banks finished runner-up in the triple jump. It was Banks who was to take his world record ten years later with 17.97m and popularize the event for television audiences.

Competing at his first Olympic Games in 1976, de Oliveira was no match for Saneyev, and, admitting to being nervous and not in the best of condition, he managed only 16.90m for the bronze medal.

The following year he was back to his winning ways, and 16.68m was enough to land him the gold medal at the inaugural World Cup in Düsseldorf. He retained the title in 1979 in Montreal where, despite fouling three of his jumps, he won with a final round leap of 17.02m.

De Oliveira managed 17.22m at the Moscow Olympics in 1980, but again he took the bronze medal behind the new champion Jaak Uudmäe of the Soviet Union, with Saneyev second. At the World Cup in Rome the following year, de Oliveira faced Uudmäe again as well as Willie Banks. The Brazilian made up for his disappointment in Moscow by winning his third title with 17.37m, just 3cm further than second-placed Zhu Zhen-Xian of China.

Olizaryenko, Nadyezda

1953–. Born USSR (URS)

A tremendously strong athlete, Olizaryenko pushed back the barriers for women's 800m running with her performances at the Moscow Olympic Games in 1980. She firstly inched inside team mate Tatyana Kazankina's world record of 1:54.9 with 1:54.85 in the semi-final and then swept to victory in the final in a new world record of 1:53:43. She followed this by claiming a bronze medal behind Kazankina in the 1500m after setting the early pace.

Two years before, as Nadyezda

Olympic Games

Despite the political and sporting boycotts of recent years, the Olympic Games remain the major athletics event for all competitors. The World Championships in 1983 and 1987 may have escaped the intrusion of politics, but it is the four-yearly Olympic Games which retain the history and glamour associated with the premier sporting occasion.

The modern Olympic movement dates back to the formation of the International Olympic Committee in 1894 by Pierre de Fredi, Baron de Coubertin. It was his ambition to resurrect the Games which had first been contested by the Greeks in the thirteenth century BC. De Coubertin, inspired by games introduced at Much Wenlock in Shropshire (UK) in 1850, was commissioned by the French government to form a universal sports association in 1889. After erxtensive research throughout Europe he announced his findings in 1892 and two years later the IOC was set up. The first Olympic Games, featuring 59 competitors from ten countries, took place in Athens in 1896.

The Games have been held every four years since then, although there was a tenth anniversary event in 1906 and gaps because of the two world wars. The four-yearly interval is known as an Olympiad.

The numbers of athletes and countries taking part have grown steadily since the first Games. Women's events were introduced in 1928 and the number of sports contested reached 23 in 1988. Athletics remain the centre piece of the Games, however.

Such is the stature of an Olympic Games that it has inevitably provided the stage for displays of fierce nationalism, as in Berlin in 1936, and has become the target of political gestures, as in Montreal in 1976, Moscow in 1980 and Los Angeles in 1984. It also, in 1972, provided the setting for terrorist killings when ten Israeli athletes were held hostage by Palestinian terrorists at the Olympic village in Munich. One Israeli athlete was shot by the terrorists and several more were killed or injured in the shoot-out which followed at a nearby airfield.

Chancellor Adolf Hitler used the 1936 Games to demonstrate to the world the power and influence of the Third Reich with grandiose displays of the Nazi regime both inside and outside the Olympic stadium. In recent years the Games have been affected by political boycotts. The black African athletes stayed away from Montreal in 1976 on the orders of their governments as a protest over New Zealand's continuing sporting links with South Africa. The Soviet invasion of Afghanistan led to a boycott by several Western countries including the USA, West Germany and Kenya in 1980. In 1984 the Eastern Bloc countries reciprocated by boycotting the Los Angeles Olympics on the pretext that the safety of their athletes could not be guaranteed. Only Romania defied the boycott and attended.

Despite the 1984 boycott, however, a record 140 countries sent athletes for all sports to Los Angeles and the number of competitors topped 7000. Needless to say, the Americans dominated the athletics events.

The IOC has made strenuous efforts since 1984 to ensure that future Games are not damaged by boycotts and has actively lobbied governments to support the Olympic ideal. A record 161 countries accepted invitations to compete in Seoul. The only countries not to accept at the time of going to press were North Korea, Cuba, Nicaragua, the Seychelles, Albania and Ethiopia.

More importantly, perhaps, the 1984 Games were a huge financial success. They were for the first time funded by commercial sponsorship and netted a profit of around $162 million. Eight years earlier the city of Montreal ran into enormous financial difficulties over its staging of the Games and is still paying off the debt incurred. LA's success provided the spur for countries to want to take on the hosting of the Games and more

Nadyezda Olizaryenko (281)

Musta, she was awarded the silver medal at the European Championships in Prague after being edged out of the gold medal spot by team mate Tatyana Providokhina, although they both shared the same time. In 1979 she finished second behind Bulgarian Nikolina Shtereva in the World Cup 800m in Montreal.

In 1980 Olizaryenko was at her peak, putting together laps of 56.41 seconds and 57.01 seconds to set a record that lasted until Jarmila Kratochvilova's 1:53.28 in Munich three years later. She closed the 1980 season by leading off a Soviet world record of 7:50.17 for the 4 x 800m.

Although she missed the next three seasons because of injury and starting a family, Olizaryenko was back in 1984 to clock a best time of 1:56.09 to rank third in the world. By 1986 she was back to gold-medal-winning form. She took the European title in Stuttgart in 1:57.15, ahead of Sigrun Wodars of East Germany and her Soviet team mate Ljubor Gurina. She qualified for the final at the World Championships a year later in Rome but could only finish seventh.

The Los Angeles Coliseum, setting for the 1984 Olympic Games

and more cities are vying to host future Olympics. The 1992 Games will be held in Barcelona and while Athens is favoured to host the 1996 centennial Olympics, several other cities will bid against it.

Venues of the modern Olympic Games	
1896 Athens	1952 Helsinki
1900 Paris	1956 Melbourne
1904 St Louis	1960 Rome
1908 London	1964 Tokyo
1912 Stockholm	1968 Mexico City
1920 Antwerp	1972 Munich
1924 Paris	1976 Montreal
1928 Amsterdam	1980 Moscow
1932 Los Angeles	1984 Los Angeles
1936 Berlin	1988 Seoul
1948 London	1992 Barcelona

Osborn, Harold

1899–1975. Born USA (USA)

Harold Osborn was the only Olympic decathlon champion ever to win an individual gold medal as well. In 1924 in Paris he not only won the decathlon with a world record 7720 points (1912 tables, 6476 on 1984 tables), but also the high jump with 1.98m, an Olympic record that was not beaten until 1936.

A high jump world record was set by Osborn in the US Olympic trials in Urbana on 27 May 1924, when he cleared 2.03m. In an exhibition in Austin, Texas the following year he cleared 2:05, an unratified mark.

The world record he set at the 1924 Olympics on 11-12 July was made up of: 100m - 11.2; long jump - 6.92m; shot - 11.43m; high jump - 1.97m; 400m - 53.2; 110mh - 16.0; discus - 34.51m; pole vault - 3.50m; javelin -

46.69m; 1500m - 4:50.0.

At the 1928 Olympics in Amsterdam Osborn finished fifth in the high jump, but ended his career that year with a world indoor best of 1.68m for the standing high jump. In all, Osborn won 18 AAU titles at six different events.

Ostermeyer, Micheline

1922–. Born France (FRA)

One of only two women to win Olympic medals at three different field events (the other is Soviet Aleksandra Chudina), Ostermeyer won the 1948 shot and discus titles in London, and also took the bronze in the high jump.

The first African-based woman to win an Olympic gold (she originated from Tunisia), she also holds the French record for the greatest number of women's titles – 19 (10 – shot put, four – discus, three – pentathlon, one

– 80mh, one – high jump). At the 1946 European Championships in Oslo she finished second in the shot and fifth in the high jump.

For the London Olympics she originally intended to enter only the shot put and high jump, but ended up winning the discus with a career best 41.92m. Her shot put mark of 13.75m was also a personal best. Two years later at the European Championships in Brussels she once again showed her sersatility. She was placed third in the shot, fourth in the discus, and won the bronze in the 80mh.

Ostermeyer had another talent which she went on to pursue after the end of her athletics career – she was a concert pianist, graduating from the Paris Conservatoire in the year of her Olympic triumphs in London.

Otkalenko, Nina

1928–. Born USSR (URS)

The leading 800m runner in the mid-1950s, Otkalenko's record suffers from the fact that between 1928 and 1960 this distance was not on the Olympic programme for women. Nevertheless she won the 1954 European Championships in Berne. She set seven world records at 800m, the greatest number ever, of which five were officially ratified.

Otkalenko lowered the world best mark from 2:12.0 set in Minsk on 26 August 1951 to 2:05.0 in Zagreb on 24 September 1955. She became the first woman to run under 2:10 in Kiev on 15 June 1952, clocking 2:08.5. She also set two world 880 yard records, the best of these being 2:06.6 set in Moscow on 10 June 1956.

Success came also at 400m, at which she was ranked number one in the world in 1956. She set one world record at this distance – 55.5 on 25 June 1954, in Kiev, and had a personal best of 55.0 in 1955. She was also an excellent 1500m runner and miler, setting a world 1500m record of 4:37.0 at the Soviet Championships on 30 August 1952. In addition she took women's mile running

to the brink of breaking the five-minute barrier, her personal best being five minutes dead.

Ottoz, Eddy

1944–. Born Italy (ITA)

Double gold medallist at the European Championships, Eddy Ottoz won the 110mh title in 1966 (13.7) and 1969 (13.5). Before the 1968 Olympics in Mexico, he was seen as the one man who might break the American domination of the event. He had run the fourth fastest time in the world and went into the competition behind the Americans Willie Davenport, Erv Hall and Leon Coleman. Having won his heat in 13.5, equalling the Olympic record, he looked set to break the Americans' stronghold and finished well in the final just losing out to Erv Hall. Both were given the same time – 10.4 – a personal best for the Italian.

In the Olympic Games of 1964 in Tokyo, Ottoz had finished fourth in 13.8 seconds in a race won by Hayes Jones (USA) in 13.6. He won three European Indoor Championships, specializing in the 50mh at which he set a world best of 6.4 three times in 1967. In all he was a three-time winner of the 50mh/60mh title between 1966-1968.

He was also the holder of 23 Italian records between 1964-1968, 19 of them at 110mh where he reduced the national record from 13.9 in 1964 to 13.4 (13.46 auto, his Olympic performance in Mexico) in 1968. He also set four national records at 200mh.

Ovett, Steve

1955–. Born England (GBR)

One of the most accomplished athletes ever to set foot on a running track, Steve Ovett has proved to be one of the sports most colourful, controversial and unpredictable characters. In his pursuit of an Olympic gold medal he shunned the press, infuriated fellow athletes with his cheeky waves along the home straight but

delighted fans with his seemingly effortless displays of running at distances from 800m to 5000m in a career stretching over 16 seasons.

As a youngster Ovett showed remarkable talent very early in his development. He won the English Schools 400m Championship at 14, clocked 11.8 for 100m and could long jump over 20ft. The following year he won the AAA Youths 400m title and ran 1:55.3 for 800m, a UK best for a 14 year old.

In 1973 his obvious potential was realized at international level when he won the European Junior 800m title in Duisburg, West Germany. In 1974, at the age of 18, he lined up in the senior European Championship 800m in Rome and was desperately disappointed at winning only a silver medal behind Luciano Susanj of Yugoslavia.

At a time when Britain was in need of winners and stars, Ovett fitted the bill perfectly. Tall and strong with powerful acceleration, he was also aggressive on the track and determined to run his own race whatever the opposition. He won the European Cup semi-final 800m in front of his home fans at Crystal Palace before going on to win in the final in Nice in 1:46.6.

His ambition remained to win an Olympic gold medal and his first chance came in 1976. He qualified for the British team at both 800m and 1500m by winning the trials and went to the Games as a genuine medal prospect. But in the 800m – where for the first and only time the first 300m were run in lanes – he found himself with too much to do after being drawn in lane eight. By the time he was allowed to run into the inside lane the giant Cuban Alberto Juantorena was already seven metres up and beginning to stretch out for the bell. Ovett mustered all his resources to close the gap but could finish no better than fifth, albeit with a personal best of 1:45.4. More disappointment was to come as he was run out of his semi-final of the 1500m.

In 1977 Ovett emerged as the finest middle-distance talent in the world.

An early season defeat at the hands of American Steve Scott over 1500m in Jamaica proved to be his last for three years as he ran the mile and 1500m 45 times undefeated until the Olympic 1500m final in 1980. His finest race came in the World Cup in Düsseldorf and it is still regarded by many, including Sebastian Coe, as one of the greatest displays of 1500m running ever seen. Running for the Europe Select team, Ovett tracked the world class field for 1300m before unleashing a devastating kick to leave them all struggling for the minor places. John Walker, the Olympic champion running for Oceania, stepped off the track. Ovett's last 100m took just 11.9 seconds and his final time of 3:34.5 was a UK record. In the home straight the wave to the crowd, which had become his trade mark, signified his delight and seemed to suggest that victory had been easy.

There seemed to be no end to Ovett's ability. The following winter he finished fourth in the nine mile English Cross-Country Championship and prepared for that summer's European Championships with a succession of increasingly impressive victories over 800m, 1500m and the mile. He was renowned for his finishing kick over the final 200m and seemed to be able to produce it in any kind of race. But the summer of 1978 saw the emergence of another major 800m talent. His name was Sebastian Coe.

The two lined up for the European Championship 800m final in Prague and it was seen as primarily a race between the two of them for the gold medal. Coe led through the first 400m in a very fast 49.3 but, although Ovett passed Coe going into the home straight, the relatively unknown East German Olaf Beyer was able to pass them both and snatch the gold medal ahead of the surprised Ovett. Ovett's time was a UK record 1:44.1 but he learned never again to focus on only one man in a race and not to leave it too late before striking out for the line. It was the first of the Coe versus Ovett races that came all too infrequently

Steve Ovett

over the ensuing years, although the supposed rivalry between the two would become the single most important talking point in the media for the next four years.

Ovett was not finished in Prague, however. He became Britain's only gold medallist when he once again sprinted for home with 200m to go to capture the 1500m title in 3:35.6. With so much running still left in his legs, he beat multi-world record holder Henry Rono over two miles at Crystal Palace in a world best 8:13.5 and took the UK mile record to 3:52.8 in Oslo five days later.

In 1979 he was beaten only once on the track as he started his preparation for the following year's Olympic Games. But Coe too was preparing well and capturing headlines with his world-record-breaking spree over

800m, the mile and 1500m. Despite claiming that he was not interested in breaking records, only winning races, Ovett did make two attempts on Coe's marks, narrowly failing with 3:49.6 in a mile at Crystal Palace and 3:32.11 in a 1500m race in Brussels. The confrontation between the two in Moscow was the most eagerly awaited clash of the Games.

Their 1980 form was equally impressive. In Oslo they both set world records, Ovett with 3:48.8 in the mile and Coe with 2:13.4 in the 1000m. Two weeks later on the same track Ovett equalled Coe's 1500m world record with 3:32.1.

In Moscow Coe chose the Olympic final to run his worst ever race at 800m while Ovett timed his finish to perfection to win with ease in 1:45.4. While Coe ran at the back of the pack for too long, Ovett followed the Russian Nikolay Kirov until the start of the home straight. Remembering his lesson from Prague, he struck out for home still surprised that he had not seen Coe for the entire race. The days between the 800m and 1500m finals gave Coe enough time to recover and he at last got it right to take the title in 3:38.4 while Ovett finished third. Ovett and Coe came away with a gold medal apiece but each had won the race in which the other had been the favourite. The issue of who was the better runner seemed undecided.

So it was to remain. The 1981 season was probably Ovett's best, with only two defeats, a spate of fast times and two world records. Although they never met in a race that year, Coe and Ovett swapped the world mile record three times, Ovett running 3:48.40 in Koblenz, West Germany to claim it briefly from Coe, who clocked 3:48.53 in Zurich and 3:47.33 in Brussels.

The two of them finally agreed to take part in a series of three races in 1982, over 800m, the mile and 3000m, but fate was against them. Ovett's season was ruined before it began when he ran into some church railings near his Brighton home while out on a training run that winter. He was unable to start proper training until the spring and ended a season dogged by illness and injury in August. Coe meanwhile also suffered injuries and illness and failed to make any of the appointed races. While an out of sorts Coe was beaten in the European Championships 800m and Ovett was reduced to commentating for television, Steve Cram (GBR) emerged as the man to challenge them both for top honours by winning both the Commonwealth and European 1500m titles.

Ovett has never regained the consistency he showed in the years between 1977 and 1981. In 1983 he was rarely at his best and at the World Championships in Helsinki ran his worst ever 1500m to finish fourth behind Steve Cram, despite a 51.9 last lap. It was not until later in the summer that he was fully racing fit and

demonstrated the fact by regaining his 1500m world record – the American Sydney Maree had snatched it briefly – with 3:30.77 in Reiti, Italy. A week later Ovett took on Cram in the mile at Crystal Palace. In a pulsating race which had the two running stride for stride to the line, victory just went to Cram, 3:52.56 to 3:52.71.

Things started well in 1984 with Ovett timing his training and racing so that he could peak for the Olympic Games in Los Angeles. But a bout of bronchitis never cleared up and left him weak and gasping for air in the heats of the 800m. He still qualified for the final though and insisted on running. He finished a distant last, collapsing soon afterwards and spending the next two days in hospital. Against all advice he ran in the heats of the 1500m and qualified for the final, only to drop out on the last lap as Coe retained his title with Cram second.

After a low key season in 1985, Ovett moved up to 5000m in 1986. He won his first Commonwealth Games gold medal in 13:24.11 but, hit by illness again, was forced to drop out of the European Championships 5000m final after 2000m. He stayed with the distance in 1987 despite the heavy training it involved. In a season when he lost more races than he won, Ovett was unable to cope with the heat and running two races in as many days at the World Championships in Rome and finished tenth.

Although Ovett has always been a target for press attention, he has never enjoyed an easy relationship with the media in general. He stormed out of a press conference at Crystal Palace in 1975 after an argument and for the next eight years granted only rare interviews. It was with some irony then that he became part of the media himself when he joined ITV's commentary team in 1986.

Owens, Jesse

1913–1980. Born USA (USA)

The choice of many experts as the

greatest-ever track and field athlete, Jesse Owens won four gold medals at the 1936 Olympics (100m, 200m, long jump, 4 x 100m relay). The previous year at Ann Arbor, Michigan, he beat or equalled six world records in the space of 45 minutes! This astonishing three-quarters of an hour went as follows: 3.15pm – 100 yards in 9.4 seconds to equal the world record; 3.25pm – 8.13m long jump, his only jump of the competition and a record that stood for 25 years; 3.45pm – a straight 220 yards in 20.3, also a world record for the shorter 200m; 4.00pm – a straight 220 yard hurdles in 22.6, also a world record for 200 metre hurdles.

One of eight children of a cotton-picker, Owens set high school records in 1932-3 at 100 yards, 220 yards and long jump, setting his first world record of 9.4 for 100 yards in 1933 (never ratified) and winning his first AAU title at long jump in 1934. A student at Ohio State University, he was coached by Larry Snyder at a time when athletics scholarships to blacks were rare. It was coach Snyder who apparently had to help Owens, who was suffering from a back injury, to the Ann Arbor Big Ten meet before and afterwards, physically lifting the multi-world-record holder to his car.

Owen's supremacy, especially at long jump, continued in 1935-6 when he cleared 26ft (7.92m) 15 times in competition 12 years before any other man did it more than once. But he found tough opposition in the sprints from Ralph Metcalfe, whom he did not beat until 1936, and Eulace Peacock, who beat them both in the 1935 AAU 100m and beat Owens four more times in 1936 before pulling a muscle and missing the Olympics.

In the outdoor season before Berlin he won all 46 competitions at sprints, hurdles and long jump before his ultimate Olympic triumph: a straight 100m in 10.3 (ahead of Metcalfe in 10.4); 200m in 20.7 (world's best around a full turn); long jump of 8.06m, only qualifying for the final on his third and last attempt; the first leg of relay to help his team to gold and a

Jesse Owens

Packer, Ann

1942–. Born England (GBR)

Ann Packer was Britain's golden girl in the 1964 Tokyo Olympics. She won silver in the 400m, then, in only her eighth race at the distance, stormed home to win gold in the 800m.

Packer started her international career as a long jumper, then won the 1959 English Schools 100 yard title. She then turned her attention to 200m and qualified for the final of the European Championships in 1962, although she placed last. She showed her versatility at the Commonwealth Games in Perth later that year, placing sixth in the 80mh final and taking silver in the relay.

In 1963 she moved in distance again to 400m and with 53.4 seconds did enough to rank fourth in the world that year. In Olympic year, 1964, she

Ann Packer

new world record of 39.8.

Turning professional after the Olympics (America in the 1930s had few opportunities for blacks, even for top athletes) he raced for various promoters against horses, dogs, even cars. But he claimed to be in good shape into middle age, achieving 100 yards in 9.7 and a 7.90m long jump in 1948, and a 9.8 100 yards in 1955, aged 41. He found further fame in middle-age when he was much in demand on the lecture circuit and a member of the US Olympic Committee.

Ozolina, Elvira

1939–. Born USSR (URS)

Married to great Soviet javelin-thrower Janis Lusis, Ozolina beat him to an Olympic gold medal in the women's javelin event in 1960 with a throw of

55.98m. Lusis did not win his Olympic title until 1968.

Before the Olympic competition in 1960, Ozolina set two world records, the first of 57.92m in the Soviet Union's national championships, the second of 59.55m in Bucharest. She won the Olympic title in Rome when Dana Zatopkova, the champion of 1952, was second with 53.78m.

Ozolina went on to win the 1962 European Championship in Belgrade with 54.92m and improved her world record to 59.78m in Moscow in 1963. She further improved the record to 61.38m (the first over 200ft) in 1964, but could only finish fifth at the Olympic Games in Tokyo. She was not able to maintain her best form for the rest of her career, however, although she rallied in 1973 to win her fifth Soviet title and to rank seventh in the world after a lifetime best of 63.96m.

moved up again to 800m, although she went to Tokyo only having run the distance five times and pinning her real hopes on the 400m. In the shorter race she met an inspired Betty Cuthbert on the come-back trail, and even a European record of 52.2 was only good enough for second place.

In the 800m final she looked well out of the medals in the last lap, but she stormed off the final bend and came through to win in a world record 2:01.1.

She then retired to marry Robbie Brightwell, who was European 400m champion and captain of the men's team in Tokyo. 'Running a home is more important than running races,' she said.

Paddock, Charles

1900–1943. Born USA (USA)

Charles Paddock held the most world records – six – for 100 yards, a record that still stands. He won the Olympic 100m title in 1920, came second in the 200m the same year and in 1924, and won a gold for the American 4 x 100m relay team that set a world record of 42.2 at the 1920 Amsterdam Games.

Paddock had a most unusual style that consisted of him hurling himself at the tape from about five metres out, but it proved extremely effective. On 23 April 1921 at the Southern California AAU meet he broke four world records in two races. First he achieved 100m in 10.4 seconds (equalling his own 100 yard record of 9.6), then in a 300m race he covered 200m in 21.2, 300 yards in 30.2, and 300m in 33.2.

Perhaps his most spectacular achievement was in 1921, when he ran 110 yards (100.58m) in 10.2. However, this was not recognized by the AAU because, according to the rules of the day, records could only be set at the distance at which the race was run. His last 100 yard world record, in 1926, was actually 9.5 but, again, rules of the day meant that records were recognized in fifths of a second, so it was rounded up to 9.6.

Paddock was a captain in the

Sabine Paetz

Marines in the Second World War. He died in action in 1943.

Paetz, Sabine

1957–. Born East Germany (GDR)

Sabine Paetz took over as the world's leading heptathlete in 1984. She came out of the shadow of her East German team mate Ramona Neubert, the former world record holder, to set two pentathlon world best scores indoors and outdoors. In Potsdam later that year she bettered Neubert's world record by 31 points in the heptathlon. Her world record score totalled 6867, which converts to 6946 on the new tables introduced in 1985.

Runner-up to Neubert at the European Championships in Athens in 1982, Paetz also had to settle for second place behind her team mate at the World Championships in 1983. Her best ever season came in 1984 when, in addition to her heptathlon performances, she excelled in her favourite events, the 100mh and the long jump. She finished second at the long jump behind Heike Drechsler (née Daute), the world champion, at the GDR Championships with 6.82m. At 100mh, she ended the season by win-

ning at the Eight Nations meeting in Tokyo in 12.72 seconds.

In 1985 she won her first individual title at the European Cup for Combined Events, after finishing fourth in 1979 and 1981. She missed the 1986 European Championships because of injury, but was back to compete in the combined events competition at Arles in France in 1987. It was a catastrophe for the East German team. Paetz was taken to hospital after suffering heat stroke on the second day, while her colleague Anke Behmer, who had won the European title the year before, fell during the 100mh and broke her collar bone. The result was that the East German team, winners of the previous four competitions, failed to finish as a team and were relegated to compete in the B Group in 1989.

Paklin, Igor

1963–. Born USSR (URS)

Since taking up the event in 1979, Igor Paklin has become the world's most consistent high jumper. He has won world and European titles, and set a new world record of 2.41m – a record 50cm above his own height. He had added a centimetre to the previous best, cleared by Rudolf Povarnitsyn a month before.

The record came at his second World Student Games in 1985, where he was the defending champion. He had already won the competition by ten centimetres and was being hurried to his world record attempt by anxious officials who wanted to prepare the stadium in Kobe, Japan, for the closing ceremony.

A year later, Paklin went to the European Championships in Stuttgart. He justified his selection, ahead of more experienced Soviet competitors, by winning the title with a jump of 2:34m. Among the men he beat were reigning champion Dietmar Mogenburg of West Germany and Patrik Sjöberg of Sweden.

His 1987 season began with two major wins, at the World Indoor Championships in Indianapolis, where he

Igor Paklin

beat fellow Soviet Gennadiy Avdeyenko after a jump-off, and at the European Cup Final in Prague. However, at the World Championships in Rome at the end of the year, he came up against an in-form Sjöberg in a closely fought competition of the very highest standard.

Paklin and Avdeyenko both ended up with jumps of 2:38m but had to share second place behind the Swede, who had cleared the height with his first attempt. Paklin needed two jumps, Avdeyenko three, while they all failed at 2.40m.

Pamich, Abdon

1933–. Born Italy (ITA)

One of the most enduring 50km walk champions, Abdon Pamich won the Olympic title in 1964, having taken bronze in 1960. He also competed in six European Championships, one of only two men to do so (the other is the Czech discus thrower Ludvik Danek), winning twice in 1962 and 1966.

Danek's international success began at the 1954 European Championships in Berne, where he finished seventh in 4:49:06.4. He finished just outside the medals at the Melbourne Olympics of 1956, in fourth place. He took European silver in 1958, clocking 4:18:00.0, and finished third in the 1960 Olympics in Rome, behind Sweden's John Ljunggren and Britain's Don Thompson. He set a world track record of 4:14:02.4 in 1961, followed by the European Championship title with 4:19:46.6 in 1962. He went on to win the Olympic title in Tokyo in 4:11:12.4, ahead of Britain's Paul Nihill (4:11:31.2). However, neither man was able to complete the course on a sweltering day four years later in Mexico City.

Abdon Pamich

He won his second European title in 1966 in 4:18:42.0, but did not finish in 1969 and came only eighth in 1971, in what was, however, his fastest European time – 4:14:36.2.

Winner of 40 Italian titles at various distances (14 at 10km, 12 at 20km, and 14 at 50km), Pamich set a 50km road best of 4:03:02 in 1960. His Olympic career came to a halt in 1972, when he was disqualified.

Pascoe, Alan

1947–. Born England (GBR)

Pascoe became a world-class high-hurdler in the wake of David Hemery's success in the 400m hurdles at the 1968 Mexico Olympics. The two were rivals until Hemery's retirement in 1972, the year that they both contributed to a British success in the 4 x 400m relay at the Munich Olympic Games.

European indoor 50mh champion in 1969, Pascoe won his first major championship medal later that year, when he won the bronze behind Hemery and the Italian Eddy Ottoz in the European Championship 110mh in Athens. Two years later, he finished runner-up to Frank Siebeck of East Germany, clocking 14.1 in the European Championships 110mh in Helsinki.

He was less successful at the 1972 Olympic Games in Munich, however, where he failed to qualify for the 110mh final after two poor runs in the heats. He did win a silver medal in the 4 x 400m relay, though. After a brilliant anchor leg by David Jenkins, the British team – which also included Hemery and Martin Reynolds equalled the European record with 3:00.5. Pascoe's leg of 45.1 convinced him that his future lay in 400m hurdling and, after advice from Hemery, he scored a significant win in the following year's European Cup Final in Edinburgh, with 50.07. The same year he also scored a notable victory over the 1972 Olympic champion, John Akii-Bua, and clocked 48.6 in a race in Stockholm.

Alan Pascoe

His most successful year was 1974. At the Commonwealth Games in Christchurch, New Zealand, he won the 400mh in 48.83, and took a silver medal in the 4 x 400m relay. He went on to win the European title in Rome in 48.82 and to take a second gold medal in the relay. He retained his European Cup Final title in 1975, running 49.00 in Nice.

Although regarded as a medal hope in the Montreal Olympic Games in 1976, he was struggling for form throughout that summer. The American Ed Moses – who was to dominate the event for ten years – won the gold medal in 47.64, and Pascoe was eighth in 51.29.

His last major competition success came at the Commonwealth Games in 1978, when he won a bronze medal behind Kimaiyo of Kenya.

He represented Great Britain 50 times between 1967 and 1978, and won a total of 13 AAA indoor and outdoor titles.

During the latter part of his athletics career he became increasingly involved in sports promotion. In 1975 he joined a sponsorship consultancy. His company, Alan Pascoe Associates, has since become the UK's most successful sports sponsorship agency, and in 1985 won the right to market athletics up to 1990.

Peters, Jim

1918–. Born England (GBR)

Although he was no more than a useful performer at 10,000m on the track (finishing ninth at the 1948 Olympic Games in London), Jim Peters became one of the most famous of all marathon runners when persuaded to move up in distance. He set a record four marathon best times and was the first

Marathon ace Jim Peters

man to go under 2:20, recording 2:18:40.2 at the Polytechnic Marathon in London on 13 June 1953, the second of his four world bests.

He set a British record at his first attempt at the distance, the 1951 Polytechnic Marathon, where he beat the evergreen Jack Holden who dropped out with a stitch. Peters finished in 2:29:24. He won the AAA title that year, and the following year set a world best of 2:20:42.2 in the Poly Marathon, which was also the AAA Championship race and the official Olympic trial.

In Helsinki in 1952, however, Peters withdrew at 30km with cramp, but returned the following year to his favourite race, the Poly Marathon, to dip under 2:20 for another world best. His third world best was set abroad in Turku, Finland, and he silenced any critics who may have doubted his ability by finishing in 2:18:34.8.

He followed a second place in the Boston Marathon in April 1954, with a further world best of 2:17:39.4 at the Poly Marathon. Peters looked set for a win at the Empire Games in Vancouver. However, although he entered the stadium with a lead of over 20 minutes in front of the next com-

Mary Peters

petitor, he collapsed in the heat 300m from the finish and went to hospital, where he remained for a week suffering from heat-stroke and dehydration.

Although he was awarded a specially-struck gold medal by the Duke of Edinburgh, he never raced again. He won eight of the 11 marathons he ran, but failed to finish in two out of the three top marathons he entered.

Peters, Mary

1939–. Born Northern Ireland (GBR)

Mary Peters won the heart of a nation with her pentathlon gold medal at the Munich Olympic Games in 1972. After finishing fourth in Tokyo in 1964 and ninth in Mexico four years later, she had dedicated her life to winning a gold medal after 17 years in athletic competition.

She went to Munich as one of the favourites, even though the competition was particularly stiff. She faced Heidi Rosendahl, the European champion, and the world record holder Burglinde Pollack, but Peters herself was in excellent form before the Games. She had not competed at all in 1969 and 1971 in order to train harder for the challenge. In between times she had won the pentathlon title at the Commonwealth Games in 1970, where she also won the shot put and finished fifth in the high hurdles. She was UK record holder for the pentath-

lon, and during the indoor season in 1972 had demonstrated her new-found prowess at the high jump, for which she had adopted the Fosbury Flop technique in preference to the straddle.

The crowd in Munich warmed to Peters from the start of the two days of events. Peters in turn produced the performance of her life, claiming personal bests in four of the five events. In the high jump, especially, she was a revelation, eventually clearing 1.82m, four centimetres above her best and 17 centimetres better than Rosendahl's effort.

When she lined up for the final event, the 200m, Peters needed to finish not more than 1.2 seconds behind Rosendahl or 0.4 seconds behind Pollack to win the gold medal. In a nerve-wracking finale, Peters was adjudged to have won the coveted gold medal by just ten points – the margin of a tenth of a second in that last event.

Peters became a national heroine and her warm, Northern Irish sense of humour made her a television favourite. She continued competing until the Commonwealth Games in 1974, when she retained her pentathlon title and finished fourth in the shot. Bel-

Gordon Pirie (left)

fast now has an athletics stadium named after her.

Pirie, Gordon

1931–. Born England (GBR)

An extremely versatile runner, Gordon Pirie held 22 British records at various times between 1952 and 1961, ranging from 2000m to 10,000m, four of which were world records.

He broke the six-mile British record in the 1951 AAA Championships, recording 29:32.0. However, at the 1952 Helsinki Olympics he finished a disappointing seventh in the 10,000m, coming fourth in the 5000m. Four years later at the Melbourne Olympics he finished one place lower in the 10,000m, and few who saw it will forget his duel with Vladmir Kuts (URS) who put in such devastating bursts of speed that only Pirie was left four laps before the finish, when he too wilted under the pressure. In the 5000m he finished second to Kuts.

Pirie and Kuts had been old rivals ever since the Briton had claimed he would one day run 5000m in under 13:40, although this was almost 20 seconds inside the current world record. Earlier in 1956, before the Olympics, he did just that, breaking Kuts' world record (which the Soviet had in the meantime brought down to 13:46.8 in 1955) with 13:36.8, against Kuts' 13:39.6.

His most successful years were 1953 and 1956. In 1953 he set a six-mile world record of 28:19.4 and ran a leg on the 4 x 1500m relay that produced another world record. At the first Emsley Carr mile in London he beat the top American miler Wes Santee in 4:06.8. In 1956 came his 5000m world record, which he followed by equalling the 3000m world record (7:55.6) then lowering it to 7:52.8, before gaining silver in the Olympic 5000m.

Pirie continued competing as an amateur until 1961, when he broke the British three-mile record for a fifth time. He then turned professional, but was reinstated as an amateur in 1980, before running his first marathon in 2:49.02.

Ponomaryeva, Nina

1919–. Born USSR (URS)

Nina Ponomaryeva (née Romashkova) won the discus at the Olympics in 1952 and 1960, taking the bronze in 1956. Her victory in the 1952 Games in Helsinki was the first ever Soviet gold in the Olympics, and her throw of 51.42m won by a massive margin of 4.34cm.

Ranked number one in the world from 1956–1960, she had set a world record 53.61m in 1952, won the European title in 1954, and had a career best 56.62m in 1955. Although third at the 1956 Games in Melbourne (52.02m), she collected a second gold four years later in Rome, beating compatriot Tamara Press into second place with 55.10m to 52.58m.

Ponomaryeva won nine Soviet discus titles between 1951 and 1959. She competed in her fourth Olympics in 1964 in Tokyo, coming eleventh. Eight years earlier in London she had been the subject of a scandal just prior to the first GB v USSR match in 1956, after being accused of shoplifting hats in C & A Modes in Oxford Street, London. The match was cancelled as a result, although Ponomaryeva never appeared in court.

Press, Irina

1937–. Born USSR (URS)

Younger sister of the great shot and discus champion Tamara Press, Irina was a star in her own right, winning the Olympic 80mh title in Rome in 1960 and the pentathlon gold in Tokyo four years later. Between 1959 and 1964 she set eight pentathlon world records and six at 80mh.

In the hurdles she took the world record from 10.6 in 1960 to 10.3 in 1965, being ranked world number one in 1960, 1961 and 1965. After her victory in the 1960 Olympics, she finished a very close fourth in 1964 (with 10.62 compared to 10.54 for winner

Irina Press

Karin Balzer of East Germany) and went on to set a personal best 10.3 in 1965, her final world record.

In the pentathlon she set the most world records ever – eight – in its various formats. She was the last world record holder in the 1948-1961 sequence. This was as follows: day one – shot, high jump, 200m; day two – 80mh, long jump. That record, set in Leningrad on 16/17 August, was the first score over 5000 points on the 1954 tables then in use (5020 points, 4486 using today's tables). She won the 1964 Olympic title, beating Mary Rand (GBR) with a world record 5246 points, and she finished sixth in the shot competition won by her sister Tamara, recording 16.71m.

She retired before the 1966 Europeans after the introduction of new sex tests.

Press, Tamara

1937–. Born USSR (URS)

Tamara Press was the dominant woman thrower of the early 1960s. She set six world records at the shot and six at the discus, was Olympic shot champion in 1960 and 1964, and discus champion in 1964 (silver medallist in 1960). Along with her sister, Irina (Olympic 80mh champion in

1960 and pentathlon gold medallist in 1964), she dominated these events until both retired when more sophisticated sex-testing was introduced in 1965.

Tamara Press first came to prominence in 1958, winning the shot and coming third in the European Championships in Stockholm. She set her first shot world record (17.25m) the following year, and had improved this to 18.59m by 1965. She became the first woman past the 60-foot barrier on 10 June 1962 in Leipzig, putting a massive 18.55m (60ft 10½ in), a 77cm improvement over the previous record. She was ranked number one in the world at shot from 1959-1966, except in 1961 when she was ranked second. Her two Olympic victories were both Olympic records – 17.43m in 1960 and 18.14m in 1964.

At discus she took the world best mark from 57.15m in 1960 to 59.70m in 1965, and won a discus and shot double at the 1962 European championships in Belgrade. She was ranked number one in the world at discus in 1961, 1962 and 1964, the year in which she produced eight of the ten longest shot puts ever and three of the top six discus throws.

Tamara Press won seven Soviet discus titles and nine at shot between 1958 and 1966.

Prinstein, Myer

1878–1928. Born USA (USA)

At the Olympic Games of 1904, in St Louis, Myer Prinstein became the first and only man to win the long jump and triple jump titles on the same day. He was the defending triple jump champion, and had won the silver in the long jump in 1900 in Paris and the gold in the long jump at the unofficial Games in 1906 in Athens. He was also a talented sprinter, finishing fifth in the 400m and the 60m in the 1904 Games.

In 1900 Prinstein was severely disadvantaged by a bizarre incident that led to his compatriot Alvin Kraenzlein winning the long jump gold. The finals of some of the field events were due to be held on a Sunday, but most of the American college authorities objected and refused to allow their athletes to take part. However, Kraenzlein, a student at the University of Pennsylvania, was one of five athletes who decided to go against the ruling. In the final he managed 7.185m, bettering the mark set by Prinstein (7.175m) in the qualifying round, a jump that still won Prinstein the silver as marks set in the qualifying rounds were carried forward into the final. However, Prinstein had the satisfaction of breaking Kraenzlein's 1900 Olympic record four years later at the Games in St Louis, with 7.34m.

He was the first man to jump 7.50m, a feat he achieved on 28 April 1900 in Philadelphia.

On the same day he hopped, stepped and jumped (now triple jumped) 14.35m to become the only athlete to achieve this double.

Puica, Maricica

1950–. Born Romania (ROM)

There seems to be no limit to the ambitions and aspirations of Maricica Puica. At the World Championships in 1987, at the age of 36, she was still battling it out, challenging the eventual winner Tatyana Samolenko in the final straight of the 3000m.

Her finest moment came in 1984, when she won the Olympic title at 3000m. She had gone to Los Angeles as one of the favourites for the gold medal, and yet her victory was almost overshadowed by the controversy surrounding the collision on the fifth lap between the American Mary Decker and Zola Budd of Great Britain. While Decker fell to the infield, injured and out of the race, and Budd ran out of steam and motivation, Puica tracked Britain's Wendy Sly for the remainder of the race until the last 300m, when she sprinted away to a well-deserved win.

Strong, experienced and able to produce a devastating finish, Puica proceeded to the 1500m final, but was

Maricica Puica

unable to counter Italian Gabriella Dorio's burst of speed over the last 80m. She did, however, pass three women in the last 50m to finish third behind team mate Doina Melinte.

Puica ran in her first Olympics, in Montreal in 1976, at the age of 26, but was eliminated in the heats of the 1500m. In 1978 she was fourth in the European Championships 3000m. Four years later she was second at 3000m and fourth at 1500m. In 1980, in Moscow, she finished seventh in the final. Since then she has come close to many titles, but has ended up with a host of silver medals and near misses. In 1986, after two hectic years in which she raced all over the world, indoors and out, she lacked the necessary finishing speed to prevent Olga Bondarenko of the Soviet Union from sprinting to a two-second margin of victory in the European Championship 3000m. She was fifth at 1500m.

A year later she was in Rome for the World Championships, and led the chase for the line with 200m to go. However, Samolenko, ten years her

junior, was too quick over the home straight and ran in a clear winner, 8:38.73 to Puica's 8:39.45.

Puica has set two world records: at the mile (4:17.44) in 1982 and at 2000m (5:28.69) in 1986. She also has a fine record at the World Cross-Country Championships. She was third in 1978, and first in 1982 and 1984, the year of her Olympic triumph.

Puttemans, Emiel

1947–. Born Belguim (BEL)

Although Lasse Viren of Finland is remembered for his remarkable record in the Olympic Games of 1972 and 1976, there is one man who enjoyed his best running in setting world records and beating the best in the world in the intervening four years. His name is Emiel Puttemans.

Puttemans went into the 1972 Olympic 10,000m final in Munich as a strong contender for a medal, even though he and Britain's David Bedford, the European record holder, had shown unnecessary haste in their semifinal, won by the Belgian in a Games and Belgian national record of 27:53.4 In the final, Puttemans stayed with Viren until the last 100m, by which time he was unable to match the Finn's finishing sprint and ended up with the silver medal in a time of 27:39.4. Viren's winning time was 27:38.4. Three days later Puttemans won his 5000m heat in 13:31.8, an Olympic record, but was lost for speed in the final, finishing fifth as Viren took his second gold medal.

Puttemans' best distance appeared to be between 3000m and 5000m, as he showed immediately after the Games. He had already set a world record for two miles of 8:17.8 in 1971, and in Aarhus, Demark on 14 September 1972 he lowered Kip Keino's world 3000m mark by two seconds to clock 7:37.6. Three days later he beat Viren in another 3000m race in Malmö, Sweden, and on 20 September 1972 he bettered the Finn's 5000m world record with 13:13.0, eclipsing Ron Clarke's six-year-old three-mile record en route. It was the last IAAF recognized world record for the three-mile distance.

Indoors, Puttemans was dominant during the winter of 1972/3. He set a new European 3000m record of 7:47 in Holland, and followed it a week later with a sensational performance over two miles in West Berlin. Aiming for the world best of 8:19.8, he set off with an opening 400m of 58 seconds, bettered Michel Jazy's 2000m world best with 4:03.2 on the way, and finished in 8:13.2, 0.8 seconds inside Viren's outdoor world record. His time at 3000m was 7:39.2, which has yet to be bettered. The following month he won the European Indoor Championship 3000m title in Rotterdam with 7:44.6.

In the summer of 1973 he ran three of the world's four sub-13:20 times for 5000m, the fastest of which was a 13:14.6 in Stockholm in August.

During the year he dominated the event, beating all the world's top distance runners. The highlight of the ensuing winter season came when he retained his European indoor title in Gothenborg.

A blood disorder upset Puttemans' racing during that summer. Although he never recovered his best form, he showed a return to something like his old speed in 1975, when he set world indoor bests for 10,000m and six miles. In 1976 he reduced his best times indoors for 5000m and three miles to 13:20.8 and 12:54.6 respectively. However, at the 1976 Olympics in Montreal he dropped out of the 10,000m final after 7000m. He also pulled out of his 5000m heat a few days later. At the 1980 Games in Moscow he failed to qualify for the 5000m final after finishing eighth in his semi-final. It was his fourth Olympic Games.

Emiel Puttemans (leading)

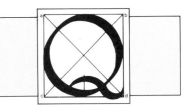

Quarrie, Don

1951–. Born Jamaica (JAM)

One of the great sprinters of all time, Don Quarrie maintained the highest of standards for 16 years. He reached his peak in 1976 at the Montreal Olympic Games. After missing out on medals at the Games of 1968 and 1972 because of injury, he finally won an Olympic title in the 200m. Leading from the gun after the best of starts, he ran a perfect bend to ease home in 20.23, ahead of Millard Hampton and Dwayne Evans of the USA.

Quarrie's gold medal trail started in 1970, when he won gold medals for 100m, 200m and 4 x 100m at the Commonwealth Games in Edinburgh. In 1971 he won gold medals in the same events at the Pan American Games, where he ran the second fastest electronically-timed 200m of all time: 19.86. His record in subsequent Commonwealth Games has been exceptional. He retained his titles in 1974 and won the 100m in 1978, when he beat the fast improving Allan Wells, destined to become Olympic champion in 1980.

Quarrie was unfortunate in his first two Olympic Games. Due to make his début as a 17-year-old with a season's best 100m time of 10.03 in Mexico in 1968, he never made the start because of injury. Four years later he was seen as one of the few men to challenge Valeriy Borzov at 200m but, once again, his chances were wrecked by injury. He pulled a muscle coming off the bend in his semi-final and was carried off the track on a stretcher.

Quarrie had a great Games in Montreal in 1976. He cruised through his 100m heat in 10.38, and was runner-up in his semi-final to Hasely

Crawford of Trinidad. The final went to Crawford, but a fast-finishing Quarrie grabbed the silver medal with 10.08. His Olympic 200m title went to Italian Pietro Mennea in 1980, as Quarrie finished third behind Alan Wells.

The Jamaican was back in 1984 for the Games in Los Angeles where he had by then made his home. He was eliminated in the heats of the 200m but added to his medal tally with a silver in the 4 x 100m. He retired after the Olympics.

In his career he set four world records: at 100m, with 9.9 seconds in 1976, and three times at 200m, with 19.8 in 1971 and the same time twice in 1975.

Don Quarrie (leading)

Rabsztyn, Grazyna

1952–. Born Poland(POL)

Grazyna Rabsztyn's world record of 12.36 seconds for the 100mh set in June 1980 lasted six years until it was broken by Yordanka Donkova of Bulgaria. Rabsztyn herself had improved the record once before, taking it to 12.48 in 1978. But despite her fast times, she seemed unable to compete well at major championships. Indoors she ran well over 50mh and 60mh, winning a handful of gold medals at European Championships, but outdoors, after becoming European Junior champion in 1970, she had a poor record in important races.

She was certainly not at her best in three Olympic Games. In 1972 she was eighth in the final, in 1976, fifth, and in 1980, when she was a clear favourite for the title, she finished fifth again behind Vera Komisova of the Soviet Union. She was eighth at the 1974 European Championships. In 1978 at the European Championships she was disqualified. She set a championship best of 12.60 in the semi-final but in the final she hit the last hurdle, strayed into the adjoining lane and collided with Nina Morgulina of the Soviet Union. The race was re-run without her.

In spite of this, Rabsztyn was still regarded as the world's leading high hurdler and emphasized her clear superiority in the World Cup competitions in 1977 and 1979. In Düsseldorf she beat the Olympic champion Johanna Klier (née Schaller) of East Germany, while in Montreal she came from behind to win in a dip finish from Tatyana Anismova of the Soviet Union, the Olympic silver medallist.

She won the European indoor title over 60mh in 1974, 1975 and 1976,

Mary Rand

won the silver in 1978, 1979 and 1980 and won a bronze medal at 50mh in 1972.

Rand, Mary

1940–. Born England (GBR)

One of Britain's best multi-event athletes, Mary Rand won the Olympic long jump title in 1964 with a world record 6.76m, finished second in the pentathlon, and won the bronze medal in the 4 x 100m relay. She won a Commonwealth long jump silver medal in 1958 and took the title in 1966, and in the 1962 European Championships long jump she took a bronze.

As Mary Bignal she was a favourite for the 1960 Olympic long jump title, especially after leading the qualifying rounds with 6.33m. But with only 6.00m in the final she finished no higher than ninth. However, she finished a good fourth in the 80mh, and still ended the year ranked number one in the world at long jump.

As Mary Rand, back in competition after childbirth in 1962, she took bronze in the long jump in the 1962 European Championships. She was ranked number one in the long jump again in 1963, as well as second in the pentathlon. She became the first woman to jump 22 feet (6.70m/22ft wind assisted) in Portsmouth on 26 September 1964, and kept this form in the Tokyo Olympics. She leapt an Olympic record 6.52m in the qualifying rounds and following this with an astonishing series of 6.59m, 6.56m, 6.57m, 6.63m, 6.76m (world record), 6.61m. Poland's Irena Szewinska took the silver with 6.60m. In the pentathlon Rand finished behind Irina Press (URS), who won with a world record 5246 points to Rand's 5035 (second on the all-time list). She continued competing after Tokyo, but injuries prevented her from making the 1968 Olympic team. In Mexico, as a broadcaster, she met and, in 1969, married decathlon champion Bill Toomey.

In all Mary Rand set 19 British records (11 at long jump, six at pentathlon, two at 80mh) and won ten outdoor WAAA titles (five long jump, two pentathlon, one each at 80mh, 100mh, high jump), and three indoors, all in 1966 (60 yard hurdles, high jump and long jump). Her best marks included: 100 yards - 10.6; 100m - 11.7; 200m - 23.9; 80mh - 10.8; 100mh - 13.4; high jump - 1.72m; long jump 6.76m; shot - 12.25m; pentathlon - 5035 points.

Rhoden, George

1926–. Born Jamaica (JAM)

A surprise winner of the 1952 Olympic 400m title, George Rhoden beat the overwhelming favourite Herb McKenley (JAM). The two men then teamed up with fellow Jamaicans Arthur Wint and Leslie Lang to win the 4 x 400m relay in a world record 3:03.9. Rhoden held the 400m world record in 1950, and won a record ten medals between 1946 and 1954 at the Central American and Caribbean Games (four golds: 4 x 400m relay, 1946/1954; 800m, 1950; 4 x 100m relay, 1954; four silvers: 400m, 1950/ 1954; 4 x 100m relay, 1950; 800m, 1954; two bronze: 400m, 1946; 4 x 400m relay, 1950).

In the Olympic 400m final in Helsinki, favourite McKenley started uncharacteristically slowly but Rhoden stormed into the lead from the gun with Arthur Wint (winner ahead of McKenley in 1948) in pursuit. Wint faded to fifth in the home straight as McKenley steamed through the last 30m, but Rhoden won by a metre despite the first two being given the same time, 45.9. (Automatic timing gave Rhoden 46.09 to McKenley's 46.20.)

Again in Helsinki, in the 4 x 400m final, the Jamaican team won the gold ahead of the USA, and after a superb relay leg by McKenley, Rhoden had a yard lead over Mal Whitfield (USA) at the start of the anchor leg, a lead he kept right to the finish with a 45.5-second lap.

His 400m world record of 45.8 was set two years before his Olympic victory, on 22 August 1950 in an international match at Eskilstuna, Sweden. It stood for nearly five years until broken at altitude in Mexico City by Louis W. Jones (USA) on 18 March 1955.

Richards, Bob

1926–. Born USA (USA)

The only man to have won three medals at the Olympic pole vault, Bob Richards won gold in 1952 and 1956 and came third in 1948. Although he never held a world record he was the second man over 15 feet, 11 years after Cornelius Warmerdam (USA), with 4.59m/15ft 1in indoors in New York on 27 January 1951.

Winner of AAU titles (1948-1952, 1954-1957) with a further eight indoor titles (1948, 1950-1953, 1955-1957), Richards won straight competitions between 1950-1952, and was unbeaten outdoors between 1953-1955. At his first Olympics in London in 1948 he took the bronze with 4.20m, but improved this to take gold in Helsinki (4.55m) and Melbourne (4.56m). By the end of his career he had cleared 15 feet (4.57m) 126 times, but never surpassed Warmerdam's best of 4.77m. His bests were 4.70m outdoors and 4.72m indoors.

Ranked world number one at pole vault for eight years, 1949 - 1956, he also held the number one ranking twice for decathlon (1951 and 1954) and won the American championships three times at that event.

Richter, Annegret

1950–. Born West Germany (FRG)

Running the third leg for the West German 4 x 100m relay team, Annegret Irrgang, as she then was, won her first gold medal at the 1971 European Championships in Helsinki. Her first Olympic gold came in the Games a year later when she joined Christiane Krause, Ingrid Mickler and Heide Rosendahl in running a world record 42.8 seconds to equal the 4 x 100m world record and win from East Germany and Cuba. She had earlier finished fifth in the 100m in 11.4 seconds behind Renate Stecher of East Germany, the world's number one sprinter.

After another fifth place in the 100m at the 1974 European Champi-

Annegret Richter (181)

onships in Rome, Richter hit her best form in 1976. In Montreal, she broke the Olympic 100m record with 11.05 in the second round and shattered the world record in the semi-final with 11.01. It took three hundredths of a second off the record set by team mate Inge Helten just over a month before. Second behind Richter in that world record run was America's Evelyn Ashford, who would become Olympic champion eight years later. In the final Richter, Stecher and Helten seemingly crossed the line together but the decision went to Richter in 11.08.

A lifetime best of 22.39 seconds was only enough for the silver medal at 200m as Richter was left a stride behind East Germany's Barbel Eckert at the line. There was another silver medal, this time in the 4 x 100m relay when the West Germans finished second to their East German rivals.

Fourth in the 100m final in Montreal was a certain Marlies Oelsner, later to become Marlies Göhr, of East Germany. Within a year she had taken Richter's world record on her way to becoming one of the all-time great women sprinters.

Ritchie, Don

1944–. Born Scotland (GBR)

Four years after his first marathon, Don Ritchie tackled his first ultra distance race in 1970. The same year he won the London to Brighton road race – a distance of just over 50 miles – but it was not until 1977 that he made a major impression on the ultra running scene.

After breaking the world best for 50km, he won the 1977 London to Brighton race and then set world marks for 150km and 100 miles. In 1978 he travelled to Hartola, Finland to set a new world best for 100km of six hours 18 minutes. He won yet another London to Brighton before setting his greatest record, running 100km in 6:10:20 and breaking the 50-mile world best en route.

In 1979 he set a new 100-mile road best but then injury began to disrupt

his career and it was not until 1982 that he began to regain some of his old form. First came a world 100km certified world best. Three weeks later he broke the world best for 40 miles on the track and in the spring of 1983, in Hendon in north London, he improved his 50-mile track record with 4:51:49. Later the same year he set his ninth world track best, this time at 200km.

Since then his best performance has been at the inaugural World 100km Championship in Belgium in 1987. He finished second in 6:40:51 behind Domingo Catalan of Spain.

Ritola, Ville

1896–1982. Born Finland (FIN)

Ville Ritola, an American-based Finn, never quite equalled the achievements of his arch-rival Paavo Nurmi. He won eight Olympic medals at the 1924 and 1928 Games, and gathered the most medals at any one Games – six in 1924. He won gold for the 3000m steeplechase, 10,000m cross-country team and 3000m team, with silvers at

Ville Ritola

5000m, second to Nurmi, and individual cross-country, second again to Nurmi. He finally beat the most famous 'Flying Finn' over 5000m at the 1928 Amsterdam Games, but finished second to him in the 10,000m, the fourth time he had done so in an Olympic final.

Ritola was the first man to go below 14 minutes for three miles, recording 13:56.2 indoors in New York on 24 February 1925. He also set records at 5000m (14.23.2 indoors to better Nurmi's official outdoor record) and two at 10,000m – 30:35.4 on 25 May 1924 in Helsinki and 30:32.2 in Paris on 6 July the same year.

His time in the 10,000m 1924 Olympic final was Ritola's second world record. Nurmi had not been entered for the race by the Finnish athletics federation, but he reportedly bettered Ritola's time on the same day, running 29.45.0 on the practice track. In 1928 Nurmi won 30:18.8 to 30:19.4, but in Amsterdam Ritola avenged his defeat at 5000m four years earlier (14:31.2 to 14:31.4) to record his first victory over Nurmi 14:38.0 to 14:41.0.

Rodgers, Bill

1947–. Born USA (USA)

The name of Bill Rodgers has been at the forefront of the running boom in the USA, where he still makes regular appearances in all the top races. At his best – during the years from 1975-80 – he was one of the world's most consistent marathon runners who was unfortunate to reach his racing peak in non-Olympic years.

He was 27 when he finished third in the International (now World) Cross-Country Championships in 1975. Although he vowed at the time never to run again, he went on to carve out a marathon career. He won the Boston Marathon (1975, 1978, 1979 and 1980) and the New York Marathon (1976-1979) four times, and in the season 1977/78 was the only man to have won those two top US marathons and the Fukuoka Marathon, in Japan, in succession.

At his only Olympic Games in 1976 he was unlucky to have incurred a foot injury while in training for the marathon. After staying with the leaders for the first half of the race, he faded to finish fourtieth. His American team mate and rival Frank Shorter, the defending champion who had beaten Rodgers in the US trial, was second behind East German Waldemar Cierpinski.

Rodgers was ranked number one in the world in 1977 after winning five of his six marathons and dropping out of the Boston race. Up to 1981, he had won 21 of his 33 marathons and he continued running in races around the world. As Americans in their thousands took up running and the number of races spiralled, Rodgers became a major draw, talking at running clinics, giving lectures and marketing his own brand of sportswear. Since turning 40 in 1987, Rodgers has set his sights on attacking veteran, or masters in the USA, records.

Roelants, Gaston

1937–. Born Belgium (BEL)

One of the best-ever steeplechasers, Gaston Roelants dominated the event in the early 1960s when he also proved himself an accomplished racer at a number of distances and over a variety of terrains.

At the steeplechase, Roelants was fourth at the 1960 Olympic Games in Rome and in 1961 began a winning sequence of 45 steeplechase finals which lasted until September 1966, when he was third at the European Championships. He became the first man to run the event inside 8:30 on 7 September 1963, when he clocked 8:29:6 at Leuven in Belgium. European champion in 1962, he further showed his superiority in 1964 when he became Olympic champion in Tokyo, winning the title in 8:30.8 from Britain's Maurice Herriot and the Soviet Union's Ivan Belyayev. He was the bronze medallist at the 1966 European Championships, when he also finished eighth in the 10,000m in

Gaston Roelants

28:59.6. At the 1968 Olympics in Mexico, he was seventh.

By 1968 he had switched to running primarily longer distances and the marathon. In 1972 he set a world record for 20km (57:44.4) while setting another for one hour (20,784m). After finishing fifth in the 10,000m at the 1969 European Championships, he went on to win a silver medal behind his great rival, Britain's Ron Hill, in the marathon, with 2:17:22. He won another medal, a bronze, in 1971, when he clocked his best-ever time of 2:16:30.

He was particularly strong in cross-country races, finishing seven times in the first three of the International Championship. He was champion on four occasions and won his last title in 1972, when he lost a shoe in the mud, made up 50 seconds on the leaders and beat Mariano Haro of Spain by 100m.

Roelants continued running well into his forties, winning five world titles in his first year as a veteran.

Rono, Henry

1952–. Born Kenya (KEN)

The only man to hold world records at 3000m flat, 3000m steeplechase, 5000m and 10,000m, Henry Rono might be described as the nearest thing to a running 'natural'. His four world records, all in 1978, were set in a spirit of adventure rather than with the help of pacemakers because, to a large extent, Rono's running depended on his moods.

Rono was born at altitude in the same area of Kenya as his hero Kip Keino, the double Olympic champion of 1968 and 1972. He took up running at the advanced age of 22 and came to prominence by qualifying as a 3000m steeplechaser in the Kenyan team for the 1976 Olympic Games in Montreal. He missed his chance to compete, however, when Kenya pulled out of the Games as part of the African boycott over the New Zealand rugby tour of South Africa. His potential was spotted, however, by coaches at Washington State University in the

Henry Rono (38)

USA and he was consequently offered a scholarship.

Rono's record-breaking year of 1978 began with a 10,000m victory in New Zealand followed by a half-marathon win in Puerto Rico, where he beat American marathoner Bill Rodgers in 1:04:46. Two good 5000m wins preceded the first of the world records on 8 April in Berkeley, California. In the previous 11 years the time for 5000m had only been reduced by 3.7 seconds. In clipping 4.5 seconds off New Zealander Dick Quax's record, Rono finished 300m ahead of the field in 13:08.4. By May he had added the steeplechase record, set in Seattle. His time of 8:05.4 took 2.5 seconds off the record set by Sweden's Anders Garderud at the Montreal Olympics.

Record number three was the 10,000m, taken from fellow Kenyan Samson Kimobwa. Taking a record 8.2 seconds off Kimobwa's mark, Rono ran 27:22.4, covering the first half of the race in 13:48.2 and the second 5000m in 13:34.2, a time that would have been a world record for the distance only 13 years before!

Two weeks later, in Oslo, Rono claimed his fourth world record. He took 3.1 seconds off Brendan Foster's 3000m best to clock 7:32.1 – a record that still stands. Once again he ran negative splits (i.e. the second half was run quicker than the first) and the final mile was run in under four minutes.

To crown his golden year, he won the steeplechase and 5000m double at the African Games and the Commonwealth Games in Edmonton. Until he was beaten by Steve Ovett, the European 1500m champion, over two miles on 15 September, Rono was unbeaten in 31 outdoor races during the year.

The following year, the pressure to study became more immediate and Rono devoted less time to his running. He put on weight and never matched his times of 1978. He missed the Olympic Games of 1980 when Kenya joined the Western boycott over the USSR's invasion of Afghanistan.

Graduation in 1981 plus the prom-

ise of the World Cup competition in Rome provided the motivation he needed to train again. But politics once more kept him away from a major occasion. He withdrew from the African team in disgust when the Ethiopian Kedir was selected in place of him to run the 10,000m, while Rono was picked for the 5000m. Kedir won a silver medal in Rome while Rono ran three races in five days, culminating in his world record-shattering 13:06.20 for 5000m in Knarvik, Norway. He ended the season with five of the ten fastest times in history over 5000m.

1982 found Rono disillusioned with athletics, running poorly and with a variety of financial problems. He retired to his farm in Kenya where he proceeded to drink heavily and to run further into debt. He went back to America in 1986 intent on a comeback and, after months of training interspersed with bouts of drinking, he managed a fine 2:19:12 in the Chicago Marathon. He also ran the New York Marathon a month later, taking more than four hours to finish after stopping at 20 miles for a meal and to watch live coverage of the race on television.

Rose, Ralph

1885–1913. Born USA (USA)

One of the great multi-event throwers at the beginning of the century, Ralph Rose won Olympic titles at the shot put in 1904 and 1908, won the two-handed shot title in 1912, silver medals at discus in 1904 and shot in 1912, and bronze at the hammer in 1904.

A giant of a man for those days, standing 1.83m (6ft 6in) tall and weighing 105kg (235lb) Rose was the first man to put the shot over 50 feet, recording 15.39m (50ft 6in) in Seattle on 14 August 1909, then 15.45m (51ft 3.4in) in San Francisco on 21 August of that year, the first official IAAF record. In fact, two months before in a non-sanctioned event in Healdsbury, northern California, he had putted 54ft 4in, but even his shorter ratified world

Heide Rosendahl

record was unbeaten for 19 years.

At St Louis in 1904 Rose won with a then-world-record 14.81m, retaining his title in London with 14.21. In all he beat the world record five times and set an unofficial hammer world record in 1909 of 54.38m.

Rosendahl, Heide

1947–. Born West Germany (FRG)

A brilliant all-rounder, Heide Rosendahl went to the 1972 Olympic Games in Munich as European pentathlon champion, long jump world record holder and as a firm favourite of the West German crowds. She emerged from the Games with two gold medals, from the long jump and 4 x 100m relay, and a silver from her epic duel with Britain's Mary Peters in the pentathlon.

She was hotly tipped to win her first Olympic medal four years earlier, when she went to the Mexico Games as the pentathlon silver medallist at the 1966 European Champ onships, where she had also won the long jump title. But illness wrecked her long jumping in Mexico – she finished eighth – and after pulling a muscle during her warm-up, she was forced to withdraw from the pentathlon.

She missed the 1969 European Championships when West Germany withdrew its team in protest over the IAAF's insistence that Jürgen May, the West German indoor 1500m champion, was ineligible to compete because he had not fulfilled residency qualifications since defecting from East Germany. The following year, however, Rosendahl claimed the world long jump record with 6.84m in Turin, and in 1971 she won her first pentathlon gold medal when she beat her East German rival Burglinde Pollak at the European Championships in Helsinki. She was also third in the long jump.

By 1972 the scene was set for a showdown between Rosendahl, the European champion, the world record holder Pollak and the Commonwealth champion, Peters. The battle for the gold medal lasted until the final event, the 200m, won by Rosendahl but without the necessary margin of victory to deprive Peters of the gold medal and the world record points score. Rosendahl took the silver, Pollak the bronze.

Rosendahl had already won the long jump competition – by a centimetre from Diana Yorgova – after a first round leap of 6.78m. She completed her medal haul by running a superb anchor leg as West Germany won the 4 x 100m relay in a world record-equalling time of 42.8 seconds. The record had been set by the Americans at the 1968 Olympics at altitude in Mexico City.

Her personal bests are: 11.3 (100m), 22.96 (200m), 13.1 (100mh), 1.70m (high jump), 6.84m (long jump), 14.27m (shot), and 48.18m (javelin).

Rudolph, Wilma

1940–. Born USA (USA)

The outstanding athlete of the 1960 Olympic Games in Rome, Wilma Rudolph won the 100m/200m sprint double and anchored the 4 x 100m relay team to victory when she was barely 20 years old. Born with polio, the 20th of 22 children, Rudolph joked that she learnt to run fast in order to get to the table first. In fact she was unable to walk without a leg brace until she was ten years old.

Incredibly, just six years later, she brought home her first Olympic medal – a bronze for the 4 x 100m relay at the 1956 Melbourne Games. Although picked for the individual 200m and recording a US record of 24.6 seconds, she was eliminated in the heats. During 1957 she won the national Junior 75-yard and 100-yard titles, missing the 1958 season to give birth.

A student at Tennessee State and a member of the famous 'Tigerbelles' track club, Rudolph won the AAU 100m title in 1959 and came third in the 200m, before taking silver in the 100m at the Pan American Games in Chicago and picking up a 4 x 100m relay gold. In Olympic year 1960 she won the AAU 100m title and in the 200m became the first woman under 23 seconds, winning in 22.9 seconds. She also won both sprints at the US Olympic trials.

In spite of twisting an ankle just before her heats in Rome she equalled the 100m world record in the semifinal (11.3) and won the final by 0.3 seconds from Dorothy Hyman (GBR) and Giuseppina Leone (ITA) in a world record 11.0 seconds that was ruled wind-assisted. Her winning time in the 200m was even greater, 0.4 seconds, as she clocked 24.0 ahead of Jutta Heine (FRG) and Dorothy Hyman (GBR). The American relay team, having set a new world record 44.4 in the heats, won the final comfortably in 44.5.

In 1961 Rudolph won the AAU 100-yard title in 10.8 seconds, equalled her own 100m record in the USA-USSR match in Moscow and helped lower the 4 x 100m record to 44.3. Finally, in Stuttgart, she took sole possession of the 100m world record with 11.2, a time that was not beaten for four years.

Ryan, Pam

1939–. Born Australia (AUS)

Dominant in the women's 80mh event during the 1960s, Pam Ryan (née Kilborn) won three Commonwealth gold medals, set two world records and won Olympic silver and bronze medals in three appearances in finals. She also set four world records over 200mh, including the last of 25.7 seconds in 1971, and won Commonwealth Games gold medals in the long jump and the 4 x 100m relay.

Her first Commonwealth Games gold medals came in Perth in 1962, when she won the 80mh and the long jump. These were followed by hurdles and sprint relay gold medals in Kingston, and in Edinburgh four years later in 1966.

In the Olympic Games, however, she was unlucky not to win gold medals. In 1964 she won a bronze medal in the 80mh after a photo-finish. The gold on that occasion went to Karin Balzer of East Germany in 10.54, silver to Tereza Ciepla of Poland in 10.55, while Ryan was clocked at 10.56. Four years later, at the age of 29, she lost out to fellow Australian Maureen Caird, 12 years her junior, who ran the fastest 80mh ever, automatically timed. Her 10.3 was an Olympic and Commonwealth record. Ryan was second with 10.4. It was a major disappointment for Ryan, who had remained unbeaten since her third place in Tokyo.

In 1972 in Munich, she had no answer to the new champion Annelie Ehrhardt of East Germany, who took the new 100mh title in 12.6. The only Westerner in the final, Ryan was fourth in 13.0.

Ranked number one in the world in 1963, 1966 and 1967, Ryan set two world records at 80mh, lowering it from 10.5 to 10.4, and in 1972 clocked her fastest ever 100mh time of 12.5, a record she shared with Ehrhardt for just a year. In Australia she won a record 17 national titles between 1963 and 1972, in the 80mh, long jump, pentathlon, 100mh, 100 yards and 200mh.

Ryun, Jim

1947–. Born USA (USA)

One of the greatest middle-distance runners never to have won a major championship, Ryun was unbeaten in 47 1500m or mile races between 1965 and 1968, the winning streak ending with his second place in the 1968 Olympic 1500m final when he finished behind a rampant Kip Keino.

With world age bests at 16 at both 1500m and the mile Ryun seemed destined for greatness, even when a cold forced him out of the 1964 Olympics in Tokyo without qualifying for the final. He won the 1965 AAU mile championships, beating Olympic champion Peter Snell (NZL) into second place, and the following year missed the world record by $^1/_{10}$ second, clocking 3:53.7 at the Compton Invitational on 4 June. The next week saw him take Snell's world 880-yard record to 1:44.9 and his 1966 season finished with a new world record mile

Jim Ryun (300)

of 3:51.3 at Berkeley, California when aged just 19 years and two months. His sensational year ended with him having run two of the three fastest miles ever, two of the three fastest half miles, and one of the three fastest 1500m.

His successes continued in 1967 with the second-fastest mile, 3:53.2 in Los Angeles on 2 June, and a new world record 3.51.1 set at the AAU final on 23 June. But his most impressive performance came against a team from the British Commonwealth on 8 July, when his 3:33.1 over 1500m not only shattered Herb Elliott's 1960 record of 3:35.6 but also destroyed rival Kip Keino (KEN) who finished a distant second in 3:37.2.

A series of leg injuries caused problems leading to the 1968 Mexico Olympics, but living at altitude in Flagstaff, Arizona, Ryun did enough to win the 1500m US Olympic trial. However, expecting that 3:39 would be enough to win in Mexico, Ryun was devastated by Keino who ran a third lap in 58.1 and then surged ahead, with Ryun six seconds adrift with 300m to go. Ryun's own sprint salvaged the silver in 3:37.89.

1969 saw some good results. He had a win at the Coliseum-Compton mile on 7 June in 3:55.9, for example. But injuries and race staleness took their toll and he withdrew until the 1971 season, when he fought with rising star Marty Liquori to be the USA's number one. A recurring health problem following glandular fever made him ever less consistent, although still capable of good results. For example, he had a good mile win over Keino in January 1972, a victory in the US 1500m Olympic trial, and then a 3:52.8 mile, the third fastest of all time.

In the heats of the Olympic 1500m in Munich he spectacularly fell when trying to overtake some back markers. When he recovered to sprint home, his Olympic chances were gone.

After these Games, his mysterious illness still present, he turned professional, but never ran faster than a 3:59.8 indoor mile.

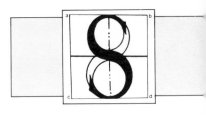

Salazar, Alberto

1958–. Born Cuba (USA)

Alberto Salazar scored a spectacular marathon début in 1980, when he won in New York in 2:09:41. For the next two years he was the most celebrated marathon runner in the world, winning his following three races and clocking what was thought to be a world best in New York in 1981. Unfortunately, his 2:08:13 could not be counted as the course was remeasured in 1984 and found to be 150m short.

Salazar moved to the USA with his parents when he was two. At 19 he was US junior champion over 5000m and 10,000m. He also showed talent at cross-country running, winning the AAU and NCAA titles in 1980. The following summer he finished third in the World Cup 10,000m behind the East German Werner Schildhauer. He enjoyed his best year in 1982, when he won the Boston Marathon with a course record of 2:08:51, set US records at 5000m (13:11.93) and 10,000m (27:25:61), and won his third New York Marathon in 2:09:29. The same year he was also runner-up to Mohamed Kedir of Ethiopia in the World Cross-Country Championship in Rome.

In Rotterdam, in 1983, he faced one of the best fields ever assembled. It included Commonwealth champion Rob de Castella of Australia and Carlos Lopes of Portugal. Salazar finished fifth in 2:10:08. In that year's Fukuoka Marathon in Japan, he also came home in fifth place in 2:09:21. In the following year's Olympic Marathon in Los Angeles, however, he was considered one of the favourites, along with the Japanese runner Toshihiko Seko (the winner of his previous five

Iberto Salazar (1)

marathons, including the 1983 Fukuoka). However, in the heat and humidity of LA, and faced with the fast pace of Britain's Charlie Speding, Salazar finished a disappointing fifteenth, one place behind Seko, as Lopes took the title in an Olympic record of 2:09:21. Salazar's time was 2:14:19.

It was his last major outing, and the American has puzzled many by his inability to run well since. He has suffered a succession of injuries and has attempted several come-backs without success.

Salminen, Ilmari

1902–. Born Finland (FIN)

One of the generation of 'Flying Finns' to succeed the great Paavo Nurmi, Ilmari Salminen won the 10,000m at the Berlin Olympics of 1936. In addition, he won the European title twice at that distance, in 1934 and 1938, and was the man who finally broke Nurmi's 10,000m record 13 years after it had been set.

At the 1934 European Championships Salminen beat his compatriot Arvo Askola with 31:02.6 to 31:03.2 to take the gold. Two years later in the Olympic final in Berlin they had another thrilling duel. At the start of the final lap Salminen broke away, only to be overtaken by Askola in the back straight. Salminen caught him with about 100m to go and the two fought neck and neck, with only a yard between them at the finish. Salminen clocked 30:15.4, Askola 30:15.6, with Volmari Iso-Hollo (FIN), the double gold-medallist steeple chaser, in third place (30:20.2). In the 5000m final, Salminen fell at the start of the last lap, in a race won by Gunnar Hockert (FIN).

The following year, in the Finnish national championships at Kouvola on 18 July, Salminen beat Lauri Lehtinen over 10,000m with Askola third, setting a world record 30:05.6 to take more than half a second off Nurmi's 1924 mark of 30:06.2. Salminen's time at six miles - 29:08.4 - was also a world record.

In the 1938 European Championships he retained his title, beating Italy's Giuseppe Beviacqua 30:52.4 to 30:53.2.

Samolenko, Tatyana

1961–. Born USSR (URS)

A strong runner with an explosive finish, Tatyana Samolenko enjoyed a tremendous season in 1987. She won the Soviet indoor titles at 800m and 1500m, before travelling to Indianapolis to win gold at 1500m and silver at 800m at the first World Indoor Championships in March. In June she won the European Cup title at 800m, in a dip finish over Czechoslovakia's Jarmila Kratochvilova, and finished second to Britain's Kirsty Wade the following day at 1500m.

Samolenko went on to win her second Soviet 1500m title and finished third in the 3000m. At the World Championships in Rome she excelled, winning the 1500m and the 3000m, both with devastating bursts of speed over the final 150m. Her winning 1500m time, 3:58.56, was a personal best.

In 1986 she was beaten only once over 1500m, at the European Championships in Stuttgart, when she finished second to team mate Ravilya Agletdinova. She was also fifth in the 3000m.

Sanderson, Tessa

1956–. Born Jamaica (GBR)

Throughout her career, Tessa Sanderson has met with both triumph and disaster with unerring regularity. She has remained, however, a dogged competitor in the world of women's javelin throwing. As the undisputed British number one in the event, she went to the 1980 Moscow Olympic Games as a gold medal favourite. Unfortunately, overcome by nerves, she was reduced to tears as throws of below 50m meant her elimination in the qualifying round. Four years later, when ranked third in the world behind Tiina Lillak of Finland and her British team mate Fatima Whitbread, Sanderson found her best form to win the Olympic title in Los Angeles.

In her first Olympics in Montreal, she finished tenth behind Ruth Fuchs, the East German world record holder, with a throw of 57m. Two years later, in 1978, she was Commonwealth Games champion. She was also run-

Tessa Sanderson

ner-up to Fuchs in the 1978 European Championships, and came within 26cm of the East German's world record in her build-up to the Moscow Olympics. An accomplished heptathlete, she set two UK and Commonwealth records in 1981. In 1982, however, injuries to her arm and Achilles tendon meant that she missed every major competition. By 1983, Britain's Fatima Whitbread had emerged as a serious rival. At the inaugural World Championships, it was Whitbread who won a medal, while Sanderson finished fourth. The rivalry between the two throwers became intense over the ensuing seasons, and the womens' javelin competition consequently took centre stage in domestic athletics meetings.

While Whitbread was expected to be Britain's main medal hope in Los Angeles in 1984, it was Sanderson who proved superior when it really mattered. Her opening throw flew out to an Olympic record 69.56m and no one was able to match it. Lillak came close with her second throw of 69m, before retiring from the competition, and Whitbread persevered to take the bronze with her fourth throw of 67.14m.

Her next 18 months were hampered by injuries and inconsistent throwing, while Whitbread continued to improve. Their next major clash was at the 1986 Commonwealth Games, where once again Sanderson proved to be the better competitor. While Whitbread led for most of the competition, Sanderson's throw of 69.80m earned her a second Commonwealth title. Whitbread was second with 68.54m, but went on to claim the European title and the world record later that year when Sanderson was ruled out by injury.

Despite slimming down and promising to return to the heptathlon in 1987, Sanderson continued with the javelin, finishing fourth at the World Championships in Rome as Whitbread took the title she had come so close to in 1983.

Sanderson's list of achievements includes ten UK javelin records between 1976 and 1983 and two silver medals in European Cup competitions (1977 and 1981).

Sanyeyev, Viktor

1945–. Born USSR (URS)

The world's greatest-ever triple jumper, Viktor Sanyeyev won three Olympic gold medals between 1968 and 1976, and came very close to winning a fourth in 1980. He dominated the event throughout the seventies and his Olympic triple has been emulated by only two other athletes, Al Oerter, who won four discus titles between 1956 and 1968, and John Flanagan, winner of the hammer title in 1900, 1904, and 1908.

Sanyeyev's first Olympic gold medal came in what was probably the finest triple jump competition ever seen, at the Mexico Games of 1968. He went into the competition with a season's best of 16.87m and yet, in a final where the world record was broken four times, Sanyeyev emerged the winner with a last jump of 17.39m. He had improved the pre-Olympic world record by 36cm.

He won the European title in 1969 with 17.34m, and finished runner-up to Jorg Drehmel of East Germany in 1971. At the Olympic Games in Munich, in 1972, the Soviet was back on top form to take the title with 17.35m – and to take revenge over Drehmel, who was pushed into second place. Later the same year, Sanyeyev regained his world record – snatched briefly the year before by Pedro Perez of Cuba – with 17.44m.

A second European title came in 1974, and two years later he completed his magnificent treble by winning at the Montreal Olympics with a fifth round jump of 17.29m. The new world record holder, Joao Carlos Oliveira, who had jumped 17.89m in 1975, was third.

Despite recurring injury problems, Sanyeyev went to Prague to defend his European title in 1978, and lost by just one centimetre to Srejovic of

Viktor Sanyeyev

Yugoslavia. In Moscow at the 1980 Olympic Games he had to be content with the silver medal, as his title went to his team mate Jaak Uudmae, 17.35m to 17.24m.

In a brilliant career, he jumped over 17m in 12 of the 13 seasons between 1968 and 1980.

Schmid, Harald

1957–. Born West Germany (FRG)

Forever in the shadow of American Ed Moses at world level, Harald Schmid has dominated 400m hurdling in Europe for a decade. He has won a record five gold medals at European Championships, five individual gold medals in European Cup competitions, won ten West German titles, and set three European records since 1979.

He was a semi-finalist at the 1976 Olympic Games, where the 400mh was won by Moses. A year later he was the last man to beat Moses before the American's 122-race winning sequence began in 1977. In all their races since, Schmid has been unable to repeat that victory. He was second to Moses at the 1983 World Championships, and at the 1984 Olympic Games he won the bronze medal behind Moses and another American, Danny Harris. It was Harris who finally ended Moses' winning streak in 1987, and later the same year just squeezed past Schmid to take the silver medal at the World Championships in Rome. The gold medal inevitably went to Moses after the most thrilling of finishes. Schmid equalled his own European record of 47.48 in finishing third. Harris was given the same time.

Schmid won his first European title in 1978, when he was also part of West Germany's victorious 4 x 400m relay team. He won both gold medals again in 1982 and, although he retained his individual title in 1986, the West Germans were beaten in the relay by Great Britain.

On the flat, he has a personal best of 44.92 for 400m, and in 1987 ran 800m in 1:44.83.

Schmidt, Josef

1935–. Born Poland(POL)

Josef Schmidt was twice European champion (1958 and 1962) and twice Olympic champion (1960 and 1964) at triple jump. He was also the first

Harald Schmid

man to clear 17m when, on 5 August 1960, at Olszlyn, he jumped 17.03m, a record that stood for eight years.

His first European title, in Stockholm in 1958, was with a new personal best of 16.43m. In Rome in 1960, as world record holder, he took on and beat the best in the world, winning with an Olympic record of 16.81m. A second European title in Belgrade in 1962, won with 16.55m, preceded a successful Olympic defence in Tokyo, where another Olympic record 16.85m showed his return to top form following a leg injury. Recurring injuries prevented him winning further titles, but he continued to compete at top level, coming fifth in the 1966 European Championships. He came seventh at the 1968 Olympics in Munich, where his 16.89m bettered his previous gold-medal-winning leaps.

Schmidt had a best 100m time of 10.4 and a long jump of 7.84m, and continued to compete internationally until 1972.

Scholz, Jackson

1897–. Born USA (USA)

One of the leading American sprinters of the 1920s, Jackson Scholz is forever immortalized in the film 'Chariots of Fire', as the man beaten by the Englishman Harold Abrahams in the 100m final of the 1924 Paris Olympics. He won the 200m in the same Games, and was part of the 4 x 100m relay team that won gold at the 1920 Games in Antwerp.

In 1920 Scholz finished fifth in the 100m, but took his first medal in the relay, running the third leg for a combined time with his team mates of 42.25, taking $^2/_5$ second off the 1912 record set by Germany. In Paris there were four Americans in the 100m final, but all were beaten by Abraham's surge from half-way. Scholz finished two feet behind the Briton, and the same distance ahead of New Zealand's Arthur Parritt.

In the 200m Scholz qualified convincingly, with Abrahams and Pad-

dock seen as his main threats. Paddock led by two feet at 150m, with Abrahams already beaten, when Eric Liddell started a surge to catch the American contingent. On the line it looked like a dead heat between Paddock and Scholz, but Paddock's last-minute look at his opponent on the line probably cost him the gold, as Scholz finished six inches ahead in a world record 21.6 (Paddock 21.7, Liddell 21.9).

In 1928 Scholz was involved in some controversy after the 200m. In a race won by Percy Williams (CAN), with Walter Rangeley second, he tied for third place with Helmut Körnig of Germany. He was offered a run-off for the bronze two days later, but Scholz declined and lost his chance of a medal.

Scott, Steve

1956–. Born USA (USA)

America's top miler for a decade, Steve Scott has missed out on championship wins simply because of the quality of the opposition. Despite his proven speed over all the middle distances, and his undoubted consistency, Scott has been unlucky in many ways to have been running at the same time as Steve Ovett, Sebastian Coe, Steve Cram, and Said Aouita.

His best times for 1500m (3:31.76) and for the mile (3:47.69) put him in the very highest class and rank him among the best of all time. Yet at major championships he has either lost out to one of the aforementioned athletes or has not been at his best because of injury.

Scott's best chance of a major win came at the World Championships in 1983 when, in the absence of Coe, he was strongly fancied to win the gold medal. He was in the best form of his life, only to find that Britain's Steve Cram, the reigning European and Commonwealth champion, was in even better form. After two slow opening laps, it was Cram who seized the initiative in following Aouita as he made a long run for the line. Scott,

Steve Scott

who had planned to hit the front himself with 300m to go found himself chasing an accelerating Cram to the line. He finished second, two metres behind Cram.

The 1984 Olympic Games were a disappointment for him. Coming back after injury problems, he was in no shape to compete in the closing stages, although he did feature briefly, hitting the front after 500m. When the Spaniard Abascal took over the lead with 600m of the race left, Scott found the pace too quick and eventually faded to finish tenth.

Five times US champion at 1500m, he has run a record eight sub-3:50 miles. He ran his one-hundredth sub-four-minute mile in May 1985, after being beaten to that particular target by the New Zealander John Walker, the 1976 Olympic 1500m champion.

Seagren, Bob

1946–. Born USA (USA)

Holder of 14 pole vault world records (eight indoors and six outdoors), Bob Seagren won the Olympic title in 1968, and took the silver in Munich four years later in controversial circumstances.

The controversy in Munich centred around the banning of certain makes of pole by the IAAF on the very eve of the competition. This meant that 14 of the finalists had to vault with 'new' poles. Seagren did not even get a chance to practise with his, but still managed to clear 5.40m. He finished second behind Wolfgang Nordwig (GDR), who vaulted a personal best of 5.50 to become the first non-American to win the Olympic pole vault. Incidentally, he won with a pole he normally used in competition.

Seagren had previously won the 1968 Olympic title in Mexico (Nordwig took the bronze) and he improved the world record outdoors from 5.32m, at Fresno on 14 May 1966, to 5.63m, at Eugene on 2 July 1972. He was the first man to clear 17 feet indoors, taking the mark from 5.18m in Albuquerque on 5 March 1966 to 5.33m (17ft 6in) on 8 February 1969 in Los Angeles.

Seagren was winner of six AAU titles (three indoors and three outdoors) and the 1967 Pan-American title. He went on after his retirement from amateur athletics to a very successful career in the Superstars competition, winning the first world title in 1977.

Sedykh, Yuriy

1955–. Born USSR (URS)

Twice the Olympic champion and six times world record holder, Yuriy Sedykh is the greatest hammer thrower of all time. Not only does he time his performances to perfection so that he is in the best possible condition for major championships, he has also shown a remarkable consistency in his throwing throughout his career. His ability to excel when throwing the hammer is based on the speed he achieves in the circle.

He went into the 1976 Olympic final already ranked second on the all-time list after an early season throw of 78.86m. Throwing against the defending champion, his coach Anatoliy Bondarchuk, and the European champion Aleksey Spiridonov, Sedykh won

Yuriy Sedykh

the competition with a second round effort of 77.52m. Spiridonov was second and Bondarchuk third.

In 1978 he won the first of his three European titles. In 1980 he returned to the Olympic arena in Moscow with another gold medal and a world record of 81.80m. It was his second world record of the season, and it came in his first throw of the final. While his team mates Sergey Litvinov and Juri Tamm completed a second successive Soviet clean sweep in the Olympic hammer competition, Sedykh had won the gold medal before they had taken their first throws.

He won his second European title in 1982, with a championship best 81.66m. He then went to Helsinki for the inaugural World Championships in 1983 as firm favourite for the gold medal, even though he would have to face the new world record holder, team mate Litvinov, the silver medallist in Moscow. In fact, it was Litvinov who proved stronger on the day, and with an opening throw of 82.68m secured the gold medal at the start of the competition, just as Sedykh had done in Moscow. Sedykh finished with the silver medal after throwing 80.94m in the fourth round.

Denied the chance to compete in

the 1984 Olympics because of the Soviet boycott, Sedykh nevertheless enjoyed a marvellous season. He took Litvinov's world record with 86.34m in Cork and went on to throw beyond 85.00m in his next three competitions. After taking time off in 1985 – when Juri Tamm headed the world rankings – he was back at his best for the European Championships in 1986. There was yet another Soviet clean sweep of the medals, but Sedykh reigned supreme. Although Litvinov opened with 85.74m – a distance only bettered by himself and Sedykh – the defending champion responded with a fourth round throw of 86.74m, a new world record. Sedykh emphasized his superiority over his younger rival by then throwing twice beyond his old world record mark. Once again – and for the thirtieth time in 41 competitions – Sedykh had beaten Litvinov.

Sedykh chose to make 1987 a low-key season in preparation for the Olympics in 1988. In his absence, Litvinov retained his World Championship title in Rome with a throw of 83.06m.

Seko, Toshihiko

1956–. Born Japan (JAP)

One of the world's most consistent marathon runners, Toshihiko Seko became a national hero after his four wins at Fukuoka between 1978 and 1983, and was a firm favourite for the gold medal at the 1984 Olympic Games. He went to LA unbeaten in his previous five marathons, but struggled in the heat and finished fourteenth in 2:14:13. However, he has won all of his marathons since, including those in London, Boston and Chicago.

In a nation that has become increasingly fanatical about its marathon runners, Seko rose to prominence through the coaching of Kiyoshi Nakamura at Washuda University. His first races brought little success – tenth in his first marathon at Kyoto in 1977, fifth at Fukuoka and sixty-eighth at Milton Keynes in 1978.

Toshihiko Seko

He began a strict training regime and an almost monastic lifestyle, supervised by Nakamura, and won his next marathon, at Fukuoka in December 1978, in 2:10:21. The following year he finished second to American Bill Rogers in the Boston Marathon, and won his second Fukuoka Marathon. He won his next four marathons, including two more at Fukuoka, another Boston and the Tokyo Marathon in 1983 in 2:08:38, a Japanese record and the fifth fastest time in history.

After his disappointment in Los Angeles in 1984, he returned to the marathon event in 1986 with wins in London (2:10:02) and Chicago (2:08:27). His only marathon in 1987 was in Boston, where he eased ahead of Britain's Steve Jones after 21 miles to win in 2:11:50.

He was unable to take part in the Japanese Olympic trial at Fukuoka in December 1987 because of injury. The Japanese selectors, who originally intended picking the first three competitors, decided to pick the first two from that race and leave a place open for Seko, in the hope that he could prove his fitness in a subsequent marathon. He was duly selected for Seoul after winning the Lake Biwa Mainichi

Marathon in March 1988, although his time, 2:12:41, was slower than the third man in Fukuoka.

Shchelkanova, Tatyana

1937–. Born USSR (URS)

The holder of the most world records for women's long jump (four), Tatyana Shchelkanova took the mark from 6.48m in 1961 to 6.70m on 19 June 1962 in Leizig. Previously, she had jumped a wind-assisted 6.50m, almost a year earlier. She won the 1962 European Championships, but could only finish third at the 1964 Olympics, won by Mary Rand (GBR) with a world record 6.76m.

Shchelkanova's second world record of 6.53m in 1962 was far behind her mark of 6.62m the same year: this was never put forward for ratification, however. She was favourite for the gold in the 1964 Olympics in Tokyo, being the existing world record holder with 6.70m, but could only manage 6.42m in the final. She regained her number one ranking in 1965, and in 1966 produced her best-ever performances: 6.73m indoors, and a wind-assisted 6.96m outdoors at the Soviet Championships.

She retired from international competition following the introduction of new sex tests in 1966.

Tatyana Shchelkanova

Sheppard, Melvin

1883–1942. Born USA (USA)

A noted front runner, Melvin Sheppard broke world records himself and helped set them up for others. He was a member of New York's Irish American Athletic Club, and first made a name for himself running indoors. At the Madison Square Garden meeting in 1906 he broke the eight-year-old indoor best for the mile with 4:25:2. Although the American Athletic Union paid little attention to indoor records at the time, it was generally thought that Sheppard had set a new indoor best for 880 yards in New York a year later, when he clocked 1:58. Sheppard was also credited with the best 1000-yard time of 2:17.5.

A year later, Sheppard demonstrated his talent at the 1908 Olympic Games in London, when he won both the 800m and the 1500m titles. After going through 400m in 53 seconds, he held on to win the 800m in 1:52.8, a new world record. His winning 1500m time was 4:03.4. He also won a gold medal as part of the USA's medley relay team, which ran legs of 200m, 200m, 400m and 800m.

Four years later, he easily qualified for the final of the 800m in Stockholm, America providing six of the eight finalists. In what was acknowledged as the greatest 800m race ever seen at that time, Sheppard set off at his customary fast pace in a bid to take the sting out of the German Braun's finishing sprint. Sheppard led through the bell, but was caught by his team mate James Meredith on the back straight. However, it was Meredith who proved the stronger, crossing the line in a new world record time of 1:51.9. Sheppard, meanwhile, was caught by another American, the pre-race favourite Ira Davenport, and they clocked the same time, 1:52.0 at the line, although Sheppard was credited with the silver medal. All three Americans had broken the previous record. Sheppard added to his collection of medals with another gold in the 4 x 400m relay.

Sheridan, Martin

1881–1918. Born USA (USA)

A multi-talented athlete at the beginning of the twentieth century, Martin Sheridan won nine Olympic medals, five of them in the unofficial Games of 1906 in Athens. He also set five discus world records in pre-IAAF days and was the first man to go over 40m.

A member of the Greater New York Irish Athletic Association, Sheridan set his first discus world record on 14 September 1901, reaching 36.77m. This he improved to 38.93 on 30 August the following year, then to 39.40 in New York on 4 October.

His first 40m throw came at the Star AC Games in New York on 2 November 1902, when he achieved a mark of 40.72m. On 10 September 1905, at the New York Irish Volunteers Athletic Association annual meet, his second throw was measured at 43.69. Sheridan was then forced to retire from the competition, having suffered an injury in the pole vault the day before.

At the 1904 Olympics, in St Louis, he won the discus, beating Ralph Rose (USA) in a throw-off after both men reached the same distance of 39.28m. Two years later in Athens, in the unofficial Games, he won both discus (41.46m) and shot (12.32m), took silvers in the standing high jump and long jump behind Ray Ewry (USA), and took silver in the stone put, reaching 19.035m with the 6.40g weight behind Nicolaos Georgantas of Greece. In 1908 in London he again dominated the discus, taking gold with 40.89m and also winning the Greek style discus with 38.00m.

Shorter, Frank

1947–. Born West Germany (FRG)

Only days after becoming the first American to break 28 minutes for 10,000m in 1972, Frank Shorter became a national sporting hero by winning the Olympic marathon in Munich by more than two minutes. Four years later he forced the pace in Montreal,

Frank Shorter

but had to be content with a silver medal as the East German Waldemar Cierpinski proved stronger on the day.

Shorter, already an established cross-country and track runner, completed his first marathon in 1971, losing in the AAU Championship by 56 seconds to Kenny Moore. Shorter had won six AAU and national collegiate titles in a two-year period, and his performance in his first marathon earned him a place in the US team for the Pan American Games later that year. There he won the 10,000m title and the marathon in 2:22:40. At the end of the year he also won the Fukuoka Marathon in Japan in 2:12:50.

After winning the Olympic trial race in the summer of 1972, he went to Munich for only his sixth race at the distance. It was a strong field, containing the world record holder (Derek Clayton), the European champion (Karel Lismont), the Commonwealth champion (Ron Hill), and the title holder (Mamo Wolde). Shorter took the lead at 15km and continued to increase it over the next 20km. Although the crowd in the Olympic stadium were fooled by a hoaxer who ran into the arena ahead of him, Shorter was a convincing winner in 2:12:19, his fastest ever time, and the first American to take the title since Frank Hayes in 1908.

He went on from Munich to win again in Fukuoka (2:10:30) and, up until the Olympic Games in Montreal, lost only two of eight races over 26.2 miles. These were at Korso, where he failed to finish in 1973, and in Honolulu, where he finished fourth in 1974. He qualified to run in Montreal after beating his rival Bill Rodgers in the trial race only two months before the Games. In Montreal, however, Cierpinski made his break at 35km and Shorter was unable to stay with him any longer. He settled for second place in a time of 2:10:45, just under a minute behind Cierpinski's Olympic record of 2:09:55.

He suffered a foot injury early in 1977, and never recaptured his best form. Further injuries and illness disrupted his racing and, although he remained a committed road runner in races over shorter distances, he never ran fast marathon times again. Now a successful businessman and a commentator on marathons for American television, Shorter has recently taken up running competitively again as a veteran.

Shrubb, Alf

1878–1964. Born England (GBR)

One of the most remarkable runners at the beginning of the twentieth century, Alf Shrubb was the forerunner of the host of 'Flying Finns' of the 1920s and 1930s who set records at various distances. Shrubb so dominated at distances from one and a half miles to one hour that Olympic medals seemed a certainty at the Games of 1904 in St Louis; however, Britain did not send a team to compete!

Shrubb was the first amateur runner to break 30 minutes for 6 miles, clocking 29:59.4 on 5 November 1904 in Glasgow during a one-hour race where he set an incredible seven world records: each mile from six to ten, 10,000m and one hour. His one-hour total of 18,742m was not beaten for 48

years and 296 days by a Briton, and it lasted for nine years as a world record. His ten-mile time of 50:40.6 lasted for 24 years and his two-mile 9:09.6 for 22 years (he had set records at two, three, four and five miles earlier in 1904).

Shrubb was national cross-country champion from 1901-1904, and he won the international race twice in 1903 and 1904. He was declared a professional in 1905 for allegedly receiving expenses payments, and he turned professional in 1906, travelling to the USA for races against other marathon stars like Dorando Pietri (ITA) and John Hayes (USA).

Shrubb became Oxford University's first professional coach before moving to Canada in 1928.

Sidlo, Janusz

1933–. Born Poland(POL)

Janusz Sidlo was twice winner of the European javelin title (1954 and 1958), and was bronze medallist in 1969. He competed at five Olympics, but only took one medal: silver in Melbourne in 1956.

Winner of 14 national titles, he set national records over two decades from 1953 to 1970. During that time he was always ranked in the world's top ten. Although not qualifying for the Olympic final in 1952, he won his first European title in Berne two years later with 76.35m. In 1956, in the Melbourne Olympics, he threw 79.98m to finish second behind Egil Danielsen (NOR), who reached 85.71m. Sidlo retained his European crown in Stockholm in 1958 with 80.18. In the 1960 Rome Olympics he threw further than any other competitor. Unfortunately his 85.14m was achieved in the qualifying rounds, and he could not reproduce this form in the final, finishing eighth with 76.46m.

He showed himself to be a consistent and durable athlete, taking seventh place in the 1962 Europeans in Belgrade, a fourth in the 1964 Olympics in 1964, and seventh again in the 1966 Europeans in Budapest. He re-

turned to the medals aged 36, in the 1969 European Championships in Athens, with 82.90 for the bronze.

In 1970 Sidlo achieved his personal best of 86.22m, 14 years after he set his only world record in Milan on 30 June 1956, with 83.66m.

Silvester, Jay

1937–. Born USA (USA)

The first discus thrower to break the 60m and 70m barriers, Jay Silvester competed at four Olympic Games (1964-1976) but won only one medal, a silver in 1972.

As world record holder in 1968 at the Mexico Games, Silvester was odds-on favourite for the title. In the qualifying rounds he threw an Olympic record 63.64m, but completely fell apart in the final and could finish no better than fifth with 61.78m. Meanwhile, Al Oerter (USA) went on to collect his fourth successive gold medal with 64.78m.

Silvester's first world record was set in Frankfurt, on 11 August 1961, the first throw over 60m (60.56m). His last was set on 16 May 1971 in Antelope Valley, California, where he became the first man over 70m with 70.38m. This mark was not ratified due to a lack of graded officials.

Jay Silvester

Sara Simeoni

Silvester, who claimed to have thrown 73.90m in practice, continued the tradition of discus thrower's longevity by competing in 1972 in Munich aged 39, finishing second to Ludvik Danek, 64.40m to 63.50m.

Simeoni, Sara

1953–. Born Italy (ITA)

In a career spanning 15 years, Sara Simeoni became one of the world's greatest-ever high jumpers. In an era which also saw Ulrike Meyfarth of West Germany and Rosemarie Ackermann of East Germany take top honours, Simeoni enjoyed her greatest success between 1978 and 1981, when she dominated the event.

At the age of 19 in 1972 she finished sixth at the Munich Olympics, when the competition was won by the 16-year-old Meyfarth and Ackermann was seventh. While it took Meyfarth several years to recapture that sort of form, Ackermann improved to become the 1974 European and 1976 Olympic champion. Simeoni placed third and second at those championships, leading the way in the Olympic final until her failure at 1.93m. The two women featured in some marvellous duels over the years. Simeoni used the Fosbury Flop technique, now the norm, while Ackermann was the last world record holder to use the straddle style.

In 1977 Simeoni won the first of four European Indoor titles, and looked set to challenge Ackermann for the position of the world's number one. The East German was in sparkling form that year, however. After winning the European Cup Final, she became the first woman to clear 2.00m in Berlin in August. A week later, Simeoni finished runner-up as Ackermann took the World Cup title with 1.98m and a 6cm margin of victory.

It was a different story in 1978, though, when Ackermann was suffering with Achilles tendon injuries. Simeoni retained her European Indoor title and, in Brescia in August, became the second woman to clear 2.00m, as she claimed the world record with 2.01m. In September, she at last turned the tables on Ackermann by beating her for the European Championships title in Prague, with yet another clearance at 2.01m. Ackermann was second.

Simeoni was second to Ackermann in the 1979 European Cup and runner-up to Canada's Debbie Brill in the World Cup. She began the Olympic year of 1980 in fine form, winning her third European Indoor title. In their final major championship clash, Ackermann failed to clear 1.94m while Simeoni was the only one in the com-

petition to jump over 1.97m. The gold medal was hers and, although she had two failed attempts at a new world record height of 2.02m, her winning jump represented an Olympic record. Ackermann bowed out of international athletics in fourth place.

After injury disrupted her 1981 season, Simeoni returned to competition in 1982 to discover that Meyfarth was once more in great form and that another jumper, the Soviet Tamara Bycova, was also in contention. The European Championships in Athens saw the gold medal go to Meyfarth. She took Simeoni's world record with 2.02m and the Italian was third behind Bycova.

Simeoni took no real part in the World Championships in Helsinki in 1983, when she was carried from the arena on a stretcher after hurting her calf while jumping 1.87m. Bycova won, with Meyfarth second.

At the age of 31, in her fourth Olympic Games, Simeoni was back at her best in Los Angeles. Left to battle it out with Meyfarth for the gold medal - plus the distinction of winning a second Olympic title - she was unable to clear 2.02m, the height that had eluded her throughout her career. She finished with the silver medal.

Simeoni was still competing in 1986, but failed to qualify for the European Championship final in Stuttgart. She retired soon afterwards. Since 1971 she had won 13 national titles, set 21 Italian records, and represented her country 62 times.

Sjoberg, Patrik

1965–. Born Sweden (SWE)

Said to have the most famous face in Sweden, Patrik Sjoberg rose to the top of the high jump rankings with a sensational season in 1987, when he cleared 2.42m for a new world record and took the World Championship title in Rome.

The world record came in his native Sweden, in front of a packed and hushed stadium in Stockholm. He cleared the bar at his third attempt, to rapturous applause. At the World Championships in September, in what was the final event, he took the gold medal from his great rivals, Igor Paklin and Gennadiy Avdeyenko of the Soviet Union, only after they had all cleared 2.38m. Sjoberg won because he had cleared every height to 2.40m at his first attempt.

Up until 1987 his career had progressed in fits and starts. He won his first Swedish title in 1981 at the age of 16 – and has won every year since – but the same year could finish only eighth in the European Junior Championships in Utrecht. At the European Championships in 1982 he finished tenth, indoors and outdoors, as the titles went to the West German Dietmar Mogenburg. While his personal best improved – he had jumped 2.33m by 1983 – he continued to disappoint in major championships. A bronze medal at the 1983 European Junior Championships in Vienna, where he cleared 2.21m, was his first medal in international competition.

Things started to go right for him in 1984. He won the silver medal at the Los Angeles Olympics with 2.33m behind Mogenburg, who won with 2.35m. Early in 1985 he cleared a world indoor best of 2.38m in Berlin, *Patrik Sjoberg*

although it was bettered two days later by his rival Mogenburg. However, by the end of the year, the Swede had captured the World Indoor Games title, the European Indoor Games gold medal, and a gold medal at the World Cup in Canberra.

He had a poor year in 1986 because of injury, finishing sixth in the European Championships, indoors and outdoors, as the titles went to Mogenburg and Paklin. Sjoberg has since won the European Indoor title in both 1987 and 1988. His world record height has been equalled indoors by the West German Carlo Thranhardt, who beat Sjoberg in a special competition staged with the accompaniment of their favourite pop music at a meeting in Berlin in February 1988.

Slaney, Mary

1958–. Born USA (USA)

Rated in an IAAF poll as the world's finest women's 3000m runner, Mary Slaney has paid for her success on the track with a series of injuries which have threatened to wreck her career on numerous occasions. So far, though, she has returned after each lay-off, stronger and faster every time. Her finest years have been 1983 and

Mary Slaney (492)

1985, when she was able to demonstrate her superiority over 1500m and 3000m against the best competition in the world.

Despite winning her first international vest as a 14-year-old, Slaney (née Decker) did not compete in a major competition until she was 25. This was mainly because she had been ruled out with injuries in 1976 - the time of the Montreal Olympics - and was prevented from competing in the 1980 Games because of the United States boycott.

At the World Championships in 1983 she demonstrated just how good she was. In the 3000m she faced the strongest possible line-up which included the great names of Soviet distance running: Tatyana Kazankina and Svetlana Ulmasova, the world record holder and European champion. But Slaney led the race from start to finish to win in 8:34.62, including a last 200m in 30 seconds. Kazankina, unable to catch Slaney in the home straight, finished third, while Ulmasova, lost for pace, was fourth. West German Brigitte Kraus pipped them both for the silver medal.

In a glorious 1500m, the story was similar. Slaney, shadowed throughout by the Soviet Zamira Zaitseva, went through 400m in 64.04, 800m in

2:10.92, and 1200m in 3:16.67. Zait-seva took the lead with 200m to go, and it looked as if Slaney would not respond until she gradually closed the gap in the last 50m and edged ahead of the Soviet with just 10m to spare. In her desperation, Zaitseva lunged for the line, toppled to the track and rolled across the finish line for the silver medal.

The scene was set for Slaney to repeat her front-running tactics at the Los Angeles Olympics, in front of an adoring American public. Billed as a race between her and South African born Zola Budd of Great Britain for the gold medal, the 3000m final also featured the Romanian Maricica Puica, an opponent Slaney feared more than Budd. However, when Budd took the lead from Slaney at 1700m, the American inexplicably tried to find a way through on the inside. The result was a collision that became the major talking point of the Games. Slaney tripped up on Budd's trailing leg, fell sideways onto the infield and lay writhing in agony as the race continued without her. She tore a groin muscle and was once again sidelined through injury for the next two months.

The recriminations following the collision rebounded badly on Slaney, who blamed Budd and was labelled a bad loser by the press and public alike. Puica went on to win the gold medal, while Budd finished a disillusioned seventh after being booed by the partisan crowd for the rest of the race.

If there were any doubts about Slaney's ability or competitiveness, she put the record straight in 1985. She went through the 1985 season unbeaten. She set a world indoor best for 2000m at the start of the year, set a new world record for the mile with 4:16.71, ran close to her 1500m best with 3:57.24, and ran the world's second fastest ever 3000m in 8:25.83. In the latter three races she convincingly beat both Puica and Budd to assert herself as the undisputed number one in the world.

After giving birth to a daughter, Ashley, in May 1986, Slaney's return

to the track was ruined as injury forced her to miss the 1987 World Championships, where she intended running 800m and 1500m.

Her record of injuries is astounding. She first came to prominence as a 14-year-old when she ran 2:02.4 for 800m and defeated the 1972 Olympic silver medallist, Niole Sabaite, in a USA v USSR match in 1973. Her demanding training and racing schedules took their toll, as Slaney's developing body seemed incapable of handling the strain. She missed 1975, 1976 and 1977 because of injury, and the whole of 1981. When she was not injured she ran a world junior 800m record of 2:02.29 in 1974, won the Pan American Games 1500m title in 1979, and set world records for 5000m and 10,000m in 1982.

Smith, Calvin

1961–. Born USA (USA)

Shorter than most sprinters, with an ungainly style, Calvin Smith has proved in recent years that appearances count for nothing. He became the fastest man in the world over 100m in 1983, when he clocked 9.93 seconds at the altitude of Colorado

Calvin Smith

Springs and went on to win two gold medals and a silver at the inaugural World Championships later that year.

Like all American sprinters of the last six years, he has run in the shadow of Carl Lewis, who took the 100m and 200m titles at the Los Angeles Olympics in 1984. However, while it was thought that Lewis would be the man to better Smith's 100m record, the honour in fact went to Ben Johnson of Canada at the 1987 World Championships, when Lewis equalled Smith's mark only to find that it was not enough for victory.

A tremendously strong athlete, Smith ran 11 races in Helsinki at the 1983 World Championships. Second to Lewis at 100m, he won the 200m by three metres in 20.14 and ran a superb third leg in the Americans' 4 x 100m world record of 37.86. The following year he only managed to make the USA Olympic team as a member of the relay team, but once again ran the third leg to win another gold medal, as the quartet improved their world record to 37.83.

He won the IAAF/Mobil Grand Prix over-all 200m title in 1985, and retained his World Championship 200m title in Rome in 1987. Coming into the home straight some two or three metres down on Britain's John Regis, Smith moved from sixth to first in the final 30m to edge past Regis and the Frenchman Gilles Queneherve (who was credited with the same time as Smith – 20.16) at the line. It was his twenty-second sub-20.70 time of the year.

Smith, Joyce

1937–. Born England (GBR)

Joyce Smith has enjoyed two athletics careers. She began as a cross-country and track athlete in the 1950s, and switched to marathon running at the age of 41 in 1979.

Three times winner of the English Women's National Cross-Country title in 1959, 1960 and 1973, and winner of the international title in 1972, Joyce was limited in the early part of her

Joyce Smith (40)

career to distances up to 1500m on the track. She represented Great Britain at 800m in her first international match in 1960.

In 1973 she set an unofficial world record of 9:23.4 at 3000m, and in 1972 reached the semi-final of the Olympic 1500m, setting UK records of 4:11.3 and 4:09.4 along the way. In 1974 she won her first major track medal, placing third in the European Championships 3000m in Rome with a time of 8:57.4. She also finished eighth in the 1500m final.

In 1977, in her first serious road race, she set a UK women's best for ten miles with 57.28, and improved it to 56.27 later in the year. After one last track season in 1978, Joyce turned to the marathon because, as she said: 'The marathon was always something I wanted to do - just to say I had done one.'

Her début at the distance came in 1979, when she won the Sandbach race in Cheshire in 2:41:37, a British best by more than nine minutes. It was to be the start of an amazing second career. Under the guidance of her husband and coach, Bryan, she continued to improve, and won her next two marathons in Waldnield, West Germany, and Tokyo.

By the time she lined up for the

first London Marathon in 1981, she had won five of her first seven races. Her time in that London Marathon marked a significant breakthrough for women's distance running in Britain. She was the first woman to run under 2:30, with 2:29:57, to rank third in the world. At the age of 43, she proved an inspiration to countless men and women, who marvelled at her achievement before taking up running themselves.

She lowered her own British record in the second London Marathon in 1982, but was unable to compete in that year's European Championship race because of injury. The following year, she travelled extensively, finishing eighth in Osaka, third in Rome and fifth in Los Angeles. She was ninth in the World Championships Marathon in Helsinki in 2:34:27.

Pre-selected for the Olympic Marathon in 1984 - the first time the race had been included in the programme - she lined up as the oldest woman competitor ever to compete in an Olympics. In a race won in spectacular fashion by America's Joan Benoit, Smith finished eleventh, second Briton to Priscilla Welch, in 2:32:48. It was a fitting performance with which to end her international career - although she did not stop running. As the invitations continue to pour in, she still runs in foreign marathons.

Smith, Tommie

1944–. Born USA (USA)

Shortly after collecting the gold medal for 200m at the 1968 Olympics in Mexico, Tommie Smith was expelled from the Games village by the US Olympic Committee for his 'black power' demonstration during the awards ceremony, along with bronze medallist John Carlos. The two of them had worn black gloves and stood with fists raised during the playing of the National Anthem. Smith had just shown his athletic power on the track, winning in 19.83, a world record that lasted for almost eleven years.

Smith became the first man to run

20 seconds around a turn in 1966, running this in Sacramento on 11 June. This he improved to 19.8 in the Olympic 200m final on 16 October 1968. He was also the first man to run a 'legal' sub 20 second time for 220 yards on a straight course, running 19.5 seconds in San José, California on 7 May. He continued his great season in 1966 by recording a world record 43.8 400m relay leg. World records continued to fall to him in 1967: 400m in 44.5 and 440 yards in 44.8 before his Olympic victory. He had also been part of the relay team that first dipped under 3 minutes for 4 x 400m in 1966.

Also a very useful long jumper (with a best of 7.90m) and short sprinter (9.3 for 100 yards, 10.1 for 100m), Smith retired after the Mexico Olympics to play American football for the Cincinnati Bengals in 1969.

Snell, Peter

1938–. Born New Zealand (NZL)

Winner of the 800m Olympic title in 1960 when largely unknown, Peter Snell not only retained his title four years later in Tokyo, but added the 1500m as well. In 1962 he became the first man since Sydney Wooderson (GBR) to hold half-mile and mile world records simultaneously, and he lowered his own mile record in November 1964. Snell also completed the 880 yard/one mile double at the 1962 Commonwealth Games.

Until he was 18, Snell concentrated on a variety of different sports, especially tennis. It was only when, aged nineteen, he came under the influence of Arthur Lydiard that he began to improve and impress nationally, winning New Zealand titles at 880 yards and the mile in 1959. Despite a stress fracture that limited his running for two months, the tough programme set by coach Lydiard – which included a regular twenty-two-mile hill run – paid dividends in Rome, where at the end of four races in three days Snell won the 800m in an Olympic record 1:46.3.

At this point he had not concen-

Peter Snell (466) wins the 1964 Olympic 800m

trated on the mile, but began to do so at the beginning of 1961. By January 1962 he planned to attempt Murray Halberg's national record of 3:57.5. On 27 January at Wanganui he ran 3:54.4, which took $^{1}/_{10}$ of a second off Elliot's world record, running the last lap in 54.8. One week later in Christchurch he set world records for 800m (1:44.3) and 880 yards (1:45.1).

Snell's fast finish was his key weapon. Against the top American milers at Modesto, California on 25 May 1963, after a moderate pace, he finished with 120 yards in 14 seconds to win in 3:54.9, only $^{1}/_{2}$ second from his world record. It was this strength that crushed the opposition in the Olympic 1500m in Tokyo: on the back-stretch of the last lap he surged to a 100m in 12.7 seconds to take the lead, and kept that pace before easing off in the final straight to win by 10 yards. Snell's last lap of his only 1500m final was 52.7, with the middle 200m in 25 seconds.

Having also won the 800m in 1:45.1, Snell became the only middle-distance runner to win three Olympic golds, and the first man since Albert Hill (GBR) in 1920 to complete the 800m/1500m double. On 17 November 1964, in Auckland, he broke his own mile record, after a very fast 880 yards in 1:54.1, to record 3:54.1. He retired in 1965.

Stanciu, Anisoara

1962–. Born Romania (ROM)

In the biggest-ever improvement on the women's long jump record, Anisoara Stanciu (née Cusmir) bettered her own record by 16cm in Bucharest on 4 June 1983 to jump 7.43m. Stanciu had, in fact, set the old record of 7.27m only moments before, as both marks came in the same competition. She became the first long jumper to land beyond 24 feet.

Earlier in the season she had improved the world record to 7.21m, again in Bucharest. The season before, in a remarkable Romanian Championship, she had set her first world record with 7.15m, but lost the competition and the world record to her rival Vali Ionescu, who jumped 7.20m. Ionescu later won the gold medal at the European Championships in Athens ahead of Stanciu, 6.79m to 6.73m.

In fourth place on that occasion was a young East German, Heike Daute, later to become Heike Dresch-ler, who was to succeed both Romanians as world record holder and the world's number one long jumper.

Stanciu was the clear favourite to win the gold medal at the World Championships in 1983. However, in one of the biggest surprises of the championships, victory went to the 18-year-old Daute, and Stanciu's 7.15m third round jump was only good enough for the silver medal.

With the East German absent from the 1984 Olympic Games in Los Angeles, Stanciu made sure of the long jump title with a 6.96m leap in the fourth round. Ionescu rescued second place with 6.81m on her last but one jump. Stanciu's world record finally fell to Dreschler in 1985 when she cleared 7.44m.

Stanfield, Andy

1927–. Born USA (USA)

One of the best American sprinters of the early 1950s, Andy Stanfield won the Olympic 200m title in 1952 and took the silver four years later in Melbourne. He also ran on the gold medal

Anisoara Stanciu

winning 4 x 100m relay team of 1952, nd set two world records at 200m.

Both his world records were 20.6, ne set at 220 yards in Philadelphia on 6 May 1951 to win the IC4A Championships, and the other to win the US Olympic trials in Los Angeles on 28 une 1952, when Thane Baker (USA) ame second in 20.9. Stanfield beat Baker in the Olympic final 20.7 (automatically timed at 20.81) to 20.8 (20.97 automatic).

Stanfield won a second gold in Helsinki, on a relay team that included three gold medallists from the 1952 Games – Harrison Dillard had won the 110mh, Lindy Remigino the 100m, and Stanfield the 200m. They joined Dean Smith to win in 40.1 (40.26 auto), beating the Soviet Union who clocked 40.3 (40.58 auto) in their first Games since 1912.

Four years later, Stanfield again peaked at the right time, coming second to Thane Baker in the AAU Championships on 23 June, finishing 0.03 second behind in a race where both men were given a time of 20.6, equalling the world record. On 30 June, in the Olympic trials, Stanfield finished third behind new sprint star Bobbyoe Morrow and old rival Baker. Morrow equalled the world record of 20.6, a feat he repeated in the Olympic final in Melbourne, and Stanfield finished second in 20.7 (20.97 auto).

Stecher, Renate

1950–. Born East Germany (GDR)

The dominant woman sprinter at the start of the 1970s, Renate Stecher won gold, silver and bronze medals in her two Olympic appearances, set nine world records at 100m, three at 200m, won a handful of European titles, and nine GDR titles.

Coached by Horst-Dieter Hille – who would later coach Marlies Gohr and Barbel Wockel – Stecher made her international début in the European Junior Championships at the age of 16. She won a gold medal as part of the East German 4 x 100m relay team. When she won silver medals in

Renate Stecher (162)

the 100m, 200m and relay at the same championships in 1968, the coach decided that she was ready for a place in the senior team at the 1969 European Championships in Athens. She duly finished second at 200m and won her first senior gold medal in the sprint relay.

In 1970 she won the first of three successive European indoor 60m titles, and outdoors that summer staked her claim as the world's best sprinter. First came an 11-second 100m to equal the joint world record of American Wyomia Tyus and Taiwan's Chi Cheng. She later won the 200m and anchored East Germany to victory in the sprint relay at the European Cup Final, after being narrowly beaten by Ingrid Mickler of West Germany in the 100m. From that meeting onwards, Stecher went undefeated over 100m or 200m until 1974, a total of 90 races.

There were double sprint victories at the 1971 European Championships in Helsinki, plus a silver medal as the East Germans finished runners-up to West Germany in the relay. In Olympic year, 1972, she began by running 100m in 11 seconds for the fourth time. In the final of the 100m at the Games in Munich, Stecher was an easy winner, clocking 11.07 ahead of Aus-

tralia's Raelene Boyle to become the fastest woman ever, according to the new automatic timing device. Her first world record in the longer sprint came as Stecher powered her way to victory in the 200m, clocking 22.40, again ahead of Boyle, as the defending champion Irena Szewinska finished third.

Stecher finally dipped under 11 seconds for 100m in 1973, when she ran a hand-timed 10.9 in Ostrava. She equalled the time twice more that season, and even reduced it to 10.8 at the East German Championships in Dresden. The time stood as a world record until automatic timing became compulsory in 1977.

Things changed in 1974, when Irena Szewinska came along to end her reign of invincibility. Szewinska first beat Stecher at the Olympic Day meeting in East Berlin, when Szewinska claimed the 200m world record with 22.0. She then beat the East German twice at the European Championships in Rome over 100m and 200m.

Nevertheless, Stecher went to the Olympic Games in Montreal in 1976 as favourite for both sprints. However, in the 100m she could only finish second, as the gold medal went to Annegret Richter of West Germany, and in the 200m Stecher faded along the home straight to finish third, as Barbel Wockel (née Eckert) and Richter took gold and silver medals. Stecher's gold medal in the 4 x 100m relay brought her athletics career to a close. Having decided that she no longer had the speed to match the new sprinting stars, she retired in 1976.

Stepanova, Marina

1950–. Born USSR (URS)

At the age of 36 Marina Stepanova became the oldest woman ever to set a world record. She upset the form book by beating Sabine Busch to win the 1986 European Championships 400m hurdles in 53.32, improving Busch's world record by three-hundredths of a second. Less than a month

Marina Stepanova

later, Stepanova took the record to 52.94 when winning her semi-final in a Spartakiade for 23-year-olds in Tashkent. Needless to say, she was running as a guest competitor and did not contest the final.

She first broke the world record in 1979, with 54.78 in Moscow, and ran faster than that in 1984 taking second place as the record was lowered to 53.58 by her compatriot Margarita Ponomaryeva. In fact, she enjoyed mixed fortunes in 1979. Winner of the European Cup Final in Turin, and top of the world rankings, she went to the World Cup in Rome as the favourite for the 400m hurdles title. However, a momentary lapse in concentration let in East German Barbera Klepp to win in 55.83.

She missed the 1984 Olympic Games – the first time the 400mh event was included – because of the Soviet boycott, but was at her very best in 1986. Her world record in Stuttgart came as she beat the finest 400m hurdlers in the world. After winning her first European title (she was sixth in 1978), she declared that if conditions had been better she might have been the first woman under 53 seconds.

Stephens, Helen

1918–. Born USA (USA)

Unbeaten in her brief sprinting career, Helen Stephens won the 1936 Olympic 100m title in Berlin, beating her more famous rival Stella Walsh. Like Walsh, she ran some extraordinarily fast times which were never ratified.

The six-foot Missouri schoolgirl was first discovered after running 50 yards in 5.8 seconds, equalling the world's best time. Two years later she beat Stella Walsh for the AAU title over 100m, running two 11.5 second times that year as well for the distance. In an extraordinary handicap race in Toronto on 2 September 1935, Stephens apparently ran 10.4 for 100 yards (official world record was 11.0) and 23.2 for 220 yards (straight), the official record being 23.6 by Stella Walsh. However, there is some doubt as to the accuracy of the timing at this meeting.

In 1936 Stephens not only defended her AAU 100m title successfully, but added shot and discus titles as well. In Berlin she powered her way to the gold ahead of Walsh, running 11.4 in the heats and 11.5 in the final, both wind assisted. She collected a second gold in the 4 x 100m relay, running a fine anchor leg to beat the German favourites, but could only finish ninth in the discus, with 34.32m.

After her retirement following the Olympics, she played professional basketball into the 1950s.

Stones, Dwight

1953–. Born USA (USA)

One of the most flamboyant and controversial characters in American athletics, Dwight Stones enjoyed the longest top-class career of all high jumpers. A bronze medallist at the 1972 and 1976 Olympic Games, he returned in 1984 to finish fourth, in a season in which he raised the US record to 2.34m.

As an 18-year-old, Stones impressed observers with his calm approach to the 1972 Olympic final. His two failures at 2.21m cost him the silver medal, as Stefan Junge of East Germany cleared it at his second attempt. The gold medal was won by Yuriy Tarmak of the Soviet Union with 2.23m.

In 1973 Stones became the first man to set a world record using the flop technique, introduced by fellow American Dick Fosbury at the 1968 Olympics. He cleared 2.30m in

Dwight Stones

Munich in an international match against West Germany and Switzerland, after using both flop and straddle styles during the competition.

He was US champion in 1973 and 1974, the same year that he won the English AAA and French national titles. In 1976, after improving his world record to 2.31m, he went to the Montreal Olympic Games as the odds-on favourite to win the gold medal. However, it was not a happy competition for him. He upset the crowd by wearing a tee-shirt carrying the slogan 'I love French Canadians', and upset officials by wearing a 1972 US Olympic vest instead of the 1976 version. Finally, persistent rain virtually wrecked his chances of winning the competition because his style depended on his being able to approach the bar much faster than other jumpers. He was unable to get into his usual rhythm and failed three times at 2.23m. Gold eventually went to Jacek Wszola of Poland (2.25m), while Canada's Greg Joy took the silver (2.23m).

Undeterred, Stones recovered from his disappointment to claim his third world record with 2.32m in Philadelphia three days later. He had already improved the world indoor record seven times from 2.26m to 2.30m between 1975 and 1976.

In 1977 he won his third US title, and finished runner-up to Rolf Beilschmidt of East Germany in the World Cup competition in Düsseldorf. He was suspended from competition by the American Athletics Union (AAU) and the IAAF in 1978 for receiving money from a television Superstars contest, but was reinstated a year later after paying the $33,400 in question to the US governing body.

After returning to competition with two poor seasons in 1980 and 1981, Stones was on the point of retiring when he cleared 2.31m in Nice. It convinced him that all was not lost and that the 1983 World Championships and even the Olympic Games in 1984 were realistic goals. He made both. He finished sixth in Helsinki in

1983, before enjoying one of his best-ever seasons in 1984. He won the US Olympic trials with a life-time best of 2.34m, and battled his way to a gallant fourth place in Los Angeles behind gold medal winner Dietmar Mogenburg of West Germany.

Stones is now an accomplished sports commentator with American television.

Szewinska, Irena

1946–. Born USSR (POL)

One of the great women athletes of all time, Irena Szewinska (née Kirszenstein) was known for much of her career as the Queen of the Track. Her record not only shows what enormous talent she possessed as a sprinter and long jumper, but also a determination to improve and a love of competition. In a brilliant career spanning five Olympic Games, she won gold, silver and bronze medals in the 100m, 200m, 400m and the long jump, as well as in the sprint relays. Above all, she will be remembered as a formidable competitor and an inspiration to the likes of Marita Koch, who succeeded her as the number one woman sprinter, and Jarmila Kratochvilova, the great 400m and 800m runner whose best performances came late in her career.

Her first international competition for Poland was aged 18 at the 1964 Olympic Games in Tokyo. Second in the long jump to Britain's Mary Rand, who broke the world record, Szewinska finished 16 centimetres behind, but ahead of the previous world record holder, Tatyana Shchelkanova. She followed with another silver medal in the 200m, behind American Edith Maguire, and a sensational gold medal in the 4 x 100m relay, as Poland beat the American favourites in a new world record time of 43.6 seconds.

In 1965, as a student at the University of Warsaw, she set world records at 100m (11.10) and 200m (22.7). She was now established as a world star and enjoyed a marvellous European Championships in 1966, when she won the 200m and long jump titles, won a

gold medal in the 4 x 100m relay, and finished second in the individual 100m. By 1967 she ranked number one in the world at 100m, 200m and the long jump. Later that year she married Janusz Szewinska.

At the 1968 Olympics in Mexico, she challenged opponents for four medals, with mixed fortunes. First of all, she failed to qualify for the long jump final, but recovered enough to equal her world record in the heats of the 100m. In the final, however, she had to be content with the bronze medal behind the Americans Wyomia Tyus, the reigning champion, and Barbara Ferrell. In the 200m, Szewinska came into her own, stretching her long legs to beat easily Raelene Boyle of Australia in a new world record of 22.5. The Poles failed to finish the sprint relay, however, as Szewinska uncharacteristically dropped the baton.

After quiet years in 1969 and 1970, when she had her son, Andrzej, Szewinska prepared for the European Championships in Helsinki in 1971. Her lack of condition showed as she finished sixth in the 100m, third in the 200m, and fifth in the long jump.

With 1972 came another Olympic Games, this time in Munich, but things would not go right for her in West Germany. Forced to pull out of the long jump because of a nagging ankle injury, she failed to qualify for the 100m final and could only finish third in the 200m, as East German Renate Stecher stormed to a new world record of 22.40.

The European Championships of 1974 meant another challenge. Now coached by her husband, Szewinska was even more effective on the track, regaining her 200m world record with 22.21 and, in her second-ever 400m, becoming the first woman to run the distance inside 50 seconds. Her time of 49.9 took an amazing 1.1 seconds off the previous mark. At the championships she won the 100m and 200m ahead of Stecher. In the 4 x 100m relay she helped Poland to third place, while in the 4 x 400m relay she ran an anchor lap of 48.6, although Poland finished out of the medals. During the year she won all of her 100m races, and 19 out of 20 of her races at 200m.

There was still more to come. At the 1976 Olympics in Montreal, she opted for the 400m, and once again took the event into new territory with another world record of 49.29 for a spectacular gold medal. Her nearest challenger, Christina Brehmer, finished almost 1.5 seconds behind.

At the 1977 World Cup she won the 200m ahead of the Olympic champion Barbel Eckert (later Wockel) of East Germany, plus the 400m, beating Marita Koch. But it was Koch who was destined to take over from Szewinska as the first lady of athletics. The East German beat her over 400m at the 1978 European Championships, with a world record 48.94, and at the 1979 World Cup in Montreal. At the 1980 Olympics in Moscow, Szewinska, now 34, pulled a muscle during her 400m semi-final and failed to make the final. The gold medal eventually went to Koch.

Her last competition was the Eight Nations meeting in Tokyo, the scene of her international début. She is still closely involved in athletics, as a member of the Women's Committee of the International Amateur Athletic Federation.

Irena Szewinska

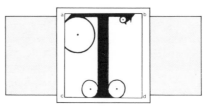

Ter-Ovanesyan, Igor

1938–. Born USSR (URS)

The dominant European long jumper throughout the 1960s, Ter-Ovanesyan won three European Championships (1958, 1962 and 1969) and took the silver in 1966 and 1971, won two Olympic bronze medals (1960 and 1964) and set two world records.

At his first Olympics in 1956 he no-jumped three times in the final, but recovered from this set-back to win the 1958 Europeans with 7.81m, and the following year was the first European over 8m, jumping 8.01m. He set a personal best of 8.04m in Rome at the Olympics won by Ralph Boston (USA), and in 1962 won the Europeans again with 8.19m, as well as setting his first world record, 8.31m. He took bronze again at Tokyo, where Lynn Davies (GBR) finished ahead of defending champion Boston. Four years later in Mexico he could only manage fourth, demoralized like the rest of the field by Bob Beamon's (USA) 8.90m leap.

Ter-Ovanesyan competed often against Ralph Boston, losing to him four times in USA-USSR matches. Lynn Davies beat him, 7.89m to 7.88m, to win the 1966 Europeans. In the 1969 Europeans, Ter-Ovanesyan beat Davies 8.17m to 8.07m, and beat him again in 1971 in the European Championships won by 1cm by Max Klauss (GDR), with Ter-Ovanesyan second with 7.91m and Davies fourth. His competitive career came to an end at the 1972 Munich Olympics, where he failed to qualify for the final.

Ter-Ovanesyan won five World Student Games titles (in 1959, 1961 - 1963, and 1965) and 12 national titles (1957, 1959 - 1960, 1962 - 1969 and 1971). After his retirement he became Soviet team coach.

John Thomas

Thomas, John

1941–. Born USA (USA)

The leading American high jumper of the early 1960s, John Thomas set four outdoor world records and 11 world indoor bests. He was not so dominant at the Olympics, winning bronze in Rome in 1960 and silver four years later in Tokyo. On 1 July 1960 he was the first man to clear 2.20m, jumping 2.22m in the US Olympic trials at Palo Alto, California.

1960 was Thomas' best year when, at 19 years old, he set all his outdoor world records and four of his indoor bests. He improved the outdoor record to 2.17m (twice), 2.18m and then his best-ever 2.22m. Indoors he jumped 2.17m (twice), 2.18m then 2.19m, this last at Chicago on 11 March. Winning the AAU title in 1959 he became the youngest world record holder this century at 17 years and 355 days, but his mark of 2.16m was not ratified as a world record as it was achieved indoors.

At the 1960 Olympics, although he was the world record holder, Thomas was beaten by 2cm (2.16m to 2.14m) by the Soviet pair Robert Shavlakadze and Valeriy Brumel. Thomas was the overwhelming favourite, having jumped seven feet or over 37 times before the championships, a mark which neither of the two Soviets had successfully cleared before. In the event Thomas only secured the bronze ahead of Viktor Bolshov (URS) who had had more failures.

Four years later in Tokyo it was Valeriy Brumel, no longer an unknown force, who took the gold. Thomas had cleared the same height, 2.18m, but lost because Brumel had fewer failures.

Thompson, Daley

1958–. Born England (GBR)

Between 1978 and 1987 Daley Thompson was quite simply unbeatable in the decathlon at a major championship. His supreme competitive spirit took him to Olympic, World, European and Commonwealth titles even when at times it looked as if his ability would let him down. At the 1984 Olympics, for instance, when it looked as if he would lose valuable points to his main rival Jürgen Hingsen in the pole vault and the discus, his determination to win kept him on course for the gold medal and a possible world record points score.

At his first Olympic Games in 1976, Thompson finished a distant eighteenth behind Bruce Jenner, but spent much of the competition learning all he could from the American. At the 1978 European Championships in Prague Thompson was runner-up to Grebenyuk of the Soviet Union. He won the Commonwealth Games title in 1978, and by 1980 he was Olympic champion, finishing the competition in Moscow more than 100 points clear of his nearest rival. He announced that his ambition was to win three Olympic decathlon titles.

He failed to finish a decathlon in 1984 but, apart from that, his progress was unimpeded as he went on to win the Commonwealth Games title twice more (1982 and 1986), the European title twice (1982 and 1986), the World Championship title in 1983 and his second Olympic title in 1984. Along

Daley Thompson

the way he set four world records and ten UK and Commonwealth records.

His winning streak came to an end in Rome at the 1987 World Championships. Beset by injury for most of the season, he went to the championships far from fully fit and could only finish ninth as his title went to East German Torsten Voss. Ironically, the two men who had regularly finished behind Thompson in the previous nine years, Jürgen Hingsen and Siggi Wentz of West Germany, could not take advantage of the champion's poor showing as they too were not at their best because of injury. But Thompson won himself a new legion of fans with the way he accepted defeat, competing to the final event and publicly saluting the new champion.

His personal bests are 100m - 10.26; 400m – 48.86; 110m – 14.04; high jump – 2.11m; pole vault – 5.25m; long jump – 8.01m; shot put – 16.10m; discus – 49.10m; javelin – 65.38m; 1500m – 4:20.3.

Thorpe, Jim

1888–1953. Born USA (USA)

Although one of the great Olympic champions – his points score in winning the decathlon in Stockholm in 1912 was not beaten for 15 years – Jim Thorpe's association with athletics was cut short soon after this. Having admitted receiving small sums of money playing college baseball in the summer vacations of 1909 and 1910, he was declared a professional by the International Committee and stripped of his gold medals.

His domination of his events (also pentathlon) was nevertheless complete – he won the decathlon by 700 points and won five of the ten disciplines. He finished fourth in the long jump, his lowest position in the decathlon. He also finished fourth in the individual high jump, and seventh in the individual long jump.

His best marks included 100 yards – 10.0; 440 yards – 51.0; 1500m –

4:40.1; 110mh – 15.0; 220 yard hurdles (straight) – 23.8; high jump – 1.95m; pole vault – 3.25m; long jump – 7.16m; shot – 14.55m; discus – 38.30m; javelin – 49.68m.

Of American Indian birth, Thorpe played professional baseball and football until he was 41, being voted in 1950 America's Greatest Sportsman of the Half-Century. Seventy years after his Olympic gold performances he was reinstated by the IOC.

Tkachenko, Nadyezda

1948–. Born USSR (URS)

After retaining her European pentathlon title in 1978, Nadyezda Tkachenko was subsequently stripped of the gold medal when the dope test showed she had used anabolic steroids. But under existing IAAF rules she was allowed to resume international competition after an 18-month ban.

On her return she won the 1980 Olympic title with a world record 5083 points. In a remarkable finish to the pentathlon competition in Moscow, the three medallists finished the final event, the 800m, to claim the world record points score in rapid succes-

Nadyezda Tkachenko

sion. Olga Kuragina won the 800m to finish with a points tally of 4875. It was a record for just 1.2 seconds as Olga Rukavishnikova crossed the line in second place to snatch the world record with 4937 points. Less than half a second later Tkachenko arrived across the line to take the gold medal and the world record. It was the first score over 5000 points. She was ninth behind Britain's Mary Peters in the 1972 Olympics and fifth behind Siegrun Seigl of East Germany in 1976.

She was World Student Games champion in 1973 and four times Soviet champion. The pentathlon – consisting of the 100mh, shot put, high jump, long jump, and 800m (which replaced the 200m after 1977) – was replaced by the heptathlon, with the addition of the 200m and javelin, in 1981.

Tolan, Eddie

1908–1967. Born USA (USA)

Winner of both 100m and 200m at the 1932 Olympics in Los Angeles, Eddie Tolan was an unlikely looking sprint champion. Only 1.63m (5ft 4in) in height, with stocky legs and spectacles, he seemed no match for the elegant Ralph Metcalfe or George Simpson. But beat them he did, although both races were surrounded by controversy.

In the 100m, although Tolan was declared the winner, both he and Metcalfe were given the same time, an Olympic record 10.3. Metcalfe remained convinced all his life that the race should at least have been a dead heat, and the photo evidence of the day suggests that he had a strong case. In the 200m Tolan powered his way to a new world record 21.2, beating George Simpson into second place by about two yards with Metcalfe a poor third. Metcalfe had apparently started the race three or four feet behind his mark, but refused the re-run offered by the officials because he did not want to jeopardize the American clean sweep of the medals.

Tolan, a college footballer whose

career was ended after a knee injury was dubbed the 'Midnight Express' by his University of Michigan team mates. He set his first world record – 9.5 for 100 yards – in 1929 at the Big Ten Championship in Illinois, and the same year won both sprint titles at the AAU Championships, and he retained the 100-yard title the following year. He won both the IC4A and NCAA 220-yard titles in 1931, and was placed second in the Olympic trials the following year behind Metcalfe.

After the Olympics Tolan took part in a sprint circus in Australia in 1935, winning the grandly labelled World Sprint title, against the best professionals of the day.

Toomey, Bill

1939–. Born USA (USA)

Olympic decathlon champion in 1968, Bill Toomey dominated the event the following year, going through the 8000 point barrier seven times. In a career that spanned 35 competitions he passed 8000 points 13 times, with a best of 8417 points set on 10 - 11 December 1969.

Toomey made his decathlon début

Bill Toomey

in 1959, scoring 5349 (on the 1952 tables) after having aspirations as a high jumper. But he found that the running events were his real strength. He ran the 400m in 45.6 during his Olympic victory in Mexico. He was hampered in the throwing events by a long-standing wrist injury.

His 8417 point total comprised the following: 100m - 10.3; long jump - 7.76m; shot - 14.38m; high jump - 1.93m; discus - 47.1m; 110mh - 14.3; 400m - 46.49; pole vault - 4.27m; javelin - 65.74m; 1500m - 4:39.4.

Torrance, Jack

1912–1969. Born USA (USA)

A huge shot putter, nicknamed 'Elephant Baby', Jack Torrance, set five world records but could finish no better than fifth at the Olympic Games in 1936 in Berlin.

Standing 1.90m (6ft 2in) tall and weighing in at around 140kg (22 stones), this student from Louisiana State University set his first world record at the start of an amazing year of competition that saw him take the mark from 16.30m to 17.40m. On 24 March he reached 16.30m at Lafayette, improving this to 16.32 in Baton Rouge on 21 April. A week later at Des Moines he shot putted 16.80m, and two months later at the AAU Championships on 30 June he reached 16.89m. But his biggest improvement came at the Bislett Stadium in Oslo during an international match on 8 August when he broke his own world record with a put of 17.40m, a record not beaten for almost 14 years.

At the Olympic Games of 1936, however, Torrance failed to impress, not even reaching the 50-foot mark in a competition won by Germany's Hans Woellke with 16.20m.

Towns, Forrest

1914–. Born USA (USA)

1936 Olympic champion over 110mh, Forrest Towns was the first man to dip under 14 seconds for the distance, which he did by taking an astonishing

0.4 seconds off his own world record.

His first record was set at the 1936 NCAA Championships in Chicago on 19 June 1936, clocking 14.1, a mark that he equalled in the semi-final in Berlin on 6 August of that year. In the final he won easily after a relatively poor start, winning in 14.2 ahead of Don Finlay (GBR) and Fred Pollard (USA), who both ran 14.4. But he saved his best performance ever for the Bislett Games in Norway on 27 August when, on a perfectly still evening, he ran 13.7, finishing almost a second ahead of the second man Larry O'Connor (CAN). Towns never again dipped under the magical 14-second barrier, but in his career he had 14 races between 14.1 and 14.2. He was also an excellent sprinter, with a personal best of 9.7 seconds for 100 yards.

Tyler, Dorothy

1920–. Born England (GBR)

Dorothy Tyler was Commonwealth Games high jump champion in 1938 and 1950. This record is impressive, but how much more impressive it would have been had the silver medals she won at the 1936 and 1948 Olympics been gold instead. On both occasions she recorded the same height as the winner but lost according to the rules of the day, whereas following today's rules she would have won.

Her first Olympics were in Berlin aged 16 and her last in Melbourne 20 years later, a record span of 20 years for British international appearances. In both Games she managed the same height, 1.60m. In Berlin, this tied for first place with Ibolya Csak (HUN), who then won in the jump-off with 1.62m. In Melbourne 1.60m was only good enough for equal twelfth.

In 1939 she set her only world record, 1.66m, but missed her chance to go for Olympic gold when the Games of 1940 and 1944 were cancelled. In the London Games of 1948 she lost to Alice Coachman (USA) (who had fewer failures) after both had cleared 1.68m, a personal best for Tyler. She was placed second in the 1950 Europeans in Brussels, seventh in the 1952 Olympics in Helsinki, and second in the 1954 Commonwealth Games in Vancouver.

In 1951 she changed her style from the scissors to the Western roll and in 1957 cleared 1.67m, just one centimetre below her best-ever mark.

Tyler was Britain's youngest female record holder, clearing 1.65m on 1 June 1936 aged 16 years and 39 days. She won 11 WAAA titles at high jump (indoors 1937-9, outdoors 1936-9, 1948-9, 1952, 1956) and won the long jump (best-ever of 5.73m) and pentathlon (best-ever 3953 points) in 1951.

Dorothy Tyler

Tyus, Wyomia

1945–. Born USA (USA)

The only athlete ever to retain the Olympic 100m title, Wyomia Tyus won in 1964 and 1968. Like Wilma Rudolph before her she competed for the famous Tennessee State Tigerbelles Track Club under coach Ed Temple. Before her first Olympics in Tokyo she was evenly matched with Edith McGuire, who ran for the same team. McGuire took the 1963 AAU title with Tyus second, and the places were reversed the following year. But once in Tokyo Tyus showed her class, tying the world record of 11.2 in the quarter final and beating McGuire by 0.2 seconds (11.4 to 11.6) for the gold. She also ran in the silver medal sprint relay team when the Americans were beaten by the Polish team that set a world record 43.6 seconds but which included Ewa Klobukowska, later disqualified retroactively after failing a sex test.

In 1965 Tyus confirmed her status, equalling the 100-yard world record of 10.3 in Kingston, Jamaica on 17 July before equalling the 100m mark of 11.1 recently set by Poles Klobukowska and Irena Szewinska. She won both AAU 100-yard and 220-yard titles the next year but came only third in 1967 before winning the Pan American Games gold at 200m.

Tyus' rivals in Mexico were from both home and abroad – Poland's Szewinska, Raelene Boyle (AUS, and Barbara Ferrell and Margaret Bailes (USA). Boyle equalled the Olympic record of 11.2 before Szewinska equalled her own 11.1 world record in the heats, but Tyus came through in the final to win in a new world record 11.0 seconds, later automatically corrected to 11.08, ahead of Ferrell and Szewinska (both 11.1). At the longer distance, though, never her favourite, she could finish only sixth as Szewinska stormed home in a new world record 22.5. But she continued winning in the 4 x 100m relay, running the anchor leg to set a new world record 42.8.

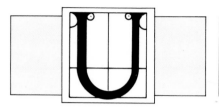

Ulmasova, Svyetlana

1953–. Born USSR (URS)

Twice the European champion over 3000m, Svyetlana Ulmasova was also ranked number one in the world in 1978 and 1982. She also broke the world record for the distance with a brilliant run in the Soviet Championships of 1982.

Her time at the 1978 European Championships, 8:33.16, was a championship record. The pace over the closing lap proved too quick for Natalia Marasescu of Romania (8:33.53) and Grete Waitz of Norway (8:34.33), a former world record holder. In 1982 Ulmasova took the record to 8:26.78. Later the same year she won her second European title.

She was a convincing winner of the 1979 World Cup race in Montreal.

Ulmasova could only finish fourth in the 1983 World Championships in 8:35.55 as the title went to Mary Decker (later Slaney) of the USA in 8:34.62.

Svyetlana Ulmasova

Viren, Lasse

1949–. Born Finland (FIN)

Winner of the 5000m and 10,000m double at the 1972 Games in Munich, Lasse Viren repeated the double four years later in Montreal, a feat that not even the great Paavo Nurmi had achieved. In 1976 he was placed fifth in the Olympic marathon only a day after the 5000m final, finishing in 2:13:10.

Viren had an uncanny knack of being able to peak at the right time, although he went into the 1972 Games as a virtual unknown. He finished seventh in the 5000m and seventeenth in the 10,000m at the 1971 European Championships, but did set a two-mile world record of 8:14.0 prior to the Games in Munich.

In the 5000m final he won in 13:26.42 after a fast last 2000m in 5:06.0 to follow a slowish pace, but he saved his most devastating form for the longer distance. On lap 12 in the 10,000m he stumbled and fell, bringing down Mohamed Gammoudi (TUN), silver medallist in 1964 and bronze medallist in 1968, but recovered himself, getting up to win in a new world record 27:38.35, ahead of Emiel Puttemans (BEL) in 27:39.58 and Miruts Yifter (ETH) in 27:40.96.

In between Olympics Viren failed to impress, although he set a world record for 5000m late in 1972 of 13:16.4. He ranked only fifteenth in the world for 10,000m and seventh for 5000m in 1973, and won only a bronze medal at 5000m in the European Championships in Finland in 1974, finishing seventh in the 10,000m. By training at altitude for part of 1976 he prepared himself for his Olympic defence, and to be the first man to take the 5000m, 10,000m and marathon

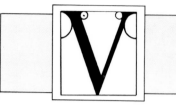

titles since Emil Zatopek in 1952.

In Montreal he retained his 10,000m title ahead of Carlos Lopes (POR) and Brendan Foster (GBR), running 27:40.38 with a second half of 13:31.3. He also beat a class field at the shorter distance, winning in 13:24.76. His preparation of one day for the marathon was assessed by one observer as the worst he had ever seen for a top-class marathon, and Viren suffered from dehydration and after finishing fifth vowed never to run the distance again. In the1980 Games in Moscow he finished fifth in the 10,000m in 27:50.5, eight seconds adrift of winner Miruts Yifter (ETH), but dropped out of the marathon after 25km. He returned to marathon running for the 1988 Los Angeles Marathon when, aged 39, he finished fifty-ninth in 2:27:31.

Viren, whose career has been dogged for years by rumours of blood doping (removing a pint of blood months before an event then replacing it just before a race to give the body the benefit of having more oxygen-carrying red blood cells, a technique of great benefit to endurance athletes but banned), was nevertheless a supreme champion at the highest level.

Lasse Viren

Waitz, Grete

1953–. Born Norway (NOR)

Such is Grete Waitz's reputation in Norway that her statue now stands outside Oslo's Bislett Stadium. For so long the first lady of distance running, her record on the track, at cross-country and on the road makes her one of the world's finest-ever women runners.

Her greatest success in recent years has been as a road and cross-country runner, but her career began on the track in the early 1970s. Her international début, in fact, was at the 1971 European Championships in Helsinki, where she was eliminated in the heats of the 800m and 1500m. She was also eliminated in the 1500m heats at the 1972 Olympic Games, and her first real success at the distance came at the 1974 European Championships, when she finished third. Four years later she was fifth. At 3000m she has fared much better, setting two world records - 8:46.6 in 1975 and 8:45.4 in 1976 - and winning a gold medal at the 1977 World Cup. She also won a bronze medal at the 1978 European Championships and a silver at the 1979 World Cup.

In 1978 she made her first appearance at the World Cross-Country Championships in Glasgow. She won it then and for the next three years. She took the title for the fifth time in 1983.

Her marathon début came in New York at the end of 1978, when her time of 2:32:30 was a world best by more than two minutes. She has since won the race a record eight times. The only other woman to win the race up to 1986 was Alison Roe in 1981, when Waitz failed to finish.

She has won the London Marathon

Grete Waitz

twice (1983 and 1986), and demonstrated her superiority at the distance by winning the first World Championship marathon in 1983 in 2:28:09. Along with fellow Norwegian Ingrid Kristiansen, she was a favourite for the inaugural women's Olympic marathon in Los Angeles in 1984. On the day, however, she allowed the American Joan Benoit to build up too much of a lead, and left it too late before starting her chase. It was an uncharacteristic tactical lapse and she ended up with the silver medal in 2:26:18, almost a minute-and-a-half behind Benoit.

She was unable to defend her World Championship title in 1987 because of a persistent leg injury. In all, she has won 11 of her 15 marathons and has dropped out of three, making Benoit the only woman to have beaten her in completed races.

Walker, John

1952–. Born New Zealand (NZL)

One of the most charismatic and popular figures in athletics since the 1970s, John Walker will go down in history

John Walker

as the first man to run the mile in under 3:50. His world record time of 3:49.4 came at Gothenburg, Sweden on 12 August 1975. A year later he won the 1500m gold medal at the Olympic Games in Montreal. A second world record, in 1976, was over 2000m, when he took 4.8 seconds off Michel Jazy's ten-year-old mark with 4:41.4.

Speaking of his achievements during that time, he said: 'In 1976 my career basically finished because I'd reached the pinnacle. I'd broken two world records, run under 3:50 for the mile and won an Olympic gold medal. I could do no more.'

In fact, he did do more. Without breaking world records or winning major championships he has gone on to become the most durable of athletes, still running world-class times and beating top-class fields at the age of 35. He was also the first man to run 100 sub-four-minute miles, a feat he achieved in 1985.

Running in the shadow of his more illustrious New Zealand colleagues Dick Quax and Rod Dixon, Walker first appeared on the European circuit in 1973. He clocked his first sub-four-minute mile in Victoria, British Columbia. His first major races came at the 1974 Commonwealth Games in Edmonton, Canada. After finishing third in the 800m, he came up against Filbert Bayi of Tanzania in the 1500m. While Bayi led for the entire race to win in a new world record time of 3:32.2, Walker chased him all the way to the line, finishing just a couple of strides behind in 3:32.5, inside the American Jim Ryun's old record.

He had his revenge over Bayi in a later race in Helsinki, where the Tanzanian – a noted front runner – ran out of steam at 1200m. Walker coasted to victory in 3:33.4. The two men dominated middle-distance running for two years, but were never to race each other again. Bayi broke the world record for the mile early in 1975 in Kingson, Jamaica, with 3:51.0, but Walker took the record into new territory only three months later.

He went to the 1976 Olympics as the favourite to win the 1500m, although the world was looking forward to another clash with Filbert Bayi. Sadly, the African boycott put paid to that, but Walker did not disappoint the crowd. He set off for the line with 250m to go, proving too strong for the chasing Ivo Van Damme of Belguim who finished second. Walker crossed the line, arms raised in 3:39.2 after a 52.7-second last lap.

His long blond hair and sun-tan made him the pin-up of the track, and he was expected to dominate the event for some time. But his fortunes changed in 1977. He ran the world's fastest 1500m (3:32.7) and mile (3:52.0), but ended his season with a disastrous appearance at the World Cup in Düsseldorf. Running for the Oceania team, he was well placed in the 1500m as Britain's Steve Ovett, running for Europe, came up on his shoulder with 200m to go. Walker inexplicably stepped off the track as Ovett swept to victory. The crowd reacted by booing him for his apparent lack of competitiveness. Walker later explained that he had taken a knock from another athlete and when he was forced off the track he momentarily lost his concentration, by which time the field had left him behind.

Injury put paid to his 1978 season and, by the time he emerged in 1979, Ovett and Sebastian Coe were the new stars of middle-distance running. In Oslo, on 7 July 1979, Walker could only finish sixth, as his world record for the mile went to Coe who lowered it to 3:49.00. Since then he has been in races when the record has been further improved by Coe, twice, and Steve Cram.

Walker opted out of defending his title at the Moscow Olympics, where victory went to Coe. He finished second to Cram in the 1982 Commonwealth Games 1500m and ninth behind the Briton at the 1983 World Championships. He moved up to 5000m for the 1984 Olympic Games in Los Angeles, but could never match the speed of his more accomplished opponents and finished eighth. A further experiment at 5000m ended with fourth place behind Ovett at the 1986 Commonwealth Games.

Walsh, Stella

1911–1980. Born Poland (POL)

Born Stanislawa Walasiewicz, Walsh spent her whole life from the age of eleven in the USA. However, she represented Poland in major championships, winning the Olympic 100m title in 1932; coming second in 1936; completing a sprint double at the 1938 European Championships (silver in the long jump); winning the 60m, 100m and 200m at the 1930 Women's World Games. She retained her 60m title in 1934, coming second over 100m and 200m.

She improved the 100m world record ten times, and the 200m world best five times. Only five were approved by the IAAF, two at 100m (11.6 in 1937, the fastest), one at 200m (23.6, which lasted for 16 years), one at 60m (7.3), and one at 220 yards (24.3). In all, she won a total of 40 AAU titles at a wide variety of events including four at 100m, 11 at 200m and long jump, two at discus and five at pentathlon.

In 1945 she ran an incredible 11.2 for 100m in Cleveland, a mark that bettered her own world record by 0.4 seconds. It was never ratified, however. 'The officials thought it was impossible for a woman to run that fast', Walsh later commented.

Although married, Walsh was discovered to have no female sex organs but only internal male ones after a post-mortem examination. She was killed as an innocent bystander in a grocery store hold-up on 4 December 1980.

Warmerdam, Cornelius

1915–. Born USA (USA)

Arguably the best pole vaulter in history, Warmerdam was the first man to clear 15 feet (4.57m), in 1940 in Berkeley, California. Until his retirement, in 1944, he raised the world record six more times to 4.77m outdoors (1942) and 4.78m indoors (1943). A 15-foot clearance is unspectacular today, but using bamboo

Allan Wells

poles in Warmerdam's era he achieved the feat 43 times before his retirement. No other vaulter succeeded in clearing that height until 1951. Robert Richards (USA) succeeded in clearing 15ft 1in (4.59m) indoors in New York on 27 January.

American champion from 1937 to 1944, excluding 1939, he first reached world class aged 19, clearing 14 feet (4.26m). Had there been Olympics in 1940 and 1944, he would have almost certainly won gold medals, such was his domination of the event. He vaulted 4.37m in an exhibition in 1952, but his own best of 4.78m was achieved at Austin, Texas on 15 June 1957. In 1975, aged 60, Warmerdam included a 3.20m vault when setting a decathlon world age record of 4328 points in Glendale, California.

Wells, Allan

1952–. Born Scotland (GBR)

Inevitably known as 'the Flying Scot', Allan Wells was singularly responsible for revitalizing British sprinting in the late 1970s, before going on to become Olympic champion in 1980. A late starter, he won his gold medal in Moscow at 28 and was still competing with world-class times at 35.

A long jumper to begin with – his best is 7.32m – Wells took up sprinting at the age of 24. However, along with every other 100m runner in the nation, he was not considered good enough to represent Britain at the 1976 Olympic Games in Montreal. The same year he joined a group of athletes trained by a professional coach who instilled in him the importance of strength training. Wells adopted the training – incorporating circuit exercises and punching a speedball – with a fanatical enthusiasm. The winter of 1977-1978 was the turning point, when Wells dedicated himself to getting stronger and faster over 100m and 200m.

The summer of 1978 saw him equal Peter Radford's 20-year-old British 100m record of 10.29. A week later the record was his when he sped

through in 10.15. At the Commonwealth Games he finished runner-up to Olympic silver medallist Don Quarrie in the 100m, with 10.07, before beating the Jamaican in the 200m for his first championship gold medal. He added another gold medal to his collection as a member of the victorious Scottish 4 x 100m relay team. His good form couldn't stretch to the European Championships later that year, however, when he finished sixth in the 100m, won by the Italian Pietro Mennea.

Coached by his wife, Margot, from then on, Wells won the European Cup 200m in 1979 and prepared for his biggest test of all, the 1980 Olympic Games in Moscow. Part of his training that winter involved using starting blocks for the first time, as they were made compulsory for the Games. In the final there was no stopping him. Pressed at the line by Silvio Leonard of Cuba, the slow motion replay on the stadium's giant screen proved that Wells had won the 100m by a whisker in 10.25. Leonard was given the same time but only the silver medal.

Next was the 200m and a remarkable sprint double was a distinct possibility. However, Mennea – the World record holder and bronze medallist in 1972 – proved the stronger, and just managed to edge Wells out of the gold medal position at the line. It was desperately close, Mennea achieving 20.19 to Wells' 20.21.

Despite the quality of his running in Moscow, Wells had to face the criticism of the top American sprinters – absent from the Games because of the US boycott – that he had won the gold medal by default. Wells responded by beating them all the following year to take the Golden Sprint title in Berlin. The same year he also won the European Cup 100m title in Zagreb and the World Cup title in Rome, beating Carl Lewis (USA) among others, who limped in ninth and last after the recurrence of a hamstring injury. It was Lewis who was to inflict Wells' heaviest defeat at the 1984 Olympics.

Running as well as ever, Wells won

the Commonwealth Games 100m in Brisbane in 1982, when he beat Ben Johnson of Canada, a man who was to make a tremendous impact on the event four years later. He also won the 200m, but had to share the title with an inspired Mike McFarlane of England, who caught Wells on the line for the first dead heat in Commonwealth Games history.

The following year saw Carl Lewis establish himself as the world's finest sprinter. Wells, however, could no longer compete with him, finishing fourth in both sprints at the World Championships in Helsinki. It was Lewis who cruised to victory in the 100m in Los Angeles at the 1984 Olympics – the first of his four gold medals – while a shattered Wells was eliminated in the semi-final. A foot injury had refused to clear up, and the unfortunate Wells ran the race with a pad inside his shoe. The desperate measure failed dismally.

Undeterred, Wells returned to top-class competition in 1986, finishing fifth in both sprints at the European Championships. He would have

Fatima Whitbread

competed at the 1987 World Championships but for injuries which forced him to pull out of the 200m and the relay.

Whitbread, Fatima
1961–. Born England (GBR)

Britain's only gold medallist at the 1987 World Championships, and the only British thrower to break a world record, Fatima Whitbread has asserted herself as the world's number one javelin thrower in the face of the stiffest competition.

As a youngster she was inspired by Tessa Sanderson, the UK record holder and winner of their first 18 confrontations. It was 1983 before Whitbread beat Sanderson in competition, and the contests between them were to become a major feature of domestic meetings in the following years.

After failing to qualify for the final at the 1980 Olympic Games, where she threw 49.74m, well below her best, she broke through into world class in 1981. Whitbread won her first UK and WAAA senior titles, improved her personal best to 65.82m and won her first international match victory. With Sanderson injured for the entire 1982 season, Whitbread improved her best again to 66.98m, beat the Olympic champion Maria Colon of Cuba, and finished eighth at the European Championships in Athens. But for problems with her shoulder, she might have done better than third place at the Commonwealth Games in Brisbane.

The competition which really brought her to the public's attention was the 1983 World Championships. Leading for the first five rounds with her opening throw of 69.14m, Whitbread could only look on in disbelief as Finland's Tiina Lillak, the world record holder, snatched the gold medal with her final throw of 70.82m. The whole nation shared her disappointment as she was consoled by her mother and coach, Margaret, the national javelin coach. Sanderson was fourth. Victory in that season's Euro-

pean Cup Final was some consolation, but her sights were set on the following year's Olympic Games in Los Angeles.

Battling against illness and the effects of an operation on her womb just days before the Olympics, she went into the final as one of the favourites in the absence of Colon and the top Eastern Europeans, ruled out by their governments' boycott. This time, though, it was Sanderson's turn to open the competition with a massive throw of 69.56m. No one could match this throw, and Whitbread finished as the bronze medallist behind Sanderson and Lillak.

It was a major disappointment for Whitbread who, although ranked number one in Britain, now faced another mighty opponent in Petra Felke of East Germany, the new world record holder with 75.40m. In 1985 Whitbread beat Sanderson on all five occasions they met and improved her best to 72.98m, regularly throwing beyond 70m. But she was yet to beat Felke.

Sanderson once again proved the better competitor in major competition in 1986, when she won the Commonwealth Games title in Edinburgh. Her 69.80m fifth round throw was better than anything Whitbread could produce and she had to be content with the silver medal. Four weeks later, though, she at last discovered her best form when it mattered. At the European Championships, in Stuttgart, she qualified for the final with a world record-breaking 77.44m, and went on to beat Felke and take the gold medal with 76.32m.

There were fears in 1987 that severe problems with her throwing arm would prevent her from competing at the World Championships. However, after last-minute treatment, she took her place in the final, where she faced Sanderson and Felke, who had regained the world record a few weeks before. This time there was no stopping her as she put together four throws beyond 70m to win with 76.64m. Felke was second, Sanderson fourth.

Whitfield, Mal

1924–. Born USA (USA)

One of the greatest 800m runners, Mal Whitfield was always more interested in winning than in records. Although he did set world records, two at 880 yards and one at one kilometre, from June 1948 to the end of the 1954 season he lost only three of his 69 races at 800m or 880 yards, a winning streak that included Olympic 800m titles in 1948 and 1952. He also won silver at 400m in 1948, and gold (1948) and silver (1952) in the 4 x 400m relay.

In both his Olympic 800m victories he beat Jamaican Arthur Wint by about two metres, each time clocking 1:49.2. Well known for his devastating turn of speed in the third 200m, he had a great range – from 10.7 for 100m to 4:12.6 for the mile.

In 1953 he set world indoor bests at 500 yards (56.6), 500m (62.9), and 600 yards (1:09.5). His one-kilometre world record that year of 2:20.8 was followed an hour later by an American record for 440 yards of 46.2.

After an unsuccessful attempt to move up in distance to the mile in 1955, and his failure to get into the US

Mal Whitfield

team for the 1956 Melbourne Olympic Games, he retired. In addition to his Olympic medals, he won the Pan American Games 800m in 1951 and the AAU 800m/880 yards title five times (1949-1951, 1953-1954).

Wilkins, Mac

1950–. Born USA (USA)

Nicknamed 'Multiple Mac' by team mates at the University of Oregon, because of his ability at all the throwing events, Mac Wilkins found his greatest success with the discus. He was Olympic champion in 1976, four times world record holder, and a silver medallist at the 1984 Olympics.

He threw his first world record in Apirl 1976, when he was apparently suffering from a back injury. Nevertheless, the discus flew out to 69.18m. A week later, at San José in California, he improved the record three times with successive throws, 69.80m, 70.24m, and 70.86m, to make him the first man to throw beyond 70m. He went on to win the Olympic title in Montreal, with a second round throw of 67.50m. The silver medal went to Wolfgang Schmidt of East Germany, who would succeed him as world record holder, and the bronze to Wilkins' fierce rival, fellow American John Powell, the previous world record holder.

Wilkins lost out to Schmidt in the World Cup competitions of 1977 and 1979, but was in tremendous form in 1980. He won the US Olympic trial and achieved a throw of 70.98m, the second furthest of all time after Schmidt's 1978 throw of 71.16m. However, he was unable to defend his title in Moscow because of the US boycott.

He finished tenth at the 1983 World Championships, where the title went to Imrich Bugar of Czechoslovakia with 67.72m. In the absence of the Eastern Bloc countries in Los Angeles in 1984, Wilkins was among the favourites for the Olympic title. He came close and led the competition until the fourth round, when West

'Multiple Mac' Wilkins

German Rolf Danneberg unleashed a throw of 66.60m. Wilkins' best response was a fifth round 61.36m for second place. John Powell was third.

His personal bests included 78.44m for the javelin, 61.36m for the hammer, and a 21.06m indoor shot put mark.

Williams, Yvette

1929–. Born New Zealand (NZL)

Winner of the 1952 Olympic long jump title, and gold medallist at the 1950 and 1954 Commonwealth Games, Yvette Williams was a multi-talented athlete who tasted success at various disciplines. She placed second in the 1950 Commonwealth javelin (shot and discus were not yet on the women's programme) sixth in the 1952 Olympic shot, and tenth in the discus. She won both the shot and the discus at the 1954 Commonwealth Games in Vancouver, Canada.

By winning individual gold medals at three different events, she equalled the 1938 achievement of Australian Decima Norman, who had won the 100 yards, 220 yards, and the long jump.

In her most successful year, 1954, she also set a long jump world record

Arthur Wint

of 6.28m. Between 1947 and 1954 she won 21 national titles at a record five events: shot – 8; long jump – 7; discus – 4; javelin – 1; 80mh – 1.

Wint, Arthur

1920–. Born Jamaica (JAM)

One of the great Jamaican runners of the immediate post-war era, Arthur Wint won the 1948 Olympic 400m title in London, and four years later formed part of the great 4 x 400m relay team that won gold in Helsinki in a world record 3:03.9. Tall and long-striding, Wint also won two silver medals at 800m, finishing behind Mal Whitfield on both occasions, 1:49.2 to 1:49.5 in 1948, and 1:49.2 to 1:49.4 in 1952.

His victory over race favourite Herb McKenley, in London in 1948, was the first of two Olympic final defeats for multi-world record holder McKenley (George Rhoden beat him in 1952). At the half-way point Wint was five metres down, but he slowly began to reach his compatriot, passing him with 20 yards to go to finish ahead by two yards, equalling the Olympic record 46.2. McKenley finished in 46.4.

In the 400m final in Helsinki in 1952, Wint went out fast in defence of his title, but faltered in the home straight to finish fifth. In the relay he ran the first leg in 46.8, handing on to Leslie Laing (47.0) before Herb McKenley (44.6) and George Rhoden (45.5) to win gold in a world record 3:03.9.

Wint was a great favourite with the British public and one of the few top Jamaican runners of the era who chose to live in England rather than the USA. He was a member of the Polytechnic Harriers.

He returned to Jamaica in 1952, but came back to London in 1974 as Jamaican High Commissioner.

Wockel, Barbel

1955–. Born East Germany (GDR)

European junior champion at 100m hurdles, 200m and in the 4 x 100m relay, Barbel Wockel (née Eckert) went on to win four Olympic gold medals in 1976 and 1980, equalling the feats of Fanny Blankers-Koen of Holland and Betty Cuthbert of Australia.

She began her athletics career as a youngster who enjoyed the sprint hurdles event, and her three gold medals at the 1973 European Junior Championships showed just how versatile she was. After being drafted into the GDR senior team in 1974, though, in time for the European Championships, she was encouraged to abandon the hurdles to concentrate on the 100m and 200m. She was initially a recruit to the formidable GDR relay team, and at the championships won a gold medal in the 4 x 100m. She was also seventh in the individual event.

Wockel was injured for most of 1975 but, as part of her preparation for the 1976 Olympics, she joined the powerful sprinting set-up at the SC Motor Jena club, which already listed Renate Stecher and Marlies Oelsner (later Gohr) among its members. Coached by Horst-Dieter Hille and guided by Stecher, Wockel went to Montreal as GDR 200m champion. In the Olympic final, she proved stronger than Stecher, the reigning champion, and West Germany's Annegret Richter, the 100m champion, to finish first in 22.37, a personal best and Olympic record. The margin of victory was just two hundredths of a second from Richter. Stecher was third. Wockel's second gold medal came in the 4 x 100m relay.

She did little of note on the track during the intervening years before the next Olympics. She married in 1979 and then took a year's maternity leave, before returning to her preparations for the 1980 Games in Moscow.

Once again, she went to coach Hille for help, and again went into an Olympic campaign as GDR champion, this time with a personal best of 22.01. The gold medal was hers in 22.03, beating Natalya Botchina of the Soviet Union who set a world junior record of 22.19. In the 4 x 100m relay Wockel earned her fourth Olympic gold medal, as the East Germans swept to a world record 41.60. It was the fifth time Wockel had been part of a relay world record. She was also a member of the GDR 4 x 200m team that set the world records in 1976 and 1980.

At the 1982 European Championships, in Athens, she finished runner-up to Gohr in the 100m and won the 200m title with 22.04 from Britain's Kathy Smallwood. A third medal, a gold, came in the relay.

Wolde, Mamo

1932–. Born Ethiopia (ETH)

Emerging from the shadows of the great Abebe Bikila, whom he had never beaten, Mamo Wolde won Ethiopia's third successive gold medal in the Olympic marathon in 1968. He had previously taken the silver medal in the 10,000m. Four years later, in Munich, he became the oldest distance running medallist when he took the bronze in the marathon, aged 40 years, 90 days.

Wolde had begun his Olympic career unsuccessfully in Melbourne in

1956, finishing last in his 800m and 1500m heat. By 1964, however, he had moved up in distance, and did well enough to come fourth in the 10,000m in Tokyo.

At altitude in Mexico in 1968, Wolde, along with other African runners, had a distinct advantage. The 10,000m, where world record holder Ron Clarke ran himself into a state of collapse, showed that advantage clearly. In a last lap sprint Wolde just lost out to Natali Temu (KEN), 29:27.4 to 29:28.0, with Mohammed Gammoudi (TUN) third in 29:34.2.

In the marathon, defending champion Bikila dropped out at 17km, but Wolde, on a very hot day with temperatures of around 27° C (80° F) and above, was content to let 10,000m winner Temu dictate the pace until he began to falter with eight miles to go. Wolde took over and was never in danger, finishing over three minutes ahead of the second man, Kenji Kimihara (JAP), 2:20:26.4 to 2:23:31.0. At 36 years, 130 days Wolde became the oldest distance running Olympic gold medallist.

Four years later, in Munich, Wolde finished third in the marathon in 2:15:08.4, almost three minutes behind Frank Shorter (USA), who had led on his own from the 15km mark to win in 2:12:19.8. Karel Lismont (BEL) had overtaken Wolde in the final stages to take the silver in 2:14:31.8.

Wooderson, Sydney

1914–. Born England (GBR)

There can have been few top athletes who looked less like champions than Sydney Wooderson: small, bespectacled and thin-chested. Nevertheless, he proved to be one of Britain's top middle and long-distance runners, winning two European Championships (1500m in 1938, 5000m in 1946), and setting world records at 880 yards and the mile.

He first impressed observers in 1933 with a 4:29.8 mile when aged 18, winning the Kent Championships

Sydney Wooderson

the following year in 4:27.8. He finished ahead of Jack Lovelock later that season in the Southern Championships and second to him in the AAA and British Empire Games, where he equalled the British record of 4:13.4.

In 1935 he beat Lovelock in the AAA mile on 13 July, 4:17.2 to 4:18.4, and again on 3 August in Glasgow in a special handicap race, 4:12.7 to 4:15.5. In all, Wooderson won five successive AAA mile titles between 1935 and 1939.

His Olympic career was brief. In 1936 he withdrew from the 1500m with a broken bone in his foot, and the war interrupted the Olympics in 1940 and 1944. Wooderson, a Pioneer Corps corporal, continued to train and race, even after spending four months in hospital with rheumatism in 1944. He raced Arne Andersson twice in 1945, first on 6 August at White City, losing 4:08.8 to 4:09.2, then on 9 September for 4:04.2 and second place in a personal best time. This time constituted his fourth British mile record, and his 1500m time of 3:48.4 was his fifth British record.

Wooderson's greatest year was

1937, when, at Motspur Park in Surrey on 28 August, he lowered the world mile record to 4:06.4, $^{3}/_{10}$ second off the American Glenn Cunningham's mark. He aimed for the 880 yards world record in 1938. He began by beating the 1936 Olympic 800m silver medallist Mario Lanzi (ITA) over the distance at White City on 1 August, setting a new British record 1:50.9. Three weeks later, again at Motspur Park, he set a new 800m world record of 1:48.4, and one of 1:49.2 for 880 yards, before winning the European 1500m championship in Paris.

After the war, aged nearly 32, he won the 1946 European 5000m title in the second fastest time ever, 14:08.6, and finished his career as national cross-country champion in 1948.

World Championships

The world governing body for athletics, the International Amateur Athletic Federation (IAAF), introduced its own World Championships in 1983. Prior to that the world championships were, in effect, incorporated within the Olympic Games, and every Olympic champion was thereby regarded as a world champion.

The IAAF sent invitations to every member federation to send athletes to the first World Championships in Helsinki. Each country was allowed to send at least one athlete who had achieved an IAAF 'B' standard in an event during the 12 months before the entry closing date, and two or three athletes who had achieved the higher 'A' standard. The IAAF also allowed countries with no qualified athletes to send one man and one woman for each event. It meant that every country was represented by at least one athlete, but with the 'A' standards being stricter than existing Olympic standards, the quality of competition was expected to be that much higher.

The result was an outstanding success, especially so since the World Championships were not subject to the political or sporting boycotts which had spoiled the previous two Olympic Games. Helsinki proved the perfect choice of location. The crowd was knowledgeable and appreciative and the climate ideal. More than 150 countries were represented. Seats in the Olympic stadium in Helsinki were sold out for four of the seven days of competition.

There were some superb performances to match the occasion. Jarmila Kratochvilova of Czechoslovakia scored a notable double at 400m and 800m, while Mary Decker (later Slaney) did the same at 1500m and 3000m. Carl Lewis of the USA won three gold medals in the 100m, 200m and the 4 x 100m relay, while Tiina Lillak delighted the home crowd with her sensational final throw to win in the javelin. The USA topped the overall medal table with 24 (eight golds, nine silver, and seven bronze), followed by the USSR, GDR, and Czechoslovakia.

There were two world records at the championships: the USA men's 4 x 100m relay team ran 37.86, and the Czech Kratochvilova captured

the 400m record with 47.99.

The second World Championships were held in Rome in 1987. After yet another boycott-hit Olympic Games in Los Angeles in 1984, the championships attracted even greater media coverage, and television audiences reached more than one billion worldwide. More than 1500 athletes competed from 160 member countries, some 300 more than four years previously. The setting was Rome's Stadio Olimpico, built for the Olympic Games in 1960. The Italians proved more partisan than the Finns had in Helsinki.

In many respects the championships were less successful. There were organizational difficulties and an appalling mix-up in the men's 10,000m, where runners were confused by a mistake in the lap counter. The championships were also clouded by numerous allegations of drug-taking, although only one positive dope test was recorded: Swiss athlete Sandra Gasser in the women's 1500m.

There were world records and a number of sensational performances. Ben Johnson of Canada ran the fastest ever 100m in 9.83 seconds, to beat the American title holder and Olympic champion Carl Lewis. Stefka Kostadinova cleared a new world record height of 2.09m just 12 minutes later. The Italians saw famous victories by Francesco Panetta in the 3000m steeplechase and Maurizio Damilano in the 20km walk. Ed Moses hung on to his title by the narrowest of margins in the greatest 400m hurdles race ever seen, and the Kenyans delighted everyone with their gold medals in the men's 800m, 1500m, 10,000m and marathon. Silke Gladisch of East Germany won the sprint double, and the Soviet Union's Tatyana Samolenko ran brilliantly to win the 1500m and 3000m.

Preparations are now underway for the next World Championships in Tokyo, scene of the 1964 Olympics, in 1991.

The first World Junior Championships were held in Athens in 1986, and the second in Sudbury, Canada in 1988. They are now held every two

years, with the European Junior Championships, initiated in 1970, taking place in the intervening years.

The IAAF established the first World Indoor Championships in Indianapolis, USA, in 1987. These championships succeeded the World Indoor Games, which had taken place in Paris in 1986.

The IAAF has also hosted the World Cross-Country Championships since 1973. There has been an international cross-country event since 1903, when just England, Scotland, Wales and Ireland took part. Other countries entered in subsequent years, but it was not until 1973 that it became a true world championship. As such it has largely been dominated by the African countries, with Kenya and Ethiopia winning the senior and junior men's team races since 1982. In 1988 John Ngugi won his third consecutive senior title. Grete Waitz of Norway won four consecutive titles between 1978 and 1981 and a fifth in 1983. The 1988 winner was her Norwegian rival Ingrid Kristiansen. The 1989 event is in Stavanger, Norway.

The IAAF World Race Walking Cup is held biennially for the Lugano

World Championships, Helsinki

Trophy (men) and the Eschborn Cup (women). The event was first held in Lugano, Switzerland in 1961, hence the trophy name, but has taken place in various locations since. It involves races over 20km and 50km for men, and 10km for women, and has been held under the auspices of the IAAF since 1977. The 1987 event was held in New York, where the USSR won both the Lugano Trophy and the Eschborn Cup.

Wykoff, Frank

1901–1980. Born USA (USA)

A remarkably consistent sprinter, Frank Wykoff's career lasted for nearly a decade, which was quite unusual for the time. Wykoff placed fourth in the 100m in the 1928 and 1936 Olympics, but ran on three gold medal-winning relay teams, in 1928, 1932 and 1936.

In 1928 he won his first AAU title, and with it a place on the US Olympic team, after a season that saw him beat multi-world record holder Charles Paddock (USA) over 100m (in 10.6) and a straight 200m (20.8). He finished fourth at the Games in Amsterdam, $^1/_{10}$ second off a medal in 11.0, but picked up his first relay gold running the first leg in a world record team time of 41.0.

1930 saw him winning his first NCAA title, the month after he had set a world record 9.4 for 100 yards (not broken until 1948). He won a second AAU title in 1931, but because of a back injury could only make the relay team for the 1932 Los Angeles Olympics. Here he anchored the team to a world record 40.0 to take the gold.

Although not having run seriously after Los Angeles, he finished third in the 100m US Olympic trials for the 1936 Games in Berlin. At the Olympics he again finished fourth in the 100m, in an event dominated by team mates Jesse Owens and Ralph Metcalfe. His third relay gold, again on the anchor leg, saw a third world record and the first sub-40 second time: 39.8.

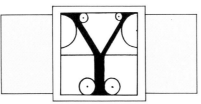

Yang, C. K.

1933–. Born Taiwan (TPE)

The best decathlete to have come out of the Far East, C.K. Yang (an Americanization of Yang Chuang-Kwang) was second in a thrilling duel to Rafer Johnson (USA) at the Rome Games of 1960, and in 1963 set the highest-ever decathlon score, 9121 points on the 1952 tables then in use.

Yang showed his athletic prowess at the Asian Games of 1954 and 1958, winning the decathlon on each occasion, taking silvers at long jump and 110mh, and gaining the bronze at 400mh in 1958.

A student at the University of California, he excelled in the 1960 Olympics, actually beating the winner, Johnson, in seven of the ten events. At the end of the first day Yang was in second place, although he had beaten Johnson in the 100m, long jump, high jump and 400m. However, the American's superiority in the shot was a key factor. On the second day, in the last event (the 1500m), Yang needed to beat Johnson by about 60m to take the gold. However, although he drew away in the final straight, his margin was no more than four metres, and Johnson won by a mere 58 points.

Yang's world record score, set over 27 and 28 April 1963 in Walnut, California, included a pole vault of 4.84m that was 2cm higher than the maximum catered for by the tables. Earlier that year (26 January in Portland, Oregan) Yang had set a world indoor pole vault best of 4.96m, almost two feet higher than his previous best. His full world record was: 100m – 10.7; long jump – 7.17m; shot – 13.22; high jump – 1.92m; 400m – 47.7; 110mh – 14.0; discus – 40.99m; pole vault – 4.84m; javelin – 71.75m; 1500m – 5:02.4.

Vladimir Yashchenko

In Tokyo four years later, although still world record holder and the favourite, he was suffering from a knee injury, and could finish no better than fifth with 7650 points. (This was on the 1964 tables, which had revised his 9121 score to 8089 points. On the 1984 tables his mark is further reduced to 8009 points.)

Yashchenko, Vladimir

1959–. Born USSR (URS)

A brilliant high jump talent, Vladimir Yashchenko leapt into the record books in an amazing series of competitions during 1977 and 1978.

His first world record was totally unexpected, as it came in a junior match between the USA and USSR at Richmond, Virginia. Yashchenko, with a previous best of 2.26m indoors and 2.22m outdoors, amazed everyone, including himself. First he broke the 16-year-old world junior record of Valeriy Brumel, and then he cleared 2.33m to break Dwight Stones' senior record by one centimetre. His victory in that year's European Junior Championships came as less of a surprise.

The following winter at the European Indoor Championships, in Milan, he took the world indoor record to 2.35m. It was, in fact, the best jump ever seen indoors or out, and came in a competition lasting over four hours.

Later that year he became the last man to set a world record using the straddle technique when he cleared 2.34m in Tbilisi. He capped a sensational year by winning the European Championship title in Prague with 2:30m, although his career was dogged from then on by recurring knee injuries and he was never to reach the same standard again.

Yifter, Miruts

1944–. Born Ethiopia (ETH)

Known affectionately as 'Yifter the Shifter' because of his electrifying pace over the final lap, Miruts Yifter crowned a glorious career by winning the 5000m and 10,000m double at the Moscow Olympics in 1980.

Despite the fact that Yifter competed internationally for more than ten years, little is known about his background, or even what his real age is. His date of birth has been listed as 1947, although 1944 is probably more accurate.

He first became an athlete in 1961, although did not start training seriously until 1968 when he was found a

Miruts Yifter

job in the Ethiopian Air Force. He later became an officer. His first notable result came in 1970, when he finished third in the East and Central African Championships 5000m. The same year he also beat Kip Keino, the 1968 Olympic 1500m champion, over 5000m. His finishing kick was first seen in 1971 when, in a USA v Africa meeting in America, he sprinted for the line in the 5000m race, only to discover that he had miscounted the laps. Forced to run another 400m, he was overtaken by the eventual winner, Steve Prefontaine of the USA. He made up for his lapse the following day, when he beat Frank Shorter in the 10,000m.

At his first Olympic Games, in 1972, he finished third behind Lasse Viren and Emiel Puttemans in the 10,000m in 27:41.0. However, he missed his heat of the 5000m.

Self-coached at altitude, Yifter was in top form by 1976 but had to miss the Montreal Olympics because of the African boycott. He later showed what might have been by beating top-class fields in the World Cup 5000m and 10,000m of 1977 and 1979. His final chance of Olympic glory came in Moscow in 1980, when he won his historic double, and became one of

the most popular figures of the Games

His 10,000m victory came with hi now familiar finishing burst in 27:42.7 including a last lap of 54.6 seconds while in the 5000m his winning tim was 13:21.0. He was the sixth winne of the long-distance double: the other were Hannes Kolehmainen, Paav Nurmi, Emil Zatopek, Vladimir Kuts and Lasse Viren.

Yrjola, Paavo

1902–. Born Finland (FIN)

Paavo Yrjola was the winner of the Olympic decathlon in Amsterdam i 1928. He set four world records, an on the 1920 tables used at the tim was the first man to exceed 800 points.

In Amsterdam he broke the worl record for the third time in two years eclipsing his earlier totals of 7820.9 (1920 tables), set over 17 and 18 Jul 1926, and 7995.19, set in Helsink exactly one year later. On the 192 tables then in use, Yrjola's Amster dam total was 8053.29 points, but o the three subsequent scoring system second-placed Akilles Jarvinen (FIN) who scored 7931.50 points on the 192 tables, is placed ahead of Yrjola. O the present tables (1984) Jarvinen i again ahead, 6645 to 6587.

Whatever the scoring complica tions, in Amsterdam Yrjola dominate the field events, winning the shot an discus, tying for first in the high jump and placing third in the javelin. Riva Jarvinen won the 400m, tied for firs in the 110mh, and came second in the 100m.

Yrjola's fourth world record 8117.300 points on the 1920 tables set in Aalborg over 9 and 10 Jul 1930, was never ratified by the IAA on the grounds that insufficient dat was submitted. On the 1984 tables i is reduced to 6700 points, but the even breakdown was: 100m – 11.6; lon jump – 6.76m; shot – 14.72m; hig jump – 1.85m; 400m – 53.2; 110mh 16.1; discus – 39.66m; pole vault 3.10m; javelin – 58.88m; 1500m 4:37.5.

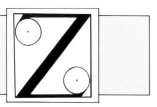

Zagorcheva, Ginka

1958–. Born Bulgaria (BUL)

After starting the 1987 season as the number two 100m hurdler in the world to compatriot Yordanka Donkova, Ginka Zagorcheva (married name Boycheva) ended the year as world champion and world record holder.

Coming out of a tremendously successful 1986 season, Donkova maintained her edge over her rival in the first seven races in which they met in 1987. However, Zagorcheva won the next series 4-2, which included her win at the World Championships in Rome, where Donkova finished out of the medals in fourth. Zagorcheva finished an easy winner in 12.34 seconds, ahead of Gloria Uibel and Cornelia Oschkenat of East Germany. Earlier in the season Zagorcheva had taken 0.01 second off Donkova's world record, with 12.25 in Drama, Greece in a match against Greece and Czechoslovakia.

At the first World Championships in 1983, Zagorcheva won a bronze medal behind the East Germans Bettine Jahn and Kerstin Knabe. She also won a 4 x 100m silver medal at the same championships.

She enjoyed an exceptional year in 1985, when she won the World Student Games title, and was unlucky not to be awarded first place in the World Cup race in Canberra. She was given the same time, 12.72, as Oschkenat, and was originally presented with the gold medal. However, an East German protest over the photo-finish was upheld, and the medal positions were reversed although the times remained the same. She did get the better of Oschkenat in the European Cup 100mh in Moscow, though, when she finished first in 12.77 and the East German came third.

Ginka Zagorcheva

At the European Championships in 1986, their positions were reversed yet again. Zagorcheva took third and Oschkenat second, as they both finished a long way behind Donkova. Indoors, Zagorcheva finished third in the 1987 World and European Championships.

Zatopek, Emil

1922–. Born Czechoslovakia (TCH)

One of the all-time great distance runners, Emil Zatopek was a phenomenal athlete, not only because of the number of world records he set, but because of the way in which he set them. His characteristically agonized style of running – with his head to one side and his shoulders hunched – seemed above all to portray the training sacrifices of a less than naturally-talented athlete.

Zatopek won the gold at 10,000m and the silver at 5000m at the 1948 Olympics, then in 1952 in Helsinki completed one of the most astonishing triples in history, winning the 5000m, the 10,000m and then the marathon, and setting Olympic records in all of them.

Zatopek trained harder than any other runner of his generation, including, unusually, during the winter. He used arduous interval sessions (fast quarter and half-miles with short intervals of jogging to recover). His first Olympics, in London in 1948, saw him destroy the 10,000m field, including world record holder Viljo Heino (FIN), with a mid-race surge, to win by almost 48 seconds in 29:59.6. In the 5000m he was 40m adrift of Gaston Reiff (BEL) at the start of the back straight in the final lap. An incredible surge almost won him the race, but Reiff countered almost on the line.

In 1952 he won the 10,000m in 29:17.0 by 100m, took the 5000m four days later in 14.06.6, then won the first marathon of his career three days later, in 2:23:03.2. He competed at the 1956 Games in Melbourne, running the marathon only six weeks after a hernia operation. He finished sixth in a race won by France's Alain Mimoun, who was runner-up to Zatopek in both his 10,000m wins and

Zatopek in Helsinki (1952)

his 5000m victory in 1952.

Zatopek's career was not limited to the Olympics, however. He won the 5000/10,000m double at the 1950 European Championships, retaining the 10,000m in 1954 and coming third at 5000m the same year. He won 261 out of 334 races at all distances, and between 1949 and 1951 won all 69 races at various distances.

He is the holder of the most world records at 10,000m – five in all – from 29.28.2 in Ostrava on 11 June 1949 to 28:54.2 in Brussels on 1 June 1954. The latter was achieved just one day after he had run a world record time of 13:57.2 for 5000m. He was the first man to break 29 minutes for 10,000m, and the first to go under 60 minutes for 20,000m. From October 1952, when he collected world records at 15 miles, 25km and 30km (to go with his ten mile, 20km and one-hour records set in September 1951), he held eight world distance records from six miles to 30km until 1955, and in 1954 for three months held the 5000m world record as well.

His best marks included 3:52.8 for 1500m; 8:07.8 for 3000m; 13:57.0 for 5000m; 28:54.2 for 10,000m; 44:54.6 for 15km; 48:12.0 for ten miles; 59:51.8 for 20km; 20,052m in one hour; 1:14:01 for 15 miles; 1:16:36.4 for 25km; 1:35:23.8 for 30km, and 2:23:03.2 for the marathon.

Zatopek is married to Dana Zatopkova (née Ingrova), Olympic javelin champion in 1952.

Zatopkova, Dana

1922–. Born Czechoslovakia (TCH)

The world's leading woman javelin thrower in the mid-1950s, Dana Zatopkova had a long and distinguished career, winning Olympic gold in 1952, silver in 1960, and two European titles, in 1954 and 1958. She was married to the distance runner Emil Zatopek.

Winner of 13 national titles between 1946-1960, Zatopkova first competed in the Olympics in London in 1948,

placing seventh with 39.64m. Four years later she won with an Olympic record 50.46m. She collected the silver in Melbourne in 1956 with 53.78m, behind Elvira Ozolina (URS) on 55.98m.

At the European Championships she scratched in 1946, and came fifth in 1950, before winning in 1954 (52.91m) and 1958 (56.02). Earlier in 1958 she had set her only world record – 55.73m – which lasted just a month, but she improved her personal best mark to 56.66m by the end of the season.

Zatopkova was Czechoslovakia's first woman Olympic gold medallist, and husband Emil was the country's first man to achieve the same feat.

Zsivotzky, Gyula

1937–. Born Hungary (HUN)

One of the most consistent hammer throwers in the 1960s, Gyula Zsivotzky competed at four Olympics, winning in 1968 after collecting silvers in 1960 and 1964. He also took part in five European Championships where he collected a complete set of medals (bronze in 1958, gold in 1962, and silver in 1966). He set two world records, in 1965 and 1968, the latter

Gyula Zsivotzky

his best ever (73.76m).

Hungarian champion for thirtee successive years (1958-1970) an AAA champion in 1965 and 196(Zsivotzky claimed the Olympic titl in Mexico in 1968, beating defendin champion Rommald Klim (URS 73.36m to 73.28m. Klim had beate him four years previously in Tokyc At the European Championships hi best-ever throw of 69.68m in Athen in 1969 only won him fourth plac« compared to 69.64m to win in 196 68.62m for silver in 1966, and 63.68r for bronze in 1958. He also compete in 1971, finishing eleventh wit 64.94m. He took fifth place at th Munich Games of 1972.

Zybina, Galina

1931–. Born USSR (URS)

Galina Zybina set the greatest numbe of women's shot records ever – 15 which were taken in succession be tween 1952 and 1956. During thi time she improved the mark fron 15.19m to 16.76m, winning the Olym pic title in 1952.

She was the first woman to p(over 50 feet, throwing 15.28m (50($1^3/4$in) on 26 July 1952 to win th gold in Helsinki. She competed i three further Olympics, finishing se(ond in 1956 (16.53m), seventh in 196 (15.56m), and third in 1964 (17.45m Eight of her shot records were ratifie by the IAAF. She also placed four in the Olympic javelin in 1952.

She competed successfully at th European Championships, finishin fourth in 1950, winning in 1954 wit 15.65m, coming third in 1962 wit 16.95 (when winner Tamara Press s(a world record 18.55m), and takin fourth in 1966. She won a bronze two other disciplines: javelin in 195 and discus in 1954.

In a bizarre incident in 1958, sh was suspended from the Soviet n; tional team accused of 'egotistica uncomradely behaviour', for refusin to accept a second-placed medal at th national championships. She was late reinstated and continued competing

The Olympic Games 1896 – 1988

The 1988 Olympic Games in Seoul, South Korea promised to be the greatest of all time. However, while the Olympic movement finally managed to avoid any major boycotts for the first time in 16 years, it could do little to combat the drugs menace that threatened to steal all the headlines from the sporting action. Despite the fact that 160 nations arrived in Seoul to find the most outstanding facilities, the Games themselves were marred by the revelation on day 10 that Ben Johnson, the 26-year-old Canadian who had won the 100m gold medal in a new world record time of 9.79 seconds, had failed a drugs test after the race. He was immediately stripped of his medal, ousted from the Canadian team, banned for two years by the International Amateur Athletic Federation and then banned for life by the Canadian authorities.

Johnson, already world record holder and world champion after his sensational run in Rome in 1987, provided the Games with the biggest scandal of their 92-year history. A urine test taken after the race was found to contain samples of Stanozolol, an anabolic steroid used to increase muscle bulk and enable an athlete to train harder and recover more quickly. Johnson was in fact one of nine athletes tested as positive for drugs at the Seoul Olympics, but the first from the athletics arena. Although his time will not be recorded as a world record, his previous world record of 9.83, set in Rome, will remain as dope tests there proved negative.

Unfortunately for the International Olympic Committee, the furore which erupted over the Johnson affair coloured much of what happened subsequently on the track. Nevertheless, the standard of competition at these Games brought some outstanding performances. America's Florence Joyner set a new world record at 200m of 21.34 – her second world record at the distance in one day – to complete the sprint double and repeat the achievement of East Germany's Renate Stecher in 1972. She added a third gold medal as part of the US 4 x 100m relay team.

America's Carl Lewis was awarded the 100m title after Johnson's disqualification, raising his hopes of repeating his 1984 feat of winning four gold medals. However, although he won the long jump, he was beaten in the 200m by countryman Joe Deloach and failed even to make the sprint relay final when the US team were disqualified for a faulty baton changeover in the semi-final.

In many ways the Games marked the end of an era in athletics with the defeat of many of the sport's top names and the arrival of new, younger talents. Edwin Moses, the American 400m hurdler and holder of two Olympic titles, two World Championship titles, with an unbeaten run of 122 races between 1977 and 1987, came third in Seoul. Mary Slaney, the former multi-world record holder and double world champion in 1983, was unable to respond to the challenge of Tatyana Samolenko of the Soviet Union, Paula Ivan of Romania and Yvonne Murray of Great Britain in the 3000m, and finished only eighth in the 1500m. Also, two great rivals from the late seventies and early eighties, Evelyn Ashford and Marlies Göhr, were eclipsed by Joyner in the women's sprints.

Ingrid Kristiansen, perhaps the greatest female distance runner of all time, failed to complete the 10,000m final. In the decathlon, Daley Thompson of Britain, holder of Olympic, World and European titles in his prime, could finish only fourth, a great disappointment to him.

The Seoul Olympics–the biggest in history–were an undoubted success, but the talk in Korea and around the world was too often about drugs and the monetary worth of a medal rather than performances inside the Chamsil Stadium.

OLYMPIC MEDALLISTS

(Where known pre-1972 automatic timings to one hundredth of a second are shown. Current world record holders – WR – are in brackets. Olympic records are indicated by OR)

MEN

100m
(B. Johnson/CAN, 9.83, WR)

	Gold			Silver			Bronze	
1896	Burke/USA	12.0	1896	Hofmann/GER	12.2	1896	Szokolyi/HUN	12.6
1900	Jarvis/USA	11.0	1900	Tewksbury/USA	11.1	1900	Rowley/AUS	11.2
1904	Hahn/USA	11.0	1904	Cartmell/USA	11.2	1904	Hogenson/USA	11.2
1908	Walker/SA	10.8	1908	Rector/USA	10.9	1908	Kerr/CAN	11.0
1912	Craig/USA	10.8	1912	Meyer/USA	10.9	1912	Lippincott/USA	10.9
1920	Paddock/USA	10.8	1920	Kirksey/USA	10.8	1920	Edward/GBR	11.0
1924	Abrahams/GBR	10.6	1924	Scholz/USA	10.7	1924	Porritt/NZL	10.8
1928	Williams/CAN	10.8	1928	London/GBR	10.9	1928	Lammers/GER	10.9
1932	Tolan/USA	10.3/10.38	1932	Metcalfe/USA	10.3/10.38	1932	Jonath/GER	10.4
1936	Owens/USA	10.3	1936	Metcalfe/USA	10.4	1936	Osendarp/HOL	10.5
1948	Dillard/USA	10.3	1948	Ewell/USA	10.4	1948	LaBeach/PAN	10.4
1952	Remigino/USA	10.4/10.79	1952	McKenley/JAM	10.4/10.79	1952	McD.Bailey/GBR	10.4/10.83
1956	Morrow/USA	10.5/10.62	1956	Baker/USA	10.5/10.77	1956	Hogan/AUS	10.6/10.77
1960	Hary/FRG	10.2/10.32	1960	Sime/USA	10.2/10.35	1960	Radford/GBR	10.3/10.42
1964	Hayes/USA	10.0/10.06	1964	Figuerola/CUB	10.2/10.25	1964	Jerome/CAN	10.2/10.27
1968	Hines/USA	9.9/9.95	1968	Miller/JAM	10.0/10.04	1968	Greene/USA	10.0/10.07
1972	Borzov/URS	10.14	1972	Taylor/USA	10.24	1972	Miller/JAM	10.33
1976	Crawford/TRI	10.06	1976	Quarrie/JAM	10.07	1976	Borzov/URS	10.14
1980	Wells/GBR	10.25	1980	Leonard/CUB	10.25	1980	Petrov/BUL	10.39
1984	C.Lewis/USA	9.99	1984	Graddy/USA	10.19	1984	Johnson/CAN	10.22
1988	C.Lewis/USA	9.92 (OR)	1988	Christie/GBR	9.97	1988	C.Smith/USA	9.99

200m
(P. Mennea/ITA, 19.72, WR)

	Gold			Silver			Bronze	
1896	Not contested		1896	Not contested		1896	Not contested	
1900	Tewksbury/USA	22.2	1900	Pritchard/IND	22.8	1900	Rowley/AUS	22.9
1904	Hahn/USA	21.6	1904	Cartmell/USA	21.9	1904	Hogenson/USA	
1908	Kerr/CAN	22.6	1908	Cloughen/USA	22.6	1908	Cartmell/USA	22.7
1912	Craig/USA	21.7	1912	Lippincott/USA	21.8	1912	Applegarth/GBR	22.0
1920	Woodring/USA	22.0	1920	Paddock/USA	22.1	1920	Edward/GBR	22.2
1924	Scholz/USA	21.6	1924	Paddock/USA	22.7	1924	Liddell/GBR	21.9
1928	Williams/CAN	21.8	1928	Rangeley/GBR	21.9	1928	Kornig/GER	21.9
1932	Tolan/USA	21.2/21.12	1932	Simpson/USA	21.4	1932	Metcalfe/USA	21.5
1936	Owens/USA	20.7	1936	Robinson/USA	21.1	1936	Osendarp/HOL	21.3
1948	Patton/USA	21.1	1948	Ewell/USA	21.1	1948	LaBeach/PAN	21.2
1952	Stanfield/USA	20.7/20.81	1952	Baker/USA	20.8/20.97	1952	Gathers/USA	20.8/21.08
1956	Morrow/USA	20.6/20.75	1956	Stanfield/USA	20.7/20.97	1956	Baker/USA	20.9/21.04
1960	Berruti/ITA	20.5/20.62	1960	Carney/USA	20.6/20.69	1960	Seye/FRA	20.7/20.82
1964	Carr/USA	20.3/20.36	1964	Drayton/USA	20.5/20.58	1964	Roberts/TRI	20.6/20.63
1968	T. Smith/USA	19.8/19.83	1968	Norman/AUS	20.0/20.05	1968	Carlos/USA	20.0/20.10
1972	Borzov/URS	20.00	1972	Black/USA	20.19	1972	Mennea/ITA	20.30
1976	Quarrie/JAM	20.22	1976	Hampton/USA	20.29	1976	Evans/USA	20.43
1980	Mennea/ITA	20.19	1980	Wells/GBR	20.21	1980	Quarrie/JAM	20.29
1984	C.Lewis/USA	19.80	1984	Baptiste/USA	19.96	1984	Jefferson/USA	20.26
1988	Deloach/USA	19.75 (OR)	1988	C.Lewis/USA	19.79	1988	Da Silva/BRA	20.04

400m
(H. Butch Reynolds/USA, 43.29, WR)

	Gold			Silver			Bronze	
1896	Burke/USA	54.2	1896	Jamison/USA		1896	Hofmann/GER	
1900	Long/USA	49.4	1900	Holland/USA	49.6	1900	Schulz/DEN	
1904	Hillman/USA	49.2	1904	Waller/USA	49.9	1904	Groman/USA	50.0
1908	Halswelle/GBR	50.0	1908	(Halswelle only finalist)		1908	(Halswelle only finalist)	
1912	Reidpath/USA	48.2	1912	Braun/GER	48.3	1912	Lindberg/SWE	48.4
1920	Rudd/SA	49.6	1920	Butler/GBR	49.9	1920	Engdahl/SWE	49.9
1924	Liddell/GBR	47.6	1924	Fitch/USA	48.4	1924	Butler/GBR	48.6
1928	Barbuti/USA	47.8	1928	Ball/CAN	48.0	1928	Büchner/GER	48.2
1932	Carr/USA	46.2/46.28	1932	Eastman/USA	46.4	1932	Wilson/CAN	47.4
1936	Williams/USA	46.5/46.66	1936	Brown/GBR	46.7/46.68	1936	LuValle/USA	46.8/46.84
1948	Wint/JAM	46.2	1948	McKenley/JAM	46.4	1948	Whitfield/USA	46.9
1952	Rhoden/JAM	45.9/46.09	1952	McKenley/JAM	45.9/46.20	1952	Matson/USA	46.8/46.94
1956	Jenkins/USA	46.7/46.86	1956	Haas/FRG	46.8/47.12	1956	Hellsten/FIN	47.0/47.15
							Ignatyev/URS	47.0/47.15
1960	O.Davis/USA	44.9/45.07	1960	Kaufmann/FRG	44.9/45.08	1960	Spence/SA	45.5/45.60
1964	Larrabee/USA	45.1/45.15	1964	Mottley/TRI	45.2/45.24	1964	Badenski/POL	45.6/45.64
1968	Evans/USA (OR)	43.8/43.86	1968	James/USA	43.9/43.97	1968	Freeman/USA	44.4/44.41
1972	Matthews/USA	44.66	1972	Collett/USA	44.80	1972	Sang/KEN	44.92
1976	Juantorena/CUB	44.26	1976	Newhouse/USA	44.40	1976	Frazier/USA	44.95
1980	Markin/URS	44.60	1980	Mitchell/AUS	44.84	1980	Schaffer/GDR	44.87
1984	Babers/USA	44.27	1984	Tiacoh/CIV	44.54	1984	Mckay/USA	44.71
1988	S.Lewis/USA	43.87	1988	Reynolds/USA	43.93	1988	Everett/USA	44.09

800m
(S. Coe/GBR, 1:41.73, WR)

	Gold			Silver			Bronze	
1896	Flack/AUS	2:11.0	1896	Dani/HUN	2:11.8	1896	Golemis/GRE	
1900	Tysoe/GBR	2:01.2	1900	Cregan/USA	2:03.0	1900	Hall/USA	
1904	Lightbody/USA	1:56.0	1904	Valentine/USA	1:56.3	1904	Breitkreutz/USA	1:56.4
1908	Sheppard/USA	1:52.8	1908	Lunghi/ITA	1:54.2	1908	Braun/GER	1:55.2
1912	Meredith/USA	1:51.9	1912	Sheppard/USA	1:52.0	1912	Davenport/USA	1:52.0
1920	Hill/GBR	1:53.4	1920	Eby/USA	1:53.6	1920	Rudd/SA	1:54.0
1924	Lowe/GBR	1:52.4	1924	P.Martin/SWZ	1:52.6	1924	Enck/USA	1:53.0
1928	Lowe/GBR	1:51.8	1928	Byléhn/SWE	1:52.8	1928	Engelhard/GER	1:53.2
1932	Hampson/GBR	1:49.7	1932	Wilson/CAN	1:49.9	1932	Edwards/CAN	1:51.5
1936	Woodruff/USA	1:52.9	1936	Lanzi/ITA	1:53.3	1936	Edwards/CAN	1:53.6
1948	Whitfield/USA	1:49.2	1948	Wint/JAM	1:49.5	1948	Hansenne/FRA	1:49.8
1952	Whitfield/USA	1:49.2	1952	Wint/JAM	1:49.4	1952	Ulzheimer/FRG	1:49.7
1956	Courtney/USA	1:47.7	1956	Johnson/USA	1:47.8	1956	Boysen/NOR	1:48.1
1960	Snell/NZL	1:46.3	1960	Moens/BEL	1:46.5	1960	Kerr/JAM	1:47.1
1964	Snell/NZL	1:45.1	1964	Crothers/CAN	1:45.6	1964	Kiprugut/KEN	1:45.9
1968	Doubell/AUS	1:44.3	1968	Kiprugut/KEN	1:44.5	1968	Farrell/USA	1:45.4
1972	Wottle/USA	1:45.9	1972	Arzhanov/SU	1:45.9	1972	Boit/KEN	1:46.0
1976	Juantorena/CUB	1:43.5	1976	Van Damme/BEL	1:43.9	1976	Wohlhuter/USA	1:44.1
1980	Olizarento/URS	1:43.53	1980	Coe/GBR	1:45.9	1980	Kirov/URS	1:46.0
1984	Cruz/BRA	1:43.00 (OR)	1984	Coe/GBR	1:43.64	1984	Jones/USA	1:43.83
1988	Ereng/KEN	1:43.45	1988	Cruz/BRA	1:43.90	1988	Aouita/MAR	1:44.06

1500m
(S. Aouita/MAR, 3:29.46, WR)

	Gold			Silver			Bronze	
1896	Flack/AUS	4:33.2	1896	Blake/USA	4:34.0	1896	Lermusiaux/FRA	4:36.0
1900	Tysoe/GBR	4:06.2	1900	Deloge/FRA	4:06.6	1900	Bray/USA	4:07.2
1904	Lightbody/USA	4:05.4	1904	Verner/USA	4:06.8	1904	Hearn/USA	
1908	Sheppard/USA	4:03.4	1908	Wilson/GBR	4:03.6	1908	Hallows/GBR	4:04.0
1912	Jackson/GBR	3:45.8	1912	Kiviat/USA	3:56.9	1912	Taber/USA	3:56.9
1920	Hill/GBR	4:01.8	1920	Baker/GBR	4:02.4	1920	Shields/USA	4:03.1
1924	Nurmi/FIN	3:53.6	1924	Scharer/SUI	3:55.0	1924	Stallard/GBR	3:55.6
1928	Larva/FIN	3:53.2	1928	Ladoumègue/FRA	3:53.8	1928	Purje/FIN	3:56.4
1932	Beccali/ITA	3:51.2	1932	Cornes/GBR	3:52.6			
1936	Lovelock/NZL	3:47.8	1936	Cunningham/USA	3:48.4			
1948	Eriksson/SWE	3:49.8	1948	Strand/SWE	3:50.4			
1952	Barthel/LUX	3:45.1	1952	McMillen/USA	3:45.2			
1956	Delany/IRE	3:41.2	1956	Richtzenhain/GDR	3:42.0			
1960	Elliott/AUS	3:35.6	1960	Jazy/FRA	3:38.4			
1964	Snell/NZL	3:38.1	1964	Odlozil/TCH	3:39.6			
1968	Keino/KEN	3:34.9	1968	Ryun/USA	3:37.8			
1972	Vasala/FIN	3:36.3	1972	Keino/KEN	3:36.8			
1976	Walker/NZL	3:39.2	1976	Van Damme/BEL	3:39.3			
1980	Coe/GBR	3:38.4	1980	Straub/GDR	3:38.8			
1984	Coe/GBR	3:32.53 (OR)	1984	Cram/GBR	3:33.40			
1988	Rono/KEN	3:35.96	1988	Elliott/GBR	3:36.15			

1932	Edwards/CAN	3:52.8
1936	Beccali/ITA	3:49.2
1948	Slykhuis/HOL	3:50.4
1952	Lueg/FRG	3:45.4
1956	Landy/AUS	3:42.0
1960	Rozsavolgyi/HUN	3:39.2
1964	Davies/NZL	3:39.6
1968	Tummler/FRG	3:39.0
1972	Dixon/NZL	3:37.5
1976	Wellmann/FRG	3.39.3
1980	Ovett/GBR	3:39.0
1984	Abascal/ESP	3:34.30
1988	Herold/GDR	3:36.21

5000m
(S. Aouita/MAR, 12:58.39, WR)
Gold

1896-1908	Not contested	
1912	Kolehmainen/FIN	14:36.6
1920	Guillemot/FRA	14:55.6
1924	Nurmi/FIN	14:31.2
1928	Ritola/FIN	14:38.0
1932	Lehtinen/FIN	14:30.0
1936	Hockert/FIN	14:22.2
1948	Reiff/BEL	14:17.6
1952	Zatopek/TCH	14:06.6
1956	Kuts/URS	13:39.6
1960	Halberg/NZL	13:43.4
1964	Schul/USA	13:48.8
1968	Gammoudi/TUN	14:05.0
1972	Viren/FIN	13:26.4
1976	Viren/FIN	13:24.8
1980	Yifter/ETH	13:21.0
1984	Aouita/MAR	13:05.5 (OR)
1988	Ngugi/KEN	13:11.70

Silver

1896-1908	Not contested	
1912	Bouin/FRA	14:36.7
1920	Nurmi/FIN	15:00.0
1924	Ritola/FIN	14:31.4
1928	Nurmi/FIN	14:40.0
1932	Hill/USA	14:30.0
1936	Lehtinen/FIN	14:25.8
1948	Zatopek/TCH	14:17.8
1952	Mimoun/FRA	14:07.4
1956	Pirie/GBR	13:50.6
1960	Grodotzki/GDR	13:44.6
1964	Norpoth/FRG	13:49.6
1968	Keino/KEN	14:05.2
1972	Gammoudi/TUN	13:27.4
1976	Quax/NZL	13:25.2
1980	Nyambui/TAN	13:21.6
1984	Ryffel/SUI	13:07.5
1988	Baumann/FRG	13:15.52

Bronze

1896-1908	Not contested	
1912	Hutson/GBR	15:07.6
1920	Backman/SWE	15:13.0
1924	Wide/SWE	15:01.8
1928	Wide/SWE	14:41.2
1932	Virtanen/FIN	14:44.0
1936	Jonsson/SWE	14:29.0
1948	Slykhuis/HOL	14:26.8
1952	Schade/FRG	14:08.6
1956	Ibbotson/GBR	13:54.4
1960	Zimny/POL	13:44.8
1964	Dellinger/USA	13:49.8
1968	Temu/KEN	14:06.4
1972	I.Stewart/GBR	13:27.6
1976	Hildenbrand/FRG	13:25.4
1980	Maaninka/FIN	13:22.0
1984	Leitao/POR	13:09.2
1988	Kunze/GDR	13:15.73

10,000m
F. Mamede/POR, 27:13.81, WR)
Gold

1896-1908	Not contested	
1912	Kolehmainen/FIN	31:20.8
1920	Nurmi/FIN	31:45.8
1924	Ritola/FIN	30:23.2
1928	Nurmi/FIN	30:18.8
1932	Kusocinski/POL	30:11.4
1936	Salminen/FIN	30:15.4
1948	Zatopek/TCH	29:59.6
1952	Zatopek/TCH	29:17.0
1956	Kuts/URS	28:45.6
1960	Bolotnikov/URS	28:32.2
1964	Mills/USA	28:24.4
1968	Temu/KEN	29:27.4
1972	Viren/FIN	27:38.4
1976	Viren/FIN	27:45.2
1980	Yifter/ETH	27:42.7
1984	Cova/ITA	27:47.5
1988	Boutaib/MAR (OR)	27:21.46

Silver

1896-1908	Not contested	
1912	Tewanima/USA	32:06.6
1920	Guillemot/FRA	31:47.2
1924	Wide/SWE	30:55.2
1928	Ritola/FIN	30:19.4
1932	Isohollo/FIN	30:12.6
1936	Askola/FIN	30:15.6
1948	Mimoun/FRA	30:47.4
1952	Mimoun/FRA	29:32.8
1956	Kovacs/HUN	28:52.4
1960	Grodotzki/GDR	28:37.0
1964	Gammoudi/TUN	28:24.8
1968	Wolde/ETH	29:28.0
1972	Puttemans/BEL	27:39.6
1976	Lopes/POR	27:45.2
1980	Maaninka/FIN	27:44.3
1984	Mcleod/GBR	28:06.2
1988	Antibo/ITA	27:23.55

Bronze

1896-1908	Not contested	
1912	Stenroos/FIN	32:21.8
1920	Wilson/GBR	31:50.8
1924	Berg/FIN	31:43.0
1928	Wide/SWE	31:00.8
1932	Virtanen/FIN	30:35.0
1936	Isohollo/FIN	30:20.2
1948	Albertsson/SWE	30:53.6
1952	Anufriyev/URS	29:48.2
1956	Lawrence/AUS	28:53.6
1960	Power/AUS	28:38.2
1964	Clarke/AUS	28:38.2
1968	Gammoudi/TUN	29:34.2
1972	Yifter/ETH	27:41.0
1976	Foster/GBR	27:54.9
1980	Kedir/ETH	27:44.7
1984	Mysocki/KEN	28:06.46
1988	Kimeli/KEN	27:25.16

Marathon
(B. Dinsamo/ETH, 2:06:50, WR)
Gold

1896*	Louis/GRE	2:58:50
1900*	Théato/FRA	2:59:45
1904*	Hicks/USA	3:28:53
1908	Hayes/USA	2:55:19
1912*	MacArthur/SA	2:36:55
1920*	Kolehmainen/FIN	2:32:36
1924	Stenroos/FIN	2:41:23
1928	El Ouafi/FRA	2:32:57
1932	Zabala/ARG	2:31:36
1936	Son/JAP	2:29:20
1948	Cabrera/ARG	2:34:52
1952	Zatopek/TCH	2:23:04
1956	Mimoun/FRA	2:25:00
1960	Bikila/ETH	2:15:17
1964	Bikila/ETH	2:12:12
1968	Wolde/ETH	2:20:27
1972	Shorter/USA	2:12:20
1976	Cierpinski/GDR	2:09:55
1980	Cierpinski/GDR	2:11:03
1984	Lopes/POR	2:09:21(OR)
1988	Bordin/ITA	2:10:32

Silver

1896*	Vasilakos/GRE	3:06:03
1900*	Champion/FRA	3:04:17
1904*	Corey/USA	3:34:52
1908	Hefferon/SA	2:56:06
1912*	Gitsham/SA	2:37:52
1920*	Lossman/EST	2:32:49
1924	Bertini/ITA	2:47:20
1928	Plaza/CHI	2:33:23
1932	Ferris/GBR	2:31:55
1936	Harper/GBR	2:31:24
1948	Richards/GBR	2:35:08
1952	Gorno/ARG	2:25:35
1956	Mihalic/YUG	2:26:32
1960	Rhadi/MOR	2:15:42
1964	Heatley/GBR	2:16:20
1968	Kimihara/JAP	2:23:31
1972	Lismont/BEL	2:14:32
1976	Shorter/USA	2:10:46
1980	Nijboer/HOL	2:11:20
1984	Treacy/IRL	2:09:56
1988	Wakihuru/KEN	2:10:47

Bronze

1896*	Kellner/HUN	3:06:35
1900*	Fast/SWE	3:37:14
1904*	Newton/USA	3:47:33
1908	Forshaw/USA	2:57:11
1912*	Strobino/USA	2:38:43
1920*	Arri/ITA	2:36:33
1924	DeMar/USA	2:48:14
1928	Marttelin/FIN	2:35:02
1932	Toivonen/FIN	2:32:12
1936	Nan/JAP	2:31:42
1948	Gailly/BEL	2:35:34
1952	Jansson/SWE	2:26:07
1956	Karvonen/FIN	2:27:47
1960	Magee/NZL	2:17:19
1964	Tsuburaya/JAP	2:16:23
1968	Ryan/NZL	2:23:45
1972	Wolde/ETH	2:15:09
1976	Lismont/BEL	2:11:13
1980	Dzhumanazarov/URS	2:11:35
1984	Spedding/GBR	2:09:58
1988	Saleh/DJI	2:10:59

N.B. Event contested at standard distance
(42,195m), except in the cases marked *

3000m Steeplechase
(H. Rono/KEN, 8:05.4, WR)
Gold

1896	Not contested	
1900*	Orton/USA	7:34.4
1904*	Lightbody/USA	7:39.6
1908*	Russell/GBR	10:47.8
1912	Not contested	
1920	Hodge/GBR	10:00.4
1924	Ritola/FIN	9:33.6
1928	Loukola/FIN	9:21.8
1932*	Isohollo/FIN	10:33.4
1936	Isohollo/FIN	9:03.8
1948	Sjostrand/SWE	9:04.6
1952	Ashenfelter/USA	8:45.4
1956	Brasher/GBR	8:41.2
1960	Krzyszkowiak/POL	8:34.2
1964	Roelants/BEL	8:30.8
1968	Biwott/KEN	8:51.0
1972	Keino/KEN	8:23.6
1976	Garderud/SWE	8:08.0
1980	Malinowski/POL	8:09.7
1984	Korir/KEN	8:11.8
1988	Kariuki/KEN	8:05.51 (OR)

Silver

1896	Not contested	
1900*	Robinson/GBR	7:38.0
1904*	Daly/GBR	7:40.6
1908*	Robertson/GBR	10:48.4
1912	Not contested	
1920	Flynn/USA	
1924	Katz/FIN	9:44.0
1928	Nurmi/FIN	9:31.2
1932*	Evenson/GBR	10:46.0
1936	Tuominen/FIN	9:06.8
1948	Elmsater/SWE	9:08.2
1952	Kazantsev/URS	8:51.6
1956	Rozsnyoi/HUN	8:43.6
1960	Sokolov/URS	8:36.4
1964	Herriott/GBR	8:32.4
1968	Kogo/KEN	8:51.6
1972	Jipcho/KEN	8:24.6
1976	Malinowski/POL	8:09.2
1980	Bayi/TAN	8:12.5
1984	Mahmoud/FRA	8:13.31
1988	Koech/KEN	8:06.79

Bronze

1896	Not contested	
1900*	Chastanieé/FRA	
1904*	Newton/USA	
1908*	Eisele/USA	
1912	Not contested	
1920	Ambrosini/ITA	
1924	Bontemps/FRA	9:45.2
1928	Andersen/FIN	9:35.6
1932*	McCluskey/USA	10:46.2
1936	Dompert/GER	9:07.2
1948	Hagstrom/SWE	9:11.8
1952	Disley/GBR	8:51.8
1956	Larsen/NOR	8:44.0
1960	Rzhishchin/URS	8:42.2
1964	Belyayev/URS	8:33.8
1968	Young/USA	8:51.8
1972	Kantanen/FIN	8:24.8
1976	Baumgartl/GBR	8:10.4
1980	Tura/ETH	8:13.6
1984	Diemer/USA	8:14.0
1988	Rowland/GBR	8:07.96

N.B. Event contested at 3000m, except in
the cases marked *

20km Walk
(A. Noack/GDR, 1:19:12, WR)
Gold

1896-1952	Not contested	
1956	Spirin/URS	1:31:28
1960	Golubnichiy/URS	1:34:08
1964	Matthews/GBR	1:29:34
1968	Golubnichiy/URS	1:33:59
1972	Frenkel/GDR	1:26:43
1976	Bautista/MEX	1:24:41
1980	Damilano/ITA	1:23:36
1984	Canto/MEX	1:23:13
1988	Pribilenic/TCH	1:19:57 (OR)

Silver

1896-1952	Not contested	
1956	Mikenas/URS	1:32:03
1960	Freeman/AUS	1:34:17
1964	Lindner/GDR	1:31:14
1968	Pedraza/MEX	1:34:00
1972	Golubnichiy/URS	1:26:56
1976	Reimann/GDR	1:25:14
1980	Pochinchuk/URS	1:24:46
1984	Gonzalez/MEX	1:23:20
1988	Weigel/GDR	1:19:60

Bronze

1896-1952	Not contested	
1956	Junk/URS	1:32:12
1960	Vickers/GBR	1:34:57
1964	Golubnichiy/URS	1:32:00
1968	Smaga/URS	1:34:04
1972	Reimann/GDR	1:27:17
1976	Frenkel/GDR	1:25:30
1980	Wieser/GDR	1:25:59
1984	Damilano/ITA	1:23:26
1988	Damilano/IIA	1:20:14

50km Walk
(R. Weigel/GDR, 3:38:17, WR)
Gold

1896 - 1928	Not contested	
1932	Green/GBR	4:50:10
1936	Whitlock/GBR	4:30:41
1948	Ljunggren/SWE	4:41:52
1952	Dordoni/ITA	4:28:08
1956	Read/NZL	4:30:43
1960	Thompson/GBR	4:25:30
1964	Pamich/ITA	4:11:13
1968	Hohne/GDR	4:20:14
1972	Kannenberg/FRG	3:56:12
1976	Not contested	
1980	Gauder/GDR	3:49:24
1984	Gonzales/MEX	3:47:26
1988	Ivanenko/URS	3:38:29 (OR)

Silver

1896 - 1928	Not contested	
1932	Dalins/LAT	4:57:20
1936	Schwab/SUI	4:32:10
1948	Godel/SUI	4:48:17

1952	Dolezal/TCH	4:30:18
1956	Maskinskov/URS	4:32:57
1960	Ljunggren/SWE	4:25:47
1964	Nihill/GBR	4:11:32
1968	Kiss/HUN	4:30:17
1972	Soldatyenko/URS	3:58:24
1976	Not contested	
1980	Llopart/ESP	3:51:25
1984	Gustafsson/SWE	3:53:19
1988	Weigel/GDR	3:38:56

Bronze

1896-1928	Not contested	
1932	Frigerio	4:59:06
1936	Bubenko/LAT	4:32:43
1948	Lloyd-Johnson/GBR	4:48:31
1952	Roka/HUN	4:31:28
1956	Ljunggren/SWE	4:35:02
1960	Pamich/ITA	4:27:56
1964	Pettersson/SWE	4:14:18
1968	Young/USA	4:31:56
1972	Young/USA	4:00:46
1976	Not contested	
1980	Ivchenko/URS	3:56:32
1984	Bellucci/ITA	3:53:45
1988	Gauder/GDR	3:39:45

110m Hurdles
(R. Nehemiah/USA, 12.93, WR)

Gold

1896	Curtis/USA	17.6
1900	Kraenzlein/USA	15.4
1904	Schule/USA	16.0
1908	Smithson/USA	15.0
1912	Kelly/USA	15.1
1920	Thomson/CAN	14.8
1924	Kinsey/USA	15.0
1928	Atkinson/SA	14.8
1932	Saling/USA	14.6/14.56
1936	Towns/USA	14.2
1948	Porter/USA	13.9
1952	Dillard/USA	13.7/13.91
1956	Calhoun/USA	13.5/13.70
1960	Calhoun/USA	13.8/13.98
1964	H.Jones/USA	13.6/13.67
1968	Davenport/USA	13.3/13.33
1972	Milburn/USA	13.24
1976	Drut/FRA	13.30
1980	Munkelt/GDR	13.39
1984	Kingdom/USA	13.20
1988	Kingdom/USA	12.98 (OR)

Silver

1896	Goulding/GBR	17.7
1900	McLean/USA	15.5
1904	Schideler/USA	16.3
1908	Garrels/USA	15.7
1912	Wendell/USA	15.2
1920	Barron/USA	15.1
1924	Atkinson/SA	15.0
1928	Anderson/USA	14.8
1932	Beard/USA	14.7
1936	Finlay/GBR	14.4
1948	Scott/USA	14.1
1952	J.Davis/USA	13.7/14.00
1956	J.Davis/USA	13.5/13.73
1960	May/USA	13.8/13.99
1964	Lindgren/USA	13.7/13.74
1968	Hall/USA	13.4/13.42
1972	Drut/FRA	13.34
1976	Casanas/CUB	13.33
1980	Casanas/CUB	13.40
1984	Foster/USA	13.23
1988	Jackson/GBR	13.28

Bronze

1896	-	
1900	Moloney/USA	
1904	Ashburner/USA	16.4
1908	Shaw/USA	
1912	Hawkins/USA	15.3
1920	Murray/USA	15.2
1924	Pettersson/SWE	15.4
1928	Collier/USA	14.9
1932	Finlay/GBR	14.8
1936	Pollard/USA	14.4
1948	Dixon/USA	14.1
1952	Barnard/USA	14.1/14.40
1956	Shankle/USA	14.1/14.25
1960	H.Jones/USA	14.0/14.17
1964	Mikhailov/URS	13.7/13.78
1968	Ottoz/ITA	13.4/13.46
1972	Hill/USA	13.48
1976	Davenport/USA	13.38
1980	Puchkov/URS	13.44
1984	Bryggare/FIN	13.40
1988	Campbell/USA	13.38

400m Hurdles
(E. Moses/USA, 47.02, WR)

Gold

1896	Not contested	
1900	Tewksbury/USA	57.6
1904*	Hillman/USA	53.0
1908	Bacon/USA	55.0
1912	Not contested	
1920	Loomis/USA	54.0
1924	Taylor/USA	52.6
1928	Burghley/GBR	53.4
1932	Tisdall/IRE	51.7/51.67
1936	Hardin/USA	52.4
1948	Cochran/USA	51.1
1952	Moore/USA	50.8/51.06
1956	G.Davis/USA	50.1/50.29
1960	G.Davis/USA	49.3/49.51
1964	Cawley/USA	49.6
1968	Hemery/GBR	48.1/48.12
1972	Akii-Bua/UGA	47.82
1976	Moses/USA	47.63
1980	Beck/GDR	48.70
1984	Moses/USA	47.75
1988	Phillips/USA	47.19 (OR)

Silver

1896	Not contested	
1900	Tauzin/FRA	58.3
1904*	Waller/USA	53.2
1908	Hillman/USA	55.3
1912	Not contested	
1920	Norton/USA	54.3
1924	Vilén/FIN	53.8
1928	Cuhel/USA	53.6
1932	Hardin/USA	51.9
1936	Loaring/CAN	52.7
1948	White/CEY	51.8
1952	Lituyev/URS	51.3/51.51
1956	Southern/USA	50.8/50.93
1960	Cushman/USA	49.6/49.77
1964	Cooper/GBR	50.1
1968	Hennige/FRG	49.0/49.02
1972	Mann/USA	48.51
1976	Shine/USA	48.69
1980	Arkhipyenko/URS	48.86
1984	Harris/USA	48.13
1988	Dia Ba/SEN	47.23

Bronze

1896	Not contested	
1900	Orton/CAN	
1904*	Poage/USA	
1908	Tremeer/GBR	57.0
1912	Not contested	
1920	Desch/USA	54.5
1924	Riley/USA	54.2
1928	Taylor/USA	53.6
1932	Taylor/USA	52.0
1936	White/PHI	52.8
1948	R.Larsson/SWE	52.2
1952	Holland/NZL	52.2/52.26
1956	Culbreath/USA	51.6/51.74
1960	Howard/USA	49.7/49.90
1964	Morale/ITA	50.1
1968	Sherwood/GBR	49.0/49.03
1972	Hemery/GBR	48.52
1976	Gavrilenko/URS	49.45
1980	Oakes/GBR	49.11
1984	Schmid/FRG	48.19
1988	Moses/USA	47.56

*Over 76.2cm hurdles

High Jump
(J. Sotomayor/CUB, 2.43m, WR)

Gold

1896	Clark/USA	1.81
1900	Baxter/USA	1.90
1904	Jones/USA	1.80
1908	Porter/USA	1.90
1912	Richards/USA	1.93
1920	Landon/USA	1.93
1924	Osborn/USA	1.98
1928	King/USA	1.94
1932	McNaughton/CAN	1.97
1936	C.Johnson/USA	2.03
1948	Winter/AUS	1.98
1952	W.Davis/USA	2.04
1956	Dumas/USA	2.12
1960	Shavlakadze/URS	2.16
1964	Brumel/URS	2.18
1968	Fosbury/USA	2.24
1972	Tarmak/URS	2.23
1976	Wszola/POL	2.25
1980	Wessig/GDR	2.36
1984	Mögenburg/FRG	2.35
1988	Avdeyenko/URS	2.38 (OR)

Silver

1896	Connolly/USA	1.65
1900	P.Leahy/GBR	1.78
1904	Serviss/USA	1.77
1908	C.Leahy/GBR	1.88
	Somody/HUN	1.88
	G. André/FRA	1.88
1912	Liesche/GER	1.91
1920	Muller/USA	1.90
1924	Brown/USA	1.95
1928	Hedges/USA	1.91
1932	Van Osdel/USA	1.97
1936	Albritton/USA	2.00
1948	Paulson/USA	1.95
1952	Wiesner/USA	2.01
1956	Porter/AUS	2.10
1960	Brumel/URS	2.16
1964	Thomas/USA	2.18
1968	Caruthers/USA	2.22
1972	Junge/GDR	2.21
1976	Joy/CAN	2.23
1980	Wszola/POL	2.31
1984	Sjöberg/SWE	2.33
1988	Conway/USA	2.36

Bronze

1896	Garrett/USA	1.65
1900	Gonczy/HUN	1.75
1904	Weinstein/GER	1.77
1908	–	
1912	Horine/USA	1.89
1920	Ekelund/SWE	1.90
1924	Lewden/FRA	1.92
1928	Ménard/FRA	1.91
1932	Toribio/PHI	1.97
1936	Thurber/USA	2.00
1948	Stanich/USA	1.95
1952	Conceiçao/BRA	1.98
1956	Kashkarov/URS	2.08
1960	Thomas/USA	2.14
1964	Rambo/USA	2.16
1968	Gavrilov/URS	2.20
1972	Stones/USA	2.21
1976	Stones/USA	2.21
1980	Freimuth/GDR	2.31
1984	Zhu/CHN	2.31
1988	Povarnitsyn/URS	2.36
	Sjoberg/SWE	2.36

Pole Vault
(S. Bubka/URS, 6.05m, WR)

Gold

1896	Hoyt/USA	3.30
1900	Baxter/USA	3.30
1904	Dvorak/USA	3.50
1908	Cooke/USA	3.71
	Gilbert/USA	3.71
1912	Babcock/USA	3.95
1920	Foss/USA	4.09
1924	Barnes/USA	3.95
1928	Carr/USA	4.20
1932	Miller/USA	4.31
1936	Meadows/USA	4.35
1948	G.Smith/USA	4.30
1952	Richards/USA	4.55
1956	Richards/USA	4.56
1960	Bragg/USA	4.70
1964	Hansen/USA	5.10
1968	Seagren/USA	5.40
1972	Nordwig/GDR	5.50
1976	Slusarski/POL	5.50
1980	Kozakiewicz/POL	5.78
1984	Quinon/FRA	5.75
1988	Bubka/URS	5.90 (OR)

Silver

1896	Tyler/USA	3.25
1900	Colkett/USA	3.25
1904	Damse/USA	3.43
1908	-	
1912	Nelson/USA	3.85
	Wright/USA	3.85
1920	Petersen/DEN	3.70
1924	Graham/USA	3.95
1928	Droegemuller/USA	4.10
1932	Nishida/JAP	4.30
1936	Nishida/JAP	4.25
1948	Kataja/FIN	4.20
1952	Las/USA	4.50
1956	Gutowski/USA	4.53
1960	Morris/USA	4.60
1964	Reinhardt/FRG	5.05
1968	Schiprowski/FRG	5.40
1972	Seagren/USA	5.40
1976	Kalliomaki/FIN	5.50
1980	Volkov/URS	5.65
	Slusarski/POL	5.65
1984	Tully/USA	5.65
1988	Gataulline/URS	5.85

Bronze

1896	Damaskos/GRE	2.85
1900	Andersen/NOR	3.20
1904	Wilkins/USA	3.43
1908	Jacobs/USA	3.58
	Archibald/CAN	3.58
	Soderstrom/SWE	3.58
1912	-	
1920	Myers/USA	3.60
1924	Brooker/USA	3.90
1928	McGinnis/USA	3.95
1932	Jefferson/USA	4.20
1936	Oe/JAP	4.25
1948	Richards/USA	4.20
1952	Lundberg/SWE	4.40
1956	Roubanis/GRE	4.50
1960	Landstrom/FIN	4.55
1964	Lehnertz/FRG	5.00
1968	Nordwig/GDR	5.40
1972	J.Johnson/USA	5.35
1976	Roberts/USA	5.50
1980	-	
1984	Bell/USA	5.60
	Vigneron/FRA	5.60
1988	Yegorov/URS	5.80

Long Jump
(B. Beamon/USA, 8.90m, WR)

Gold

1896	Clark/USA	6.35
1900	Kraenzlein/USA	7.18
1904	Prinstein/USA	7.34
1908	Irons/USA	7.48
1912	Gutterson/USA	7.60
1920	W.Pettersson/SWE	7.15
1924	D.Hubbard/USA	7.44
1928	Hamm/USA	7.73
1932	Gordon/USA	7.64
1936	Owens/USA	8.06
1948	Steele/USA	7.82
1952	Biffle/USA	7.57
1956	Bell/USA	7.83
1960	Boston/USA	8.12
1964	Davies/GBR	8.07
1968	Beamon/USA	8.90 (OR)
1972	R.Williams/USA	8.24
1976	Robinson/USA	8.35
1980	Dombrowski/GDR	8.54
1984	C.Lewis/USA	8.54

Year	Gold	
988	C.Lewis/USA	8.72

Silver

Year		
896	Garrett/USA	6.18
900	Prinstein/USA	7.17
904	Frank/USA	6.89
908	Kelly/USA	7.09
912	Bricker/CAN	7.21
920	Johnson/USA	7.09
924	Gourdin/USA	7.27
928	Cator/HAI	7.58
932	Redd/USA	7.60
936	Long/GER	7.87
948	Bruce/AUS	7.55
952	Gourdine/USA	7.53
956	Bennett/USA	7.68
960	Robertson/USA	8.11
964	Boston/USA	8.03
968	Beer/GDR	8.19
972	Baumgartner/FRG	8.18
976	R.Williams/USA	8.11
980	Paschek/GDR	8.21
984	Honey/AUS	8.24
988	Powell/USA	8.49

Bronze

Year		
1896	Connolly/USA	6.11
1900	P.Leahy/GBR	6.95
1904	Stangland/USA	6.88
1908	Bricker/CAN	7.08
1912	Aberg/SWE	7.18
1920	Abrahamsson/SWE	7.08
1924	Hansen/NOR	7.26
1928	Bates/USA	7.40
1932	Nambu/JAP	7.45
1936	Tajima/JAP	7.74
1948	Douglas/USA	7.54
1952	Foldessy/HUN	7.30
1956	Valkama/FIN	7.48
1960	Ter-Ovanesyan/URS	8.04
1964	Ter-Ovanesyan/URS	7.99
1968	Boston/USA	8.16
1972	Robinson/USA	8.03
1976	Wartenberg/GDR	8.02
1980	Podluzhniy/URS	8.18
1984	Evangelisti/ITA	8.24
1988	Myricks/USA	8.27

Triple Jump
(W. Banks/USA, 17.97m, WR)

Gold

Year		
1896	Connolly/USA	13.71
1900	Prinstein/USA	14.47
1904	Prinstein/USA	14.32
1908	T.Aherne/GBR	14.91
1912	Lindblom/SWE	14.76
1920	Tuulos/FIN	14.50
1924	Winter/AUS	15.52
1928	Oda/JAP	15.21
1932	Nambu/JAP	15.72
1936	Tajima/JAP	16.00
1948	Ahman/SWE	15.40
1952	F. Da Silva/BRA	16.22
1956	F. Da Silva/BRA	16.35
1960	Schmidt/POL	16.81
1964	Schmidt/POL	16.85
1968	Sanyeyev/URS	17.39
1972	Sanyeyev/URS	17.35
1976	Sanyeyev/URS	17.29
1980	Uudmae/URS	17.35
1984	Joyner/USA	17.26
1988	Markov/BUL	17.61 (OR)

Silver

Year		
1896	Tuffère/FRA	12.70
1900	Connolly/USA	13.97
1904	Englehardt/USA	13.90
1908	MacDonald/CAN	14.76
1912	Aberg/SWE	14.51
1920	Jansson/SWE	14.48
1924	Brunetto/ARG	15.42
1928	Casey/USA	15.17
1932	Svensson/SWE	15.32
1936	Harada/JAP	15.66
1948	Avery/AUS	15.36
1952	Shcherbakov/URS	15.98
1956	Einarsson/ICE	16.26
1960	Goryayev/URS	16.63
1964	Fedosyeyev/URS	16.58
1968	Prudencio/BRA	17.27
1972	Drehmel/GDR	17.31
1976	Butts/USA	17.18
1980	Sanyeyev/URS	17.24
1984	Conley/USA	17.18
1988	Lapchine/URS	17.52

Bronze

Year		
1896	Persakis/GRE	12.52
1900	Sheldon/USA	13.64
1904	Stangland/USA	13.36
1908	Larsen/NOR	14.39
1912	Almlof/SWE	14.17
1920	Almlof/SWE	14.27
1924	Tuulos/FIN	15.37
1928	Tuulos/FIN	15.11
1932	Oshima/JAP	15.12
1936	Metcalfe/AUS	15.50
1948	Serialp/TUR	15.02
1952	Devonish/VEN	15.52
1956	Kreyer/URS	16.02
1960	Kreyer/URS	16.43
1964	Kravchenko/URS	16.57
1968	Gentile/ITA	17.22
1972	Prudencio/BRA	17.05
1976	de Oliveira/BRA	16.90
1980	de Oliveira/BRA	17.22
1984	Conner/GBR	16.87
1988	Kovalenko/URS	17.42

Shot Put
(U. Timmermann/GDR, 23.06m, WR)

Gold

Year		
1896	Garrett/USA	11.22
1900	Sheldon/USA	14.10
1904	Rose/USA	14.81
1908	Rose/USA	14.21
1912	McDonald/USA	15.34
1920	Porhola/FIN	14.81
1924	Houser/USA	14.99
1928	Kuck/USA	15.87
1932	Sexton/USA	16.00
1936	Woellke/GER	16.20
1948	Thompson/USA	17.12
1952	O'Brien/USA	17.41
1956	O'Brien/USA	18.57
1960	Nieder/USA	19.68
1964	Long/USA	20.33
1968	Matson/USA	20.54
1972	Komar/POL	21.18
1976	Beyer/GDR	21.05
1980	Kiselyov/URS	21.35
1984	Andrei/ITA	21.26
1988	Timmermann/GDR	22.47 (OR)

Silver

Year		
1896	Gouskos/GRE	11.20
1900	McCracken/USA	12.85
1904	Coe/USA	14.40
1908	Horgan/GBR	13.62
1912	Rose/USA	15.25
1920	Niklander/FIN	14.15
1924	Hartranft/USA	14.89
1928	Brix/USA	15.75
1932	Rothert/USA	15.67
1936	Barlund/FIN	16.12
1948	Delaney/USA	16.68
1952	Hooper/USA	17.39
1956	Nieder/USA	18.18
1960	O'Brien/USA	19.11
1964	Matson/USA	20.20
1968	Woods/USA	20.12
1972	Woods/USA	21.17
1988	Barnes/USA	22.39
1976	Mironov/URS	21.03
1980	Barishnikov/URS	21.08
1984	Carter/USA	21.09
1988	Barnes/USA	22.39

Bronze

Year		
1896	Papasideris/GRE	10.36
1900	Garrett/USA	12.37
1904	L.Feuerbach/USA	13.37
1908	Garrels/USA	13.18
1912	Whitney/USA	13.93
1920	Liversedge/USA	14.15
1924	Hills/USA	14.64
1928	Hirschfeld/GER	15.66
1932	Douda/TCH	15.61
1936	Stock/GER	15.66
1948	Fuchs/USA	16.42
1952	Fuchs/USA	17.06
1956	Skobla/TCH	17.65
1960	Long/USA	19.01
1964	Varju/HUN	19.39
1968	Gushchin/URS	20.09
1972	Briesenick/GDR	21.14
1976	Barishnikov/URS	21.00
1980	Beyer/GDR	21.06
1984	Laut/USA	20.97
1988	Guenthoer/SUI	21.99

Discus
(J. Schult/URS, 86.74m, WR)

Gold

Year		
1896	Garrett/USA	29.15
1900	Bauer/HUN	36.04
1904	Sheridan/USA	39.28
1908	Sheridan/USA	40.89
1912	Taipale/FIN	45.21
1920	Niklander/FIN	44.68
1924	Houser/USA	46.15
1928	Houser/USA	47.32
1932	Anderson/USA	49.49
1936	Carpenter/USA	50.48
1948	Consolini/ITA	52.78
1952	Iness/USA	55.03
1956	Oerter/USA	56.36
1960	Oerter/USA	59.18
1964	Oerter/USA	61.00
1968	Oerter/USA	64.78
1972	Danek/TCH	64.40
1976	Wilkins/USA	67.50
1980	Rashchupkin/URS	66.64
1984	Danneberg/FRG	66.60
1988	Schult/GDR	68.82 (OR)

Silver

Year		
1896	Paraskevopoulos/GRE	28.95
1900	Janda-Suk/BOH	35.25
1904	Rose/USA	39.28
1908	Giffin/USA	40.70
1912	Byrd/USA	42.32
1920	Taipale/FIN	44.19
1924	Niittymaa/FIN	44.95
1928	Kivi/FIN	47.23
1932	Laborde/USA	48.47
1936	Dunn/USA	49.36
1948	Tosi/ITA	51.78
1952	Consolini/ITA	53.78
1956	Gordien/USA	54.81
1960	Babka/USA	58.02
1964	Danek/TCH	60.52
1968	Milde/GDR	63.08
1972	Silvester/USA	63.50
1976	Schmidt/GDR	66.22
1980	Bugar/TCH	66.38
1984	Wilkins/USA	66.30
1988	Ubartas/URS	67.48

Bronze

Year		
1896	Versis/GRE	28.78
1900	Sheldon/USA	34.60
1904	Georgantas/GRE	37.68
1908	Horr/USA	39.44
1912	Duncan/USA	42.28
1920	Pope/USA	42.13
1924	Lieb/USA	44.83
1928	Corson/USA	47.10
1932	Winter/FRA	47.85
1936	Oberweger/ITA	49.23
1948	Gordien/USA	50.77
1952	Dillion/USA	53.28
1956	Koch/USA	54.40
1960	Cochran/USA	57.16
1964	Weill/USA	59.49
1968	Danek/TCH	62.92
1972	Bruch/WE	63.40
1976	Powell/USA	65.70
1980	Delis/CUB	66.32
1984	Powell/USA	65.46
1988	Danneberg/FRG	67.38

Hammer
(S.Litvinov/URS, 84.80m, WR)

Gold

Year		
1896	Not contested	
1900	Flanagan/USA	49.73
1904	Flanagan/USA	51.23
1908	Flanagan/USA	54.74
1912	McGrath/USA	54.74
1920	Ryan/USA	52.87
1924	Tootell/USA	53.29
1928	O'Callaghan/IRE	51.39
1932	O'Callaghan/IRE	53.92
1936	Hein/GER	56.49
1948	I.Nemeth/HUN	56.07
1952	Csermak/HUN	60.34
1956	Connolly/USA	63.19
1960	Rudyenkov/URS	67.10
1964	Klim/URS	69.74
1968	Zsivotzky/HUN	73.36
1972	Bondarchuk/URS	75.50
1976	Syedikh/URS	77.52
1980	Syedikh/URS	81.80
1984	Tiainen/FIN	78.08
1988	Litvinov/URS	84.80 (OR)

Silver

Year		
1896	Not contested	
1900	Hare/USA	49.13
1904	DeWitt/USA	50.26
1908	McGrath/USA	51.18
1912	Gillis/CAN	48.39
1920	Lind/SWE	48.43
1924	McGrath/USA	50.84
1928	Skiold/SWE	51.29
1932	Porhola/FIN	52.27
1936	Blask/GER	55.04
1948	Gubijan/YUG	54.27
1952	Storch/GER	58.86
1956	Krivonosov/URS	63.03
1960	Zsivotzky/HUN	65.79
1964	Zsivotzky/HUN	69.09
1968	Klim/URS	73.28
1972	Sachse/GDR	74.96
1976	Spiridonov/URS	76.08
1980	Litvinov/URS	80.64
1984	Riehm/FRG	77.98
1988	Sedykh/URS	83.76

Bronze

Year		
1896	Not contested	
1900	McCracken/USA	42.46
1904	Rose/USA	45.73
1908	Walsh/USA	48.50
1912	Childs/USA	48.17
1920	Bennet/USA	48.25
1924	Nokes/GBR	48.87
1928	Black/USA	49.03
1932	Zaremba/USA	50.33
1936	Warngard/SWE	54.83
1948	R.Bennett/USA	53.73
1952	I.Nemeth/HUN	57.74
1956	Samotsvetov/URS	62.56
1960	Rut/POL	65.64
1964	Uwe Beyer/FRG	68.09
1968	Lovasz/HUN	69.78
1972	Khmyelevskiy/URS	74.04
1976	Bondarchuk/URS	75.48
1980	Tamm/URS	78.96
1984	Ploghaus/FRG	76.68
1988	Tamm/URS	81.16

Javelin
(J. Zelezny/TCH, 85.90m, OR)
(J. Zelezny/TCH, 87.66m, WR)

Gold

Year		
1896 - 1904	Not contested	
1908	Lemming/SWE	54.82
1912	Lemming/SWE	60.64
1920	Myyra/FIN	65.78
1924	Myyra/FIN	62.96
1928	Lundqvist/SWE	66.60

1932	M.Järvinen/FIN	72.71
1936	Stock/GER	71.84
1948	Rautavaara/FIN	69.77
1952	C.Young/USA	73.78
1956	Danielsen/NOR	85.71
1960	Tsibulenko/URS	84.64
1964	Nevala/FIN	82.66
1968	Lusis/URS	90.10
1972	Wolfermann/FRG	90.48
1976	M.Nemeth/HUN	94.58
1980	Kula/URS	91.20
1984	Härkönen/FIN	86.76
1988	Korjus/FIN	84.28

Silver

1896 - 1904	Not contested	
1908	Halse/NOR	50.57
1912	Saaristo/FIN	58.66
1920	Peltonen/FIN	64.50
1924	Lindstrom/SWE	60.92
1928	Szepes/HUN	65.26
1932	Sippala/FIN	69.80
1936	Nikkanen/FIN	70.77
1948	Seymour/USA	67.56
1952	Miller/USA	72.46
1956	Sidlo/POL	79.98
1960	Kruger/GDR	79.36
1964	Kulcsar/HUN	82.32
1968	Kinnunen/FIN	88.58
1972	Lusis/URS	90.46
1976	Siitonen/FIN	87.92
1980	Makarov/URS	89.64
1984	Ottley/GBR	85.74
1988	Zelezny/TCH	84.12

Bronze

1896 - 1904	Not contested	
1908	Nilsson/SWE	47.10
1912	Koczan/HUN	55.50
1920	Johansson/FIN	63.09
1924	Oberst/USA	58.35
1928	Sunde/NOR	63.97
1932	Penttila/FIN	68.70
1936	Toivonen/FIN	70.72
1948	Varszegi/HUN	67.03
1952	Hyytiainen/FIN	71.89
1956	Tsibulenko/URS	79.50
1960	Kulcsar/HUN	78.57
1964	Lusis/URS	80.57
1968	Kulcsar/HUN	87.06
1972	Schmidt/USA	84.42
1976	Megelea/ROM	87.16
1980	Hanisch/GDR	86.72
1984	Eldebrink/SWE	83.72
1988	Raty/FIN	83.26

Decathlon
(D.Thompson/GBR, 8847pts, WR)
Gold
N.B. First figure shows the official score under the table used at the time; second figure shows the reconverted score as per 1962 table

1896 - 1908	Not contested	
1912	J.Thorpe/USA	8412/6756
1920	Løvland/NOR	6804/5970
1924	Osborn/USA	7710/6668
1928	Yrjola/FIN	8053/6774
1932	Bausch/USA	8462/6896
1936	G.Morris/USA	7900/7421
1948	Mathias/USA	7139/6825
1952	Mathias/USA	7887/7731
1956	Campbell/USA	7937/7708
1960	Johnson/USA	8392/8001
1964	Holdorf/FRG	7887
1968	Toomey/USA	8193
1972	Avilov/URS	8454
1976	Jenner/USA	8618
1980	Thompson/GBR	8495
1984	Thompson/GBR	8797 (OR)
1988	Schenk/GDR	2448

Silver

1896 - 1908	Not contested	
1912	Wieslander/SWE	7724/6161
1920	Hamilton/USA	6770/5912
1924	Norton/USA	7350/6340
1928	Järvinen/FIN	7931/6815
1932	Järvinen/FIN	8292/7038
1936	Clark/USA	7601/7226
1948	Heinrich/FRA	6974/6740
1952	Campbell/USA	6975/7132
1956	Johnson/USA	7587/7568
1960	Yang/TPE	8334/7930
1964	Aun/URS	7842
1968	Walde/FRG	8111
1972	Litvinyenko/URS	8035
1976	Kratschmer/FRG	8411
1980	Kutsenko/URS	8331
1984	Hingsen/FRG	8673
1988	Voss/GDR	8399

Bronze

1896 - 1908	Not contested	
1912	Lomberg/SWE	7413/5943
1920	Olsson/SWE	6579/5825
1924	Klumberg/EST	7329/6260
1928	Doherty/USA	7706/6593
1932	Eberle/GER	8030/6830
1936	Parker/USA	7275/6918
1948	Simmons/USA	6950/6711
1952	Simmons/USA	6788/7069
1956	Kuznyetsov/URS	7465/7461
1960	Kuznyetsov/URS	7809/7624
1964	Walde/FRG	7809
1968	Bendlin/FRG	8064
1972	Katus/POL	7984
1976	Avilov/URS	8369
1980	Zhelanov/URS	8135
1984	Wentz/FRG	8412
1988	Steen/CAN	8328

4 x 100m
(USA, 37.83, WR)
Gold

1896 - 1908	Not contested	
1912	GBR	42.4
1920	USA	42.2
1924	USA	41.0
1928	USA	41.0
1932	USA	40.0
1936	USA	39.8
1948	USA	40.6
1952	USA	40.1/40.26
1956	USA	39.5/39.59
1960	FRG	39.5/39.66
1964	USA	39.0/39.06
1968	USA	38.2/38.23
1972	USA	38.19
1976	USA	38.22
1980	URS	38.26
1984	USA	37.83 (OR)
1988	URS	38.19

Silver

1896 - 1908	Not contested	
1912	SWE	42.6
1920	FRA	42.6
1924	GBR	41.2
1928	GER	41.2
1932	GER	40.9
1936	ITA	41.1/41.13
1948	GBR	41.3
1952	URS	40.3/40.58
1956	URS	39.8/39.92
1960	URS	40.1/40.23
1964	POL	39.3/39.36
1968	CUB	38.3/38.39
1972	URS	38.50
1976	GDR	38.66
1980	POL	38.33
1984	JAM	38.62
1988	GBR	38.28

Bronze

1896 - 1908	Not contested	
1912	-	
1920	SWE	42.9
1924	HOL	41.8
1928	GBR	41.8
1932	ITA	41.2
1936	GER	41.2/41.30
1948	ITA	41.5
1952	HUN	40.5/40.83
1956	GER	40.3/40.34
1960	GBR	40.2/40.32
1964	FRA	39.3/39.36
1968	FRA	38.4/38.42
1972	FRG	38.79
1976	URS	38.78
1980	FRA	38.53
1984	CAN	38.70
1988	FRA	38.40

4 x 400m
(USA, 2:56.16, WR)
Gold

1896 - 1904	Not contested	
1908	USA	3:29.4
1912	USA	3:16.6
1920	GBR	3:22.2
1924	USA	3:16.0
1928	USA	3:14.2
1932	USA	3:08.2
1936	UK	3:39.0
1948	USA	3:10.4
1952	JAM	3:03.9
1956	USA	3:04.7
1960	USA	3:02.2
1964	USA	3:00.7
1968	USA	2:56.1
1972	KEN	2:59.8
1976	USA	2:58.7
1980	URS	3:01.1
1984	USA	2:57.91
1988	USA	2:56.16 (OR)

Silver

1896 - 1904	Not contested	
1908	GER	-
1912	FRA	3:20.7
1920	SA	3:24.2
1924	SWE	3:17.0
1928	GER	3:14.8
1932	GBR	3:11.2
1936	USA	3:11.0
1948	FRA	3:14.8
1952	USA	3:04.0
1956	AUS	3:06.2
1960	FRG	3:02.7
1964	GBR	3:01.6
1968	KEN	2:59.6
1972	GBR	3:00.5
1976	POL	3:01.4
1980	GDR	3:01.3
1984	GBR	2:59.13
1988	JAM	3:00.30

Bronze

1896 - 1904	Not contested	
1908	HUN	-
1912	GBR	3:23.2
1920	FRA	3:24.8
1924	GBR	3:17.4
1928	CAN	3:15.4
1932	CAN	3:12.8
1936	GER	3:11.8
1948	SWE	3:16.0
1952	GER	3:06.6
1956	GBR	3:07.1
1960	W.INDIES	3:04.0
1964	TRI	3:01.7
1968	TRI	3:00.5
1972	FRA	3:00.7
1976	FRG	3:02.0
1980	ITA	3:04.3
1984	NGR	2.59.32
1988	FRG	3:00.56

WOMEN

100m
(F. Joyner/USA, 10.49, WR)
(F. Joyner/USA, 10.62, OR)
Gold

1928	Robinson/USA	12.2
1932	Walasiewicz/POL	11.9
1936	Stephens/USA	11.5
1948	Blankers-Koen/HOL	11.9
1952	Jackson/AUS	11.5/11.65
1956	Cuthbert/AUS	11.5/11.82
1960	Rudolph/USA	11.0/11.18
1964	Tyus/USA	11.4/11.49
1968	Tyus/USA	11.0/11.08
1972	Stecher/GDR	11.07
1976	Richter/FRG	11.08
1980	Kondratyeva/URS	11.06
1984	Ashford/USA	10.97
1988	Joyner/USA	10.54

Silver

1928	Rosenfeld/CAN	12.3
1932	Strike/CAN	11.9
1936	Walasiewicz/POL	11.7
1948	Manley/GBR	12.2
1952	Hasenjager/SA	11.8/12.04
1956	Stübnick/GDR	11.7/11.92
1960	Hyman/GBR	11.3/11.43
1964	McGuire/USA	11.6/11.62
1968	Ferrell/USA	11.1/11.15
1972	Boyle/AUS	11.23
1976	Stecher/GDR	11.13
1980	Göhr/GDR	11.07
1984	Brown/USA	11.13
1988	Ashford/USA	10.83

Bronze

1928	E.Smith/CAN	12.3
1932	Von Bremen/USA	12.0
1936	Krauss/GER	11.9
1948	Strickland/AUS	12.2
1952	Strickland/AUS	11.9/12.0
1956	Matthews/AUS	11.7/11.94
1960	Leone/ITA	11.3/11.48
1964	Klobukowska/POL	11.6/11.64
1968	Szewinska/POL	11.1/11.19
1972	Chivas/CUB	11.24
1976	Helten/FRG	11.17
1980	Auerswald/GDR	11.14
1984	Ottey-Page/JAM	11.16
1988	Drechsler/GDR	10.85

200m
(Joyner/USA, 21.34, WR)
Gold

1928 - 1936	Not contested	
1948	Blankers-Koen/HOL	24.4
1952	Jackson/AUS	23.7/23.89
1956	Cuthbert/AUS	23.4/23.55
1960	Rudolph/USA	24.0/24.13
1964	McGuire/USA	23.0/23.05
1968	Szewinska/POL	22.5/22.58
1972	Stecher/GDR	22.40
1976	Eckert/GDR	22.37
1980	Eckert-Wockel/GDR	22.03
1984	Brisco-Hooks/USA	21.81
1988	Joyner/USA	21.34 (OR)

Silver

1928 - 1936	Not contested	
1948	Williamson/GBR	25.1
1952	Brouwer/HOL	24.2/24.25
1956	Stübnick/GDR	23.7/23.89
1960	Heine/GER	24.4/24.58
1964	Szewinska/POL	23.1/23.13
1968	Boyle/AUS	22.7/22.73
1972	Boyle/AUS	22.45
1976	Richter/FRG	22.39
1980	Bochina/URS	22.19
1984	Griffith/USA	22.04
1988	Jackson/JAM	21.72

Bronze

1928 - 1936	Not contested	
1948	Patterson/USA	25.2
1952	Khnikina/URS	24.2/24.37
1956	Matthews/AUS	23.8/24.10
1960	Hyman/GBR	24.7/24.82
1964	Black/AUS	23.1/23.18
1968	Lamy/AUS	22.8/22.88
1972	Szewinska/POL	22.74
1976	Stecher/GDR	22.47
1980	Ottey/JAM	22.20
1984	Ottey/JAM	22.09
1988	Drechsler/GDR	21.95

00m
1. Koch/GDR, 47.69, WR)

old

928 - 1960	Not contested	
964	Cuthbert/AUS	52.0/52.01
968	Besson/FRA	52.0/52.03
972	Zehrt/GDR	51.08
976	Szewinska/POL	49.29
980	Koch/GDR	48.88
984	Brisco-Hooks/USA	48.83
988	Bryzgina/URS	48.65 (OR)

ilver

928 - 1960	Not contested	
964	Packer/GBR	52.2/52.20
968	Board/GBR	52.1/52.12
972	Wilden/FRG	51.21
976	Brehmer/GDR	50.51
980	Kratochvilova/TCH	49.46
984	Cheeseborough/USA	49.05
988	Mueller/GDR	49.45

ronze

928 - 1960	Not contested	
964	Amoore/AUS	53.4/-
968	Pechenkina/URS	52.2/52.25
972	Hammond/USA	51.64
976	Streidt/GDR	50.55
980	Lathan/GDR	49.66
984	Cook/GBR	49.42
988	Nazarova/URS	49.90

00m
M. Kratochvilova/TCH, 1:53.28, WR)
N. Olizaryenko/URS, 1:53.5, OR)

Gold

928	Radke/GER	2:16.8
932 - 1956	Not contested	
960	Shevtsova/URS	2:04.3
964	Packer/GBR	2:01.1
968	Manning/USA	2:00.9
972	Falck/FRG	1:58.6
976	Kazankina/URS	1:54.9
980	Olizaryenko/URS	1:53.5
984	Melinte/ROM	1:57.6
988	Wodars/GDR	1:56.10

ilver

928	Hitomi/JAP	2:17.6
932 - 1956	Not contested	
960	Jones/AUS	2:04.4
964	Dupureur/FRA	2:01.9
968	Silai/ROM	2:02.5
972	Sabaité/URS	1:58.7
976	Shtereva/BUL	1:55.4
980	Mineyeva/URS	1:54.9
984	Gallagher/USA	1:58.6
988	Wachtel/GDR	1:56.64

ronze

928	Gentzel/SWE	2:17.8
932 - 1956	Not contested	
960	Donath/GDR	2:05.6
964	Chamberlain/NZL	2:02.8
968	Gommers/HOL	2:02.6
972	Hoffmeister/GDR	1:59.2
976	Zinn/GDR	1:55.6
980	Providokhina/URS	1:55.5
984	Lovin/ROM	1:58.8
988	Gallagher/USA	1:56.91

500m
T. Kazankina/URS, 3:52.47, WR)

old

928 - 1968	Not contested	
972	Bragina/URS	4:01.4
976	Kazankina/URS	4:05.5
980	Kazankina/URS	3:56.6
984	Dorio/ITA	4:03.25
988	Ivan/ROM	3:53.96 (OR)

ilver

928 - 1968	Not contested	
972	Hoffmeister/GDR	4:02.8
976	Hoffmeister/GDR	4:06.0
1980	Wartenberg/GDR	3:57.8
1984	Melinte/ROM	4:03.7
1988	Baikauskaite/URS	4:00.24

Bronze

1928 - 1968	Not contested	
1972	Pigni-Cacchi/ITA	4:02.9
1976	Klapezynski/GDR	4:06.1
1980	Olizaryenko/URS	3:59.6
1984	Puica/ROM	4:04.1
1988	Samolenko/URS	4:00.30

3000m
(T. Kazankina/URS, 8:22.62, WR)

Gold

1928-1980	Not contested	
1984	Puica/ROM	8:35.96
1988	Samolenko/URS	8:26.53 (OR)

Silver

1928-1980	Not contested	
1984	Sly/GBR	8:39.47
1988	Ivan/ROM	8:27.15

Bronze

1928-1980	Not contested	
1984	Williams/CAN	8:42.14
1988	Murray/GBR	8:29.02

10,000m
(I.Kristiansen/NOR, 30:13.74, WR)
N. B. Event contested for the first time at an Olympics in 1988

Gold

1988	Bondarenko/URS (OR)	31:05.21

Silver

1988	McColgan/GBR	31:08.44

Bronze

1988	Zhupieva/URS	31:19.82

100m Hurdles
(Y. Doncova/BUL, 12.21, WR)
N.B. Held at 80m until after 1968

Gold

1928	Not contested	
1932	Didrikson/USA	11.7
1936	Valla/ITA	11.7/11.74
1948	Blankers-Koen/HOL	11.2
1952	Strickland/AUS	10.9/11.03
1956	Strickland/AUS	10.7/10.96
1960	I.Press/URS	10.8/10.94
1964	Balzer/GDR	10.5/10.54
1968	Caird/AUS	10.3
1972	Ehrhardt/GDR	12.59
1976	Schaller/GDR	12.77
1980	Komisova/URS	12.56
1984	Fitzgerald/USA	12.84
1988	Donkova/BUL	12.38 (OR)

Silver

1928	Not contested	
1932	Hall/USA	11.7
1936	Steuer/GER	11.7/11.809
1948	Gardner/GBR	11.2
1952	Golubnichaya/URS	11.1/11.24
1956	Birkemeyer/GDR	10.9/11.12
1960	Quinton/GBR	10.9/10.99
1964	Ciepla/POL	10.5/10.55
1968	Ryan-Kilborn/AUS	10.4
1972	Bufanu/ROM	12.84
1976	Anisimova/URS	12.50
1980	Klier-Schaller/GDR	12.63
1984	Strong/GBR	12.88
1988	Siebert/GDR	12.61

Bronze

1928	Not contested	
1932	Clark/SA	11.8
1936	Taylor/CAN	11.7/11.818
	Testoni/ITA	11.7/11.818
1948	Strickland/AUS	11.4
1952	Sander/GER	11.1/11.38
1956	Thrower/AUS	11.0/11.25
1960	Birkemeyer/GDR	11.0/11.13
1964	Ryan/AUS	10.5/10.56
1968	Chi Cheng/TPE	10.4
1972	Balzer/GDR	12.90
1976	Lebedyeva/URS	12.80
1980	Langer/POL	12.65
1984	Turner/USA	13.06
1988	Zackiewicz/FRG	12.75

400m Hurdles
(M. Stepanova/URS, 52.94, WR)

Gold

1928-1980	Not contested	
1984	El Moutawakil/MAR	54.61
1988	Flintoff–King/AUS	53.17 (OR)

Silver

1928-1980	Not contested	
1984	Brown/USA	55.20
1988	Ledovskaia/URS	53.18

Bronze

1928-1980	Not contested	
1984	Cojocaru/ROM	55.41
1988	Fiedler/GDR	53.63

High Jump
(S. Kostadinova/BUL, 2.09m, WR)

Gold

1928	Catherwood/CAN	1.59
1932	Shiley/USA	1.65
1936	Csak/HUN	1.60
1948	Coachman/USA	1.68
1952	Brand/SA	1.67
1956	McDaniel/USA	1.76
1960	Balas/ROM	1.85
1964	Balas/ROM	1.90
1968	Rezkova/TCH	1.82
1972	Meyfarth/FRG	1.92
1976	Ackermann/GDR	1.93
1980	Simeoni/ITA	1.97
1984	Meyfarth/FRG	2.07
1988	Ritter/USA	2.03 (OR)

Silver

1928	Gisolf/HOL	1.56
1932	Didrikson/USA	1.65
1936	Odam/GBR	1.60
1948	Odam-Tyler/GBR	1.68
1952	Lerwill/GBR	1.65
1956	Pisaryeva/URS	1.67
	Hopkins/GBR	1.67
1960	Jozwiakowska/POL	1.71
	Shirley/GBR	1.71
1964	Brown/AUS	1.80
1968	Okorokova/URS	1.80
1972	Blagoyeva/BUL	1.88
1976	Simeoni/ITA	1.91
1980	Kielan/POL	1.94
1984	Simeoni/FRG	2.07
1988	Kostadinova/BUL	2.01

Bronze

1928	Wiley/USA	1.56
1932	Dawes/CAN	1.60
1936	Kaun/GER	1.60
1948	Ostermeyer/FRA	1.61
1952	Chudina/URS	1.63
1956	-	
1960	-	
1964	Chenchik/URS	1.78
1968	Kozir/URS	1.80
1972	Gusenbauer/AUT	1.88
1976	Blagoyeva/BUL	1.91
1980	Kirst/GDR	1.94
1984	Huntely/USA	2.00
1988	Bykova/URS	1.99

Long Jump
(G. Chistyakova/URS, 7.52m, WR)

Gold

1928 - 1936	Not contested	
1948	Gyarmati/HUN	5.69
1952	Williams/NZL	6.24
1956	Krzesinska/POL	6.35
1960	Krepkina/URS	6.37
1964	Rand/GBR	6.76
1968	Viscopoleanu/ROM	6.82
1972	Rosendahl/FRG	6.78
1976	Voigt/GDR	6.72
1980	Kolpakova/URS	7.06
1984	Stanciu/ROM	6.96
1988	Joyner–Kersee/USA	7.40 (OR)

Silver

1928 - 1936	Not contested	
1948	De Portela/ARG	5.60
1952	Chudina/URS	6.14
1956	White/USA	6.09
1960	Krzesinska/POL	6.27
1964	Kirszenstein/POL	6.60
1968	Sherwood/GBR	6.68
1972	Yorgova/BUL	6.77
1976	McMillan/USA	6.66
1980	Wujak/GDR	7.04
1984	Ionescu/ROM	6.81
1988	Drechsler/GDR	7.22

Bronze

1928 - 1936	Not contested	
1948	Leyman/SWE	5.57
1952	Cawley/GBR	5.92
1956	Dvalishvili/URS	6.07
1960	Claus/GDR	6.21
1964	Shchelkanova/URS	6.42
1968	Talisheva/URS	6.66
1972	Suranova/TCH	6.67
1976	Alfeyeva/URS	6.60
1980	Skachko/URS	7.01
1984	Hearnshaw/GBR	6.80
1988	Chistyakova/URS	7.11

Shot Put
(N. Lisorskaya/URS, 22.63m, WR)

Gold

1928 - 1936	Not contested	
1948	Ostermeyer/FRA	13.75
1952	Zibina/URS	15.28
1956	Tishkyevich/URS	16.59
1960	T.Press/URS	17.32
1964	T.Press/URS	18.14
1968	Gummel/GDR	19.61
1972	Chizhova/URS	21.03
1976	Khristova/BUL	21.16
1980	Slupianek/GDR	22.41(OR)
1984	Losch/FRG	20.48
1988	Lisovskaya/URS	22.24

Silver

1928 - 1936	Not contested	
1948	Piccinini/ITA	13.09
1952	Werner/GER	14.57
1956	Zibina/URS	16.53
1960	Lüttge/GDR	16.61
1964	Garisch/GDR	17.61
1968	Lange/GDR	18.78
1972	Gummel/GDR	20.22
1976	Chizhova/URS	20.96
1980	Krachevskaya/URS	21.42
1984	Loghin/ROM	20.47
1988	Neimke/GDR	21.07

Bronze

1928 - 1936	Not contested	
1948	Schaffer/AUT	13.08
1952	Tochonova/URS	14.50
1956	Werner/GER	15.61
1960	Brown/USA	16.42
1964	Zibina/URS	17.45
1968	Chizhova/URS	18.19
1972	Khristova/BUL	19.35
1976	Fibingerova/TCH	20.67
1980	Pufe/GDR	21.20
1984	Martin/AUS	19.19
1988	Meisu/PRC	21.06

Discus
(G. Reinsch/GDR, 76.80m, WR)

Gold

1928	Konopacka/POL	39.62
1932	Copeland/USA	40.58
1936	Mauermayer/GER	47.63
1948	Ostermeyer/FRA	41.92
1952	Romashkova/URS	51.42
1956	Fikotova/TCH	53.69

1960	Romashkova/URS	55.10
1964	T.Press/URS	57.27
1968	Manoliu/ROM	58.28
1972	Myelnik/URS	66.62
1976	Schlaak/GDR	69.00
1980	Schlaak-Jahl/GDR	69.96
1984	Stalman/HOL	65.36
1988	Hellman/GDR	72.30 (OR)

Silver

1928	Copeland/USA	37.08
1932	Osborn/USA	40.12
1936	Wajsowna/POL	46.22
1948	Gentile/ITA	41.17
1952	Bagryantseva/URS	47.08
1956	Beglyakova/URS	52.54
1960	T.Press/URS	52.59
1964	Lotz/GDR	57.21
1968	Westermann/FRG	57.76
1972	Menis/ROM	65.06
1976	Vergova/BUL	67.30
1980	Vergova-Petkova/BUL	67.90
1984	Deniz/USA	64.86
1988	Gansky/GDR	71.88

Bronze

1928	Svedberg/SWE	35.92
1932	Wajsowna/POL	38.74
1936	Mollenhauer/GER	39.80
1948	Mazéas/FRA	40.47
1952	Dumbadze/URS	46.29
1956	Romashkova/URS	52.02
1960	Manoliu/ROM	52.36
1964	Manoliu/ROM	56.87
1968	Kleiber/HUN	54.90
1972	Stoeva/BUL	64.34
1976	Hinzmann/GDR	66.84
1980	Lyesovaya/URS	67.40
1984	Craciunescu/ROM	63.64
1988	Kristova/BUL	69.74

Javelin
(P. Felke/GDR, 80.00m, WR)
Gold

1928	Not contested	
1932	Didrikson/USA	43.68
1936	Fleischer/GER	45.18
1948	Bauma/AUT	45.57
1952	Zatopkova/TCH	50.47
1956	Jaunzeme/URS	53.86
1960	Ozolina/URS	55.98
1964	Penes/ROM	60.54
1968	A.Nemeth/HUN	60.36
1972	Fuchs/GDR	63.88
1976	Fuchs/GDR	65.94

1980	Colon/CUB	68.40
1984	Sanderson/GBR	69.56
1988	Felke/GDR	74.68 (OR)

Silver

1928	Not contested	
1932	Braumuller/GER	43.49
1936	Krüger/GER	43.29
1948	Parviainen/FIN	43.79
1952	Chudina/URS	50.01
1956	Ahrens/CHI	50.38
1960	Zatopkova/TCH	53.78
1964	Rudas/HUN	58.27
1968	Penes/ROM	59.92
1972	Todten/GDR	62.54
1976	M.Becker/FRG	64.70
1980	Gunba/URS	67.76
1984	Lillak/FIN	69.00
1988	Whitbread/GBR	70.32

Bronze

1928	Not contested	
1932	Fleischer/GER	43.00
1936	Kwasniewska/POL	41.80
1948	Carlstedt/DEN	42.08
1952	Gorchakova/URS	49.76
1956	Konyayeva/URS	50.28
1960	Kalediene/URS	53.45
1964	Gorchakova/URS	57.06
1968	Janko/AUT	58.04
1972	Schmidt/USA	59.94
1976	Schmidt/USA	63.96
1980	Hommola/GDR	66.56
1984	Whitbread/GBR	67.14
1988	Koch/GDR	67.30

Pentathlon/Heptathlon
(Heptathlon: J. Joyner/USA, 7291pts, WR)
N. B. 80mh replaced by 100mh in 1972;
200m replaced by 800m in 1980
Gold

1928 - 1960	Not contested	
1964	I.Press/URS	5246
1968	I.Becker/FRG	5098
1972	Peters/GBR	4801
1976	Siegl/GDR	4745
1980	Tkachenko/URS	5083
1984*	Nunn/AUS	6390
1988	Joyner/USA	7291 (OR)

Silver

1928-1960	Not contested	
1964	Rand/GBR	5035
1968	Prokop/AUT	4966
1972	Rosendahl/FRG	4791

1976	Laser/GDR	4745
1980	Rukavishnikova/URS	4937
1984*	Joyner/USA	6385
1988	John/GDR	6897

Bronze

1928 - 1960	Not contested	
1964	Bistrova/URS	4956
1968	Toth/HUN	4959
1972	Pollak/GDR	4768
1976	Pollak/GDR	4740
1980	Kuragina/URS	4875
1984*	Everts/FRG	6363
1988	Behmer/GDR	6858

* Heptathlon (7 events) staged for the first
time to replace previous 5-event pentathlon

Marathon
(I. Kristianson/NOR, 2:21:06, WR)
Gold

1928–1980	Not contested	
1984	Benoit/USA	2:24:52 (OR)
1988	Mota/POR	2:25:40

Silver

1928–1980	Not contested	
1984	Waitz/NOR	2:26:18
1988	Martin/AUS	2:25:53

Bronze

1928–1980	Not contested	
1984	Mota/POR	2:26:57
1988	Doerre/GDR	2:26:21

4 x 100m
(GDR, 41.37, WR)
Gold

1928	CAN	48.4
1932	USA	47.0
1936	USA	46.9
1948	HOL	47.5
1952	USA	45.9/46.14
1956	AUS	44.5/44.65
1960	USA	44.5/44.72
1964	POL	43.6/43.69
1968	USA	42.8/42.87
1972	FRG	42.81
1976	GDR	42.55
1980	GDR	41.60 (OR)
1984	USA	41.65
1988	USA	41.98

Silver

1928	USA	48.8
1932	CAN	47.0

1936	GBR	47.6
1948	AUS	47.6
1952	GER	45.9/46.18
1956	GBR	44.7/44.70
1960	FRG	44.8/45.00
1964	USA	43.9/43.92
1968	CUB	43.3/43.35
1972	GDR	42.95
1976	FRG	42.59
1980	URS	42.10
1984	CAN	42.77
1988	GDR	42.09

Bronze

1928	GER	49.0
1932	GBR	47.6
1936	CAN	47.8
1948	CAN	47.8
1952	GBR	46.2/46.41
1956	USA	44.9/45.04
1960	POL	45.0/45.19
1964	GBR	44.0/44.09
1968	URS	43.4/43.41
1972	CUB	43.36
1976	URS	43.09
1980	GBR	42.43
1984	GBR	43.11
1988	URS	42.75

4 x 400m
(USR, 3:15.18, WR)
Gold

1928 - 1968	Not contested	
1972	GDR	3:23.0
1976	GDR	3:19.2
1980	URS	3:20.2
1984	USA	3:18.29
1988	URS	3:15.18 (OR)

Silver

1928 - 1968	Not contested	
1972	USA	3:25.2
1976	USA	3:22.8
1980	GDR	3:20.4
1984	CAN	3:21.21
1988	USA	3:15.51

Bronze

1928 - 1968	Not contested	
1972	FRG	3:26.6
1976	URS	3:24.2
1980	GBR	3:27.5
1984	FRG	3:22.9
1988	GDR	3:18.29

(Data reproduced by kind permission of the IAAF.)

OLYMPIC UPDATE

Kenya reaffirmed its place in international athletics with four gold medals, two silver and a bronze in 1988 in Seoul. After missing two Olympic Games because of boycotts in 1976 and 1980, the Kenyans returned as a world force at the 1987 World Championships.

They went to Seoul without two of their world champions, Billy Konchellah (800m) and Paul Kipkoech (10,000m), but there were equally talented runners to take their places. The 20-year-old unknown Paul Ereng won a superb 800m final, while the inexperienced Peter Rono upset the form books by taking the 1500m title. John Ngugi, the three-time World Cross-Country champion, won the 5000m, and Julius Kariuki and Peter Koech took gold and silver in the 3000m steeplechase. In the marathon, world champion Douglas Wakihuru came close to his second major championship win with a silver medal, after a fierce battle with Gelindo Bordin of Italy.

While Carl Lewis became the first man in history to retain his Olympic 100m title, the race in question will always be remembered for the disqualification of Canada's Ben Johnson, who finished first in what was to thought be a new world record of 9.79 seconds. His positive drugs test meant that his gold medal was subsequently presented to Lewis, the silver went to Britain's Linford Christie, the European champion, and the bronze to former world record holder Calvin Smith of the USA.

There were sensational wins for the Americans in the flat 400m and 400m hurdles. Steve Lewis, at 19 years old the third youngest ever Olympic champion, beat world record holder Harry Butch Reynolds with a breath-taking display of sprinting over one lap. André Phillips became the first man to beat Ed Moses in an Olympic race when he won the 400mh title in 47.19, a new Games record. Moses finished third while the silver medal went to Hadj Dia Ba of Senegal.

Christian Schenk of East Germany became the new Olympic decathlon champion. Defending champion Daley Thompson of Great Britain–who wanted to be the first man to win three successive titles–was fourth.

The highlight of the women's events was the running of Florence Joyner. She won the 100m and 200m titles, the latter with a world record of 21.34 seconds, and took a gold medal in the 4 x 100m relay and a silver in the 4 x 400m. The East German women were somewhat overshadowed at these Games, although Sigrun Wodars won the 800m, Martina Hellman the discus, and Petra Felke the javelin.